The Common Wor

The Common Worship Lectionary

A Scripture Commentary Year B

Edited by

Leslie Houlden

and

John Rogerson

Published in Great Britain in 2002
Society for Promoting Christian Knowledge
36 Causton Street
London SW1P 4ST
www.spckpublishing.co.uk

British Library Cataloguing-in-Publication Data
A catalogue record for this book is available from the British Library

ISBN 978–0–281–05326–1

Typeset by Wilmaset Ltd, Birkenhead, Wirral
First printed in Great Britain by
The Cromwell Press, Trowbridge, Wiltshire
Subsequent digital printing in Great Britain

Contents

Introduction

The purpose of this book is to offer a particular kind of help and stimulus to those who must address congregations and other groups where the Revised Common Lectionary is followed. We provide entries for all the Sunday readings for Year B and for the readings put down for a selection of major Holy Days.

The tone aims to be decently academic, not in the sense that readers are to feel led back to their earlier education, with examinations in the offing, but in the hope of helping them to read a passage in terms of its context and intentions. Of course it would be confusing, and is not possible in the space available, to give a full range of current ways of understanding a text, but the interpretation offered is meant to be neither eccentric nor shallow.

Given this kind of treatment, the entries are emphatically not designed to give instant sermon-fodder; rather, they offer one element in preparation. To it, the speaker will add pastoral experience and a sense of local need – and of course creative imagination. The underlying 'philosophy' of preaching is that, far from being an exegetical plod, it should be seen as, in effect, an art form, with its own special characteristics. The content is the gospel, and the resources and approaches are manifold – but always so that, by way of rhetorical art, hearts and minds are moved. Of course, sometimes a point from the kind of material given here may make a direct appearance in the spoken address, but that will be because it is a telling way of conveying a particular message.

This philosophy seems to downgrade expository preaching as once commonly practised and sometimes still found in (it is to be hoped) appropriate circumstances. But, despite the unparalleled number of opportunities now available for various kinds of formal biblical study, most congregations do not include many people able to slot in, at a moment's notice, to the world of a passage of Scripture that has just been read – at least, as that passage is currently discussed in the academy. Anyway, it is scarcely desirable that this should be the sermon's primary focus. It is an existential act of speech, offered to particular people, here and now.

A further factor is the character of modern biblical scholarship itself – with which the Christian community has always had a guarded relationship. One might say that it exists, for good or ill, and it takes forms that are sometimes informative, sometimes edifying, but often technical and seemingly remote from life and from modern issues. More seriously, it is widely believed to be inimical to faith, especially in the tendency of some of its historical judgements. It is no part of this book's task to enter into a defence or assessment of modern scholarship, and it is unlikely that those who suspect or reject such scholarship, more or less on principle, will be among those who use the book. In part, we simply take it as an inescapable feature of the current scene. But we do also see it as offering great opportunites for the understanding of the ancient writings that make up the Bible, as well as steering us away from modernizing subjectivism. Our attitude is positive. We also believe that the attempt to grasp the sense of Scripture more clearly is necessary if serious mistakes are not to be made in its use and if mere intuition is not to prevail. The preacher has a responsibility to the text in its own right and decisions to make about its style of relevance, perhaps only of an oblique kind.

Of course modern scholarship is vast in range and multiple in method. The writers of this book have sought to avoid one possible way of reacting to this situation, the method of bland generality. Rather, there has been an attempt to present some of the more stimulating approaches currently in use and to show them working out in practice. The attempt is not rigorously organized. Contributors have written as they thought appropriate to the particular case.

Perhaps the most striking development of recent decades has been to move away from constant attention to questions of mere historicity to an understanding of the minds, intentions and social setting of the numerous writers of Scripture, as well as to seek a grasp of the sheer literary 'flow' of what they wrote. Such approaches are more easily and fruitfully adopted in some writings than in others. Often, in the Old Testament especially, there is too little agreement about the dating or make-up of many of the books that finally emerged. In other cases, notably the Gospels, there is enough discernible homogeneity of mind to offer real illumination if we work along these lines. With the newly adopted sequential reading of one synoptic Gospel in course per year, there is every encouragement to help both preachers and congregations to enter into the thought-forms, ideas and spiritualities of each evangelist in turn – though of course weekly 'doses' of a few verses do not make sermons necessarily the best medium for the conveying of such understanding. (In this respect, liturgists and biblical scholars are not exactly working in tandem.) Our contributors, all experienced scholars and preachers, are identified by initials. They do not conform to one particular method or school of biblical interpretation, and there has been no narrow editorial policy in this respect.

Contributors to the Old Testament readings are Richard Coggins and Rex Mason, in addition to contributions from the overall editor, John Rogerson. The New Testament contributions are from Charles Cousar, Ruth Edwards, John Fenton, Sophie Laws, Beverly Gaventa, Anthony E. Harvey, David Horrell, Robert Morgan, John Muddiman and the overall editor, Leslie Houlden. The contributions from Charles Cousar and Beverly Gaventa have been included by kind permission of Westminster John Knox Press, and are taken from *Texts for Preaching, Year B*, The author's initials are at the end of each entry.

The First Sunday of Advent

Isaiah 64.1–9; 1 Corinthians 1.3–9; Mark 13.24–37

Isaiah 64.1–9

This passage, which actually begins at 63.19b, is part of the long communal lament that starts at 63.7. It expresses a mixture of the hope and frustration of the Jerusalem community in the period 540–520 BC. The hope sprang from the fact that politically, the rebuilding of the temple and the restoration of its worship had become a possibility. The frustration arose from an apparent lack of progress and, worse, no apparent sign that God would crown the new possibilities with a spectacular intervention. It is an appropriate passage for the beginning of Advent – a season that lives with the frustration of hoping and waiting for a new world that is beyond the capacity of the human race to achieve.

The opening cry to God for an appearing, an epiphany, draws on traditional language that associates the coming of God with the shaking of the powers of nature and the awestruck terror of the nations. This cry leads to an affirmation of the incomparability of God (vv. 4–5a) and to a confession of the people's unfaithfulness (vv. 5b–7). The second part of v. 5 (v. 4 in the Hebrew) is difficult, and NRSV 'because you hid yourself we transgressed' is based upon a conjectural emendation as well as importing a degree of self-justification into the passage that is foreign to it. On the other hand the statements of vv. 6–7 employ exaggerations that are in order in liturgical language even if they overstate what is actually the case. Does *no one* actually call on God's name?

A dramatic change comes with v. 8, 'and now, O LORD . . .'. Whether NRSV 'yet' quite gets the force of this is arguable. It is much rarer for God to be called 'Father' in the Old Testament than might be expected, and the force of the word here has less to do with gender than with the idea of kin relationships in general, relationships that provide a safe context in which children can grow up. Yet the image that is pursued is not that of parental relationships but that of potter and clay. In a way, both images have their difficulties. Parents often do not want their children to grow up, or want to fulfil in them their own frustrated ambitions. Clay has no control over what the potter makes of it. The frustrated hopes of the community in this passage and of the Church today, are related to the paradox – implicit in these images – that humans desire freedom but do not know how to cope with it. They desire God to order things, but not at the expense of their own decisions. In prayerful lament before God we explore these paradoxes. We do not get immediate answers, but we may be in a better position to cope with the paradoxes than those for whom, unfortunately, worship is an alien experience. JR

1 Corinthians 1.3–9

Because Paul follows a standard format in the openings of his letters, the preacher may experience a strong temptation to skip past these lines and into the 'meat' of the letter itself. This temptation needs to be resisted, however, since the salutations and thanksgivings reflect some of Paul's most fundamental theological convictions and also provide clues to major topics of the letter.

In the opening lines of 1 Corinthians one theological conviction that emerges is that of calling. The first word with which Paul identifies himself is the word 'called'. By the will of God, Paul was called as an apostle. Calling belongs not only to what we might term 'professional church leaders', however. Already in v. 2 Paul speaks of Christians in Corinth as those who are 'called to be saints' and who in turn 'call on the name of our Lord Jesus Christ'. That this designation is no mere nod in the direction of the laity emerges in 1 Cor. 1.26 and 7.17–24, where Paul uses the language of vocation to describe God's summons of persons to obedience. For Paul each and every Christian is such because of God's calling.

As in other letters, the thanksgiving (vv. 4–9) identifies ways in which Paul is grateful for this particular community of believers. He thanks God for God's grace, specifically for the gift of 'speech and knowledge of every kind'. The Corinthians lack no 'spiritual gift'. These words sound odd if we know the discussions that lie ahead in this letter, where it is precisely the Corinthians' knowledge and gifts that provoke Paul's wrath. A suspicious first reading of the thanksgiving might lead us to conclude that these words carry an ironic tone, but they are in fact guarded and carefully chosen. The thanksgiving, after all, addresses God and thanks God for these gifts – not for the accomplishments of the Corinthians. The question that dominates part of the letter is not whether the Corinthians have the gifts, but how they interpret them and how they use them.

Debate about the origin of the difficulties at Corinth continues unabated. Whatever had occurred there, Henry Joel Cadbury's description of the Corinthians as 'overconverted' seems apt. Their enthusiasm led at least some of them (perhaps those from the higher social strata) to conclude that they had already arrived at the fullness of Christian life. Nothing more could be added to them (see e.g. 1 Cor. 4.8f.). Paul responds to this situation throughout the letter, but one element in his response appears already in vv. 7–8, 'you are not lacking in any spiritual gift as you wait for the revealing of our Lord Jesus Christ. He will also strengthen you to the end, so that you may be blameless on the day of our Lord Jesus Christ.' In common with all Christians, one task of the Corinthians is to *wait*. The ultimate revealing or apocalypse of Jesus Christ lies in the future, not in the past. Only when God has completed that apocalypse can believers expect their own completion, their own 'arrival'. The reference to a future judgement ('the day of our Lord Jesus Christ') underscores the fact that the Corinthians are not yet to regard themselves as perfected or mature. That decision will come.

Another element in Paul's response to the 'overconversion' of the Corinthians comes in v. 9: 'You were called into the fellowship of his Son, Jesus Christ our

Lord.' The vocation of the Christian is a vocation to 'fellowship' (Greek, *koinōnia*). In contrast to the factionalism that appears to plague the Christian church in Corinth, Paul asserts the commonality of believers. Over and over in this letter he will insist that considerations about the community as a whole outweigh the prerogatives of individuals or small groups (see e.g. 10.23–30). The reason for this insistence lies not in the inherent good of the group, but in the fact that the fellowship is that of 'his son, Jesus Christ our Lord'. Because all members of the community belong to the God who has called them in Jesus Christ, the community merits upbuilding.

While it is a kind of table of contents for the remainder of the letter, 1 Cor. 1.1–9 has far more than merely pragmatic significance for contemporary Christians. The insistence on the calling of all Christians challenges our professionalism, which threatens to treat the laity as qualitatively different from the ordained. If all Christians are called, although to differing tasks (as emerges in the body image of 1 Cor. 12), then the gospel's most radical claims intrude into the lives of every believer. Finally, if all Christians are called, they enter alike into a community that requires full participation. BG

Mark 13.24–37

Advent Sunday, the beginning of the Christian year, but what is the subject of the Gospel? – the coming of the Son of Man at the end of the world. It may seem odd to us, to begin by thinking about the end, but it was not so for Mark, or for those for whom he wrote. His book contains only one section of continuous, direct speech of Jesus of great length, and today's passage is the final paragraphs of it. The subject is the return of Christ in glory, as it was explained to the first four disciples in private, shortly before his death, for them to pass on to everyone (v. 37). Such final words of famous people were highly valued in the ancient world among Jews and among others.

Mark, like Matthew and Luke after him, believed that Christ would come soon, during the lifetime of some of the contemporaries of Jesus (Mark 9.1; 13.30). It may also have been the case, though this is still much disputed, that Jesus too expected the end of the present age and the beginning of the age to come within a short period. Apocalyptic expectations are usually set within a brief future; this is why Mark's congregation is commanded to keep awake (v. 37).

That is not the whole truth. Today's section of Mark 13 should not be read in isolation from the previous 19 verses (5–23), in which the emphasis is on not thinking that the end is near (e.g. vv. 5–7, 21f.). The coming of Christ will be unmistakable; it will be preceded by cosmic disasters, about which there can be no doubt. Notice also v. 32: only the Father knows the day and the hour. Mark's purpose, in part, is to contradict those who are saying that 'the day of the Lord is already here' (2 Thess. 2.2, which seems to presuppose a similar situation).

The earliest followers of Jesus looked forward to an age to come on a new earth, in resurrected bodies. Jesus would gather his chosen from all over the world, and they would be changed; Mark has shown his readers how Jesus is the one to deliver people from sickness and death, and to overcome the wind and the storms. The oldest Christian prayers that we know were for this to happen soon: *Marana tha*; thy kingdom come; come, Lord Jesus.

A good case can be made that the best way to read Mark's Gospel is to begin with ch. 13. JF

The Second Sunday of Advent

Isaiah 40.1–11; 2 Peter 3.8–15a; Mark 1.1–8

Isaiah 40.1–11

The opening verses of Deutero-Isaiah, proclaimed and/or written during the exile in Babylon (587–540 BC), are among the best-known passages in the Old Testament. This is partly because of their use in the New Testament with reference to John the Baptist (see today's gospel), and because they begin Handel's *Messiah*. Yet while they may have 'messianic' overtones, concentration upon these should not be allowed to obscure the many wonderful features of the passage. From the outset, there is an element of mystery as an unnamed speaker calls upon unspecified people in the plural (cf. the familiar 'comfort ye' of the Authorized Version) to comfort Jerusalem. 'Comfort' in Hebrew here is much stronger than in English, and conveys a promise of action, and of hope for the future. It is like a political prisoner unexpectedly being told about imminent freedom on the grounds of an amnesty. The mystery is continued by another voice summoning unspecified people to build a highway for God in the desert (v. 3). The image may derive from the processional routes in Babylon along which the images of the gods were ceremonially taken. While for modern readers the command may conjure up the swathes of destruction wrought by bulldozers upon an innocent countryside during the construction of motorways, it must be remembered that nature was a hard taskmaster in the ancient world, and that even a route that made travelling easy had to be traversed on foot, if one were poor. The image is complex: the route will be a highway for God but, by implication, a route along which God will lead his people from exile in Babylon to freedom in their own land.

Another voice commands (v. 6), this time ordering the prophet to cry out. He gives the only reply that any human preacher can give who relies upon human resources. Humankind has no message of hope, such is human frailty and lack of constancy (vv. 6–7). Fortunately, the preacher has another resource, in the 'word of our God' (v. 8). This is best understood as the accumulation of traditions about God's faithfulness to his people in the past. They give hope by indicating that God will never forsake a people that he has called and formed especially for his glory.

There is one more voice in the passage, this time addressing the female personification of Zion/Jerusalem. She is to ascend a high mountain so as to be both witness and herald of the coming of God to Judah. The language in v. 11 about God feeding his flock is the language of kingship (cf. Ps. 23). As applied to God it means the use of power to establish situations of graciousness. It is this idea which brings us closest to the idea of Messiahship as embodied in the ministry of Jesus. JR

2 Peter 3.8–15a

2 Peter is not a book from which preachers regularly draw texts. Its brevity and the issues it addresses make it a scarce commodity in the contemporary Church. Yet it wrestles with one of the critical problems the early Church faced – the delay of Jesus' return and the moral laxity that regularly accompanied a sceptical stance. During the Advent season, when the liturgical spotlight falls on the second as well as the first coming of Jesus, we do well to return to 2 Peter and listen to the implications of an eschatological faith. While the usual apocalyptic images appear in the text (the thief in the night, cosmic dissolution, fire, and new heavens and a new earth), the text struggles with more than a mere repetition of the old mythology, perhaps in an effort to speak to hellenized readers for whom the ancient symbols no longer held meaning.

The beginning of the chapter sets the tone for the argument and appeals that follow (3.1–4). Not unexpectedly (since they had been anticipated by the prophets and apostles), sceptics scoff at the delay of the longed-for return and live as if there will be no judgement. They cynically ask what has happened to the promise, and suggest that the created order from its very beginning has happily rocked along without any divine intrusion on God's part (v. 4).

The writer's first response is to address the issue of God and creation (vv. 5–7). God has been active not only in the establishing of the heavens and the earth but also in preserving and maintaining the present order. It would be disastrously short-sighted to assume that the world operates without God. Look at the flood. God essentially destroyed the earth with water, and in fact is the one who has thus far kept the present world from being destroyed again by fire.

Then the writer faces head-on the matter of the delay of the *parousia*. First, there is the problem of human limitations. Psalm 90 meditates on the inestimable gap between God's perspective and the time and mortality of humans, and the writer of 2 Peter in 3.8 recalls a verse from Ps. 90.4 for the sceptics who assume their own perspective is so certain. God does not reckon time the way humans reckon time. When humans grow itchy and impatient, then doubting and cynical, God remains committed to the divine promise. In fact, God's patience is a measure of divine grace. God is not eager to destroy and punish disobedient children. God wants sufficient time for all to repent.

Rather than interpreting the delay as an indication of a failed promise, the writer follows the prophets and Paul (2 Pet. 3.15b; cf. Rom. 2.4–5) in pointing to the divine mercy, which holds back the judgement and prolongs the time to enable true remorse. This explanation of the delay may not satisfy every question we have about the return of Christ, especially the questions of the oppressed and marginalized, who yearn for the end so as to have vindication and a relief from their predicament. But then it was not written for such a group, but for scoffers and cynics whose presumptuous perspective needs challenging. The challenge is that they live faithfully in the present and 'regard the patience of our Lord as salvation' (2 Pet. 3.15a).

Second, once the writer has reminded readers of God's viewpoint on history,a reaffirmation of the traditional 'day of the Lord' is made (cf. Amos 5.18–20; Joel 2.28–32). Two features stand out. On the one hand, the image of the thief suggests suddenness and unexpectedness. There is no need for speculation. Preparation for the final day is critical, but it does not consist of developing timetables and calculating precise moments. On the other hand, the traditional language of the dissolution of the created order with fire is not without meaning. 'Fire' connotes testing, the burning of what is peripheral and the continuance of what is lasting, valuable and worthy. This leads to the third and final movement in the passage.

The writer asks what all this means for the present lives of the readers. Given the prospects of a future dissolution of this order, they go about their business in a mood of expectancy ('waiting for and hastening the coming of the day of God', 3.12–14). In place of scepticism and cynicism, they hope for what lies beyond dissolution: new heavens and a new earth (v. 13). A proper preparation for the future consists not in speculation, but 'in leading lives of holiness and godliness' (v. 11), in striving for peace (v. 14).

The new world is a place 'where righteousness is *at home*' (v. 13, emphasis added). Admittedly, in the present world 'the way of righteousness' (2.21) is hard to maintain, given the hostile and enticing context that threatens to overpower believers, but the future promises something better. Just as Noah, at this time of the first dissolution of the world, was 'a herald of righteousness' (2.5), so now 'the righteousness of our God and Saviour Jesus Christ' (1.1) will prevail beyond the second dissolution into the new order, where it is 'at home.'

Holiness, godliness, peace, and righteousness are four ingredients characterizing the waiting mood of the Advent season. They include both personal and social dimensions, both attention to the self and attention to the broader community. CC

Mark 1.1–8

Familiarity with the birth narratives of Matthew and Luke and the elegant Prologue of John makes the beginning of Mark's Gospel seem not only abrupt but vaguely disappointing. Here no angelic pronouncements anticipate the birth of Jesus. No word of the Christ's place in creation itself signals the importance of the narrative that is to follow. A careful reading of this passage, however, reveals that Mark also begins with detailed attention to an antecedent of Jesus, this time in the person of John the Baptist.

The first verse of Mark's Gospel teems with ambiguity: Who or what constitutes the 'beginning of the good news of Jesus Christ'? Does Mark here simply identify the beginning of the story? Is the whole of what follows in Mark merely 'the beginning'? Another possibility is that John himself is the beginning, or that the beginning lies in the prophecy concerning John as forerunner of Jesus. Whatever the nuances of v. 1, clearly Mark understands John as the one who prepares 'the way of the Lord'.

In at least four ways, Mark identifies John the Baptist as the forerunner of Jesus, the one who prepares his way. First, and perhaps most obvious, the arrival of John is itself an object of prophecy, and he in turn prophesies the advent of Jesus. The biblical quotations in vv. 2–3, taken from Mal. 3.1 and Isa. 40.3 (despite the introduction's identifying the quotation solely with Isaiah), serve in this context as prophecies of the activity of John, and the description of John's dress identifies him with the tradition of Elijah (see 2 Kings 1.8). The major activity associated with John in Mark's account, of course, is his announcement of the One who is to come.

John is not simply the forerunner of Jesus in the sense of announcing his imminent arrival, however. John and Jesus share a common location in the wilderness. Mark's insistence on the wilderness as the location of John the Baptist, probably in conformity to the quotation from Isa. 40.3, makes the description of Joh's activity puzzling. If John appeared in the *wilderness*, as Mark 1.4 indicates, and if John did his preaching there, how is it that people were aware of his activity or went out to hear him and be baptized by him? The location is thematic or theological rather than geographical, as is confirmed in 1.12, when Jesus is driven into the wilderness, and later in Mark, when Jesus repeatedly retreats to the wilderness (1.35, 45; 6.31, 32, 35).

A third way in which John serves as forerunner of Jesus is in the act of proclamation. The only words attributed to John in this passage are the pronouncement about the coming of Jesus, and the first words attributed to Jesus are, again, words of proclamation. The content of their preaching differs, in that John proclaims Jesus and his baptism and Jesus proclaims the nearness of the kingdom. Yet both call for repentance (1.4, 15), which again connects the two figures.

The final way in which John serves as forerunner of Jesus stands outside this immediate passage, but it nevertheless impinges on Mark's understanding of John. John becomes the forerunner of Jesus in being handed over for death. The same word (*paradidōmi*) describes John's arrest or betrayal in 1.14 and that of Jesus later in Mark's Gospel (for example, 3.19; 9.31; 14.18). More significantly, the reference to John's arrest in 1.14 comes well before the actual story of John's arrest and execution in Mark 6.14–29. One reason for that untimely reference is that it foreshadows not only *John's* death but also that of Jesus.

These parallels between Mark's presentation of John the Baptist and that of Jesus serve more than a merely decorative or mnemonic function. Mark's story invites disciples (and probably readers as well) to follow in the way of John and Jesus. Late in the gospel story, the disciples accompany Jesus into the wilderness (the 'deserted place' of 6.31). Part of their task is to engage in the proclamation of the gospel (6.12; 13.10). And, as 13.9–13 makes painfully clear, disciples will also be handed over or betrayed (*paradidōmi*). What Mark creates, then, is not a simple identification, in which disciples *become* John or Jesus or their equivalent. Instead, disciples follow in the *way* of John and Jesus, as Bartimaeus is invited to do following his healing (10.46–52). BG

The Third Sunday of Advent

Isaiah 61.1–4, 8–11; 1 Thessalonians 5.16–24; John 1.6–8, 19–28

Isaiah 61.1–4, 8–11

Compared with last Sunday's reading from Isa. 40.1–11, there has been a shift of time and place with Isa. 61, if modern scholars are correct. The setting is not Babylon between 560 and 540, but Palestine between 540 and 520 BC. The passage is addressed not to exiles wanting to return home, but to returned exiles living among ruins (v. 4). In this situation of partly fulfilled but also of dashed hopes, the prophet announces that he has been filled with the Spirit of God and thus anointed to proclaim good news. Such a claim by someone in the first person singular is virtually unparalleled in the Old Testament (cf. Mic. 3.8), and may have arisen from a challenge to the prophet's authority from people who doubted his message. Whatever the passage's origins, it remains one of the high points of the Old Testament, and one used by Jesus in his preaching in Nazareth (Luke 4.18–19).

At first sight, the opening verses do not seem to fit the setting proposed by modern commentators. Who were the captives and prisoners in the Jerusalem of the returned exiles? The similarity of the language with that of the so-called servant songs in chs. 40–55 (cf. 42.1–4) has provided the suggestion that these verses come originally from the time of the exile. Whether or not this is true, vv. 1–4 can best be understood as a proclamation of the imminent beginning of the reign of God. Changes of dynasty in the ancient world were often occasions when amnesties were announced for prisoners; and if a previous regime had been oppressive, its ending brought hope for a new future. Such ideas are addressed here to a community returned to a ruined country. The ending of a war and the need for repairing the damage it has caused are the nearest experiences in today's world.

In v. 8 there is a change of speaker. As though to confirm what the prophet has said, God announces his love of justice, which is right dealing in all its manifestations, and his hatred of all forms of deceit and oppression. His imminent rule will result in a new covenant with his people, an everlasting one. This raises a question about the former covenant. Was it not everlasting? Did the obstinacy and lack of co-operation of the people doom a covenant made and guaranteed by God? The focus is less upon a contrast between a limited and an everlasting covenant and more on the fact that God will leave witnesses to his graciousness throughout the people and their generations (v. 9). These witnesses will be to the world what the prophet is to his people in the opening words of the passage, inspired messengers of hope.

The prophet's response to God's promise comes in vv. 10–11 in the form of a hymn of praise. It uses imagery that powerfully expresses hope for the future: wedding garments that bespeak the new life together of bride and bridegroom;

new shoots that promise a harvest. The people are bidden to look not at the ruined land in which they find themselves, but at the fact that they are once more at home, with all that this implies about God and the future. JR

1 Thessalonians 5.16–24

Each of the epistolary texts for the first three Sundays of Advent binds the expectation of the second coming of Jesus to the demand for faithful living. The text for this third Sunday, which concludes a letter particularly concerned with eschatological expectations, makes the demand a special matter through a series of short injunctions.

It may be hard to sense the urgency of the injunctions, because we do not know enough about the original readers to know how the injunctions immediately addressed their lives. We can, however, appreciate that short, pointed exhortations like these, with a certain immediacy, invite the reader to accept their message, to see what life would be like if they were followed. They indicate directions in which one moves in obedience. The demands are directly put to the reader, no ifs, ands or buts. At the same time, the injunctions are general. They do not define the 'good' that is to be sought or the 'evil' to be avoided. Nor do they prescribe circumstances under which the injunctions are especially relevant. Readers are not relieved of making ethical decisions. They are faced with a new kind of discernment as they are forced to determine the particularity of the will of God in the challenges of their everyday lives.

The injunctions at the end of 1 Thessalonians concern three related matters. First, there is *the specific call to a life of worship* (5.16–18). Rejoicing, prayer and thanksgiving are not designated here as Sunday activities. They are each identified by the repeated adverbial emphasis: 'always', 'without ceasing', 'in all circumstances'.

The injunctions indicate an existence oriented to God, where believers recognize in every moment of their lives, in every decision they face, that they have to do with the reality of God. Life cannot be simply divided into the God-related and non-God-related dimensions of human activity; the latter do not exist. Writing cheques, marking ballots in the voting booth, relating to family members in the home, making business decisions – as well as private and public worship – are the ways in which God seeks to be glorified.

It is intriguing that verbs for worship are used (rather than verbs like 'obey', 'serve', 'submit to'). The manner of life imagined here is characterized by delight, by gratitude, by confidence. We may not be inclined to give thanks *for* all the circumstances of our lives, but the next envisions no situation *in the midst of which* we cannot recognize expressions of divine mercy and give God thanks. (Note that the original readers had known considerable persecution; see 2.14–16.)

Second, there is *a specific call to a life of discernment* (5.19–22). Aspects of the Christian experience are ambiguous, even frightful. The Spirit is the divine activity in human life over which we have no control. Believers can deny the Spirit's presence or fail to heed the Spirit's promptings, but believers (though they may often presume to do so) cannot ultimately manipulate the Spirit. Paul, therefore, urges readers not to quench the Spirit.

Precisely because the Spirit's activity is mysterious and often ambiguous, believers are enjoined to a life of discernment. As in Rom. 12.2, they are to test and prove the will of God; but more, they are to test and prove 'everything'. All of human experience – events, practices, relationships – invariably demands discrimination to determine the 'good' that is to be clung to and the 'evil' to be avoided. Prophets, who speak with authority and insight, are to be listened to, though not necessarily heeded. They may or they may not disclose the divine will. They, along with every source of direction, have to be tested.

The verbs throughout this passage as well as the second-person pronouns are all plural. Since the letter is also addressed to a congregation, the notion seems clear that the Christian community is the locus for this discerning and discriminating activity. It is not that the individual has to make all the weighty, burdensome ethical decisions alone. Rather the church is called to be a community of moral discernment, to test the various voices who speak the wisdom of the age to see if there is divine guidance for the confusing decisions of life.

Third, there is *a specific call to a life of holiness* (1 Thess. 5.23–24). The verb 'sanctify (make holy)' may send shudders through us if we have had much experience with legalistic brands of religion that organize life around a list of dos and don'ts. We quickly counter that we want no part of such moralism. There is no question that 'holy' (both in Hebrew and in Greek) does carry with it the notion of separation, but in Paul's framework it describes life oriented to the new age that has come in Jesus Christ as distinguished from the old age. It depicts a separation from the transitory, passing order, a break with the illusionary power brokers who have not heard or will not accept the radical newness God has promised.

Rather than through a list of dos and don'ts, the call to a life of holiness comes through a prayer. Only God can 'sanctify' us completely. Only God can make our whole selves 'sound' and keep us 'blameless at the coming of our Lord Jesus Christ'. At heart, sanctification is first and foremost a gift of God, not an act of human will. The faithful God guarantees a positive response to a prayer for holiness. CC

John 1.6–8, 19–28

Of all the Gospels, John's gives the most sustained attention to the testimony of John the Baptist, and this lection consists of two segments of that testimony. The prose of vv. 6–8 interrupts the poetry of the Prologue, perhaps indicating that these verses were inserted into an existing poem (see also v. 15, which again interrupts the poetic structure). Verses 19–28 contain the first part of the Baptist's testimony, which continues through v. 34.

Despite the emphasis on the testimony of John, at first glance what is most striking about these passages is not the positive assertions John the Baptist makes concerning Jesus, but the negative assertions made about John, both by the narrator and through the direct speech of John himself. As early as v. 8, the narrator insists that 'he [John] was not the light'. The repeated and formal assertions in vv. 19–28 seem calculated to limit John's role: 'He confessed and did not deny it, but confessed, "I am not the Messiah."' While John's testimony ostensibly concerns 'the light', the content of vv. 19–28 has more to do with *John's* identity – or with denying certain identities to John – than with that of *Jesus*.

Historically, an explanation for these negative assertions regarding John the Baptist comes readily enough. Apparently at least some of John's followers understood him to be superior to Jesus, and a rivalry developed between the two groups. The story of Jesus' baptism by John easily lends itself to the inference that Jesus thereby yields to John's greater authority, making it important for Jesus' interpreters to explain how it is that the Christ came to be baptized by John. Although they treat the issue differently, Matthew and Luke also appear to downplay John's significance, either by having John himself resist the notion of baptizing and then having Jesus explain the reasons for his baptism (Matt. 3.13–17) or by placing John in prison at the time of Jesus' baptism (Luke 3.18–22). By negatively stating John's identity (he is *not* the light [John 1.8], nor is he the Messiah, Elijah, or the prophet [vv. 20–21]), the Fourth Gospel counters any attempt to rank John above Jesus.

Polemic against the followers of John the Baptist is not, however, the sole function of these passages. They also serve to emphasize the importance of the one about whom John gives his testimony. Indeed, John's authority (like that of all proclaimers) appears to consist of his honest denial of exalted titles for himself in favour of pointing the way to Jesus. Throughout the Fourth Gospel, characters who encounter Jesus serve largely to illuminate him in some way and, thus, the reader learns little about them as individuals. The treatment of John the Baptist is but an extreme example of that tendency.

Theologically, what the character John the Baptist does in this Gospel is to point ever away from himself and toward Jesus. The narrator explicitly gives that role, the role of witness, to John in 1.6–8, and John acts it out in the scenes that follow. John's rejection of titles for himself serves as prelude to his assertion about the one who follows him: 'Among you stands one whom you do not know, the one who is coming after me; I am not worthy to untie the thong of his sandal' (vv. 26–27). Just beyond the confines of this lection, John elaborates on Jesus' identity as 'Lamb of God', and concludes with the formal assertion, 'I myself have seen and have testified that this is the Son of God' (v. 34), an assertion that circles back to and fulfils the vocation of John as witness (giver of testimony) in v. 7.

John the Baptist's comments about Jesus here differ from those in the Marcan account of the Second Sunday of Advent, primarily in the assertion that the one who comes is 'one whom you do not know'. This signals an important Johannine theme. Indeed, throughout John's Gospel Jesus remains one whom people either do not know or do not understand. Nicodemus (3.4) and the Samaritan woman (4.11–12) understand his words but not their meaning. The high priest understands him only as a threat to the status quo (11.45–53). Pilate gives him the right title, but for the wrong reasons (19.19–22). Even the disciples consistently reveal their misunderstandings.

John's proclamation of Jesus as the one who is unknown challenges the Church to acknowledge its presumptuous assumption that it does know who Jesus is. Whether it portrays Jesus as innocuous infant, as dispenser of salvation (however currently understood), as revolutionary leader, as spiritual guru, or in any of a dozen other ways, the Church and its people claim to understand Jesus. Each of those understandings, however, like the understandings of various characters in the Fourth Gospel, at best grasps only one facet of Jesus' identity.

As the Church waits during the season of Advent, anticipating the birth of the infant Jesus, it needs to recall the startling fact that Jesus continues to make his appearance in ways that are surprising, unexpected, even unwelcome. The gentle baby of the Christmas story shortly becomes the one who challenges the religious authorities, overthrows the temple's status quo, offers the people teachings that make little or no sense, dismisses his own family, and finally provokes the suspicion of the government. BG

The Fourth Sunday of Advent

2 Samuel 7.1–11, 16; Romans 16.25–27; Luke 1.26–28

2 Samuel 7.1–11, 16

See Proper 11 on p. 191.

Romans 16.25–27

The doxology that concludes Paul's letter to the Romans seems an unlikely choice for a sermon text on a Sunday so close to Christmas. It contains nothing of the romance of the season – no angelic choirs, no weary shepherds, no seeking Magi. In fact, there is no narrative quality to the text at all, and we need stories at Christmas. Furthermore, these three verses have a disputed textual heritage. Some Greek manuscripts locate them at the end of ch. 14 or at the end of ch. 15; others omit them entirely. A number of reputable commentators will argue that the verses were probably added after Paul's time by a later editor. All these considerations may scare the preacher off, sending them to the more familiar words of Luke.

But the doxology should not be summarily dismissed. It provides a fitting ending to Romans and, even if added by a later editor, it picks up the themes developed throughout the complex argument of the letter and expresses them liturgically. All good theology ultimately must come to expression in worship, and what better time to express it than the Christmas season! In the context of praise, the heart of God's intentions in the sending of Jesus Christ into the world is a matter of adoration – 'to the only wise God, through Jesus Christ, to whom be the glory for ever!'

First, a word about liturgical language. We shall try to identify the movements in the doxology that undoubtedly led the shapers of the lectionary to select this text for this Sunday. But the words of worship always tend to be effusive rather than precise, expressions of heartfelt emotion rather than analytical argumentation. It is impossible to outline the prayers in the Book of Common Prayer or to diagram their sentences. So with this doxology. Critical to any interpretation must be the recognition of its liturgical quality.

We can observe three movements in the passage that distinguish this doxological expression. First, there is elaboration of Paul's gospel and the proclamation (kerygma) of Jesus Christ as *the revelation of the mystery, long kept secret but now revealed.* The gospel as disclosure has to be taken seriously. The story of Jesus Christ does not have the kind of rational basis that makes it possible for people to 'think' their way into becoming believers. Without denigrating theology, it is critical to recognize that the gospel is not an intellectual exercise. The shepherds (who might be stereotyped as nonthinkers) and the Magi (who might be labelled thinkers) each got to Bethlehem by means of disclosure – the shepherds from an angel, the Magi from the scribes at Jerusalem. And so it has been ever since.

To speak of the revelation of a mystery is another way to speak of grace. The divine initiative that makes Christmas possible does not stop with the birth of Jesus, but continues in the unveiling of the meaning of the birth for generations that follow. The penny drops, the light dawns, eyes are opened in the experiences of people who are given to see beyond the trappings of Christmas the significance of the One strangely born.

A second movement in the doxology is a backward movement – to *the prophetic writings* where the mystery was hidden that is now made known *to all the Gentiles.* No specific text in the prophets is cited in the passage (though it is legitimate to think of the Old Testament reading from 2 Sam. 7 as 'prophetic'). The letter to the Romans, however, is filled with citations of Old Testament texts that anticipate the revelation of the mystery. The point is that the story of Jesus, odd as it may seem (remember, Paul called it 'foolishness' and 'a stumbling block', 1 Cor. 1.23), is not an accident of history. The gospel is both planned ('according to the command of the eternal God') and anticipated. As said earlier in Romans, the disclosure of the mystery proves that God's faithfulness is not invalidated (3.3; 15.7–13), that God can be fully trusted (3.21–26).

What about the specific mention of the inclusion of 'all the Gentiles'? It is difficult to recapture the force of such a disclosure today, when the Church has become exclusively 'Gentile'. Yet Christmas is an appropriate time to recall that *we* are the outsiders (not the Jews), who have been drawn into the family of God and made recipients of the revealed mystery. The very mention of the word 'Gentiles' reminds us of brothers and sisters in the family who during December celebrate Hanukkah.

From gospel to revealed mystery, from revealed mystery to prophetic writings – and the third move is from prophetic writings to human response, '*the obedience of faith*'. The phrase serves as the interpretive brackets that begin (1.5) and end (16.26) this significant letter describing what the gospel is to evoke in the lives of those to whom the mystery is disclosed.

Though commentators do not universally agree on the grammatical analysis of the phrase 'unto obedience of faith' (literally), the expression nevertheless reminds us that the two words 'obedience' and 'faith' are inexorably bound together, almost synonymous. An obedience not born of faith is inevitably prone to legalism and to becoming a burden too heavy to bear. Likewise, a faith that fails to obey is empty and vain, no more than mere lip service.

The text, then, confronts us with the wonder and demand of the Christian gospel, expressed in the language of worship and offered as an act of adoration to the God of Christmas. CC

Luke 1.26–38

The annunciation of Jesus' birth has as its focus just that fact – the advent of Jesus Christ. If modern Christians come to the text with a number of historical, biographical, even biological questions, those are not the questions Luke addresses. Gabriel's extended identifications of the child who is to be born indicates where the focus lies for Luke: 'You will name him Jesus . . . Son of the Most High . . . the throne of his ancestor David . . . holy . . . Son of God.' First and foremost, Luke here identifies Jesus as the subject matter of his entire two-volume work.

Within this annunciation of Christ's advent, three themes take on particular importance. The first theme Gabriel states explicitly: 'For nothing will be impossible with God' (1.37). Gabriel's final words to Mary sum up the birth stories both of John the Baptist and of Jesus. Although the conception of John the Baptist is highly unusual, his parents being old and his mother barren, that story nevertheless recalls similar stories from the Hebrew Bible, so that the reader knows what to anticipate. Like Sarah and Abraham, surely Zechariah and Elizabeth will find their hopes fulfilled. But if their hopes are for that which is improbable, the pregnancy of a virgin is manifestly impossible; yet it is just that impossibility which Gabriel says has been overcome.

These words from Gabriel interpret not only the annunciation of Jesus' birth but the whole sweep of Luke–Acts. If Luke's is an 'orderly account' (1.3), it is also – and first – an account of the impossible things that God has in fact done. The healing of the sick, the resurrection of Jesus, the gift of the Holy Spirit, the formation of community, the release of the captive apostles – again and again Luke tells of the impossible things actually accomplished by God. The 'events that have been fulfilled among us' (v. 1) are events that cannot be believed and yet *must* be believed.

A second theme in this story, and a theme too often neglected, is that of grace. Gabriel greets Mary with the words 'Greetings, favoured one! The Lord is with you', and assures her, 'You have found favour with God.' The Greek verb and noun (*charizomai* and *charis*), here translated 'favour,' could equally well be translated as 'grace'. Mary is the object of God's grace.

What is it about Mary that makes her appropriate as an object of God's grace? Startlingly, nothing in the text provides even a hint to the answer to that question. Luke identifies her simply as a young girl who was engaged to be married. More is said about Joseph (he is of the house of David) than about Mary. Even in the case of Zechariah and Elizabeth, Luke explains that they are righteous and blameless, that they kept God's commandments and prayed to God (1.6–7, 13). Yet not a single word describes the virtues or vices of Mary or explains why God might have chosen her.

That is, of course, precisely the point: God chooses because God chooses. Mary does not earn or deserve the honour of becoming the mother of Jesus any more than would any other woman. This text might profitably be read alongside Romans 9.6–29, where Paul articulates the right of God as God to make whatever choices God elects to make. The biblical story is not one of virtue rewarded – or vice punished – but of the relentlessly unmerited nature of God's grace.

What is Mary's response to this grace? The answer to that question touches on the third theme of the passage. Following Gabriel's announcement, Mary first identifies herself as 'the servant of the Lord'. A better translation would be 'slave of the

Lord' since the Greek word (*doulos*) certainly connotes the involuntary relationship of slavery, not one in which an individual has agreed to service for a wage. Mary's first response, then, recognizes that she has been selected by God and that God's choosing leaves no room for her own volition. Like others within Luke's story, most notably the apostle Paul, Mary's service comes about as a result of God's plan, not her own.

Nevertheless, with the second part of her response, Mary consents to God's plan: 'Let it be with me according to your word.' In the Magnificat that follows immediately upon this scene, Luke places in Mary's mouth words that powerfully interpret the birth of Jesus Christ as the triumph of God for God's people. Later still, she puzzles over events surrounding her child's birth and his behaviour. Here at the beginning, however, Mary signals her 'yes' to God's action, a consent that she cannot fully understand.

Contemporary Christians sometimes balk at the passivity attributed to Mary in this scene, especially in light of the fact that she is sometimes invoked as a model for all women. What needs to be recalled, however, is that Mary later does take initiative, when she interprets events in the Magnificat and when she seeks after her child in the temple. It is also important to recall that Luke portrays most of his characters, both women and men, as the passive objects of God's intervention. Luke's is, beginning to end, a story of God's plan and God's action for the salvation of the whole people of God; given that starting point, it is little wonder that human characters appear quiescent. BG

Christmas Day and Evening of Christmas Eve

Set I

Isaiah 9.2–7; Titus 2.11–14; Luke 2.1–14 (15–20)

Isaiah 9.2–7

This passage illustrates how God's word in Scripture can prove relevant at different times, and in very varied circumstances. The many parallels to the 'royal psalms' show that this passage could have been used at the coronation of any of the Davidic kings. Such an occasion was seen as the dawn of a bright new epoch (v. 2, cf. 2 Sam. 23.4; Ps. 110.3). The joy of hope the occasion brought, like the joy of harvest or the division of the spoils of war (v. 3) finds echo in 1 Kings 1.39–40; Ps. 132.9. The overthrow of national enemies (vv. 4–5), the responsibility of the king (1 Sam. 8.19–20), is assured because of the promise of God to his 'son' (Pss. 2.8–9; 89.23). Indeed, at his accession the king was 'born', given birth as a son by God (v. 6, cf. Ps. 2.7). As Egyptian pharaohs at their accession were given a number of titles, so the king here is given four. He will govern in divinely given wisdom of counsel; he will be a god-like warrior; he will be a 'father' to the nation for a long period and, by his military prowess and just rule (v. 7), he will establish conditions of 'peace', that is both security from the nation's enemies and all that makes for fullness of life (cf. Ps. 72.1–4, 8–11, 16). Indeed, such conditions will endure 'for ever' (v. 7, cf. Ps. 72.5), as conventional a wish as 'O king, live for ever'.

This passage may, therefore, consist of a number of very general themes from the royal worship of the pre-exilic Jerusalem temple. Yet Isaiah may have composed it particularly for the accession of Hezekiah to the throne, in which case the 'darkness' and distress of the later part of ch. 8 (see especially v. 32, cf. 9.2) would have referred to the ravages caused by the Assyrians under Tiglath-Pileser III. Yet such times of darkness often returned. Job uses the same word as that in v. 2 to describe the darkness of the underworld and the despair of death (Job 10.21–22). Again and again the people of God would have felt the need for the birth of a great deliverer who would fill the conventional phrases of the enthronement ceremonies with new and real meaning, especially when the Davidic line proved a failure and came to an end. A passage like this would furnish 'messianic' hopes for the Jewish people after the exile. And Christians found in the birth, life, death and resurrection of Jesus the perfect fulfilment of all that is merely promised in this passage (Matt. 4.15–16). Nevertheless, at each level it reinforces the truth that, only when the king's sovereign rights are acknowledged, can people know the blessings of his reign.

The promise rests on God's 'zeal'. The word can denote the 'ardent' love of a lover

(Song of Sol. 8.6) and God's burning concern for the well-being of his people (Zech. 1.14). RM

Titus 2.11–14

This passage is one of a small number of more doctrinal interludes in the largely pastoral, ethical and organizational topics that occupy the greater part of the Pastoral Epistles. This proportioning of the theological and practical themes is one factor that leads us to think of these writings as coming from the post-Pauline church world of the late first or early second century: practical concerns were now even more pressing for the Christian communities, and so was the need to find ways of developing cohesion in holding to basic Christian beliefs that could be succinctly stated.

It is hard to think of a more succinct statement of those beliefs than that presented here, with its mixture of doctrine and, immediately, its moral implications. And (v. 15) all is to be propagated with authority, the arrangements for which are of major importance for this writer, in the closely interwoven spheres of Church and household (1.5–9; 2.1–10; cf. 1 Tim. 3).

Nevertheless, despite the community concerns, the vision remains universal ('salvation to all', v. 11), even if God's practical goal has an Israel-like quality – the creation of a purified people (v. 14).

The vocabulary in which the doctrine is couched owes something to Scripture and something to the wider religious terminology of the day. 'Has appeared' (v. 11) and 'manifestation' (v. 13) belong to the same family of words: *epiphaneia* conjures up the drama of a visit by the deified emperor, with its excitement and hope of tangible benefits. All the more so with Christ. This idea of his appearance (however expressed) had tended to be associated with the hope of his return, but now the two statements refer to the first and the second comings, as if in balance. They are the brackets within which Christian life is lived.

'Saviour', though a scriptural word, is also characteristic of the imperial cult. It is a favourite with this writer to refer to both God and Christ. The translation of v. 13, it has to be said, presents problems. That commonly given ('our great God and Saviour, Jesus Christ'), which seems to affirm Christ's divinity, would be unique in this (and probably, in fact, any other New Testament) writer, and it is hard to imagine quite what might have been in his mind (he is not the most daring of theologians) – unless the context is indeed that of other cults, and Jesus Christ is being affirmed as *our* deity and saviour (as opposed to those worshipped by others): he, and he alone, is the centre of our full devotion. Less dramatically, the translation could and perhaps should be: 'the glory of the great God and of our saviour Jesus Christ'. It is God who sent Jesus as a supreme act of 'grace' (v. 11); and the writer's perspective appears plainly in 1 Tim. 2.5. LH

Luke 2.1–14 (15–20)

This passage, so beautifully crafted in Luke's narrative, certainly counts among the most familiar passages in the Bible. Dramatizations of the Christmas story as well as repeated readings make it a well-known text. People who know little or nothing about the Christian faith know about the shepherds and the angelic chorus. For that reason, the text presents a challenge to the preacher to hear and declare a fresh word that probes the familiar and yet moves beyond it.

What immediately emerges from the early portion of this story is the political context in which the birth of Jesus is recounted. We are told that Emperor Augustus had ordered an enrolment and that Quirinius was governor of Syria. Despite the problems surrounding the historical accuracy of this beginning (dealt with in most commentaries), the narrative setting cannot be ignored. It is not against the background of the reign of Herod, the local ruler who is known for his heavy-handed and brutal ways, that the story of Jesus' birth is told (as in Matthew's Gospel), but against the background of the Roman Empire.

The Emperor Octavian was a prominent figure, who solidified the somewhat divided loyalties of the various regions of the empire and ushered in the famous Pax Romana. In 27 BC, the Roman senate gave him the title 'the August One'. Poets wrote of his peaceful ideals and anticipated that his reign would signal a golden age based on virtue. Ancient monuments even ascribed to him the title 'saviour'. He represented a high and hopeful moment in Roman history.

Luke gives Octavian his familiar title and recognizes his authority by noting that 'all the world' (actually the Roman Empire) is encompassed by his decree. Often in ancient times the demand for a census evoked rebellion and opposition, but Luke records a dutiful response: 'All went to their own towns to be registered.' The mention of Augustus not only provides an indispensable time reference to help readers date the events that are being narrated, but also enables Luke to explain how Mary and Joseph, who lived in Nazareth, had a baby born in Bethlehem.

The introduction, however, provides a much more important function than this. It sets the stage for the birth of one who is Saviour, Christ the Lord. Octavian is not pictured as an evil, oppressive tyrant, a bloody beast 'uttering haughty and blasphemous words' (Rev. 13.5). The Roman state in Luke's narrative simply does not represent the enemy against which Christians must fight. The backdrop for Jesus' birth is rather a relatively humane and stable structure, the best of ancient governments, which led to dreams of a peaceful era and aspirations of a new and wonderful age. The decades between the time of Jesus' birth and the time of Luke's narrative, however, exposed the failed hopes and the doused aspirations. Octavian is succeeded by caesars who turn the imperial dreams into nightmares.

Against the horizon of disillusionment, we read of the birth of another ruler, from the lineage of David, whose meagre beginnings, on the surface, do not compare with the promise and hope of Augustus. All the world obeys the caesar, but Jesus' parents are rejected and relegated to a cattle stall. Yet the birth of Jesus is good news for all the people, ensuring a new and lasting promise of peace and goodwill.

The narrative does not present us with a confrontation between Augustus and Jesus, but with a contrast between vain expectations and true hope, between the disappointment that follows misplaced anticipations and the energy born of a divine promise, between the imposing but short-lived power of Caesar's rule and the humble manifestation of the eternal dominion of God, between the peace of Rome and the peace of Christ. The titles for Jesus, found later in the narrative (Luke 2.11) – Saviour, Christ and Lord – stand out starkly against the claims made for Augustus, and in the ensuing story become titles interpreted in fresh and surprising ways.

The setting for Luke's birth narrative clarifies for us the distinction between false hopes and true ones. Relatively humane, stable structures that contribute to the well-being of others often tend to promise more than they can deliver. Their very positive nature becomes seductive and generates impossible expectations. In contrast, Jesus is the anchor for reliable hope, for dependable promises, for anticipations that are more than fulfilled. CC

Set II

Isaiah 62.6–12; Titus 3.4–7; Luke 2.(1–7), 8–20

Isaiah 62.6–12

It is usually thought that chs. 56—66 come from the time shortly after some had returned from the Babylonian exile and were addressing the tasks of rebuilding city, temple and national life so poignantly mirrored in the book of Haggai. Some of the great promises of return in chs. 40—55 had, therefore, been fulfilled, but the reality fell painfully short of the kind of pictures of salvation promised there. So the words and imagery of chs. 40—55 are used a great deal in these chapters to reassure them and renew those hopes.

In the light of v. 1 it is probably the prophet and his circle who are called upon for such an active ministry of intercession in vv. 6–7. The idea of the prophet as 'watchman', looking, like the sentry on the walls of a besieged city, for the first signs of deliverance and proclaiming news to the people, is a familiar one (e.g. Ezek. 3.17; Isa. 21.6–12; 52.8, cf. 2 Sam. 18.24–27). Here the prophet calls for a more strenuous response to the situation than a resigned 'How long, O Lord?' It brings us face to face with the mystery of God's self-limitation in calling for active human participation in the accomplishment of his work, in both deeds and, as here, in prayer.

The response from God is as emphatic as could be imagined, reinforcing the promise of deliverance from the crippling economic hardship which comes from political subservience with an oath of the most solemn nature (vv. 8–9). The promise envisages the restoration of worship in the rebuilt temple as they praise God and know fellowship with him there (v. 9). The same link between economic prosperity and the centrality of God among them in the rebuilt temple is made by Haggai (Hag. 2.4–9).

Again active human participation is called for in a clear allusion to the promise of 40.3–5 that God would miraculously make a highway by which his exiled people could return home (v. 10). Here prophet and people are called on to make all ready for the great things God is going to do in their midst. Presumably, what is in mind is being ready by repentance and faith and doing all in their power to rebuild a new community. Again the mystery of divine sovereignty which yet makes use of human cooperation is stressed.

The promise of that divine sovereign initiative is that God himself will be present in power and grace among his people (he himself is described as their 'salvation' in v. 11). To know him *is* salvation, yet he always brings his 'reward' and 'recompense' with him, v. 11, cf. 40.10. Among the 'rewards' of fellowship with him is the giving of a new nature ('name', v. 12, cf. v. 2). His people will have been 'redeemed' from their bondage by their divine kinsman (cf. Lev. 25.25–28); they will be God's people because he has 'sought' them (cf. Ezek. 34.11–16) and they will live as God's chosen bride (cf. v. 4, and Eph 5.25–27). RM

Titus 3.4–7

Like the other virtually formulaic, brief doctrinal passages in the Pastoral Epistles, these verses are a concise statement of basic Christian faith. Many of the characteristic words of these writings are here: 'appeared', 'saved', 'saviour'. Therefore much that was said about 2.11–14 (see p. 19) is equally relevant here.

But there is in these verses, in this surely post-Pauline writing, rather more Pauline vocabulary than in the other passage: notably in v. 7, where we are reminded of the language of Rom. 5.1f.; 8.17. Equally Pauline is the putting of the contrast between righteous works and God's mercy (v. 5). However, the linking of the mercy of God and baptism is unique. And this is the only reference to baptism in the Pastoral Epistles, perhaps rather surprisingly in view of their interest in the practicalities of Christian life.

'Rebirth' is not used elsewhere in the New Testament explicitly in relation to baptism, though a parallel idea of the utterly transformative meaning of the rite occurs in Romans 6.4, and in the closer parallel in John 3. It is akin to Paul's sense of Christ's coming as giving a new creation. The link between baptism and the Spirit is common early Christian teaching: cf. 1 Cor. 12.13 and numerous passages in Acts. The rite is far more than one's initiation into Christianity or the Church in a purely formal sense: it is a making new – an entry to the life of the new age, in the here and now. The Spirit is a recognized symptom of the presence already of the new state of affairs to which both Jewish and Christian hope looked and which Christian faith saw as now available as the fruit of Christ's saving life and death. It is one of the most powerful verbal means used in early Christianity to express the experience of radical newness and strength of fulfilment which were major features of the Christian community. LH

Luke 2.(1–7), 8–20

The birth of Jesus is the centre of Christmas. What one learns about Jesus from the narratives that relate his birth comes, however, from the actions and words of the other characters of Christmas – in Luke, from the shepherds, the angelic messenger, the heavenly chorus, the mysterious bystanders (2.18), and Mary; in Matthew, from repeated angelic messengers, Joseph, the wise men, Herod, the chief priests and scribes. Nowhere is that more evident than in the Lucan story, where a bare statement of the birth of Jesus is followed by the intriguing account of the nameless shepherds. They are traced from their location in the field tending their flock through their visit to Bethlehem and back to where they originated. From their actions and their interactions with the angelic messenger and the heavenly host, we learn about the character and significance of Jesus' birth.

We first meet the shepherds doing what shepherds are supposed to be doing – tending their flocks. They no doubt remind Luke's readers of the shepherding done once in these same regions by Jesus' famous ancestor, David. The routineness of these shepherds' lives is abruptly interrupted by the appearance of the angelic messenger. Their world, circumscribed at night by the wandering of the sheep, is exploded by the awesome presence of this one who brings news of Jesus' birth. The manifestation of the divine glory, the shepherds' fright, the announcement of the messenger disrupt their order and uniformity and set them on a journey to hear and see earth-changing events.

Three things we note about the intrusive announcement of the messenger. First, the good news includes great joy for 'all the people'. It is not merely the shepherds' small world that is changed by the word of Jesus' birth, but it is Israel's world. While Luke sets the story of the birth in the context of the Roman Empire (2.1–2), he has a primary interest in the destiny of Israel and 'the falling and the rising of many' for whom this baby is set (v. 34). Jesus' relevance for the world, in fact, begins in the city of David as the fulfilment of Jewish expectations. It includes the acceptance of Jewish traditions (vv. 21, 22–40, 41–52), and only from this very particular origin does its universal character emerge.

Second, the announcement focuses on three astounding titles this baby is to carry – Saviour, Messiah and Lord. 'Saviour' has meaning in the narrative because original readers would recognize that the exalted Emperor Augustus had borne such a title. Unfortunately, the eager anticipations for a brighter, more peaceful day stirred by his rule were long since dashed by the brutality and weakness of his successors. Now a true and promise-fulfilling Saviour appears. 'Messiah' (or 'Christ') reminds us of Israel's hope for the anointed figure and God's grand design that he will inaugurate. 'Lord', interestingly, occurs four times in our passage, and in the other three instances is used for God (2.9 [twice], 15). It is inescapable in such a context, then, that divine associations be attached to Jesus (in v. 11).

Third, the angelic announcement designates the sign that will assure the shepherds that they have found 'a Saviour, who is the Messiah, the Lord'. But such a strange sign! Hardly fitting for one bearing such honoured titles! The babe 'wrapped in bands of cloth and lying in a manger', however, is only the beginning of the story of God's unusual ways in accomplishing the divine rule. Not by might or coercive tactics, but in submission and humbleness, Jesus fulfils his vocation.

Perhaps it is the perplexity caused by such a menial sign for such an exalted baby that evokes the immediate confirmation of the heavenly chorus, who join the angelic messenger in a doxology. God is praised for the birth of this child because the birth begins God's reign of peace on earth. The creatures of the heavenly world, in a context of praise, announce God's good plans for this world.

Having heard the heavenly witnesses, the shepherds now decide to go to Bethlehem and 'see' this revelation. Like other disciples who abruptly leave fishing boats and tax tables, they go 'with haste'. We are not told what happened to the flocks, apparently left in the fields. The shepherds' old world has been shattered by the appearance of the messenger, and now they are in search of a new one, one centred in the event that has occurred in Bethlehem.

When the shepherds find Mary, Joseph and Jesus, the narrator records that they report the message that had been made known to them about the baby. To whom did they give their report? To Mary and Joseph? Perhaps. Perhaps the shepherds in responding to the angelic messenger in fact become a confirmation to Mary and Joseph of the significance of this baby so unusually born. But there must have been a wider audience for the shepherds' report too, since 'all who heard it' were astonished – not believing or thoughtful or adoring, just 'amazed'. Apparently nothing spurred them to ask questions or pursue the matter further. In contrast, Mary clings to what has happened. She continues to ponder the events and the words (the Greek word is inclusive of both) of the shepherds' visit.

Finally, the shepherds go back to where they came from, apparently back to fields and to flocks, but not back to business as usual. What was told them by the angelic messenger has been confirmed. They have heard and seen for themselves. Their old world is gone, replaced by a new world. Whatever the structure and order of life before, their world now is centred in the praise and glorifying of God. The nights in the field will never be the same. CC

Set III

Isaiah 52.7–10; Hebrews 1.1–4 (5–12); John 1.1–14

Isaiah 52.7–10

The prophet predicts the certainty of coming deliverance for God's people in a graphic poem depicting the arrival of the messenger bearing news of victory to a besieged and beleaguered city. To share the suspense which precedes it and the intoxicating sense of relief which follows it we need only to read of David and his people anxiously waiting for news from the battlefield (2 Sam. 18.24–28).

First comes the single messenger, running from Babylon, the place of Israel's defeat and misery, appearing over the 'mountains', i.e. the Mount of Olives. At a distance it is impossible to say whether he brings good news or bad. Until he comes within hailing distance it is like watching a doctor coming in to tell us the result of a medical examination. Then the body language and shout tell that the news is good, victory has been gained (cf. 2 Sam. 18.28). God's victorious kingship over hostile forces has been established. The faith and hope expressed in their worship (Pss. 96.10; 97.1; 99.1) has been realized in fact.

Now the city watchmen take up the good news of the messenger (v. 8). In place of anxious hope they have now seen for themselves evidence of victory. 'Eye to eye' they see God returning to his city and his people, just as Job, who had 'heard of God with the hearing of the ear' could say 'but now my eye sees you' (Job 42.5).

The song of salvation, begun as the messenger's solo, then swollen by the concerted shouts of the watchmen, is taken up by the whole chorus of God's people. They are apostrophized as 'the waste places of Jerusalem' (v. 9) because they live in the ruins of their former buildings and among the shattered disillusionment of their former hopes. When God comes as saviour it is the 'waste places' of human suffering, sin and despair that are the first to be so transformed that they become the scene of praise and joy. The promise of the prophet that God would 'comfort' his people (40.1) has been fulfilled, and he has shown that, in their need and failure, they are still 'his' people as he takes on the role of nearest relative and 'redeems' them from their slavery (cf. Lev. 25.25–28).

God has taken his arm from his mantle and acted in power on behalf of his oppressed people (v. 10, cf. Ezek. 4.7). And this is no introverted, domestic matter within the small family of Israel only, but is accomplished on a universal scale. It is because he is the only God of all the earth, victorious over all other powers, that God can redeem his people and fulfil his purposes for all the nations through them (v. 10).

All is of God. Effective messengers and watchmen serve their people best by speaking of God and what he has achieved. RM

Hebrews 1.1–4 (5–12)

The document known as the Epistle to the Hebrews opens with none of the address and greetings that characterize the Pauline letters, but with a polished and highly rhetorical statement of the person and work of Christ; more like the text for a sermon or the proposition for an argument. Ideas are introduced that will be expounded later in the epistle: the continuity between the old and the new, as in chs. 11—12.1; the sacrificial work of Christ and his exaltation to heaven, as in chs. 8—10. God has spoken through 'a Son', and in 2.10–14 the author will describe him as a son among many brethren, fully identified with them. He will clearly affirm Jesus' humanity, but here at the outset needs to express the deeper significance of that individual human life. There are obvious comparisons to be made with the Prologue to the Gospel of John and both authors draw on the language of wisdom, as in Prov. 8; here most closely echoing Wisdom of Solomon 7.26.

Scholars disagree as to whether 'wisdom' in Jewish tradition was understood as a heavenly being, present with God at creation as his agent, or as a personification: a way of talking about the creative work of God himself; but here it hardly matters, for whatever is meant by the wisdom of God is now seen in the person of Christ.

The opening statement is followed by a series, or catena, of quotations, loosely linked by verbal echoes in a manner familiar in Jewish exegesis, and all taken to demonstrate the Son's superiority to angels. There is no need to employ the conspiracy theory of interpretation and to suspect a veiled attack on a contemporary deviant group who held Christ to be an angel, of whom there is no evidence at all. All the texts are ones that may have been used as messianic texts in Judaism and came early into Christian use, and so would have been familiar to the readers. There is some suggestion later in the epistle that the author was dealing with an educated audience who were, however, failing to grow in their faith (5.11–14). They need to be 'stretched' to explore the meanings of familiar texts, and the exposition of such texts as Ps. 110.4 will shape the course of his later argument. SL

John 1.1–14

Beyond the sentimentality and romance of Christmas, we encounter in the baby born at Bethlehem, so the passage tells us, nothing less than God's decision to become human.

One notable feature of the Prologue to the Fourth Gospel is the prominence of visual language (a particularly relevant feature for the Epiphany season). 'Light' and 'glory' are terms associated with the Word, and 'seeing' (alongside 'receiving' and 'believing') is the verb used for the perception of faith. Even before a statement of the incarnation, we read that the life found in the Word illuminates human experience, that the light continually shines in the darkness, and that the darkness has neither understood nor succeeded in extinguishing the light. (The Greek verb in 1.5 translated in the NRSV as 'overcome' has a double meaning: 'comprehend' and 'seize with hostile intent.' Perhaps an appropriate English word retaining the ambiguity would be 'grasp', or 'apprehend'.)

The mention of John the Baptist, who is a kind of lesser luminary or reflected light (5.35) and is contrasted with the true light, signals the movement from a pre-incarnate lumination to the historic advent of the light in Jesus. It is in this context that we understand that the coming of the light into the world 'enlightens everyone' (1.9). This universal reference has sometimes been taken to refer to the ancient notion that every individual possesses a spark of the divine, a measure of a universal conscience. The function of religion (any religion?) is to nurture the inextinguishable spark until it glows with understanding, so the argument goes. But such a reading hardly coheres with the evangelist's use of the image of light throughout the Gospel. Jesus claims in a specific way to be the light of the world (8.12), without whom people grope in the darkness (12.35). The coming of the light entails judgement, because it discloses that people prefer darkness to light (3.19). What seems to be implied in the Prologue is that all people, whether they believe it or not, live in a world illuminated by the light just as they live in a world created by the Word. What they are called to do is to trust the light, to walk in it, and thereby to become children of light (12.36).

Whether as a bolt of lightning in a dark sky, or as a distant beam toward which one moves, or as a dawn that chases the night, what light does is to push back darkness. The Prologue, however, gives no hint that the light has totally banished the darkness, that life now is a perpetual day. In fact, the story John tells reiterates the powerful opposition of the darkness in the ministry of Jesus and beyond. But the promise of the Prologue is that the darkness, despite its best efforts, including even a crucifixion, has not put out the light.

The last paragraph of the prologue has to be understood in terms of the many references to the book of Exodus, which it reflects. In a sense its background is the statement that 'no one has ever seen God' (1.18). Though in fact there are places in the Hebrew Bible where people 'see' God (e.g. Exod. 24.9–11; Isa. 6.1), the statement seems to recall the occasion where Moses, eager to behold the divine glory, is not allowed to view the face of God, only God's backside (Exod. 33.23). In contrast, now God is seen in 'the only Son'.

Furthermore, the seeing of the divine glory is made possible by the incarnation of the Word, who 'tabernacled among us'. The Greek verb translated in the NRSV (John 1.14) as 'lived' more specifically means 'tented' or 'tabernacled', and recalls the theme of God's dwelling with Israel, in the tabernacle of the wilderness wanderings and the temple at Jerusalem. In the humanity of Jesus, the Christian community has beheld the very divine glory Moses wished to see, that unique and specific presence of God that hovered over the tabernacle as a cloud by day and a fire by night.

Terms like 'light' and 'glory' tend toward abstractions and become very difficult to communicate in concrete language to a contemporary congregation. What, then, does it mean to 'see' God, to behold the divine glory? Two other words repeated in the Prologue help in the translation: grace and truth. To behold God is to be a recipient of wave after wave of the divine generosity (grace) and to experience God's faithfulness to the ancient promises (truth). 'Seeing' includes but goes beyond mere sense perception; it has to do with becoming children of God, with discovering the divine benevolence and reliability. Revelation in the Fourth Gospel has a strongly soteriological cast (17.3). CC

The First Sunday of Christmas

Isaiah 61.10—62.3; Galatians 4.4–7; Luke 2.15–21

Isaiah 61.10—62.3

The opening verse of this passage concludes the chapter that begins 'The spirit of the Lord God is upon me . . .' (see the Third Sunday of Advent). They express the hope of the prophet, addressed to newly returned exiles living amid the ruins of their land (cf 61.4), that a new era is about to dawn. The image of being clothed with garments of salvation can best be understood in terms of investiture. Clothes denote office and task, both of which are a gift, looking forward to the future. In a similar way, the image of bride and bridegroom preparing for their wedding expresses the idea of change of status, and new opportunities in new relationships. God's purposes will come to fruition as surely as the earth brings forth its produce (cf. 55.10–11).

The second part of the passage (62.1–3) is a section of a longer poem whose first stanza extends to 62.5. It is a pity that the lesson does not extend to this point, because vv. 4–5 spell out the implication of v. 2, that Jerusalem will be called by a new name. The designations 'Forsaken'; and 'Desolate' will be replaced by 'My delight is in her' and 'Married'. The poem begins with a type of lament in which the prophet exclaims that his entreaty to God on behalf of the people will not cease until he sees their vindication accomplished. In reply the divine assurance is given not only that the vindication will be seen universally, but that Jerusalem will be seen as the crown of God's achievements, and a vital instrument in the fulfilment of his purposes (v. 3). The tension between promise and entreaty is important. To hope for a better world is not simply to sit back and wait for God to do everything. It involves strenuous efforts, including prayer and intercession, carried out in the assurance of the office and task with which all believers have been invested. JR

Galatians 4.4–7

Paul rarely mentions the Incarnation, and lectionaries provide little from his authentic epistles in the Christmas season. However, he plainly presupposes the story of Jesus prior to last supper and crucifixion, and understands the coming of the Messiah (here and Rom. 8.3, God's sending of his Son) as the climax of God's history with Israel and the fulfilment of his design to save the world. This reference to the birth of Jesus is remarkably brief. It does not even name Mary and shows no knowledge of the Matthean and Lucan story of a virgin birth. Paul's use of the title 'Son of God' implies pre-existence but is only indirectly related to later trinitarian developments. Jesus was a Jewish male, born under the Law (of Moses), subject to the requirement of circumcision – a point which relates this epistle to the gospel that follows (Luke 2.21).

Paul's missionary position, that Gentile converts do not have to be circumcised, was later accepted and so his negative argument against what the Galatians were being persuaded to do became superfluous. Later readers have therefore either given 'the law' a wider application to make Paul attack moralism (Augustine) or medieval catholicism (Luther), or else have been interested only in his positive claim: that salvation is through faith in our Lord Jesus Christ. Membership of God's people no longer depends on observing the Law of Moses but on holding fast to the God of Israel by holding fast to God's Messiah, the recently crucified and vindicated Son of God. Trusting obedience to Jesus Christ, reflecting his own faith in God, is the proper response to the gospel through which both Jews and Gentiles are rescued from the present evil age (1.3), and transferred into God's new age. Paul's metaphor of 'redemption' or 'buying back' from slavery contrasts believers' former 'slavery' with their new birth of freedom. His next metaphor is even more suggestive. He describes the transfer from one realm to another here and at Rom. 8.15 (that whole chapter is the best commentary on this passage) as 'adoption' because the new status of believers is a matter of personal relationship to a heavenly Father. The reality of the new age is constituted by God's Spirit, the power enabling believers to live and work to God's praise and glory. The Spirit leads them to pray to their heavenly Father, echoing (as at Rom. 8.15) the Aramaic of Jesus' own prayer (cf. Mark 14.36) which probably lies behind the Lord's Prayer at Luke 11.2. The new relationship to God constituted by the Spirit bears promise for the future. As at Rom. 8.17 this is expressed through the language of inheritance.

Setting Paul's theological reflection alongside the Christmas story can teach us to appropriate that story in terms of its meaning for ourselves. Our new life in the Spirit as brothers and sisters of Jesus (Rom. 8.29) means sharing his freedom (Gal. 5.1, 13, and cf. 2 Cor. 3.17). It is contrasted with old patterns of life, including outdated religious practices. It is not hard to identify the greed and self-absorption that are contrasted with life in the Spirit in ch. 5, but Galatians challenges us to bring even our religious practices to the test of the Spirit and the freedom given us in Jesus. RM

Luke 2.15–21

Reading this passage, it is hard not to see it in terms of the many classical paintings that depict it. All through these first two chapters indeed, Luke's writing has a visual quality. But the passage is also part of the larger literary whole, and we note how the John the Baptist sections of the chapters run (though not slavishly) in tandem with those concerning Jesus. So compare these verses with 1.57–80. In both, there is the linking of circumcision and naming, the giving of acclaim to the child, and a response from a patient. But there are also differences. Jesus' birth has been greeted and validated by the appearance of no less than a host of angels (vv. 9–14), who made clear precisely who he is. And Mary's reaction (v. 19; cf. v. 51), describing her in almost sage-like terms, shows her role as a unique link onwards to the ministry of Jesus that follows (8.21; 11.28, which does not 'down' her but re-describes her, cf. 1.37) and still further to the first Christian community in Jerusalem (Acts 1.14). Luke says nothing about the content of her pondering, though his reticence has not prevented the making of 'helpful' suggestions.

Nor does Luke give any clear sign of the significance of shepherds, though later persons (painters included) have juxtaposed them, as the poor balancing the rich in nice social comprehensiveness, with the Magi from Matthew 2. Perhaps Luke sees them as a first instance of Jesus' acceptance of the outcast or disreputable, one of his recurring themes; but he does not say so. Or perhaps they make an allusion to David, the greatest shepherd of all, whose messianic heir Jesus is; see vv. 4, 11. Similarly, though later generations have seen Jesus' circumcision as a sign of his humble submission to the law of God (cf. v. 46), Luke does not make this point here, leaving it to the following episode. And Luke is no advocate of circumcision's permanence for Christians; see Acts 15. Here, he seems to be concerned only with the giving of the name, already commanded by the angel in 1.31. Jesus' identity and role are Luke's overriding concern. LH

The Second Sunday of Christmas

Jeremiah 31.7–14 or Ecclesiasticus 24.1–12; Ephesians 1.3–14; John 1.(1–9), 10–18

Jeremiah 31.7–14

These are probably not the words of the prophet Jeremiah, but the work of a disciple whose outlook was similar to that of the author of Isa. 40—55. They were probably composed towards the end of the Babylonian exile, which lasted from 597 to 540 BC, and were meant as a comfort and challenge to those in exile. Where they were spoken/written and precisely to whom they were addressed is uncertain.

The opening words are either a command to the people to lead into the prayer 'Save, O Lord, your people', or, more likely, a declaration that God's victory is already accomplished, in which case a preferable translation would be 'the Lord has saved his people' (so NEB, REB).

God affirms that he is about to bring the exiles home, no matter how far away they might be. It is noteworthy that explicit mention is made of precisely those groups who would find the journey, mostly on foot, of some thousand miles (if only Babylon is envisaged) most arduous and forbidding: the blind, the lame, pregnant women and those giving birth. Their journey will be made possible because God will provide an even path (rather than a straight path) which is well provisioned with water. Behind this language is the image of the shepherd leading his flock, finding the best pasture, and paying particular attention to its weakest members (cf. Ezek. 43.16).

The description of the life of the returned community in Jerusalem is one which draws on those images that most adequately express a perfect existence in the harsh world of subsistence farming. 'Life shall become like a watered garden' (cf. the description of paradise in Gen. 2.10), and those things that sustain the necessities of life (grain, wine, oil, flocks and herds) will be abundantly blessed. The dancing of young women and the rejoicing of young and old men symbolize the peace (i.e. the lack of danger from enemies) that Jerusalem will enjoy.

Was this prophecy fulfilled? The answer must be 'no'. The actual restoration after 540 BC was nothing like what is envisaged here. Will it be fulfilled? The answer must again be 'no', at any rate at the level of its details, which concern the restoration of a peasant and not an industrial or technological society. What, then, is the value of the passage? Its value is that it is a sublime expression of the compassion of God: a God who, because he regards his people as his very offspring, can never be indifferent to their plight and their sufferings; a God who, because he has scattered, will gather his people. Then why has he scattered, or allowed his people to be scattered? The parent image partly answers this question. How can children grow up if they are always to be under parental control? The good news is that God will never give up on his people – including ourselves. JR

Ecclesiasticus 24.1–12

This poem, in which personified Wisdom speaks in the first person, draws upon other parts of the Old Testament, most notably Gen. 1 and Prov. 8.22–36; but it also contains original ideas. The opening introduction (vv. 1–2) sets the scene for Wisdom's oration. There is a twofold scenario. In v. 2 she is standing in the divine assembly, surrounded by God's angels and his heavenly armies (the stars). In v. 1 she is speaking to 'her people', i.e. Israel. How she combines these two stances is explained by the two parts of the passage.

The first part of Wisdom's speech in vv. 3–6 describes her privileged position in relation to God and the created order. That she 'came forth from the mouth of the Most High' has made Jewish interpretation identify her with the Law (Torah), and Christian interpretation identify her with the Logos (cf. John 1.1). 'Mist' in v. 3 translates the Greek, whereas the Hebrew version discovered in Cairo in the 1890s has a word meaning 'dark cloud'. This takes us closer to Gen. 1 as does the Hebrew word rendered as 'abyss' in v. 5, the same word translated as 'deep' in Gen. 1.2. The idea of 'covering the earth' in v. 3 is also similar to the spirit of God hovering over the waters in Gen. 1.2. Combined with allusions to the Genesis creation narrative is one from the exodus and wilderness wanderings traditions. The 'pillar of cloud' in v. 4 alludes to the symbol of the divine presence at Exod. 13.21 and elsewhere. The word 'alone' in v. 5 is important, because it excludes other deities from the governance of the universe and firmly anchors Greek ideas of wisdom (Sophia) into Israel's monotheistic faith.

The second part of the poem describes how universal Wisdom entered into a special relationship with Israel and Jerusalem. The idea that God chose Israel as the particular nation for which he would care is found in Deut. 32.8–9. Here, he cares for Israel through his surrogate, Wisdom. Initially, Wisdom is represented as ranging over the whole universe seeking a resting place (v. 7; and cf. again the hovering spirit of God in Gen. 1.2) until God commands her to go to Israel (the Jacob of v. 8) and Jerusalem. Three times in vv. 7–8 come words based upon the Hebrew verb *shakan*: 'where should I abide?', 'place for my tent', 'make your dwelling'. In later Judaism this verb is used for the noun *shekinah* denoting the divine presence, while in John 1.14 'dwelt among us' (*eskēnosen*) uses the Greek verb that usually renders the Hebrew *shakan,* including here in the Septuagint. Thus does the poem nobly express the transcendence and imminence of the divine principle, embodied for Jews in the Law (Torah) and for Christians in the incarnation. JR

Ephesians 1.3–14

Paul customarily opens his letters with an expression of thanksgiving for God's action in the lives of the congregation he addresses. Ephesians, which was probably written by a disciple of Paul rather than by Paul himself, not only continues that practice but expands it. Virtually the whole of chs. 1—3 is taken up with expressions of praise and thanksgiving. Eph. 1.3 introduces this dominant mood of doxology with an ascription of praise to God for God's gifts to humankind. Since the word 'blessing' in Greek can refer both to an act of thanksgiving or praise and to an act of bestowing some gift on another, the play on the word in this verse sets the tone for what follows: God is to be blessed for God's blessings. The extent of these blessings comes to expression in the phrase 'every spiritual blessing in the heavenly places'. God's goodness takes every conceivable form.

Verses 4–14 detail the form of God's blessings and focus on God's choosing of the elect. First, the author points to the agelessness of God's election: 'He chose us in Christ before the foundation of the world.' This bit of eloquence need not be turned into a literal proposition about God's act of election. Instead, the author asserts that God's choosing has no beginning. Just as it is impossible to identify the beginning of God's Christ (John 1.1), so it is impossible to conceive of a time when God did not choose on behalf of humankind.

God's election creates a people who are 'holy and blameless before him'. Verse 5 elaborates this characterization of God's people. They become God's children through Jesus Christ, but always what happens is 'according to the good pleasure of his will'. Everything that has occurred comes as a result of God's will and results in 'the praise of his glorious grace that he freely bestowed on us in the Beloved'. In the face of God's eternal choice on behalf of humankind, in the face of God's revelation of his Son, Jesus Christ, in the face of God's grace, the only appropriate response is one of praise (v. 6).

Verses 7–14 continue the exposition of God's gifts to humankind – redemption, forgiveness, wisdom, faith. The exposition culminates with repeated references to the inheritance believers receive through Christ (vv. 11, 14). That inheritance carries with it the responsibility already articulated in v. 6, which is to praise God's glory. Primary among the Christian's responsibilities is the giving of praise to God. With v. 15, the writer moves from this general expression of thanksgiving for God's actions on behalf of humankind to particular expressions of thanks relevant to his context. He constantly keeps the Ephesians in his prayers, asking for them 'a spirit of wisdom and of revelation as you come to know [God]' (v. 17). The prayer continues in v. 18 with the petition that believers might be enlightened so that they know the hope to which they have been called and the riches that are part of God's inheritance. This mood of doxology continues throughout ch. 2 and most of ch. 3, as the author celebrates the nature of God's action in Christ Jesus.

For Christians in the West, these words may have an alien and perhaps even an exotic tone. They run counter to at least two of our most deeply held values. First, these verses insist over and over again that humankind is utterly dependent on God. To assert that God creates, God destines, God wills, God reveals, God accomplishes God's own plan means that human beings, in and of themselves, accomplish nothing. This assault on the Western sense of independence and autonomy poses not only a challenge, but also a significant opportunity for preaching.

The second way in which this text cuts against the grain of Christianity in a modern context derives from its insistence on the obligation to praise God. Our thoroughgoing pragmatism inclines us to respond to the claim that God has acted on our behalf with the question, 'What are we to *do?*' If we stand in God's debt, then we understand ourselves to be obligated to pay back the amount owed. The text, however, stipulates no repayment, for the debt can never be paid. Instead, the exhortation is to give God thanks and praise. To our way of thinking, this is no response at all, and yet it is fundamental to our existence as God's creatures. The reading of Ephesians should prompt us to recall the words of the Westminster Larger Catechism, that the chief end of human life is 'to glorify God, and fully to enjoy him for ever'. BG

John 1.(1–9), 10–18

See Christmas Day, Set III, pp. 26–27.

The Epiphany

Isaiah 60.1–6; Ephesians 3.1–12; Matthew 2.1–12

Isaiah 60.1–6

This passage introduces a section (chs. 60—62, and especially 60.1–22) that announces the good news of deliverance for stricken Israel. The imperatives 'arise', 'shine', are feminine singular and so it is 'Zion' which is addressed, that is the community whose life is centred on the still poor and unreconstructed city. The future action of God is announced in a series of 'prophetic perfects'. It is seen as so certain that it can be described as having happened already.

They are to 'rise' from the lethargy of despair and to 'shine', but with the reflected light of God for it is his 'glory', that is, his manifested presence, which is 'rising' on them, ushering in a new age as the rising sun brings a new day. Three times in vv. 1 and 2 the words 'on you' are repeated, emphasizing that it is these very defeated, fearful people who are being summoned to reflect the light of God who comes among them, just as Moses' face shone with the reflected glory of God (Exod. 34.29–35, cf. 2 Cor. 3.18).

By contrast, the other nations are still in deep darkness (v. 2a). This might be an allusion to the 'darkness' which covered the face of the earth before God said 'Let there be light' at creation (Gen. 1.2–3). More likely, however, it is recalling the exodus story when God's presence ensured the Israelites had light by which to travel while the pursuing Egyptians were frustrated by darkness (Exod. 10.21–23). So, attracted by what they see of the miracle transforming Zion, these Gentile nations come to seek the source of that light for themselves (v. 3) so fulfilling the original promise to Abraham that 'all the families of the earth' would be blessed through him (Gen. 12.1–3).

Nor do these nations come empty-handed. They bring back all the dispersed Israelite exiles whom they have taken away captive (v. 4), a sight destined to bring such joy that, when the people see it, they will be radiant with the light of God's presence and power (v. 5, cf. Ps. 34.5, the only other instance of this word in the Old Testament) and their hearts will be enlarged to accommodate all their joy.

Further, the prophet pictures caravans of camels trekking across the desert bearing rich gifts of gold and frankincense, just as the Queen of Sheba brought tribute to Solomon, having heard of his great reputation (1 Kings 10.1–2). This inspired a continuing hope for the Davidic king (Ps. 72.15). Verse 6 here has probably also influenced the account in Matthew's Gospel of the coming of the wise men from the east bearing gifts (Matt. 2.1–11).

If all this sounds the note of nationalist chauvinism we have at least to remember that the Gentiles are attracted, not by Israel's splendour, but by the degree to which they reflect God's splendour (cf. Matt. 5.16). Further, the nations are envisaged as coming, not as servants of Israel, but as fellow worshippers in the temple (v. 6). RM

Ephesians 3.1–12

Following the first two chapters of Ephesians, with their extensive thanksgiving to God, in 3.1 the author takes up Paul's ministry in the context of God's mystery. Verses 1–3 characterize Paul's calling as his 'commission'. Verses 4–6 elaborate on the nature of God's mystery that is now revealed, and this section provides the most obvious entrance into a discussion of the Epiphany. In vv. 7–9, the focus is once again on Paul's ministry concerning that mystery, and in vv. 10–12 it is on the ministry of the Church as a whole.

The opening statement breaks off awkwardly after the identification of Paul as 'a prisoner for Christ Jesus for the sake of you Gentiles'. Verse 2 verifies Paul's calling as prisoner on behalf of the Gentiles by referring to the gift of God's grace that bestowed on him a 'commission' on behalf of Gentiles. Verse 3 makes specific the nature of this gift of grace, in that the mystery became known to Paul through revelation. In common with all believers, Paul's knowledge of God's action comes to him solely through God's own free gift.

Verse 4 returns to the term 'mystery', which is initially described only as a 'mystery of Christ'. The newness of the revelation of this mystery emerges in v. 5, which emphasizes that only in the present time has the mystery been revealed. This assertion stands in tension with statements elsewhere in the Pauline corpus regarding the witness of the prophets to God's action in Jesus Christ (e.g. Rom. 1.2; 16.26). What the author celebrates is the present revelation of God's mystery, and the contrast with the past helps to emphasize that fact but should not become a critique or rejection of past generations. Similarly, the second part of v. 5 identifies the 'holy apostles and prophets' as recipients of revelation, not because revelation confines itself to those individuals but because of their central role in proclamation.

Verse 6 identifies the 'mystery of Christ': 'the Gentiles have become fellow heirs, members of the same body, and sharers in the promise in Christ Jesus through the gospel'. Given the previous few verses, we might anticipate that the 'mystery' refers to the mystery of Jesus' advent. For this letter, however, the 'mystery of Christ' has a very specific connotation, namely, the inclusion of the Gentiles. Each word identifying the Gentiles in v. 6 begins with the prefix *syn*, 'together', emphasizing the oneness created through the mystery. We might convey this phrase in English as 'heirs together, a body together, sharers together'. For the writer of Ephesians, central to the 'mystery of Christ' is the oneness of Jew and Gentile.

The emphasis here on the social dimension of the gospel, the unification of human beings, needs specific attention. Certainly Ephesians does not limit the mystery to its social component, as if the only characteristic of the gospel is its impact on human relations. The extensive praise of God and of Jesus Christ in chs. 1 and 2 prevents us from reductionism. Nevertheless, here the radical oneness of Jew and Gentile who become one new humanity (2.15) becomes a necessary ingredient in the larger reconciliation of humankind to God (2.16). Any separation between 'vertical' and 'horizontal' dimensions of faith here stand exposed as inadequate.

Verses 7–9 return us to Paul's role with respect to the gospel. He, despite his own standing as 'the very least of all the saints', receives the gift of preaching among the Gentiles and, indeed, among all people (v. 9). Proclamation of the gospel comes not from Paul and his fellow apostles alone, however. Verse 10 identifies the role of the whole Church in proclamation. The Church, both through its verbal proclamation and through its actions, makes known God's wisdom. Here that wisdom is addressed to 'the rulers and authorities in the heavenly places'. The gospel addresses not only human beings but all of God's creation.

Verses 11–12 affirm once again the purpose of God in the proclamation of Paul and of the Church. God's purpose has its final goal in Christ Jesus our Lord, 'in whom we have access to God in boldness and confidence through faith in him'. These last terms connote more in Greek than the English translations can convey. To speak 'boldly' (*parrēsia*) is to speak without regard for the consequences, and to have 'access' (*prosagōgē*) is to have, through Jesus Christ, a means of drawing near to God. In other words, the revelation, or epiphany, of Jesus Christ carries with it both the obligation of proclaiming the gospel and the strength needed for carrying out that obligation. BG

Matthew 2.1–12

The Book of Common Prayer explained Epiphany as the manifestation of Christ to the Gentiles, and this is certainly how Matthew understood his story of the wise men. He never describes them explicitly as Gentiles, but the way in which they are presented by Matthew indicates that this is how he meant them to be understood. Thus they ask where the child is who has been born king of the Jews, in contrast with the Jewish chief priests and scribes, who know the answer from the Scriptures; they say 'king of the Jews', whereas Jews usually referred to themselves as Israelites. Notice that Herod rephrases their title with 'the Messiah'.

The story presents a contrast between Gentile 'wise men' (astrologers, whom Matthew surely values as among the intellectual elite of their day, a plus mark for the Christian cause) worshipping the true king and a Jewish false king seeking his apparent rival's death. Antitheses of this kind are characteristic of Matthew's Gospel: destruction–life; wheat–weeds; good servants–bad servants; etc.

There is another point which confirms this view of the wise men. Matthew seems to have arranged his whole book as a diptych, with the beginning matching the end; e.g. God is with us (1.23) and I am with you always (28.20). Similarly, the coming of Gentiles in ch. 2 is matched at the end by the command to make disciples of all the nations (*ethné*, Gentiles). In one of the very few healing stories that Matthew adds to what he had received from Mark, the contrast is made between the faith of a Gentile and the faithfulness of Israel, and between the final salvation of Gentiles and the damnation of Jews (8.5–13).

The presence of this theme in Matthew's Gospel is extraordinary, and calls for some explanation. The book as a whole seems to come from a church or churches where the law of Moses was still regarded as authoritative (5.17–20). We might therefore have assumed that these 'Jewish Christians' would have disapproved of a mission to Gentiles. Moreover, the Gospel does contain the prohibition, 'Go nowhere among the Gentiles' (10.5f.). The Twelve are to preach to Israel, and to Israel alone (perhaps, however, just for the present, during Jesus' lifetime, with 28.20 providing for the rest of time). There remains, however, something of a puzzle about how Matthew quite held these two attitudes together; and we can also note his use from time to time of 'Gentiles' as a term of abuse or at least as an expression of superiority: 5.47; 6.32; 18.17: is that just an unthinking and unregenerate reflex?

Perhaps, like Paul, he was convinced of the rightness of preaching to Gentiles, by the bare fact that they had received the Spirit. And, also like Paul, by the fact that Jews, on the whole, were less likely to become Christian believers than Gentiles were. Perhaps, even as a Jew, he was on the 'liberal' wing that saw a positive future in God's purposes for at least some Gentiles.

Whatever the reason for it, Matthew's book contains both a high belief in the Jewish elements of Christianity and a conviction that these are to be made available to those who were not physically descended from Abraham. Though Jesus himself had few contacts with Gentiles, Matthew, like Paul before him, and like Luke and John later, believed that the mission to the Gentiles was according to the will of God. For him this must have been in many ways a costly belief to hold. JF

The Baptism of Christ

(The First Sunday of Epiphany)

Genesis 1.1–5; Acts 19.1–7; Mark 1.4–11

Genesis 1.1–5

The reason why this passage has been chosen for the baptism of Christ is because of the reference to the Spirit of God moving over the face of the waters in 1.2. It is therefore particularly unfortunate that the translation printed in the lectionary, from the NRSV, has adopted the rendering 'a wind from God'. Those responsible for worship will therefore be well advised either to use the RSV, NIV or REB for this passage, or to substitute the NRSV marginal reading 'while the spirit of God swept . . .' If it is asked how 'the spirit of God' can become a 'wind from God', the answer is that the Hebrew word *ruach* means both spirit and wind; and it has to be added that 'wind' is an excellent way of understanding 'spirit'. Just as we can see and feel the effects of the wind without being able to see the wind itself, so the effects of God's Spirit (cf. Gal. 5.22–3) can be seen without the Spirit being visible. This does not make the NRSV rendering correct, however, and although its translation evokes a picture of brooding, primordial chaos, early Christian and Jewish interpreters certainly took 1.2 to refer to the Spirit of God.

Significant for today's readings is the fact that the verb translated 'swept' is also used at Deut. 32.11 of an eagle fluttering over its young. The image is that of attentive, concerned and protective hovering. In the context of the opening of Genesis, then, the primordial chaos out of which God brings order, i.e. creates, is one over which God's Spirit hovers and flutters expectantly, protectively, prior to light appearing in obedience to the divine command. The combination of primordial waters, hovering Spirit and creation provides an excellent backcloth for the account of Jesus' baptism. JR

Acts 19.1–7

It is evident from the Gospels that the figure of John the Baptist, though always highly valued, was nevertheless in some ways disturbing for the early followers of Jesus; and it is not always easy to see quite how and why this was so. In a general way, it was to do with the relationship between John and Jesus. John was on the scene first and it is likely that Jesus was among his adherents before stepping into his own path. Hence a question: did that make John superior to Jesus? So it might seem. But Jesus had gone his way, with a distinct message and a distinct style of presenting God's purpose and God's rule, apparently less ascetic than John (Luke 7.18–35) and perhaps less threatening and severe. So for the followers of Jesus, the role of John was reduced – to that of herald or preparatory voice, and Scripture justified that judgement (Mark 1.2–8; Luke 3.15–17). Yet the bond was never severed and sometimes it was strengthened. Luke says that they were blood relations (Luke 1.36).

This picture of closeness between the two, and yet the incompleteness of John, persisted into the early decades of the Church – at least according to Luke in Acts. John's Gospel too sees disciples of John as on the edge of the movement around Jesus and in some cases joining it (1.35–37), and so finding a fuller truth; for the evangelist, the link seems still to live, especially if you read the Gospel as reflecting concerns of the writer's situation.

Here in Acts, the inadequacy of John the Baptist (and his inheritance) is located in the matter of the manifestation of the Spirit, notably as made observable in ecstatic speech: there, one had a visible and audible touchstone. For Luke, a Pentecost-like experience is needed to guarantee full faith centred on Jesus (and Luke does not lack modern Christians to see as he saw). It was true also in the equally contestable case of Cornelius (10.44) – and the Spirit made acceptance now beyond challenge. Here too the clear signs of the Spirit (v. 6) end all doubt and the new 'full Christians' even turn into a sort of shadow apostolate, twelve strong (v. 7). It goes unremarked by Luke that followers of John the Baptist, presumably Jews, were to be found in Ephesus; not, one would think, a place to find Jews of what we might see as the distinctly un-Hellenistic kind associated with John. For Luke, it is as if the one thing that matters is tidying up a persisting anomaly left over from Jesus' lifetime in Galilee. And he had just told of a similar piece of clarification over Apollos, also stuck at the John the Baptist stage, for all his (again Hellenistic in style?) learning (18.24, 28). Paul saw him as a fellow-missionary and makes no reference to any problem over his genuineness or adequacy (1 Cor. 1—3). He had given no hint of what Luke may be getting at and it remains obscure. But plainly Luke is determined that due order must be observed, in whatever ways seemed right in his time and place. LH

Mark 1.4–11

It was not kind to the evangelist to urge us to read this passage without what precedes and follows it. The first 11 or, more likely, 13 or even 15 (and perhaps 20, see pp. 270–271) verses of Mark's Gospel have the character of a prologue. This is a theological even more than a literary judgement. It means that the idea is to present us with cameos of doctrine, each brief and full of allusion and symbol, and together epitomizing the message of the Gospel as a whole, rather than quasi-historical episodes.The passage is more akin in function to the Johannine Prologue than appears at first sight and more than has generally been recognized.

After words from prophecy in vv. 2–3, which proclaim, as if with a fanfare, the herald-role of John the Baptist in preparing 'the way' that will lead to Calvary, Mark establishes that role in vivid pictorial terms. John looks like Elijah, the great prophet of the coming age whose return Malachi had foretold (2 Kings 1.8; Mal.

4.5); and his preaching of a new start for all ('repentance for remission of sins') is greeted with amazing enthusiasm by everybody, in the first of Mark's crowd scenes; no doubt stirring the hearts of his readers in their little Christian groups – for whom he has, total innovator, taken up his pen.

But this is only preliminary. Jesus will baptize 'in Holy Spirit', just as he will himself receive the Spirit (v. 10). It is the evidence of the new world's coming. As, in Mark, Jesus does no baptizing at all, this must surely look ahead to the life and practice of the Church; the hearers of the book know what it means and they are beneficiaries of the promise. Mark has a dual focus: both on his story and on its wonderful outcome. His originality was to write of the present faith of himself and his friends – but by way of the tale of Jesus' words and deeds.

Jesus of Nazareth appears and is himself baptized. Mark's successor-evangelists found this puzzling to the point of embarrassment and even scandal, for Jesus needed no repentance. Mark felt no such difficulty, and perhaps 10.38 enables us to see why. For him, baptism was a metaphor for death; compare Paul in Rom. 6.3–11 (Mark shows many signs of thinking Paulinely). So Jesus' baptism foreshadows his death, and Mark is getting that death on the agenda from the start. The word 'beloved', inserted into the quote from Ps. 2.7 with which Jesus is addressed from heaven, has the same effect. It is, in the Septuagint, the repeated description of Isaac, mysterious almost-victim in sacrifice in Gen. 22 (cf. English from Hebrew, 'only'). It was a passage that helped early Christians to grasp the sense in Jesus' death (cf. Rom. 8.32; John 3.16), just as it was also a lively subject of Jewish theological imagination in the period (but perhaps in reaction to Christian use of it).

Finally, Mark encloses his Gospel in brackets of meaning: the 'splitting' of the heavens and the recognition of Jesus as the 'Son of God' reappear at the crucifixion that makes all his message plain and finally effective (15.38–39). Heaven and earth, God and humankind, are united by God's act and Jesus is his all-sufficient agent, somehow recognized in his dying by his executioner, ostensibly the most flagrant sinner of all, yet representing us all. LH

The Second Sunday of Epiphany

1 Samuel 3.1–10 (11–20); Revelation 5.1–10; John 1.43–51

1 Samuel 3.1–10

It is likely that we are intended to read the books of Joshua, Judges, Samuel and Kings (that is, excluding Ruth) as one continuous story of the people's past from their entry into the 'promised land' to their defeat at the hands of the Babylonians. Its particular viewpoint is close to that found in the book of Deuteronomy, and so it is often described as the 'Deuteronomistic History'. It certainly contains historical elements, though scholars are sharply divided as to the historical plausibility of much of the material. In any case it is not history in any modern sense, but is a story deliberately organized to show God's hand at work. One way of doing this is to set out the material in distinct phases, with important transitions between them.

One such transition is the change from rule by judges to the establishment of a monarchy, and in that development an important role was played by Samuel. We know little or nothing about him historically, and even the stories in which he is pictured present him in different ways. Here he is involved with both prophecy and priesthood.

The priesthood is presumably that attached to the sanctuary at Shiloh, though that is not specified in our story. The priest there was Eli, and readers of the early chapters of 1 Samuel have been given several hints that all was not well with Eli and his family. (In ch. 1 he had supposed Samuel's mother Hannah to be drunk; in ch. 2 he had failed to control his own sons, and he had been warned that his family was doomed.) Probably in the present story we are meant to see his failing eyesight as symbolizing his failure to see God's will.

A new intermediary between God and the people is needed, and that brings out the prophetic aspect of this story. Samuel is being prepared for his task in a way reminiscent of the stories of the calling of prophets, for example Isaiah, who also receives a vision of God in a holy place (Isa. 6). Like the other prophetic call-stories, the account of Samuel's call is brought out in a very dramatic way: the call is repeated three times, and at last Samuel responds obediently, 'Speak, Lord.' The fact that Samuel did not recognize the origin of the voice in the night is not due to weakness on his part; like the later prophets he has not yet been taught what will be required of him (v. 7). Fortunately Eli's spiritual blindness is not yet total, for 'he perceived that the LORD was calling the boy' (v. 8). RC

Revelation 5.1–10

In his vision of heaven, John is shown a sealed scroll, unread for want of an agent to unseal it. When it is progressively unsealed, in ch. 6, things happen; and they are terrible things involving human suffering on a vast scale and from all manner of causes. John weeps because it cannot be opened; yet surely it were better to remain closed. The scroll contains a vision of the future, terrifying, yes; but it is held in the hand of God, and opened through the agency of the Lamb, Christ. In the introduction of God's agent, traditional messianic images are used: he is the Lion of Judah (Gen. 49.9–10) and the heir of the house of David (Isa. 11.1). Such a Messiah may be expected, as he often was in contemporary Judaism, to be a ruler and a conqueror, delivering God's people by the power of military might; and indeed John uses the language of warfare and victory for the work of Christ, as here in v. 5, and again in ch. 19. Yet in the dramatic juxtaposition of images characteristic of this author, although he 'hears' the Lion, he 'sees' the Lamb. This image inevitably evokes the language of sacrifice, echoing the acclamation of Jesus as 'the Lamb of God' in the Gospel of John 1.36, where he dies as the Passover lamb. Interestingly, the author of Revelation avoids explicitly sacrificial language: his Lamb is seen as 'slaughtered', violently butchered as his followers will be in 6.9. This Lion/Lamb Messiah shares in the suffering of the world, and it is his death that is the means of redemption from it (v. 9). He will create a messianic people of God from all the peoples of the world, and they will share his reign; this does not mean that they will escape the world's suffering any more than he does for, as the author will make clear, the closest followers of Christ are the martyrs. The explanation of the means of this Messiah's victory is given in the words of a 'new song' sung by the inhabitants of heaven and introduced with the same acclamation, 'You are worthy', as was offered to the one seated on the throne in 4.11. The Lamb who died as man is addressed as God; and the eyes of the Lamb are the spirits of God; in the imagery of Revelation is some of the 'raw material' for trinitarian theology. Finally, as the inhabitants of heaven offer their new song to the Lamb, they hold a bowl of incense that is the prayers of the saints: the worship of the Church on earth is joined to that of heaven. SL

John 1.43–51

The call of the disciples necessarily stands near the beginning of the story in every Gospel. But in John's Gospel it has a particular slant. It comes after a long section devoted to John the Baptist, who is introduced as a key 'witness' to the true nature of Jesus; and the disciples, instead of responding to a direct and personal call from Jesus, are men who recognize something unique in him and add their own testimony to John's, calling him 'the Messiah', or (as here) the one 'about whom Moses in the law and also the prophets wrote'. This series of witnesses culminates in Nathanael.

Why is his testimony valuable? His first reaction shows some scepticism: 'Can anything good come out of Nazareth?' But Jesus, when he meets him, describes him as 'without guile'. Deceitfulness was the mark of a false witness (Prov. 12.17); this man could be relied on to speak the truth. It was a culture in which proof depended far more on the reliability of witnesses than on physical evidence. The first chapter of John's Gospel builds up an impressive list of witnesses to the crucial proposition that Jesus is Messiah and Son of God.

Nathanael does not appear in any list of the apostles, but reappears after the resurrection (John 21.2). What brought him to the point of being able to say about Jesus, 'You are the Son of God! You are the king of Israel!'? Was it really Jesus' apparent gift of second sight, by which he had identified him previously 'under the fig tree'? For a moment it is as if Jesus, not Nathanael, is the one who gives the precious evidence. When a witness was cross-examined, he might be asked, 'What tree did it happen under?' – as Daniel asked the perfidious elders in the story of Susanna (Susanna 54). Jesus forestalls the question, and Nathanael immediately sees something so exceptional in him that he acclaims him as the one whom his religion has taught him to look forward to.

But one of the themes of all the Gospels is that though Jesus was indeed this expected Messiah, he was also profoundly different from what people had imagined this figure would be. 'Messiah' meant simply a man 'anointed' – that is appointed and empowered by God – for the purpose of inaugurating a new era. But in John's Gospel Jesus is clearly not just a man with a mission. He is more: he has a quite special relationship with his heavenly Father. The story of Jacob's dream (Gen. 28.10–17) offers some imagery in which this special relationship can be expressed. Jacob dreamt that he saw a ladder set up between heaven and earth and the angels of God 'ascending and descending on it'. But the words 'on it' could also mean 'on him'. Nathanael would soon discover that Jesus' intimate access to heavenly realities made it appropriate to speak of angels 'ascending and descending upon him'. AEH

The Third Sunday of Epiphany

Genesis 14.17–20; Revelation 19.6–10; John 2.1–11

Genesis 14.17–20

Chapter 14 has long been regarded as an erratic block in the Genesis story. It seems to describe a situation in which the leading rulers of the known world all converged on the area of the Dead Sea. In the story Abraham is introduced at a late stage and is envisaged as a warrior, with an extensive retinue, engaged in battles with large-scale enemy coalitions. This is a very different picture from the family story of surrounding chapters. The older source-critics were quite unable to assign this chapter to any of their preferred sources. Most modern scholars regard the chapter as a late addition to the main Genesis material, perhaps aimed at drawing out Abraham's connection with Jerusalem (assuming that 'Salem' here is a short form of Jerusalem), but no consensus has been reached.

Within this larger context the verses of our reading pose their own problems. Many have taken them to be an entirely separate unit, unconnected with the remainder of the chapter. Nothing is known of Melchizedek in historical terms; he is presented here both as king and as 'priest of El Elyon' ('God Most High'). This became a name applied to Yahweh, especially in the Psalms (cf. Pss. 7.17; 91.1). Whether this was the name of an originally Canaanite deity or simply one mode of describing Israel's own God remains unclear.

Melchizedek became an important symbolic figure within later traditions. He is mentioned at Ps. 110.4 as the typical priest, and is also mentioned in the Dead Sea Scrolls. The theme of Melchizedek as the true priest is taken further in the Epistle to the Hebrews, where Jesus is credited with priestly status 'according to the order of Melchizedek' (Heb. 6.20), and the links between Melchizedek and Jesus are imaginatively developed in the following chapter.

In Christian liturgical tradition these verses have played another important part, because the 'bread and wine' (v. 18) have been seen as prefiguring the eucharistic elements. Overall, one may say that this is one of those passages that will prove frustrating for those who wish to have a clear historical account, of the kind that can be backed up by reliable supporting evidence. By contrast it will be a delight for those who treasure literary allusions and traditions and are not greatly concerned about historical details. RC

Revelation 19.6–10

The vision of John has unfolded with three great cycles of disaster, and now God's judgement is celebrated and a new age anticipated in a great Hallelujah chorus. As usual with Revelation, there is a blend of images. The new age as a great banquet may be found in Isa. 25.6 and became commonplace in Jewish eschatology; and Israel the people of God as God's bride appears in Isa. 61.10 (cf. the unfaithful wife in Hos. 2). Jesus draws on the former tradition in his parable of the great supper in Luke 14.16–24, which becomes a marriage feast in Matt. 22.1–14, cf. 25.1–12. In the Gospel the identity of the bridegroom is not stated, though it may have been inferred by the readers; here it is explicit. The heart of the vision of the new age is the union of Christ the Lamb with his Church as bridegroom with bride. In Revelation this union belongs to the future, when Christ's people are ready for him, clothed with what is required of the saints (the usual translation 'righteous deeds' suggests a moral preparation; comparison with 7.13–14 might rather suggest a sharing in Christ's suffering). It is part of the vision of the coming together of the new heaven and earth (21.1–2). In Ephesians the husband/wife image for Christ and the Church is used of the present experience of Christ's love and care, and to undergird advice on human relationships (5.22–33).

An odd little exchange between the seer and his interpreting angel interrupts the vision. The invitation to this new age seems so to overwhelm John that he falls in worship before the angel, only to receive a sharp rebuke. Human beings and angels alike are merely servants: worship is reserved for God. This implicitly underlines what is clear from passages like 5.9: worship is only for God, yet worship is also offered to Christ the Lamb; and properly so. John and his fellows must hold the testimony of Jesus: this may mean that they should testify *to* him or that they hold fast to the testimony that he, the 'faithful witness' (1.5), bore; most particularly in his death. This holding to the testimony of Jesus is what led John to share in persecution, what brought him to Patmos, and what made him a prophet. The inspiration for Christian prophecy is the work of Christ; its role is to explore and expound that work, and it can have no other content or focus (compare the role of the Spirit as interpreter in John 15.26 and 16.12–15). In the troubled times in which John lived there may have been many attempting to explain the present and anticipate the future: but unless their visions were anchored in an understanding of the work of Christ they could only be false prophecy. Christianity has no place for new revelations. SL

John 2.1–11

John calls the great deeds of Jesus 'signs', directing our attention to their inner meaning, beyond their role as mere 'wonders'. So, in this Gospel, 'sign' is almost always a positive word (but see 4.48 where it is linked to 'wonders' in its disparaging sense, typical of the other Gospels). Here is the first of the succession of signs that occupy much of chs. 2—12 (which C. H. Dodd called John's 'Book of Signs'); and then the passion is perhaps to be seen as the greatest of all, to which, in various ways, the rest point. Here, that hint of the passion is to be found in the final verse: Jesus shows forth his 'glory', his God-given splendour that is seen in its highest degree in his death by crucifixion (e.g. 13–31f.).

We are given this story to read at this season of Epiphany, by centuries-old association, as a result of v. 11: Jesus 'manifested' his glory; and surely because of its theme of the widening of God's bounteous provision beyond the confines of Judaism (water), into the headier reaches of the new salvation in and through Jesus (wine). As in the scene at the cross (19.25–27), perhaps the (unnamed) mother of Jesus signifies Israel, from which Jesus springs (as indeed, therefore, does 'salvation', 4.42), even as he then transcends it. This transcending of old Israel explains what (despite various attempts at mollifying) remains the harsh candour of v. 4: in this Gospel particularly, the place of the old dispensation rarely avoids negativity; for Jesus, we remember, has in truth been at work from the very start (1.1–3). Hence, the 'glory' (i.e. his true nature and role in all its radiance) that Jesus displays here in this action is one with that which believers continue to 'behold' (1.14). He is 'light', and the light of glory is there to be seen, though of course not all perceive (v. 10). So the faith that is evoked (in the disciples, v. 11) by this act is not at all the cheap product of sheer amazement at so much wine so miraculously produced (the quantity is huge – like the abundance of grace in 1.16 (cf. v. 17) and of bread in 6.1–14: God's saving generosity is without bounds). It is rather the faith that binds his own to him and brings them into the new dispensation – whose character is woven into them in the supper discourse of chs. 13—17, words achieving life. In the Christian mystery, newness is always to the fore and the sense of it must not be lost. In the hierarchy of the signs, this, worked on inanimate matter rather than a human being, is sometimes seen as the 'lowest' (with the raising of Lazarus in ch. 11 as the topmost); but it contains in fact the whole gospel message, in its own idiom and manner. LH

The Fourth Sunday of Epiphany

Deuteronomy 18.15–20; Revelation 12.1–5a; Mark 1.21–28

Deuteronomy 18.15–20

The main issue in this passage is that of authority. In the incident in Deut. 5.22–7 referred to in v. 16, the people are so terrified at the manifestation of divine power at Mount Horeb (Sinai) that they request Moses to be their intermediary. They promise to do all that God had commanded via Moses, if this means that they are spared the potentially fatal encounter with God's glory and greatness. Moses, however, is a human being, with a limited lifespan. What will happen after his death? Will there be no communication between God and Israel? Moses promises that God will raise up a prophet to succeed him, whose words must be taken to be as authoritative as those of Moses himself. But it has to be asked whether the text has only one prophet in mind, or a succession of prophets; and some modern interpreters have certainly taken the view that the text justifies the belief of the deuteronomistic theologians in the importance of prophets. Throughout the books of Samuel and Kings in their deuteronomistic edition, prophets play a key role in interpreting and explaining events; and what is often regarded as a deuteronomistic comment at Amos 3.7 declares that God does nothing without declaring his secret purposes to his servants the prophets. If this line of interpretation is correct, the usual understanding of 'prophet' must be broadened to include that of lawgiver; and both ideas of prophet, those of foreteller and lawgiver, are present in this chapter (see 18.20–22).

However, authority is a difficult concept. While Deuteronomy accepts that Moses' words are authoritative because directly received from God, it also acknowledges that there are situations in which it is impossible at the time to know whether someone is speaking in the name of God or not (see v. 22). There is also abundant evidence from books such as Jeremiah that prophets were ignored or threatened (Jer. 20.7–10). It is therefore no surprise that today's passage came to be understood not with regard to a succession of prophets but to a single Mosaic successor who, at a future date, would resolve all the issues that had arisen in the meantime. That this hope was alive in the first century AD is indicated at John 1.25 where John the Baptist is asked whether he is 'the prophet'. In Christian perspective, Jesus is like 'the prophet' since, like Moses, his authority comes from a relationship to God granted to no other. He does not provide conclusive answers to all questions, however. He tells parables and out of their implications commands us to go and do likewise. As with Moses, we discover authority as we work out the implications of obedience, for our own situation. JR

Revelation 12.1–5a

This is one of the most difficult and tantalizing passages in the Apocalypse. Although there are elements in the vision that echo biblical passages, overall it seems much closer to the non-Jewish world. Signs 'in heaven' with sun, moon and stars, sound like the constellations of popular astrology – Virgo and Draco maybe. The heavenly mother and her threatened child seem to belong in Greek or Egyptian myths familiar in John's contemporary pagan world: the stories of Leto and Apollo or of Isis 'Queen of Heaven' and Horus. As for the great dragon, though it may be related to the Greek Python or the Egyptian Set, it seems more at home in the Babylonian creation myth of Tiamat the chaos-monster. What are these alien images doing in John's vision? It is tempting to cut through them and find a simpler equation for the image, especially in the season of Epiphany when we are still thinking of a marvellous birth and the portent of a star. Maybe Herod could be cast in the role of the dragon, like Pharaoh in Ezek. 32! Yet the woman cannot simply be Mary, for she is a heavenly symbol, nor can the birth be simply that of Jesus. As the vision continues, the newborn child is snatched away to heaven, out of danger. For Jesus it was his death that led to his exaltation, as the image of the Lamb in ch. 5 (the Second Sunday of Epiphany) has shown. Moreover, in the further continuation, the woman is seen to have other children (12.17), so the birth of the heavenly child associates him with others.

The passage must have to do with the fulfilment of messianic hope, for its last words clearly allude to Ps. 2.7–9, and one popular reading of the passage is that it is a vision not just of the Messiah but of the messianic *community*, brought into being with the birthpangs of the new age, faced with hostility and danger but assured of deliverance. The heavenly woman is then like Paul's 'Jerusalem which is above, which is the mother of us all' (Gal. 4.26). The Christian messianic community is, however, the community of the Messiah, Jesus, whose way to heaven was by the cross. Those who belong to his community know that they must follow him in that way. Popular mythology may supply the imagery for the hope of salvation, but the images have to be 'unpacked' in the context of Christian faith, so that the vision of heaven will strengthen John's readers to endure their trials on earth. SL

Mark 1.21–28

When contemporary Christians read the stories of Jesus healing people of disease or exorcising demons, the tendency is to see these actions as signs of Jesus' compassion for the afflicted or as proofs that Jesus is God's Son. Occasionally the Gospels support these interpretations, as when Jesus is said to act out of strong emotion (e.g. Mark 1.41). The designation of Jesus' miracles as 'signs' in the Fourth Gospel does support the notion that they demonstrate his divinity (e.g. John 2.11). On the whole, however, the Gospel writers treat Jesus' miracles as acts that raise questions about who he is and whose power he employs.

This lection, the first miracle in the Gospel of Mark, provides an excellent illustration of this understanding of miracle. The man who is afflicted with the unclean spirit is, to say the least, not the focus of the story. Indeed, he comes 'on stage' only as the carrier of the unclean spirit. Nothing is said about the man himself, his background, his faith or lack thereof. Jesus' conversation is with the spirit, and Jesus' action is on the spirit. After the exorcism, the man is not even mentioned. While Gospel miracles often treat the healed person more as a prop than as a character, this story carries that custom to an extreme degree.

Not only does the man who is afflicted and then healed receive little attention, but the exorcism itself is treated with haste. Jesus is teaching, he casts out the unclean spirit that presents itself, and the final report returns to the issue of Jesus' authoritative teaching. For Mark, then, what makes this event important stems from the teaching of Jesus and the issue of authority rather than from the exorcism alone.

When the story opens, Jesus enters the synagogue in Capernaum, where his teaching amazes people because he teaches 'as one having authority, and not as the scribes' (1.22). The contrast between Jesus and the scribes is noteworthy, since the scribes were regarded as important and knowledgeable teachers in the Jewish community. When Mark says that Jesus' teaching has 'authority', then, he may mean something other than its credibility or reliability. Exactly what 'authority' means here remains to be seen.

The unclean spirit bursts into the synagogue and confronts Jesus with a challenge ('Have you come to destroy us?' or another translation that is equally possible, 'You have come to destroy us!') and with a title ('the Holy One of God'). As elsewhere in Mark, unclean spirits and others who are outside the religious power structure recognize who Jesus is, while those who might be expected to know Jesus do not. Despite this display of knowledge on the spirit's part, it obeys Jesus' rebuke. (See Acts 19.11–20; unclean spirits did not acquiesce to the demands of every would-be exorcist!)

Most miracle stories, including exorcisms, conclude with a demonstration of the effectiveness of the cure and the response of those who have observed it. Here the demonstration drops out altogether and the response that comes from bystanders is a curious one: 'What is this? A new teaching – with authority! He commands even the unclean spirits, and they obey him.' Jesus' power over the unclean spirits reinforces the earlier judgement that his teaching is authoritative.

Again, based on a contemporary understanding of healing as an act of compassion, we might anticipate that Jesus' exorcism would prompt bystanders to rejoicing and celebration. Jesus brings gifts that we imagine ourselves receiving with outstretched arms, but nothing in this story indicates that he was so received. Instead, the story concludes with 'At once his fame began to spread', but the word translated as 'fame' can also be rendered 'report'. It signifies only that word went out regarding this event, but not how it was received.

The story culminates, then, in a kind of question. The earlier question, 'What is this?' calls up another, more profound question: 'Who is this?' If the 'who' question is not asked here explicitly, it surely lies just below the surface. Who is this man? What is the source of his power? What do these events mean? If the reader of

Mark's Gospel knows who Jesus is because of 1.11, and if the unclean spirit knows because it recognizes superior power, and if the disciples at least know the authority of the Master who has called them, those standing by do not know what is at hand. The answer is not obvious, and in fact the question will continue through most of Mark.

What makes the question raised by Jesus' exorcism the more intriguing is that so many contemporary Christians believe that miraculous events, if ever witnessed first-hand, would produce unerring and unwavering faith. The Gospel writers know otherwise. They know that miracles demonstrate power, but power can come from a variety of sources, both good and evil. The Gospel writers also know that understanding who Jesus is and what his mission entails involves far more than simply witnessing a miracle. As with every aspect of Jesus' ministry, the miracles and the teaching raise as many questions as they provide answers. BG

The Presentation of Christ

(2 February)

Malachi 3.1–5; Hebrews 2.14–18; Luke 2.22–40

Malachi 3.1–5

The book of Malachi, evidently dating from the late fourth century BC, was written or compiled within a society that contained sorcerers, adulterers, perjurers, and corrupt employers and landowners (cf. v. 5). This state of affairs, together with other unsatisfactory conditions, produces a series of charges and counter charges in the book, as God and the people engage in a dialogue of questions and answers. The passage in 3.1–5 is best seen as God's reply to what immediately precedes (2.17), where God takes objection to the view that he approves of, or is powerless to deal with, evil-doers.

The Hebrew of 'I am sending' implies that something is about to happen. A messenger or angel (the same word in Hebrew) will precede the coming of God to his temple. The function of the messenger is unclear. If it is to prepare the people for the divine coming, then why will it be necessary for God to refine and judge (vv. 2–5)? Perhaps the messenger's function will be to warn the people of the imminence of the divine judgement. At any rate, the divine coming will be painful for those who experience it. People may desire God, but will they be able to endure his judgement?

This judgement will begin with the temple and its worship (v. 3), with the place that ought to know better because it supposedly exists to mediate between the people and God; the place where the experts in prayer, sacrifice and holiness are supposed to be found. The judgement will then pass to the social sphere. A religion in which the cult is acceptable but which tolerates social injustice is an abomination to the Old Testament prophets. True religion is neither an acceptable cult without social justice nor social justice without a worthy cult. The two must go together because they belong together. People who fear God but are indifferent to their fellow human beings, especially those most socially disadvantaged, do not really fear God. People who are only humanitarian workers fail to recognize that the deepest instincts of human sympathy and compassion are God-given.

Although this reading is selected to go with the Gospel story of Christ's presentation in the temple 40 days after his birth (cf. Lev. 12.2–8) it is arguably the story of the cleansing of the temple (Mark 11.15–18) that comes closest to a fulfilment of this prophecy in the ministry of Jesus. JR

Hebrews 2.14–18

No writer in the NT was more dedicated to the sense of Jesus' identification with the human race, 'his brothers and sisters in every respect', than the author of Hebrews. In ch. 1, using a barrage of Scripture quotations, he had established his heavenly status as God's Son, occupying the role of God's 'wisdom' and above the angels, seated at God's right hand. But then the writer had shifted his gaze – to Jesus who, in the role foretold in Ps. 8, had become (to take the words in a convenient sense that the Greek version could bear) 'for a little while' below the angels, a human among humans (2.7). (In the Hebrew, the sense was spatial, not temporal.)

Yet in that place, he had a task that was unique: he was to bring 'many sons to glory', by being 'the pioneer of their salvation' (2.10) – an image found also in Acts 3.15 and 5.31. Again, scriptural texts demonstrated that Wagnerian hero-role: Ps. 22.22 and Isa. 8.17–18. It is made plain that his position in relation to the angels, temporarily put aside, was now incidental. Instead, his significance related to human beings, specifically 'the descendants of Abraham': this writing functions, it now emerges, within Jewish horizons, however wide some of its language.

The leadership role of Jesus prompts the first appearance of the image or analogy that comes to dominate the later chapters: that of the high priest who, human as he is, has the role of making 'expiation for the sins of the people', above all on the Day of Atonement. Whether the actual high priests of Jerusalem saw themselves quite thus is another question; here, it is their very identity with everybody else, in temptation and suffering, that qualifies them to perform their vital and sacred task. Humility and leadership are not incompatible. LH

Luke 2.22–40

The narratives in Luke 1—2 evoke the atmosphere and world of old Israel, sometimes (as in the echoes of Sarah in the aged Elizabeth and in the near repeat of Hannah's song from 1 Sam. 2 in the Magnificat) very old Israel indeed. It is a literary old Israel, for Luke writes here in the style and vocabulary of the Septuagint. The evocation occurs also in the depiction of the characters – not just Elizabeth and Mary, but Zechariah and the rest; in the dominant temple scenario, and indeed in the nature of the episodes themselves. We are to understand that, new and decisive in God's purposes as Jesus is, he is no novelty or bolt from the blue. Even if his saving significance is for all, Israel can still be seen as 'thy people' (v. 32).

Simeon and Anna (Luke works in pairs of persons throughout these chapters) are typical of the venerable holy sages of Israel, and their great age ratifies their wisdom and their power to speak God's truth. And as through all Luke's history, they are Spirit-led. Paralleling Zechariah in relation to John, Simeon reminds us of Eli in relation to Samuel and Anna of Judith in the second-century BC tale of piety. Both are obscure figures, exemplifying the divine favouring of the poor and simple, as the Magnificat said. (In the figure of Anna, Luke may also have an eye on the status of Christian widows in his own day, as described and regulated in 1 Tim. 5.) They are in effect oracular persons, and Simeon's words are almost a catena of scriptural allusions. All this is more important to Luke than the precise details of the ritual which the parents of Jesus carry out and in fact he has not wholly understood the law's requirements. The 'presentation' of a new firstborn carried no visit to the temple and was distinct from the mother's 'purification' which entailed sacrifice: it is the latter which Luke is really describing.

It is hard to know whether Luke is keen to show Jesus as rooted in scriptural validation for reasons of doctrine (God's work is uninterrupted from start to finish) or, also perhaps, for reasons connected with his church situation in the later first century, when Jewish Christians were becoming more plainly a minority and needed reassurance, perhaps in the face of some Gentile-Christian intolerance: it is a message of balance and reconciliation that Acts is at pains to reiterate, notably in the council of Acts 15.

All the same, as the annunciation story and the shepherds' vision have already made clear, Jesus is the focus of faith and hope: the one who brings 'salvation', a word resonant for Jews and pagans alike, and virtually confined to Luke among the evangelists. Yet the child's purpose will only be carried out through suffering which Simeon also foresees. The suffering will also devastate Mary: in the image in v. 35 we have one more example of how Luke is the true originator of what would eventually flower as Marian devotion. LH

The Fifth Sunday of Epiphany

Isaiah 40.21–31; 1 Corinthians 9.16–23; Mark 1.29–39

Isaiah 40.21–31

The questions with which the passage begins are part of a series of questions that begins at v. 12. They all tend in the same direction, towards the incomparability of God. In the present passage they imply that the exiles, to whom they are addressed, should know, should hear and should have been told; but it is one thing to know in theory and quite another to put theory into practice. It was all too easy for the exiles in Babylon around 560 BC to have been so overwhelmed by the splendour of the capital city and the wonders of Babylonian civilization to have forgotten what they had been taught about the God of Israel, or to have regarded it as meaningless. The need to awaken new hope in a dispirited people partly explains the magnificent and exalted language of the passage; and there is an explicit criticism of the astral religion of the Babylonians in vv. 25–26. The night sky is especially impressive in the region of present-day Iraq and, not surprisingly, affected local religious expression. The exiles are bidden to look up in order to experience the sublimity of the spectacle they behold. Can any human work of art adequately represent what the skies contain, and do they not lead to a feeling of human nothingness in the face of an overwhelming majesty?

But the idea of creation in the Old Testament includes the moral order as well as the natural order, which is why the fate of princes is mentioned in vv. 23–24. God's treatment of princes is not arbitrary. Although this is not explicitly stated, the removal of princes is probably to be understood in terms of God's exercise of justice in the world. It is also a sublime expression of human transience in relation to divine permanence.

The moral aspect of creation leads to the thought of the final verses. If creation were simply about the ordering of the natural world, Jacob-Israel would have grounds for feeling abandoned (v. 27); but the truth is that the unwearying God cares for justice, and gives strength to those who long to see it triumph. Yet patience, persistence and not growing weary in well-doing are also involved. Humanity expects immediate answers and instant solutions. The ways of the incomparable creator are past human understanding (v. 28a). What is important is that God's concern to establish justice never grows weary, and that those who cling to that truth will be sustained in their earthly journey, whether they feel that they are borne on eagles' wings, or consigned to mundane human running and walking. JR

1 Corinthians 9.16–23

One of the reasons the apostle Paul is not a favourite figure with many Christians is because he is difficult to understand (and in many cases is misunderstood). Another reason for his unpopularity, however, is because he is all too readily understood. His message comes through loud and clear and, in doing so, annoys and disturbs the patterns of life and thought to which we have become accustomed. He repeatedly nudges the comfortable accommodations we have made with the surrounding culture. Though Paul, of all the New Testament witnesses, is the theologian of grace, he refuses to let his readers rest easy with the gospel as if it were a take-or-leave-it matter, or as if it were a reality to be tacked on to the rest of our concerns, another charity to be supported. Paul constantly confronts us with the life-orienting character of the gospel, its absolute centrality.

The matter of Christian identity is at the heart of the reading assigned for this Sunday. The two issues that occupy Paul in connection with the passage are: eating food associated with the worship of idols (1 Cor. 8 and 10.23–33) and the right of an apostle to receive monetary support from the people being served (9.1–15). Neither issue seems all that momentous, and neither is likely to disturb or annoy modern readers, except that Paul describes his own behaviour regarding each issue in terms of the mandate of the gospel. His way of defending himself (since he was probably being criticized in each case) tells us a great deal about what really matters.

First, for Paul there is *the compulsion of the gospel*. 'An obligation is laid on me, and woe to me if I do not proclaim the gospel!' (9.16). The compulsion spoken of here does not refer to an irresistible impulse of the psyche, an irrational drive that coerces him into preaching against his better judgement. The compulsion derives from the nature of the gospel and from Paul's sense of his own place in the economy of God. The gospel is not intended only to be heard and enjoyed; it is to be lived and preached. By its very nature, it is a story that demands retelling. And that surely goes for all 'garden-variety Christians' as well as for apostles.

The critical importance of retelling the story emerges in the way Paul justifies his decision not to accept financial support from the Corinthians. He recognizes that support is a 'right' due an apostle (and his readers no doubt agree). In fact, 'the Lord commanded that those who proclaim the gospel should get their living by the gospel' (v. 14). But in his circumstances (and we are not clear what they were) the urgency of proclamation causes him to forgo his 'rights'. The life-and-death character of the gospel dictates that no unnecessary hindrance should stand in the way of retelling the story. Even what is justly due is waived if the situation seems to warrant it. The compulsion of the gospel determines the exercise or non-exercise of rights – a novel idea!

The text also speaks of *the freedom of the gospel*. From the stance Paul takes on the matter of eating food consecrated to idols one could get the impression (and undoubtedly some in Corinth did) that Paul was wishy-washy, that this 'play it either way' attitude masked a lack of principle.

Paul reaffirms his position by saying he can become like a Jew when with Jews or like a Gentile when with Gentiles. His 'right' to eat marketplace food that has been sacralized in the pagan cult can be exercised or not exercised as the situation warrants. It is a clear statement of Christian freedom with regard to moral issues.

Each particular decision is made, however, not according to one's personal whims but in order to 'win' Jews or Gentiles: 'I do it all for the sake of the gospel' (v. 23). Christian freedom is not unrestricted autonomy. In fact, Paul in characteristic fashion juxtaposes the terms 'free' and 'slave' (v. 19). Submitting to the freedom of the gospel means making oneself a slave to Jews and Gentiles alike, letting their real needs dictate behaviour. The two statements put in parentheses in the NRSV show the paradox of Paul's position: 'I myself am not under the law' (v. 20); 'I am not free from God's law but am under Christ's law' (v. 21).

To put the matter in a less paradoxical way, the text confronts readers with the gospel as the controlling reality in Christian identity. The sensitivities, intuitions and discernment of the Church and individuals within the Church are shaped and informed by the Christian story. As moral issues arise, they are confronted by people who know about the compulsion and freedom of the gospel. Such people may respond to a given crisis in one situation one way and to the same crisis in another situation in a different way (as Paul does), but their responses always emanate from the central identity.

The decisive issue, then, comes with the shaping of identity, with the question of who we really are, with what controlling role the gospel plays in moulding us. That often becomes an unpopular question to raise. CC

Mark 1.29–39

A first reading of this passage could send the preacher scurrying after another passage, for this one appears to lack direction or even coherence. Three distinct scenes comprise the passage: the first a terse miracle story (Mark 1.29–31), the second a summary of Jesus' activity as healer (vv. 32–34), the third a mild conflict between Simon and Jesus over what should be Jesus' next action (vv. 35–39). Little is said that holds the three scenes together, and no one of them offers an obvious starting point for preaching.

Mark has tightly connected these three with one another, however, despite the initial impression of disjointedness. The healing of Simon's mother-in-law occurs on the Sabbath, probably in the afternoon (see v. 21). It is a private event, witnessed presumably by only a few. The second scene takes place that same evening (see v. 32), and contrasts with the first in that it is public ('the whole city', v. 33). The third scene occurs the following morning and implicitly refers back to the second (vv. 35, 37). These careful links among the three scenes press us to look again at what each accomplishes and how the three interpret one another.

Although Mark tells of the healing of Simon's mother-in-law with notable brevity, all the customary features of a miracle story are included: the description of the illness, the healing itself and the demonstration of the healing. This last feature takes place when the woman 'began to serve them', proving that she was sufficiently recovered to resume her daily routine. (Ironically, her behaviour is exactly that called for in Jesus' later teaching on discipleship, teaching elicited by the request for power by James and John, who are present in Simon's house but who do not understand the importance of the mother-in-law's action. See Mark 10.35–45.)

In the second scene, the healing powers of Jesus have become a matter of public knowledge. People bring to Jesus 'all who were sick or possessed with demons', and 'the whole city' gathers in the doorway (1.32–33). Such claims, surely exaggerated, serve notice to the reader that Jesus is now a public figure. His real identity as Son of God remains concealed, however, for the demons (and presumably only the demons) know who he is, and he forbids them to speak. (On possible reasons for this prohibition, see the commentary on Mark 1.40–45, the Sixth Sunday of Epiphany.) In other words, Jesus is sought for his power to heal, but his teaching is not acknowledged, nor is his real identity.

The third scene confirms that Jesus is misunderstood, even by Simon and other disciples. Jesus seeks a deserted place for prayer and is 'hunted' by them, with the demand that Jesus return, a demand implicit in the words, 'Everyone is searching for you.' But Jesus rejects the demand. He does not return to Capernaum, but moves instead toward other towns in Galilee so that he may resume his task of proclamation.

Why does Jesus reject the request for more miracles, the demand even of those who are closest to him? There appear to be at least two reasons, one negative and one positive. First, what Jesus rejects seems to be a response to himself that focuses exclusively on his miracles. While the miracles demonstrate his power, and force questions about his identity, they do not reveal who he is. This theme becomes more prominent later in the Gospel, but it emerges even here.

Second, Jesus appears to reject the request because he understands his vocation to lie elsewhere: 'I may proclaim the message there also; for that is what I came out to do' (v. 38). Jesus came to preach the gospel (vv. 14–15) and to challenge the power of Satan (vv. 13, 39). However good and pleasant and popular it may be for him to heal large numbers of people, he understands that his real vocation lies elsewhere. The miracles do not in and of themselves conflict with that vocation, but the uncomprehending response of people to the miracles does conflict with that vocation.

Since we customarily read the Gospels with the expectation that every move of Jesus should be accepted as right and proper, we may well miss the cutting edge of this text. A contemporary analogy might be useful. Imagine that a pastor is a poweful counsellor, so gifted that her office overflows day and night with those seeking insight and understanding. She, however, firmly believes that her vocation lies in a ministry of teaching, and decides to cut back on counselling in order to fulfil that vocation. The complaints would quickly emerge: 'She has no time for people' . . . 'What happened to her compassion?' . . . 'Why doesn't she care for the needs of people the way she did earlier?'

The analogy is admittedly limited, but it illustrates what is at stake in this lection. Jesus subordinates his power for healing and exorcism to the greater need for proclamation of the kingdom of God. He does so because that is his primary task. He also does so because proclamation of the kingdom is the only context in which the power of healing gains its true meaning. BG

The Sixth Sunday of Epiphany

2 Kings 5.1–14; 1 Corinthians 9.24–27; Mark 1.40–45

2 Kings 5.1–14

This passage belongs to the cycle of stories of miracles worked by Elijah and Elisha, and probably originates in popular stories about these figures, who were active in the northern kingdom, Israel, in the period roughly 860–810 BC. In the literary form in which the story now appears there is great artistry and several surprises. The first surprise is the claim that God had enabled Naaman, the Syrian Commander, to defeat Israel (v. 1). This is probably because the biblical compilers regarded the dynasty of kings Omri and Ahab as unfaithful to God (the unnamed king in this account is presumably one of their successors, such as Jehoram), and wanted to indicate that God was not indifferent to their apostasy, which also included social abuses (cf. 1 Kings 21). Naaman, indeed, is portrayed in the continuation of the chapter (vv. 15–19) as far more faithful to the God of Israel than Israel's kings of the time. The 'leprosy' from which Naaman suffered was not necessarily the scourge familiar in the Middle Ages in Europe, but probably a skin disease such as psoriasis. While it did not inhibit Naaman's effectiveness as a soldier, it was no doubt unpleasant, and could also be regarded as a sign that the gods of Syria did not favour him.

This is the background to the witness of the young Israelite captive, whose faith in Elisha leads to an embassy being sent to the king of Israel. The latter's suspicious response is typical of a harassed ruler; but the narrative is also making a deeper point, that the king of Israel seems to know neither the power of his God nor that of the prophet Elisha. How Elisha comes to hear of the king's reaction is not stated, nor does it need to be from the narrative point of view. The story moves easily to its climax, in which Naaman feels let down because his cure is not effected in a spectacular manner. Not for the first time in the story (cf. v. 3) wisdom lies with a servant, who makes the sensible point that if Naaman were willing to do something difficult when commanded by the prophet, he ought equally to be prepared to do something simple.

This is a profound story. It claims that God's action and favour are not restricted to Israel and Israelites; it attributes wisdom and insight to a captive girl and a Syrian servant; it portrays the king of Israel and, to some extent, Naaman, as ignorant in comparison with them. Yet the bottom line is that if, from the human point of view, Syria is ascendant, the reality is that the last word rests with the God of Israel and his prophet (cf. v. 8). The feared commander does not even *see* the prophet (cf. vv. 9–10 – another reversal in the scales of greatness). The truth that it seems more appropriate to do something hard and spectacular in obedience to God than to do something simple, has many ramifications in Christian life, and the whole narrative could be easily and effectively dramatized by children and adults. JR

1 Corinthians 9.24–27

At the end of a chapter defending his non-stipendiary ministry against those who see it as inferior to paid ministries, and so explaining his missionary practice, Paul concludes with two commonplace illustrations from athletics; namely, running and boxing. The games were a feature of life in Hellenistic cities, especially in Corinth which hosted the biennial Isthmian Games. This metaphor of struggle (*agon*) or competition was often used in popular moral philosophy and comes easily to Paul (cf. 1 Cor. 15.32; Phil. 2.16; 3.13f.) and his imitators (1 Tim. 4.7; 2 Tim. 2.5; 4.7). Boxing, however, appears only here, and might seem too violent for comfort to contemporary sensibilities. Fighting the good fight and muscular Christianity, like military metaphors as in 'Onward Christian soldiers', seem out of tune in a Church rightly committed to non-violence and seeing this at the heart of the gospel. (The military reference in v. 7 is a harmless analogy, and therefore inoffensive.) The language of competition is equally problematic in a social and economic order based on this in ways that are deeply opposed to any just and humane Christian society, and it is possible to question Paul's need to succeed by labouring more abundantly than them all (1 Cor. 15.10). However, Paul's point is 'training in Christianity' (Kierkegaard) and self-discipline. Asceticism is suspect in an age made aware by psychology of its dangers and distortions, an age itself inclined to hedonism. Self-mortification sounds close to masochism. But it is hard to envisage a serious religious commitment without self-discipline, and Paul's metaphors might challenge us to consider its appropriate forms for today.

Bonhoeffer's *Cost of Discipleship* directs us back to the Sermon on the Mount. In an overfed society fasting, for example, might well be thought an essential, if silent, act of witness. If the ultimate test of martyrdom is (thankfully) not required of us, it should at least remind us that discipleship of the crucified Jesus is by definition costly. If it seems to make no demands on us, we are perhaps missing the point now and unlikely to be prepared to meet whatever test the future has in store. Paul's tone is mostly encouraging, not threatening. He can point to himself as an example, and his metaphor of the prize provides a reminder that the Christian life is going somewhere; it has a goal. But he ends with an admonition that the clergy above all need to hear. RM

Mark 1.40–45

Healing stories in the New Testament have as their unrelenting focus the person and power of Jesus. As a result, few details are given about the nature of the diseases involved except to underscore their severity and the difficulty of the healing. For the most part, then, the disease itself is of little interest. An important exception to this general state of affairs is that of leprosy, for leprosy involves not only disease, but ritual purity laws and theological understandings as well.

As the explanatory note at Mark 1.40 of the NRSV indicates, 'leprosy' in the Bible includes a broad range of skin ailments. The regulations regarding leprosy in Lev. 13—14 clearly cover a variety of diseases. Those regulations also demonstrate that leprosy, whatever its form, involves a violation of ritual purity laws. Since ritual purity laws often come into play because something is thought to be abnormal or out of place, various diseases of the skin probably were regarded as violations of ritual purity simply because they looked unusual or strange. The consequences of this violation were serious, in that persons with skin diseases would be separated from much that constituted normal society. (As always, it is difficult to determine how precisely the Levitical code was observed in day-to-day life.) Complicating matters even further for the individual so afflicted, leprosy was often interpreted as punishment for sin and healing from leprosy as an act of God (see e.g. Num. 12.10–15; Deut. 24.8–9; 28.27, 35; 2 Kings 5.19–27; 2 Chron. 26.16–21).

The person who approaches Jesus in Mark 1.40, then, may not have been stricken with a grave physical disease, but his situation was nevertheless a severe one. His words to Jesus convey complete confidence in Jesus' ability to heal him, but they also reveal a question about whether Jesus will wish to heal him: 'If you choose, you can make me clean.' Given that the leper was probably understood to be a sinner and an outcast, the question in his approach to Jesus is more than polite. He knows that many would not heal him even if they could.

Jesus' response emphatically rejects the walls erected between this man and himself. First, the narrator describes Jesus as being 'moved with pity' or 'moved with anger' (NRSV margin). A difficult text-critical problem creates the divergent translations here, and a number of scholars think the better reading is 'moved with anger'. Even if that reading is rejected, 'moved with pity' translates a strong Greek verb (*splagchnizomai*) that literally refers to having one's intestines turn. The feeling described is more than a superficial kind of sympathy – Jesus is deeply moved. Second, he touches the man. Healings often involve touch, of course, but touching a person with a skin disease identifies Jesus with that person, making him outcast as well. (Although the situations differ in many ways, the contemporary hysteria about touching persons afflicted with AIDS offers some telling parallels.) Third, Jesus' response, 'I do choose', emphatically connects him with the leper's plight.

The healing itself accomplished, Jesus gives the man two instructions, instructions that almost of necessity conflict with each other. He directs the former leper to show himself to the priest and make the offering required of him. This command places Jesus in conformity with Lev. 14, which specifies the procedure and the offerings appropriate for various persons, depending on their economic standing. That this action is said to be 'a testimony to them' (Mark 1.44) may mean that Jesus is hereby vindicated from charges of being hostile or indifferent to Mosaic Law. In view of the various conflict stories in 2.1—3.6, however, it could also mean that Jesus challenges the authorities to acknowledge his powerful act of healing.

The first instruction Jesus gives the former leper ('Say nothing to anyone') is more difficult to understand. How could this man return to his home without explaining the origin of his cure? Surely the priest who examined him would immediately ask how he came to be healed. The man in question apparently thinks nothing of violating this injunction, since the story closes with a report about his proclamation of the event and its impact on Jesus. Several such instructions in Mark (e.g. 5.43; 8.26; 8.30), customarily identified as the Messianic Secret, prompt much perplexity on the part of students of this Gospel. The injunctions to silence appear to be connected with Mark's understanding of the place of miracle in identifying Jesus. Jesus' miracles evidence his power, but they do not adequately explain who he is or what his mission is, for that explanation comes only in light of the cross (see e.g. 8.27–31; 9.9).

Whatever the explanation for the command to silence, the end of the story finds Jesus once more besieged. Earlier he fled Capernaum because 'the whole city' was at his doorstep. Now no town offers him refuge, and he must stay in the country (literally, 'deserted places'). The question of what the miracles mean is once again eclipsed by the people's hunger for the power itself. BG

The Seventh Sunday of Epiphany

Isaiah 43.18–25; 2 Corinthians 1.18–22; Mark 2.1–12

Isaiah 43.18–25

At first sight, the logic of this passage is confusing, if not contradictory. While it begins with a call to forget former things (v. 18), it then seems to dig up the past as God complains that the people did not bring him the appointed sacrifices (vv. 22–24). A further difficulty is that elsewhere in the Old Testament and Isaiah (cf. 1.12–15; 66.3) there seems to be a repudiation of the idea that God requires sacrifices. These difficulties can be overcome if we assume that vv. 22–4 are a divine reply to a complaint of the people (cf. v. 26, not included in the reading, which mentions a disputation). The complaint is that the sacrifices and offerings *were* duly made, but that in spite of this Jacob was given to destruction and Israel to reviling (v. 28). In reply, God says in effect that even if the sacrifices and offerings were made according to the letter, they were not made according to the spirit. What the people actually brought before God was their sins and iniquities (v. 24b), for which their insincere offerings effected no forgiveness. In this context, v. 23b is at first sight confusing, because God appears to be saying that *he* did not make offerings to *Israel*! It is almost impossible to reproduce the subtlety and wordplay of the Hebrew here. REB has: 'I did not exact grain-offerings from you, or weary you with demands for frankincense', which reads more logically.

There is a second part to the divine response to the people's complaint about their plight, and this is that, all along, they have misunderstood the nature of their relationship with God. They have sought, through their offerings, to make him indebted to them; he, however, is the incomparable one (cf. v. 25a) who forgives sins and blots out the past. They must learn to be thankful for his mercy.

This thought returns us to the beginning of the passage, because whatever else forgiveness is about, it is about facing a future which is no longer encumbered by the past. The people are to set out on a new journey, one in which the desert provides not dangers from wild animals and lack of water, but new opportunities and the protection of the God who has formed a people for himself (v. 21). This journey can be thought of physically, as applied to the return of exiles from Babylon to Judah in the sixth century BC, or as representative of the spiritual journey of a forgiven people; that is, a people always facing a future unencumbered by the past. JR

2 Corinthians 1.18–22

Paul's relationship with the church at Corinth was not always a happy one. Misunderstanding and conflict characterized it almost from the beginning. Paul speaks of postponing a visit to Corinth so as to avoid the pain that had marked a previous visit, and he describes writing a letter 'out of much distress and anguish of heart and with many tears' (2 Cor. 2.4). And yet, ironically, this context of conflict evokes one of the most positive affirmations of the Christian faith and its meaning for human life that we have in the New Testament.

Such is the epistolary assignment for this Sunday – 2 Cor. 1.18–22. Paul cancelled a promised visit to Corinth and apparently was sharply criticized by some in the community for doing so. Not carrying through with his plans exposed him as an unreliable messenger of the gospel, a figure the Corinthians could not count on. On the surface, such a criticism hardly seems worth responding to, except that it may have eroded confidence in the gospel preached. An undependable messenger means an undependable message.

Paul's reply is twofold. On the one hand, he defends his decision not to come by saying he did not want to make another trip that would create more pain for himself and for the Corinthians (1.23—2.5). He wants them to know that he has not been talking out of both sides of his mouth at the same time, as some evidently accuse him of doing. On the other hand, Paul calls attention to the gospel he has preached to them, a gospel at whose heart is not a vacillating, unreliable word, but the full 'Yes' of God. It is this positive affirmation of the gospel that warrants our special reflection.

Three observations about Paul's positive thinking are in order. First, he speaks of the faithful God who can be counted on to fulfil all the divine promises. The advent of Jesus Christ reveals that God is trustworthy. In Christ 'every one of God's promises is a "Yes"' (1.20). In the liturgy the worshipping community can say 'Amen' because they can trust God.

Paul's strategy here is not to cite a single Old Testament passage and argue that Jesus has fulfilled it, but rather to make a blanket affirmation about 'every one of God's promises'. The issue is bigger than this or that text. The long and involved story of God's engagement in human history finds its climax in Jesus Christ, the one preached by Paul, Silvanus and Timothy.

Now this turns out to be a critical word for an age like ours, which sets a high value on positive thinking – in business, athletics, education and even the Church. Christians have their reasons for optimism about the course of human history and even about their own personal lives, but not because they trust in the indomitable human spirit or the infinite capacity of human achievement, not because they have learned to psych themselves up to perform outstanding feats or to endure excruciating pain. Christian hope emerges from a confidence in the reliability of God, who in Jesus Christ proves to be utterly dependable – both in human history and in our personal lives.

Second, the faithful God establishes people in community (1.21). We note with interest Paul's strategy here with his initial readers: the community God establishes is composed of 'us' and 'you'. Some in Corinth may criticize Paul for his change of plans, but they need to know that what binds them together is not his behaviour or their response, but God's action.

Beyond the rhetorical move Paul makes, we can observe the remarkable intention of God – to create a single people composed of such diversity and conflict as represented by Paul and his readers. Despite all the tensions between Paul and the Corinthians and among the Corinthians themselves, God's plans have not changed, and these plans include the creation of a community in Christ. Amid the pressures and pluralism of the contemporary Church, whether local or global, Paul's positive words to Corinth offer reassurance.

Third, Paul's optimism includes the confirming activity of God's Spirit. The language of 1.21–22 suggests that the notion of baptism may not be far from Paul's mind, but his emphasis lies on experience ('in our hearts'). The dependable presence of God is not limited to one moment in history, but continues in the lives of the people God has established in community.

The phrase in v. 22 translated in the NRSV as 'first instalment' (in the RSV as 'guarantee') has particular significance in a passage that concentrates on the promises of God. It represents the down payment, or pledge, that pays part of the purchase price in advance and obligates the contracting party to the remaining payments. The experience of the Spirit in human lives functions like this.

Often the Christian community finds itself with what seem like good reasons to conclude that God has abandoned the divine promises. The vicious presence of evil in the world, the constant conflict within the Church, the struggle with inexplicable tragedies would lead any reasonable person to infer that God has taken a long holiday or drastically changed the script – except for the persistent rumblings of the Spirit 'in our hearts', rumblings that remind us of God's commitments to complete the story.

The gospel of Jesus Christ, the reality of the Christian community, the experience of the Spirit are grounds for positive thinking of a Pauline sort. CC

Mark 2.1–12

After the brief and straightforward miracle stories of Mark 1.29–31 and 1.40–45, this story of the healing of a paralysed man comes as a surprise. Its setting elaborately details the effort required to bring the man into the presence of Jesus. Jesus' comments concerning the forgiveness of sins introduce some confusion about what the relationship is between forgiveness and healing. Little has prepared readers to anticipate the serious conflict between Jesus and the scribes. These features of the text reflect the fact that it forms a bridge between the miracle stories that run from 1.21 to 2.12 and the controversy stories that run from 2.1 to 3.6.

While this story, like all gospel miracle stories, has Jesus rather than any other character as its focus, the actions of the people who bring the paralysed man to Jesus catch our attention because of the detail Mark lavishes on them. The setting in 2.1–2 makes clear that simply getting near Jesus is a challenge. He has returned to Capernaum, the town he earlier left because of the crowds (1.21, 32–34, 38–39). Now the number of those gathered makes it impossible even to get near the door to hear him (cf. 1.33). Despite these difficulties, a paralysed man is carried to Jesus.

Mark's awkward introduction of this event already draws attention to the effort required: 'Then some people came, bringing to him a paralysed man, carried by four of them.' The picture Mark evokes is a comic one; a sea of people, over which four individuals are carrying the man who is paralysed. When they cannot enter through the door, they expend the additional effort required to make a hole in the roof and lower him to Jesus.

The result of this effort Mark describes with the simple phrase, 'Jesus saw their faith.' In other Marcan miracle stories as well, faith is ascribed to the action involved in coming to Jesus for healing (5.34; 10.52). No affirmation about the person of Jesus or the nature of God accompanies these actions; the actions themselves speak of confidence in Jesus' ability. Equally important, these faithful or trusting actions precede healing rather than coming as the result of healing.

Another prominent feature of this story is the relationship between forgiveness and healing. In response to the faith of those who bring the paralysed man to him, the expectation is that Jesus will tell the man to walk or pronounce him healed. Instead, Jesus announces, 'Son, your sins are forgiven.' This, of course, prompts the controversy that follows, as a result of which Jesus then claims for himself the authority to forgive sins and then effects the cure. What is the relationship between these two actions, forgiveness and healing?

As in other biblical texts, the assumption at work is that illness or affliction comes about as the result of sin (e.g. Ps. 103.3; John 5.14; 9.2; Jas. 5.15–16). Because that connection has often been twisted to inflict needless guilt on persons, it is important to consider carefully what is said here. Jesus' statement that the man's sins are forgiven may indeed suggest that his paralysis results from sin, but the man does not rise and walk when he is forgiven. More important, Jesus' initial proclamation in 1.14–15 and the tenor of the Gospel as a whole also suggest that everyone stands in need of repentance. There are no exemptions from that category. The paralysed man simply becomes a specific instance where two major features of Jesus' ministry, forgiveness and healing, come together. To put it another way, this remains a story about Jesus, not a story about the origin of disability.

In this particular story, where bystanders challenge Jesus' authority to make the claim that sins have been forgiven, the healing becomes Jesus' way of demonstrating that he does have this authority. The question, 'Which is easier?' points to the fact that, unlike forgiveness, healing is verifiable. When healing is accomplished, Jesus' power cannot be denied, as is clear in the people's amazement at the story's conclusion.

The relationship between forgiveness and healing provides the pretext for the emergence of controversy surrounding Jesus. Even in the first healing story, the comparison between Jesus and the scribes raises eyebrows (1.21–28), and questions about Jesus' authority begin early (1.27). Here accusations come to the surface of the story, and the specific accusation of blasphemy is extremely serious, as blasphemy carried with it the death penalty (Lev. 24.15–16). If Jesus' statement,'Your sins are forgiven', is a 'divine passive', a circumlocution that avoids the more direct 'God forgives you', then the scribes correctly challenge Jesus' claim. His response, which takes the customary form of a question and then the act that demonstrates his authority, tosses the controversy back into the faces of his opponents.

Despite the seriousness of the charge against Jesus in this passage, it is worth recalling that the scribes do not yet speak out against him. Mark carefully says that Jesus perceives what the scribes are thinking ('questioning in their hearts'). The section that follows will bring these controversies into the open, as Pharisees begin to challenge particular actions of Jesus. The section as a whole culminates in 3.6 with the conspiracy to bring about Jesus' death. BG

The Second Sunday Before Lent

Proverbs 8.1, 22–31; Colossians 1.15–20; John 1.1–14

Proverbs 8.1, 22–31

For ancient Israelites the natural world was not benign. The sentence passed on the man in Gen. 3.17–19 promises him toil and sweat in producing the food necessary for survival, and famine plays its part in the stories of Abraham, Joseph and Ruth, to name but three. The claim here, that Wisdom was present with God when he created the world, is a claim both that there is a rational basis to an otherwise ambiguous world, and that this rational principle is accessible to humankind.

As an alternative account of the creation to that in Gen. 1—2, our passage is a useful reminder that none of the biblical creation narratives can be made to conform to modern scientific accounts of the origin of the universe. There is no 'big bang' here; rather, there is a charming picture of God with a female companion (Wisdom is feminine in Hebrew) perhaps helping him (the meaning of the word translated as 'master worker' in v. 30 is uncertain) but certainly playing (rather than 'rejoicing' cf. v. 30b–31a) with the created order as though with new toys. There are resonances with the Genesis creation stories. The word translated 'depths' in v. 24 is the same word that is rendered 'deep' in Gen. 1.2, and it recurs in Prov. 8 in vv. 27 and 28. The idea that one of the purposes of creation is to ascribe limits, essentially to the sea (cf. v. 29), is implicit in Gen. 1 (and cf. Job 38.8–11) in that these limits are removed when God brings a flood upon the earth (Gen. 7.11).

Scholarly speculation has naturally focused upon the origin of the figure of Wisdom, with possible candidates being the Egyptian idea of *maat* 'justice' and the Greek figure of *Sophia*. The passage also undoubtedly comes from a later period in the growth of the Old Testament, when there was a felt need for an intermediate figure between a transcendent God and humankind. It may also have been necessary to counteract the challenge presented to Judaism by Greek philosophy.

Granted all this, the passage injects a marvellously light touch into the process of creation. It shows us a designer enjoying the work in company with someone who expresses her approval of what is done by playing with it. There is no 'first cause' or 'unmoved mover' here; and the presence of Wisdom and her especial delight in the human race ensure that the creation is far more than a machine that is left to run on its own once it has been made. The figure of Wisdom personifies God's unwearying care for the created order, and for the well-being of the human animal that is so destructive of what God has made. This is one reason why Jewish interpretation has connected Wisdom with the Torah, God's revealed law for every facet of the life of his people, and why Christian interpretation has made a connection with the divine Logos, the Word made flesh. JR

Colossians 1.15–20

Theologically profound and memorable as it is, and influential as it has been in Christian thought, this passage cannot be said to lend itself to a ten-minute sermon or to be heard, momentarily, between psalm and Gospel.

There is little doubt that we should see these verses as standing apart from their context; the passage was included as a quotation from some other use. Was it perhaps a hymn or a sort of creed? First-century Christians did not distinguish between the two (and maybe it would be an advantage if we could imitate them). The 'hymn' is frequently seen in this light alongside Phil. 2.5–11 (see p. 102), and in both cases structural analyses abound. Pretty clearly, it divides into two halves: vv. 15–17 concerning Christ's role in creation; and vv. 18–20 concerning his salvific and ecclesial triumph. Like the Philippians partner, it is one of the loftiest statements of Christ's status and role in the whole of early Christian literature – and one of the earliest, especially if we suppose it to antedate Colossians itself. It is to be compared to the Johannine Prologue, 1.1–18, with which it shares not only general import, but also conceptual background.

This should probably be sought in the Jewish tradition of 'wisdom' writings, Proverbs, Job, Ecclesiasticus and, most recently, the Wisdom of Solomon; together with reflection on the figure of Adam and the sense that the 'beginning-times' would be replicated in the 'end-times'. Jesus is seen as the key to such replication – 'the image' of God (cf. Gen. 1.26). Yet he is not just the end-times replica: he was God's agent in the original creative act. Here, there are precedents in Jewish speculation about the 'pre-existence' of the great mediatorial agencies of God's purpose, like his word and the Law. So vital are they that there cannot have been a time when they were not 'with God'. Jesus is included in their number and indeed subsumes them for, to the Christians, he is the comprehensive expression of God and his purposes. So any lesser view of him would, in this perspective, be inappropriate and unreasonable (using the term in a sense far from that of the eighteenth century).

What we have in this 'hymn' is what we may call an advanced instance of the general and inevitable (in that thought-world) early Christian methods for identifying who Jesus was and what he signified. They were Jews, of one kind or another, so must necessarily see him as stepping into as many roles and images as possible whereby they were used to thinking of the communication between God and humankind. It was a process which, in certain ways, Jesus himself probably initiated. To view the phenomenon as a whole: it is of course the sheer concentration of such images (Messiah, Son of man, Word, etc.) that is so striking and that testifies so forcibly to the theological revolution that Jesus occasioned. This passage plays an important part in the development of the process.

It is the idea of Christ as agent in creation (corresponding to God's 'word' or 'Wisdom' in Jewish thought, see Prov. 8.22f.; Wisd. 9.1) that is likely to seem to us a step too far. But once you embarked on the conviction of Christ as your all-sufficient route to God and his mediator to you, how could you omit the most pervasive feature of all, the created order that surrounded you? There, surely, God leaves his Jesus-shaped mark and not only in the human soul. LH

John 1.1–14

See Christmas Day, Set III, pp. 26–27.

The Sunday Next Before Lent

2 Kings 2.1–12; 2 Corinthians 4.3–6; Mark 9.2–9

2 Kings 2.1–12

At 1 Kings 19.16, Elijah was commanded to anoint Elisha to be his successor. The immediate sequel to this passage records that Elijah found him ploughing, and threw his mantle upon him, whereupon Elisha followed him. Elisha then disappears from the narrative until 2 Kings 2; the present passage can be seen both as the public endorsement of Elisha's succession as well as the climax of Elijah's career.

There are only two people in the Old Testament who do not die, but who are taken to heaven: Enoch (Gen. 5.24) and Elijah. The tradition that Moses' burial place was known to no one (Deut. 34.6) later gave rise to the idea that he, too, did not die.

The present passage is artistically constructed, with not a little air of mystery. The reader is told from the outset that Elijah is to be taken to heaven by a whirlwind (v. 1). Whether Elisha knows this, is left in doubt. Elijah, apparently, does not wish Elisha to witness his ascension and three times tries to persuade him to stay behind. Three companies of prophets do know what is to happen and inform Elisha, who in turn ('keep silent') tries to conceal his knowledge from his master. Perhaps the incidents are a kind of test, designed to discover the strength of Elisha's loyalty. The exact manner of how Elijah is to be 'taken' is perhaps known only to the narrator and the readers (cf. v. 1) so that Elisha's triple declaration of undying loyalty (vv. 2, 4, 6) indicates his willingness to face anything that may happen to Elijah. Elisha having passed this test, Elijah grants him a wish. He does not make a selfish request. A 'double share' (Hebrew *pi shnayim*) normally means the two-thirds of an estate that the eldest son inherits from his father (Deut. 21.17). Elisha therefore wants to be Elijah's heir. Although possession of some of his spirit – that is, some of his power – will be a personal endowment, its use will be to further the cause of the prophetic groups in their service of the God of Israel. The wish is granted, on condition that Elisha sees Elijah's translation. The chariot of fire and horses that separate the two men symbolize the unseen forces that surround God's servants, according to the Elijah–Elisha stories (see 2 Kings 6.17). They may also have been a title for Elijah and, if so, this would explain the despairing cry of Elisha in v. 12 as his master disappears (cf. the same despairing cry when Elisha is on his deathbed, 2 Kings 13.14). The loss of the prophets' great champion is grievous; in the present instance, the combination of divine providence and human persistence has provided a successor. JR

2 Corinthians 4.3–6

Year B provides most readings from 2 Corinthians (Propers 3–9) but still only a fraction of this rich and difficult epistle. Paul's apostolic authority has been challenged in Corinth and he defends himself by speaking of the gospel itself. The character of his ministry derives from that, and he himself and his ministry team are merely servants of God – suffering servants even – and so they are their servants for the sake of Christ and the communication of the gospel. This gospel is publicly proclaimed and yet a mystery, hidden to those who do not see it. Paul has no problem in combining belief in malign powers governing human destiny with his assumption that anyone is free to respond to his message. His sharp dualism between those who are in and those who are not (cf. 1 Cor. 1.18) here draws on a personification of the evil power that later opened a door to Christian gnosticism's demiurge who created this present evil world. How far that is from Paul's intention is clear in his allusion to the Gen. 1 creation narrative (v. 3) in v. 6. Christ is the image, or likeness, of God (v. 4), and to know him is to know God (cf. John 8.19; 14.9).

Paul gives eloquent expression to the Christian understanding of revelation, echoing the language of Isa. 9.2 in his allusion to Gen. 1.3. Light is a natural symbol of revelation (illumination, enlightenment) found in several religions. The knowledge that is spoken of here is a personal knowledge that can be contrasted with what counts as knowledge in some modern epistemologies, but the word reminds us of the intellectual dimension in authentic Christian religious responses. The specifically Christian content of what Paul describes is contained in the reference to Jesus. He had formerly known enough about Jesus to persecute his followers, but a christophany (1 Cor. 9.1; 15.8) persuaded him that God had indeed vindicated this crucified man, and the exalted Lord was now the centre of his transformed but still Jewish religious life (cf. Gal. 2.19f.). The slightly later *merkabah* Jewish mysticism might help us to make sense of Paul's experience. (See J. Ashton, *The Religion of Paul the Apostle*, Yale, 2000.) Even without exploring the historical analogies, many readers will feel drawn into the magnetic field of the apostle's religious experience by the power of his language and allusion. Most of this passage is repeated under Proper 4 (pp. 161–162). RM

Mark 9.2–9

A great deal has been written about the transfiguration, an event in the Synoptic Gospels that has no obvious parallels: the miracle happens to Jesus, rather than being done by him. Some points are clear. For instance there are other occasions in Mark when Jesus takes three or four disciples apart from the Twelve: the raising of Jairus' daughter (5.37), the final speech of Jesus (13.3), and in Gethsemane (14.37). On each of these occasions some aspect of Jesus is revealed: his power over the dead; his coming to gather the elect; his obedience to the Father's will. What is it then that is revealed to the three on the mountain?

The emphasis of the story is on Peter's words: 'Rabbi, it is good that we are here.

Shall we make three shelters, one for you, one for Moses, and one for Elijah?' Both the address (Rabbi; see e.g. Mark 14.25, where Judas Iscariot uses it) and the evangelist's comment ('He did not know what to say, they were so terrified') show that, as so often in Mark, Peter and the other disciples have failed to understand who Jesus is. The fact that he specifies why three shelters were needed, one for each, only adds to the inappropriateness of the question. That is what is being revealed: Jesus is not one of three, of whom the other two are Elijah and Moses; he is greater than both of them, as Elijah himself (in the person of the Baptist, cf. 9.13) has already said: 'After me comes one mightier than I am' (1.7).

Similarly, the voice from heaven declares Jesus to be God's one and only Son, and commands attention to him, rather than to Elijah or Moses (see Deut. 18.15f.). And the final line confirms and stresses the point: Jesus and no one else was with them, there was no longer anyone else to be seen.

Mark is fond of sharp contrasts: the clothes of Jesus are more white than those of anyone else on earth; the leaders of Israel in the past are no longer to be attended to and disappear; Jesus exceeds all others and is not to be placed alongside any of them; he is not one rabbi among others. Faith in Jesus exceeds all other kinds of faith in the limitlessness of its demands. He will die for everybody, and what he requires of his followers is willingness to give him total assent. JF

Ash Wednesday

Joel 2.1–2, 12–17 or Isaiah 58.1–12; 2 Corinthians 5.20b—6.10; Matthew 6.1–6, 16–21 or John 8.1–11

Joel 2.1–2, 12–17

The book of Joel appears to have been occasioned by a devastating plague of locusts round about the year 400 BC. These locusts and the havoc they have wrought are explicitly described in 1.4–7, one effect of the plague being that some of the regular offerings in the temple have been interrupted (1.13). While ch. 1 describes the threat to the land of Judah, ch. 2 envisages the plague approaching Jerusalem itself. The city is put on a war footing with the blowing of the trumpet, and the sky darkened by the dense cloud of the flying locusts, seems to be a portent of the coming day of the Lord (v. 2), an event that prophetic tradition had come to associate with judgement. Just as the locusts were unstoppable by any human agency, so nothing could forestall the day of the Lord.

In the verses omitted from the reading (vv. 3–11) the oncoming unnatural army is described in vivid and terrifying poetic images, leading to frightened reactions from heaven and earth, and sun, moon and stars (v. 10). Such phenomena elsewhere accompany descriptions of God's coming in judgement, and the army of locusts is seen as one commanded by God (v. 11).

In the face of this terror, God offers respite. If the people return to God, if they proclaim a solemn fast, and if they pray to God to spare them, he may alter their fortunes for good. The book, from 2.18 onwards, implies that the times of prayer and fasting have been noted by God, who now promises his blessing on the land.

This material prompts two questions. Was the plague averted as a result of the prayer and fasting? If it was, did the people remain faithful once the danger was over, or was theirs a temporary piety prompted more by the instinct of self-preservation than a genuine desire for repentance?

The closest point of contact between the text and modern readers lies in the fact that, when confronted by overwhelming forces of nature, humankind becomes aware of its limitations and seeks help from the divine. If we can learn to live our lives as what we really are – creatures with limits to our strength, our intellect and, ultimately to our lives – we may be able to achieve the kind of genuine dependence upon God that is not generated solely by emergencies, special occasions or self-interest. JR

Isaiah 58.1–12

At the heart of this passage is the complaint of the people in v. 3a that God is failing to act in their present distress. Verses 1–2 state God's call to the prophet to go to the heart of their need – their sin. He is to speak with the vehemence and urgency that is the hallmark of all authentic prophecy (for the voice like a trumpet, cf. Hos. 8.1, and for the task of showing the people their true need, cf. Mic. 3.8).

In this case the clarity and insistence are all the more necessary because the people are armour-plated in a complacency built on the fervour of their religious and devotional activity (vv. 2–3). The fact that only fasting is mentioned and not sacrifices suggests that the temple is not yet rebuilt (cf. v. 12). Probably this dates the oracle early after the return in 538 BC, before the rebuilding instigated by Haggai and Zechariah in 520 BC.

Fasting was practised in times of crisis and was regarded as a sign of humility before God and dependence on him in times of crisis (cf. Joel. 1.14; Jer. 36.9). It appears to have been constantly repeated during the time of the exile, for people came to Jerusalem to ask if they should continue this practice of 'many years' now that Zechariah assures them the new age is dawning (Zech. 7.3).

The prophet gives two reasons why their fasting is ineffectual. The first is that it is self-regarding (v. 3). The words may mean that they are more concerned with their own business interests than the rights of others but, possibly, that they have been looking more for religious 'kicks' than true relationship with God.

The second is that it is a cloak for their failure to live in the way God requires (cf. Isa. 1.10–17). Verses 3b–4 describe their internecine strife and their exploitation of those dependent on them.

Verses 6–8 contain one of the finest descriptions of true religion to be found anywhere in the Old Testament. The practice of fasting is not rejected, but a true spirit behind it is expressed only when it is backed by concern for 'doing' righteousness (cf. v. 2), especially for the poor and 'little people' of society.

It is when they truly express such an attitude towards God (a relationship always affecting and being affected by the attitude shown towards other people) that God will arise as light for them (cf. 60.1) and heal them (cf. 57.18–19). Indeed, their need is for inner healing rather than change of circumstances. For then, even as they travel like Israel earlier through their own wilderness, they will find God's presence guiding them just as their fathers did (v. 8, cf. Exod. 14.19–20). Restoration is promised in the expansion of vv. 9b-12 but, meanwhile, it is those who keep faith in the dark times who are the real 'builders' of any community (v. 12). RM

2 Corinthians 5.20b—6.10

Contemporary Christians sometimes look back to the early days in the Church's life with rose-tinted glasses. That period seems to have been inhabited by believers who were filled with zeal, who knew the necessity of evangelism, who had the advantages of a new and innocent faith. Read with care, Paul's letters reveal another side to the story, one in which there are conflicts, struggles and misunderstandings. In the present passage, Paul pleads with baptized Christians, people whom he elsewhere characterizes as being 'in Christ' and belonging to the 'body of Christ', to become reconciled to God. The need for reconciliation is inherent in the

Christian faith – it is not a symptom of degeneracy in the latter days of the Church's life.

Set against the other texts assigned for Ash Wednesday (e.g. Ps. 51) and other reflections on the need for reconciliation between God and humankind, 2 Cor. 5 sounds a distinctive note. Here human beings do not cry out to God for forgiveness and reconciliation, for it is God who seeks reconciliation. In the sending of Jesus Christ, God acts to reconcile the world to God (5.20a). Paul characterizes the gospel itself as God's making an appeal to human beings to be reconciled to God (5.20; 6.1). Consistent with Paul's comments elsewhere (Rom. 1.18–32), the point he makes here is that it is not God who must be appeased because of human actions; but human beings, who have turned away from God in rebellion, must accept God's appeal and be reconciled. Even in the face of the intransigence of human sin, it is God who takes the initiative to correct the situation; human beings have only to receive God's appeal.

The urgency of the appeal for this reception comes to the fore in 6.1–2. Without accepting God's reconciliation, the Corinthians will have accepted 'the grace of God in vain'. Moreover, the right time for this reconciliation is now: 'Now is the acceptable time; see, now is the day of salvation!' This comment about time lays before the Corinthians the eschatological claim of the gospel. As in 5.16 ('from now on'), Paul insists that the Christ-event makes this appeal urgent. There is also, however, a very specific urgency that affects the Corinthian community. It is time – or past time – for them to lay aside their differences and hear in full the reconciling plea of God made through the apostles. Time is 'at hand' (NRSV 'near'), both for the created order as a whole and for the Corinthians in particular.

Throughout the text, Paul asserts that it is God who brings about this reconciliation, but he also points to the role of Christ. God reconciles the world 'in Christ', that is, by means of Christ. Specifically, God 'made him to be sin who knew no sin' (5.21). To say that Christ 'knew no sin', consistent with Paul's understanding of sin as a state of rebelliousness against God, means that Christ was obedient to God, that Christ submitted to God's will. That God 'made him to be sin' suggests, in keeping with Rom. 8.3 and Gal. 3.13, that Christ's death on the cross had redemptive significance. Through it human beings are enabled to 'become the righteousness of God' (2 Cor. 5.21b); in Christ's death the reconciling act of God becomes concrete.

Paul's eloquent plea for reconciliation stands connected to comments on the ministry that he and his co-workers are exercising among the Corinthians. Throughout this entire portion of the letter (1.1—7.16), in fact, the focus is on both the nature of the gospel and the nature of the Christian ministry. That dual focus exists not simply because Paul is once more defending himself against his critics (although he certainly is defending himself!), but because the ministry can be understood rightly only where the gospel itself is understood rightly. Paul's ministry, like his gospel, has to do with reconciling human beings to God. In 6.3–10 he expands on that role, insisting that he and his colleagues have taken every measure that might enhance the faith and growth of believers in Corinth. Ironically, he begins his itemization of the things that commend him with a list of things that would certainly not impress many readers of a résumé or letter of recommendation – afflictions, hardships, calamities, beatings, imprisonments . . . For those who see the gospel as a means of being delivered *from* difficulties rather than *into* difficulties, Paul's commendation of the ministry will have a very negative sound. As earlier in the letter, he insists on the contrast between how the apostles are viewed by the world and how they stand before God. If the world, with its standards of measure, regards them as impostors, unknown, dying, punished, those assessments matter not at all. Before God, the apostles know that they are in fact true, well-known, alive and rejoicing.

This aspect of the passage makes powerful grist for reflection for those engaged in Christian ministry today, but it is equally relevant for all Christians, especially on Ash Wednesday. The reconciliation God brings about in Jesus Christ obliges not only ordained ministers but all Christians to proclaim the outrageous, universal, reconciling love of God. BG

Matthew 6.1–6, 16–21

It was perhaps not very respectful towards the author of this Gospel to omit from this lection the Lord's Prayer that is at its centre, but at least we can be led to focus on a particular aspect of Matthew's teaching, here and elsewhere: his use of financial language in his exposition of the good news. That use is down-to-earth: for example, the noun 'reward' (coming four times in our passage) can mean payment for work done, and the corresponding verb can mean to pay workers for what they have done (e.g. 20.8, where both words occur). In the whole section, 6.1–21, Matthew presents Jesus as an accountant advising clients to invest in long-term securities rather than in those that mature sooner, and to do without interest payments in the meantime.

For all our love of money – or perhaps because of it and of our feelings of guilt about it – we find this way of thinking embarrassing when it is applied to God. Should not our love for him be pure? ('Not with the hope of gaining aught, not seeking a reward . . .') Matthew appears not to have thought so. His characteristic emphasis on reward can be seen by comparing the frequency with which he and the other evangelists use the noun: Matthew 10 times, Mark once, Luke three times, John once. He has created problems for moral theologians.

But there is another aspect of Matthew's language that must be borne in mind. In vv. 4, 6 and 18, he refers to God as 'your Father' (see also 7.7–11). God's rewards are presents; there is no need to think of them as payments for work done. In Matthew, the language of commerce gives way to that of family. We are not employees in a faceless business, but sons and daughters of a father. It is a sad fact that 'paternalism' became a term of abuse in the late nineteenth century. No New Testament writer calls God 'father' more than Matthew, normally with a possessive 'my', 'your' or 'our'.

Matthew believed that to love God was the greatest and first commandment (22.34–40). There is some evidence that in Judaism at the time of Jesus there were reckoned to be three pious acts through which one fulfilled this command: almsgiving, prayer and fasting (see e.g. Tobit 12.8). If they are performed in order to acquire a good reputation in the sight of others, then they lose their reality as deeds of love *for God*. Matthew is very clear on this aspect of the matter. But there is more to it than that. If they are done in order to receive payment from God, they cease to be acts *of love* for God. There is a saying from the Jewish fathers: be not like servants who serve the master on condition of receiving a gift, but be like servants who serve the master not on condition of receiving. It is entirely the result of God's love that he repays according to their work (Ps. 62.12, quoted, in its darker aspect, at Matt. 16.27; see also 20.1–16).

Matthew has not, therefore, transferred the language of payments and earnings to the relationship between God and his family without transforming it. It is a happy fact that God's love for his creatures expresses itself in gifts, embarrassing though we find such excessive generosity. JF

John 8.1–11

It is dispiriting (but perhaps not wholly surprising) that this passage has traditionally been known as 'the pericope concerning *adultery*', when so many readers have been glad to find it the story about Jesus' generous forgiveness and his shaming of the censorious. It has indeed been the comfort of sinners and the banner of the liberally minded, even though there are always those to wag a cautionary finger with the final words: 'go, and do not sin again'. But from a pastoral point of view, it has been a prime model, leaving its mark notably on the practice of sacramental confession. And, in another dimension, who can forget, once having seen it, Guercino's picture in the Dulwich Picture Gallery, with the look of piteous contempt on the face of Jesus as he confronts the woman's tormentors? As the word goes, it says it all.

From a more academic point of view, however, the story is remarkable for a quite different reason. It is unique in the gospel tradition in being demonstrably an example of what form criticism has seen as the earlier stage of all the stories. It truly is a floater and came to rest in this location in the Gospel of John only late and, as it were, by accident. The oldest manuscripts do not have it at all, while others put it after 7.36, and still others place it at various locations in the Gospel of Luke. Indeed, it has often been felt that in ethos and tendency this is a Luke-type story, with its loving generosity of spirit. It certainly has no Johannine 'feel'.

Yet if its floating character presses us to dub this story apocryphal, that seems unsatisfactory, for it has none of the magical features which tend to characterize those episodes from the life of Jesus to be found in the later apocryphal Gospels. Quite the contrary: it is among the most believable (as well as welcome) episodes in the entire canon. It is not surprising that critics have put forward the case for its authenticity as a genuine memory from Jesus' life. After all, if Jesus' teaching and behaviour left a special mark, must it not have been precisely for striking, generous and unusual acts of this kind? It was an inspired move that the designers of the lectionary gave it to be read on Ash Wednesday.

Guercino also painted a picture of the scene in the garden on Easter Day. He used the same man as model and dressed him in the same clothes. I do not know whether he was making a deliberate point about the identity, the sameness, of Jesus across all divides of time, place and state; but in any case we can ponder the point. And in another way, the presence of this story in the still-read canon (even by the skin of its teeth – it might so easily have slipped into oblivion) speaks of the eternal freshness of the truth of its winning message. LH

The First Sunday of Lent

Genesis 9.8–17; 1 Peter 3.18–22; Mark 1.9–15

Genesis 9.8–17

With Gen. 9.2–4 we reach the world of human experience, a world in which humans can now eat not only things that grow (see Gen. 1.30) but all other creatures, minus their blood. The distinction between clean and unclean creatures is not yet given to Israel, although the distinction is anachronistically introduced at the beginning of the passage (8.20).

Two matters call for especial comment: the reason for God promising never again to destroy the creatures of earth (8.21) and the significance of the rainbow (9.13). On the face of it the logic of 8.21 is odd. God promises never again to destroy the earth's living creatures 'for the inclination of the human heart is evil from its youth'. However, given that the perversity of the human heart was the cause of the flood and the destruction that it caused in the first place, it seems odd that this same perversity is given as the reason for God promising *not* to destroy living creatures in the future! The NEB translation 'however evil his inclinations may be' is an attempt to soften the difficulty. The odd logic is best taken as a declaration of God's grace. There are two ways of dealing with human perversity. One way is to destroy the human race and the rest of creation with it. The other way is to wean the human race from perversity to the love of peace and justice. But this cannot be done in the benign, vegetarian world of Gen. 1.30. It can only be done in the new, and compromised creation of Gen. 9.2–3.

The rainbow of 9.13 has become a universal symbol of peace; but is this its function in Gen. 9? The bow in the Old Testament is a sign of war; the broken bow is the sign of peace (cf. Ps. 46.9: he [God] breaks the bow, and shatters the spear). Because of this, it has been suggested that the bow in Gen. 9 is not a promise of peace but a warning to the human race that God will not be indifferent to human behaviour if it threatens to destroy the earth. God will not again bring a flood; but this does not mean that he will do nothing to preserve his creation.

It must be admitted that this interpretation seems to go against the concluding words of the passage, that the bow and the clouds will remind God of his covenant – a covenant, let it be noted, not just with humanity but with all living creatures. The bow can probably remain, then, as a promise not only of peace, but as an example of the way in which Old Testament narratives can exert powerful influence upon today's world. JR

1 Peter 3.18–22

Christ has ascended into heaven, but his followers continue to live in the world, and it is a world that is often hostile and suspicious. Peter gives his readers practical guidance on how to live in this situation. They have every right to expect that if they behave well, they will have nothing to fear: and good behaviour is necessary not just for their own protection but so that their faith may not be brought into disrepute (4.15). There is a general confidence here in the ability of the non-Christian world to recognize goodness and to respond to it. Christians have no monopoly on morality and justice: that is why it is possible and proper for them to obey lawful secular authority (2.17). Conscience, a term more reminiscent of Stoic philosophy than distinctively Christian morality, is a general guide. However, the conscience of society is not an infallible safeguard. Christians may find themselves suffering precisely for doing what they see to be right. Here their guide for behaviour must be the model of Christ. The author has already appealed to this in his specific advice to the Christian slaves of unjust masters (2.18–25). The imitation of Christ has a long history as a basis of Christian morality, but in both passages in this epistle it is clear that the story of Christ is not just an example to be followed, but a transforming, saving event that makes a new way of living possible. So the advice on practical living is followed by an almost credal statement of the death, resurrection and ascension of Christ, as the means of dealing with human sin and of establishing a new relationship with God, appropriated through baptism.

The somewhat stylized statement of faith may well represent a form familiar to the readers, but allusions that they would no doubt have understood are unclear to us. Who are the 'spirits in prison' to whom Christ is said to have preached, when did he preach to them, and what is the connection with 'the days of Noah'? The reference may be to the period between death and resurrection, in which Christ 'descended into hell' and proclaimed the gospel to the dead from the time of the flood onwards; this may be echoed later at 4.6, and is how it is understood in the apocryphal Gospel of Peter (10.39). Alternatively, the spirits in prison might be seen as the powers of the underworld, maybe identified with the giants of the pre-flood period (Gen. 6.4) so that the passage serves as the foundation for the idea of the 'Harrowing of Hell' as portrayed in icons and medieval mystery plays. Again, Christ's proclamation might be located not in the time between death and resurrection, but in the sequence of both, seen as a victory over the demonic forces in the world (as v. 22 and Col. 2.15, 1 Tim. 3.16). The analogy between baptism and the flood is also unclear, since the waters of the flood themselves were hardly 'saving'. Noah and his companions, however, came through the waters of death to salvation and a new life; there may be a suggestion here in Peter of the Pauline interpretation of baptism as an incorporation into the death and resurrection of Christ, being 'buried with him in baptism' (Rom. 6.4). The mythological language provides a happy hunting ground for commentators, but the relation of the doctrinal statement to the practical advice remains clear: the risen and ascended Christ is the Lord of the Church, empowering it to face the world. SL

Mark 1.9–15

For vv. 9–11, see pp. 40–41. The rest of the passage is made up of two parts, vv. 12–13 and vv. 14–15. Following on from the baptism of Jesus, these two brief sections are full of meaning for, like the baptism, they place central Marcan themes on the agenda at the beginning of the work and, together, they therefore make a kind of epitome of the book as a whole. For that reason, we speak of the whole passage, at least from v. 1 down to the end of these episodes, as fulfilling the role of a prologue. (Some critics prefer to stop speaking of a prologue at v. 13; others might go on to v. 20. See p. 40.)

We call vv. 12–13 the story of the temptation of Jesus, though the word does not quite capture the drama of what is told or the message Mark wants us to hear through it. Matthew and Luke both expanded this brief story and did indeed describe three temptations undergone by Jesus. They are thus elaborating what Mark gave – and in the process losing what Mark wished to convey. He gives us a story full of symbolic sense.

The wilderness is the place of exile and distress and, above all, testing. There Israel spent forty years en route to the Land of Promise; there too Elijah went in exile, again to suffer the testing of his calling to the service of God. Psalms like 78, 106 and 107 embedded the theme in Israel's consciousness. In the wilderness Jesus is 'tested'; and the passage looks on in Mark to Gethsemane, 14.32–42, where the final crisis occurs, for which this passage gives a foreshadowing, establishing the theme for us readers and encouraging us to see it as hanging over the book as a whole. *Peirazo*, *peirasmos* are the key words in both passages. It is not possible to be sure whether the wild beasts are unpleasant (and therefore part of the testing) or friendly and tamed. If the latter, then Jesus has shifted from being a symbol of Israel to being a new Adam, and the wilderness becomes a kind of Eden restored as the animals that were the friendly subjects of unfallen Adam resume their place (Isa. 11.6–9); and the angels who were set to bar Adam's way at the gate of Eden now serve their lord. One may be encouraged to discern this doctrine if (on very many grounds) one sees Mark as formed by Pauline thought (Rom. 5.12ff; 1 Cor. 15.22, 45–49).

The final two verses are a summary of Jesus' whole message and ministry. That 'the time is fulfilled' and that 'the kingdom has come near' – these ideas are the heart of his purpose. Where he is, God's rule or sovereignty is and his purpose fulfilled; and its completion is assured. For those who read or hear, the response can only be to accept this best of news. A *euaggelion* indicated an exciting message, like an emperor's approach. Paul and Mark use it naturally for the coming of the kingdom of God himself. LH

The Second Sunday of Lent

Genesis 17.1–7, 15–16; Romans 4.13–25; Mark 8.31–38

Genesis 17.1–7, 15–16

Promises by God to Abram have already been made at Gen. 12.2 and 15.5. Further, a mysterious ceremony reminiscent of covenant-making has occurred at 15.9–10, 17–18. Chapter 17 is therefore widely regarded as the work of the priestly tradition, summing up what has gone before, and giving prominence to the notion of covenant. The Hebrew word for covenant, *berit*, occurs 13 times in the chapter.

In its particular theological and literary articulation, the chapter emphasizes the initiative and graciousness of God. Ninety-nine, for the original readers of the passage, was an age which hardly any of them were likely to reach, let alone one at which they would become a parent. In verses not included in the reading, incredulity is expressed that the 90-year-old Sarah could bear a child (vv. 16–17). The understanding of the logic of vv. 1–2 is also important here. The 'and' at the beginning of v. 2 is not conditional; that is, walking before God and being blameless is not a condition that has to be fulfilled before God will make the covenant. The 'and' could just as well be omitted, as in the German Catholic-Protestant Translation (*Einheitsübersetzung*).

A further sign of divine initiative and grace is the granting of the new names, Abraham and Sarah. The standard translations give meanings for the old and new names. Abram means 'high father' while Abraham has the sense of 'father of many'. Sarai, perhaps meaning 'mockery' (cf. v. 17) becomes Sarah, 'princess'. Probably more important than the meanings of the names, assuming that ancient readers understood Hebrew etymologies in the same way as modern scholars do, is the simple fact of the change. Kings adopted new names at their accession (as did British monarchs even in the twentieth century!), and new names denoted new status and responsibility. To have a name bestowed by God was the ultimate divine honour.

The verses selected for the reading omit material that is integral to the chapter, such as the institution of the rite of circumcision as the outward sign of the covenant, the promise of the land of Canaan, and the promise to Ishmael. It is also interesting to contrast what is actually said in the chapter about Abraham's response (vv. 17–18) with what is made of it in Romans 4.13–25 (today's epistle). The Genesis version is both more true-to-life and honest, and may provide a more realistic view of what it means to trust God than Paul's implication that Abraham had no doubts! JR

Romans 4.13–25

Paul is determined to show that the inheritance promised to Abraham's seed is a promise for all who believe, both Jew and Gentile, a theme which runs like a refrain through much of his letter to the Romans. If the promise is only 'to those who are of the law' (the New American Standard Version's rendering of *hoi ek nomou* in v. 16) then Paul's gospel, he reckons, is empty and void; if the promise given to Abraham is for the Jewish people alone then salvation for the Gentiles could only come by their entering the law-defined identity of Israel. But Abraham, Paul is clear, is the 'father of us all', those of the law and those who share Abraham's faith, the father of both Jews and Gentiles.

Following a formulaic statement about God 'who gives life to the dead and calls into being the things that are not', Paul turns his thoughts to the fact that Abraham and his wife Sarah were as good as dead by the time God's promise was fulfilled in the birth of their son Isaac (the Greek in v. 19 literally refers to the deadness of Sarah's womb). Despite the impossibility seemingly inherent in their physical condition, Abraham was unwavering in his faith in God's promise and ability to fulfil his word (at least according to Paul: Gen 17.17 may suggest otherwise!). This steadfast faith was 'reckoned to him as righteousness' (v. 22; Gen. 15.6). Paul has already explained that this idea of righteousness being 'reckoned' to someone reflects its character as gift and not as wage (Rom. 4.3–5). And here he declares that the words 'it was reckoned to him' were written not just for Abraham's sake but for all believers who follow the pattern of his unwavering faith in the God who brings life from the dead. All such believers are made righteous through faith as the gift of God. There is a clear thematic link running through from v. 17 to vv. 24–25. Abraham entrusted himself to the God who brings life from the dead, and such was indeed in effect what took place, since both Abraham and Sarah were as good as dead when the promised new life was given to them. Likewise, Christians place their faith in this life-giving God, who raised Jesus from death. This leads Paul into the final acclamation, probably an established Christian formulation, concerning the death and resurrection of Christ. This is the first mention of Christ's resurrection since the opening comments in Rom. 1.3–4, and signals a further stage in Paul's extended argument: having considered the 'justification' which comes about through the death of Christ (see Rom. 3.21–26) and shown, by the example of Abraham, that this gift is for all who have faith, Paul now turns more to the new life which is lived 'in Christ' and which, he will later explain (7.6; 8.4f.), is empowered by the Spirit. DH

Mark 8.31–38

See Proper 19, pp. 226–227.

The Third Sunday of Lent

Exodus 20.1–17; I Corinthians 1.18–25; John 2.13–22

Exodus 20.1–17

Recent research on the ten commandments has reached two conclusions: that the commandments are a literary distillation of laws from several social settings in ancient Israel, and that this distillation played an important role in shaping other parts of the Old Testament. This second point can be illustrated in several ways. First, there are two fairly similar versions of the ten commandments, the other version being in Deut. 5.6–21. Second, the ten commandments stand at the head, i.e. the most important position of, the so-called Book of the Covenant, the laws contained in Exodus 20—23. Third, a case can be made that Deut. chs. 12—26 largely follow the order of the ten commandments, and are a kind of elaboration and enlargement of them. Fourth, passages such as Lev. 19 and Ps. 50 are arguably based upon or allude to the ten commandments.

The various backgrounds from which the ten commandments have been taken may be indicated by changes in the form of address. Verses 2–6 are a speech of God in the first person singular, vv. 7–12 talk about God in the third person while vv. 13–17 could be spoken either by God or a human representative. The second section, vv. 7–12, has been thought to represent the standpoint of the exile, with the particular emphasis on the sabbath, while the origin of vv. 13–17 has been sought in family law, the purpose of these verses being to protect the family and its property. The opening section is more difficult to place, presupposing as it does belief among the people in the existence of other gods and the attractions of idolatry. The general consensus of critical scholarship, however, is that in their present form, the ten commandments date from the exilic or post-exilic periods.

The fact that the ten commandments have been distilled from other laws and have then become the basis of further elaboration and expansion in the Old Testament indicates that they should not be regarded as a last word incapable of alteration. A reason given for observing the sabbath in Exod. 23.12 is that it will enable the ox and the ass to rest; and Lev. 19 adds further laws designed to protect the poor and needy. Christian tradition, too, has used the commandments creatively. The sabbath law, concerning Friday night to Saturday night, has been applied in various ways to Sunday; and Calvin's exposition of the ten commandments in the *Institutes of the Christian Religion* Book 2, Ch. 8 are a fine example of how their spirit can lead to more profound ethical reflection. JR

1 Corinthians 1.18–25

In this remarkable passage Paul asserts that the cross of Jesus Christ reveals the power of God. While for Christians some 20 centuries removed from Paul, and accustomed to the cross as a symbol in churches and even in jewellery, this assertion may seem inoffensive, it must have struck some of Paul's contemporaries as the ravings of a madman. The cross was, in fact, the antithesis of power – except as it revealed the power of the Roman Empire to crush those regarded as its opponents. Even so, this humiliating death was reserved for slaves, criminals, social outcasts – those who were deemed to be outside the boundaries of ordinary human society. Only the powerless died on the cross.

Yet Paul, who knew these brutal facts of crucifixion and its victims far better than we do, nevertheless asserts that the cross reveals God's power. God chose this act of foolishness because the world was unable to recognize God's wisdom (vv. 19–21). Instead of meeting the expectations of the world, either Jew or Greek, God offers the good news of 'Christ crucified', good news in the form of a scandal. Even so, God's foolishness is wiser than human wisdom. The cross is the point at which the conflict between God's ways and human ways is revealed to be irreconcilable; human wisdom is utterly bankrupt.

Alongside this assertion that the cross is God's power and God's wisdom (v. 24) runs the recognition that not everyone 'sees' the cross in this way. It is those 'who are being saved', in contrast to 'those who are perishing', who are able to see God's power in the crucifixion. The precise expression 'who are being saved' is important because it touches on the way in which salvation occurs: human beings do not save themselves, they are the recipients of God's salvation; and salvation is not a past event but a continuous one ('being saved').

Those who are being saved are those whom God has 'called', as Paul asserts in vv. 26–31. This passage serves as an extended illustration, based on the experience of the Corinthians, of the point Paul has been making in vv. 18–25. Paul asks the Corinthians to consider their own calling: 'Not many of you were wise by human standards, not many were powerful, not many were of noble birth.' Interpreters have often understood this verse to mean that early Christians came almost exclusively from the poor and uneducated elements of society, but Paul's statement, as well as the rest of the letter, indicates that indeed *some* of the Corinthians were from the ranks of the well-established. The point Paul is after is not primarily social, but theological: God did not choose you because you deserved to be chosen. God chose those who are undeserving, by the world's logic, in order to confound the logic of the world. The Corinthians, then, may look to their own experience to see that God does not act by human rules.

Later in this letter, Paul hints (not always subtly) that the Corinthians are boasting in their own accomplishments. They have achieved honour because of their wisdom (e.g. 4.8–13); in the gospel they have been freed from restrictive rules and regulations (5.1–3). Throughout the present passage Paul urges a different understanding of boasting, namely, the only boasting that belongs to a Christian is boasting in the cross. The only boasting rightly done is boasting in what God has given believers through Jesus Christ (1.31). Boasting in human wisdom and power is rejected, for it is precisely human wisdom and power that bring about the crucifixion of Jesus Christ and are thereby revealed to be utterly bankrupt.

It may strike us as curious, at first glance, that Paul does not interject in this passage a reference to the resurrection. Surely it is the resurrection rather than the crucifixion that reveals God's true power. In ch. 15, he does explain how the resurrection guarantees God's final triumph over all other powers, but here, in ch. 1, the resurrection is carefully, perhaps even intentionally, omitted. There may be two reasons for this omission. First, Paul understands that the Corinthians, with their emphasis on their own wisdom and their own spiritual gifts, needed to understand that the gospel is not about human accomplishments and being a Christian does not mean that one has already arrived at a life of glory. By issuing this forceful reminder about the centrality of the cross Paul places the entire Christian life in the context of the cross itself. Second, a central theological issue is at stake here – namely, the place of the cross in Christian faith. For Paul this is not merely a persuasive step through which he can bring the Corinthians over to his side. The cross, for Paul, is not a human error that God corrected through the resurrection or an embarrassment to be overcome. It is, instead, the point at which God's own and God's wholly other wisdom and will are revealed. BG

John 2.13–22

At this point John's Gospel presents us with a choice. The episode of 'the cleansing of the temple' in the Synoptic Gospels (and so in most people's minds) stands at the beginning of Holy Week, straight after Jesus' entry into Jerusalem. Here it is at the other end of Jesus' ministry, his very first moment of public confrontation with the religious authorities. From the point of view of chronology there is no way of reconciling the two accounts. We just have to choose.

But is chronology the most important thing? By the time the Gospels were written the exact sequence of events may have been forgotten (it is usually the first thing to get muddled in people's memories). The two traditions may represent two decisions on how best to tell the story. The Synoptics chose to separate Jesus' confrontations in Jerusalem from his preaching and healing ministry in Galilee by grouping them all together at the end, whereas John wove these two aspects of Jesus' activity together through relatively frequent visits to Jerusalem (which is in fact the more plausible pattern historically). The point, at any rate, is not so much to determine exactly when these events took place, but what they *meant*.

And John packs a great deal of meaning into his account. Jesus' action against the traders was in the tradition of the Old Testament prophets, a physical demonstration (of a distinctly aggressive kind in this Gospel) followed by a verbal explanation. He was explicitly fulfilling a prophetic protest made by Zechariah (14.21): 'There shall no longer be traders in the house of the Lord' – there is some evidence that trading had begun to exceed proper limits in the precincts, even if certain commercial activities (such as changing money into the special coins required for temple dues) were necessary and perhaps officially sanctioned.

But the Gospel goes on to offer more meanings than this. 'Zeal for your house will consume me' is an allusion to Ps. 69.9, the song of a nameless righteous sufferer who had had even his devotion to the temple turned against him. The disciples are said to have begun to see a similar destiny for Jesus. But there is a further meaning introduced in a way typical of this Gospel. On several occasions something Jesus says is taken in a literal and superficial sense by his hearers, only for Jesus to confound them by showing that it has a deeper meaning. Jesus certainly made some prophecy about the temple's destruction: there is a number of reports of it scattered through the New Testament. Here his opponents are the ones who take it literally. Jesus does not immediately correct them; it was his disciples who gradually came to see what he may have meant when, after the resurrection, they experienced that, through their life in the Church, they belonged to the 'body of Christ', a 'temple not made with hands'. AEH

The Fourth Sunday of Lent

Numbers 21.4–9; Ephesians 2.1–10; John 3.14–21

Numbers 21.4–9

This narrative has long intrigued interpreters, and given rise to bold expositions. As early as the Wisdom of Solomon (first century BC) the point was firmly made that it was not the brazen serpent that saved those who looked at it. The serpent was merely a symbol; God was the actual saviour (Wisd. 16.5–7). Another ancient Jewish interpretation took the importance of Moses' action to be to get the people to look upwards; that is, to God; and in this regard comparison was made with Exod. 17.8–13, where Moses held up his hand to heaven, to enable Israel to prevail in battle over Amalek. The same connection was made in the second-century AD Letter of Barnabas 12.2, 5–6, and by Justin Martyr (died *c.* AD 165) in his Dialogue with Trypho 112.2. The latter Christian writers also connected both incidents (i.e. Num. 21.4–9 and Exod. 17.8–13) with the passion of Jesus.

Modern commentators have tended to regard the story as a justification for the worship of a brazen serpent in Jerusalem, which Hezekiah is said to have destroyed during his reign (727–698 BC; cf. 2 Kings 18.4). The difficulty with this is that if Numbers reached its present form in the sixth to fifth centuries, we are left wondering why justification would still be needed for an object destroyed 200 years previously. Other lines of interpretation have noted the healing cult of Asclepios, whose symbol was a serpent, or the practice of using like to cure like, as in the story of the Philistines manufacturing golden tumours and mice to deliver themselves from these afflictions (1 Samuel 6.4–5). The discovery of a copper snake in a Midianite tent shrine from ancient Timnah has also been cited as a possible origin for the serpent symbolism in the story.

If the narrative itself is examined, it is one of many in the wilderness wanderings stories that describe the impatience of the very group of people whom God had delivered from slavery. The reference to 'miserable food' is to the manna and quails that God had provided. The ordeal that follows – that only those who are prepared to obey God's instructions survive – has the effect of distinguishing between those who are capable of trust in God, and those who are not. Although it must not be overlooked that many Israelites died before the serpent was set up (modern commentators have noted the difficulty of casting and smelting a metal object in the wilderness situation), once the serpent was lifted up, there was no need for anyone to die who wished to live. The implication is that some did die, however, being unwilling to carry out what was perhaps seen as an irrational act. The narrative therefore explores profound themes: why is it hard to respond to divine grace, and why does a liberated people hate freedom? Is it enough merely to provide a means of grace, or must God create in us the possibility of responding in faith? JR

Ephesians 2.1–10

In ch. 1 the writer has given us his picture, painted in the most vivid colours, of the triumphant work and present status of Christ, enthroned over all. Now, he turns to his audience and depicts the contrast between their former and their present conditions. It is, in effect, a grand statement, made in the Pauline manner, of the whole doctrine of the salvation and the new life brought by Christ.The subject is seen in terms of the ending of human alienation and sin; and then, in the rest of ch. 2, it is a matter of the special case of the removal of the division between Jews and Gentiles. In both respects reconciliation has come about, and those essential struggles are over. This is then a jubilant and confident statement of faith; and the rest of Ephesians will work out its ecclesial and ethical implications.

All through, the language is Pauline, even hyper-Pauline, though the ethos is more concentratedly cosmic and mythological (v. 2) than in Paul's undoubted letters. It is, however, a difference of emphasis rather than basic outlook; but Paul is more concerned to explore the subtleties and conflicts of the human heart. It is not surprising that a liturgical purpose or source has been suggested for this writing. At the same time, there are differences from Paul's typical usage; he, mostly, reserves 'save' and 'salvation' for the future completion of the process begun by and in Christ; here, in vv. 5 and 8, we have the tense of finished process. And the imagery of justification makes no appearance.

The contrast between 'before' and 'after' comes in the strongest terms: from death to life; from the devil to God; from wrath to mercy; from 'the course of this world' (v. 2) to 'the heavenly places' (v. 6). There is then a sense in which the believers' continued presence in the ordinary world is illusory: outwardly, we shop and cook and earn our living, but in real truth, we have our being elsewhere, on a different plane. God's long-laid purpose has at last broken through (v. 10). LH

John 3.14–21

'God so loved the world'. Is Jesus still speaking? Ancient manuscripts had no inverted commas, and there is no means of knowing whether this is a continuation of Jesus' conversation with Nicodemus or a paragraph of commentary by the evangelist. Translators simply have to make a choice; and NRSV (unlike RSV) has gone back to the Authorized Version's decision (familiar from the 'Comfortable Words' in the Book of Common Prayer) to assume that these are intended to be read as words of Jesus.

Perhaps from a critical perspective it makes little difference. The discourses of Jesus in John's Gospel, even if they go back to Jesus in some form, have been heavily edited to bring out their meaning, and these verses have no less significance as an authoritative commentary than they would if they were a transcript of Jesus' words. But one advantage of assuming that Jesus is still speaking is that what is said about 'the Son' can be interpreted in the light of what has just been said about 'the Son of man'. In the Synoptic Gospels this title (in so far as we can be sure of its meaning) denotes a figure who, after a period of suffering and humiliation, will be vindicated and glorified. If this figure is modelled, at least in part, on the 'one like a son of man' in Daniel 7, then his glorification will be accompanied by the judgement that is to be passed on all human beings at the end of the age. But this Danielic image presupposed the traditional scenario: the present is for doing right and wrong, for repentance and good works; in the future there will be judgement, fixing every person's destiny for eternity.

John's Gospel offers a radical reinterpretation of this scheme. Much of what was traditionally imagined as belonging to the future in reality takes place in the present. The appearance of Jesus creates an opportunity to anticipate the divine judgement. As Son of man, Jesus is not merely the judge before whom we will one day appear; his activity in the present provides an opportunity here and now to align oneself with the light against the darkness and to be saved from the threat of ultimate judgement.

But what does it mean to be 'saved', and how does it happen through Jesus? The question has remained unresolved for two millennia, sometimes causing bitter division among Christians. There can be no single authoritative answer. Nor does John's Gospel offer one. It prefers to work with images. Moses 'lifting up' the bronze serpent in the wilderness, by which, when they looked at it, the Israelites were 'saved' from a plague of snakes (Num. 21.8–9), is a suggestive one. Conventionally, a Son of man figure was imagined as having been 'lifted up' to the right hand of God at the judgement. But 'lifting up' could also be a description of what happened to Jesus on the cross; and by looking at that, contemplating it and making it their own, believers could find in this Son of man, not just a judge, but a saviour (cf. 12.32–33). AEH

Mothering Sunday

Exodus 2.1–10 or 1 Samuel 1.20–28; 2 Corinthians 1.3–7 or Colossians 3.12–17; Luke 2.33–35 or John 19.25b–27

Exodus 2.1–10

The name 'Moses' is probably part of an Egyptian name, as found in the name of Pharaoh Thutmose(s), and connected with the verb *msy* 'to be born' and the noun *mes* 'child'. It is remarkable that the greatest founder of the Israelite nation should have a partly Egyptian name, and it suggests that Moses is not an invented figure.

In the present passage, however, the Egyptian name has been forgotten, even if Moses' Egyptian origins have not. The end of the story, in which Moses' name is explained as 'I drew him out of the water' depends on the similarity of the name Moses (Hebrew *moshé*) and the Hebrew verb *mashah* 'to draw (out)'. A further implication is that the story of Moses' preservation (the passage must be set in the context of the pharaoh's order that all Hebrew baby boys must be killed) belongs more to the realm of folk tale than that of fact. Stories from elsewhere in the world about the miraculous preservation of a future ruler while a child have been cited, including the close parallel relating to Sargon of Akkad, whose mother laid him in a basket of rushes.

But if it is correct to see the story as an instance of the genre of the miraculous deliverance of the future ruler when a child, what must not be overlooked is the realistic and resourceful human female side of the story. The bonds between the mother and her child, and between the child and his sister, are so strong that they lead to bold and imaginative action. Moreover, such is the nature of human sympathy, especially that evoked by a helpless baby, that when the pharaoh's daughter discovers the child, she deliberately overlooks the facts both that he is 'foreign' and that helping the child will involve disobeying her father's expressed decree. Far more instances of brave and self-sacrificing action by mothers on behalf of their own and other children must exist than parallels to the story of the delivered future ruler!

The function of this passage in the story of Moses is to explain how the future deliverer of the Israelite nation grew up in the Egyptian court. Its deeper message is that God works through the emotions and the determined and resourceful action of women, especially mothers. JR

1 Samuel 1.20–28

Motherhood and childhood as understood today in the West is a comparatively modern invention. In ancient Israel, as in the rest of the ancient world, women were expected, along with tackling arduous routine daily tasks such as fetching water, to bear as many children as possible, preferably males. They could expect to be constantly pregnant and childbearing and rearing from the time of their marriage, at 13 or 14, until they were around 40.

A barren woman was an economic liability as well as a failure in the eyes of her family and society. Perhaps the reason why Elkanah had two wives (1 Sam. 1.2) was because he could not afford economically and for social reasons to have one wife who bore him no children. Peninnah may therefore have been a second wife, who was married when Hannah produced no offspring. The tender way in which Hannah's husband treated her (1 Sam. 1.5, 8) needs also to be understood against the harsh realities of life in ancient Israel.

The birth of the son to Hannah, therefore, did more than remove a social stigma. Although we are not told whether Hannah had other children after the birth of Samuel, the possibility must be entertained.

Hannah's decision to dedicate her precious son to the service of God at Shiloh indicates how heavy the burden of her barrenness had been, and how important to her its ending was. She probably suckled her son, as was normal, for two or three years before bringing him to Shiloh, years that she would have relished in the circumstances. The offerings that accompanied the bringing of the child to Shiloh were lavish. A three-year-old bull would be an especially valuable animal.

The purpose of the narrative is to prepare readers for the remarkable career that the boy born in response to the divine answering of prayer will have. Modern readers will sympathize with pressures placed upon Hannah to conform to the social and economic expectations of women of her day. Such pressures are not unknown in today's world, where people are not accepted for what they are, but for how they measure up to norms of career, motherhood or physical beauty. God, fortunately, sees things differently. JR

2 Corinthians 1.3–7

In literary form, the passage follows a convention of the time, normal in Paul's writings, whereby a letter's opening greeting is followed by some form of thanksgiving. Here (alone, but see 1 Pet. 1.3f. and the dubiously Pauline Eph. 1.3f.), he uses a Jewish variant: a 'blessing' (*berakah*) – 'Blessed be God who . . .'

The content is dominated by two groups of words, which engage in an elaborate, interwoven dance: comfort or encourage, encouragement (*parakaleō*, *paraklēsis*); and affliction, suffer, sufferings (*thlibō*, *thlipsis*, *paschō*, *pathēmata*). The effect is clearest if the passage is read aloud, as, certainly, it was meant to be. The very repetition would have made it memorable. The first group is one of Paul's favourites (65 occurrences, but chiefly in this letter); note especially the link with the Spirit in 2 Cor. 13.13. As the Gospel of John shows, the theme and the linkage caught on (via the related *paraklētos*). In Paul himself, it is a powerful word, to which the English 'comfort' scarcely does justice.

'Affliction' and 'sufferings' make the natural counterweight. And of course the pattern corresponds to the fundamental one of death-resurrection, founded in the pattern of Christ, that is so pervasive in Paul (see e.g. 4.7—5.5). And God, father of Jesus, is praised for the assurance that comfort (encouragement, strengthening) will prevail. As the pattern is that of Christ, so it is also ours, for we live 'in him'. What is more, the life and its pattern are mutual, with Paul on the one hand and his converts on the other as partners to the roots of their existence. In relation to this Christian community, Paul had ample reason to hold on doggedly to this fact of life. LH

Colossians 3.12–17

The two final chapters of Colossians (like the latter parts of other Pauline letters) are largely devoted to moral teaching. Here, following the establishing of a doctrinal base in the 'risen' standing of Christian people and a list of vices which are, therefore, to be 'put to death' (v. 5), and then a statement, akin to others in Paul, of the multi-ethnic, multi-status composition of the community for whom 'Christ is all' (v. 11), we have an uncomplicated list of virtues, of the kind common in the literature of the time. Again, the list contains few surprises and is comparable to passages elsewhere. There are also few exegetical difficulties, and the passage invites reflection rather than head-scratching.

All the same, it is important to note the presence of a number of well-known features. The previous verses drew the familiar contrast between the new way of life and the old: 'in these you once walked' (v. 7), and put the whole ethical instruction in an eschatological perspective: because of the prevalence of vice (sex, greed and idolatry), 'the wrath of God is coming' (v. 6).

Now the contrary virtues are headed by humility and its dependent social quality of forgiveness, which has God's forgiveness as its driving motive (cf. the Lord's Prayer). But love is the head of the moral pyramid, as in all the Gospels, as well as in Paul himself.

Then we have a practical note, referring to actual practice at Christian meetings: teaching, admonition and (in a reference virtually identical to Eph. 5.19–20, and therefore important in discussions of the connection between the two writings) music. Little can be said with certainty about the hymns referred to, though the New Testament is studded with possible examples, not least Col. 1.15–20 (see also Phil. 2.6–11; Eph. 5.14; and numerous passages in the Revelation of John). For the context of their use, 1 Cor. 14 provides the most vivid evidence. It must remain open whether 'the word of Christ' (v. 16) refers to something as precise as the tradition of his teaching and whether the giving of thanks (v. 17) refers to something as formal as the Eucharist: whether it does or not, the words 'to the Father through him' give a succinct statement of the structure and point of later eucharistic prayer. LH

Luke 2.33–35

For the passage from which this is a brief extract, see pp. 53–54. It is a detail which, though pregnant and moving, is easily passed over in the flow of Luke's Gospel. It is a vignette, whose place in Christian life and imagination lay ahead, in the Middle Ages and since, and in the artistic and devotional tradition rather than the academic; also more Catholic than Protestant. It is one of the roots of Marian devotion, in particular that which centres on Mary as the suffering mother, forever alongside her Son, with his death implicitly yet cryptically foretold from the start by Simeon, and her involvement at the end and afterwards foreshadowed in these ominous words.

Their significance for Luke and his narrative remains mysterious. In one sense, however, this is not so: Luke is the effective founder of the 'cult' (however understood) of Mary; the first Christian writer to make her a Christian heroine, with a clear and emphatic role (yet almost in her own right) in the coming of Jesus. But this particular aspect, that is, her being associated with Jesus' suffering, now foreshadowed for the first time, is new. It is hard not to read it without the interposing of innumerable medieval and renaissance paintings of Mary's place in the dying of Jesus and its aftermath. This is already (but surely anachronistically?) the Mary of the *pietà*.

If however we stick to Luke's own context, there is more to be said, or at any rate there is an adjustment of perspective. Simeon, prophet-like, utters two oracles, first the Nunc Dimittis, with its general assurance of universal salvation now at hand, and now, in vv. 34–35, a more specific statement of Jesus' own part and his mother's association with his fate. The word rendered 'thoughts' is usually used, in the New Testament, in a pejorative sense: it is judgement that Jesus will bring, the 'fall' as well as the 'rise' of 'many in Israel'. He will be the instrument of God's sundering of his people into the genuine and the false, a common idea in apocalyptic and not here elaborated. It is in line with the frequent quoting of Isa. 6.9, making intelligible the rejection of Jesus by his own people. The passage occurs significantly, in relation to Paul's apostolate, in Acts 28.26. So the theme can be said to bracket Luke's work as a whole. The reference to the sword is obscure – despite numerous attempts to interpret it down the centuries. In any case, with its centring on death and division, this is a sobering reading for the normally rather cheerful atmosphere of Mothering Sunday, though even so it has its own realism. LH

John 19.25b–27

Since early days Christians have been touched by Jesus' tender love for his mother as he hangs dying on the cross. Traditionally in the words, 'Woman, behold your son', he is seen as commending his mother to the care of the disciple whom he specially loves, knowing that he – her firstborn – can no longer provide for her. In fact, this passage is about much more than this. Jesus is creating a new relationship: Mary is given a new 'son', and the beloved disciple a new 'mother'.

Many questions have been raised about this passage. Why does John alone mention the beloved disciple at the cross? According to Mark, when Jesus was arrested, all the (male) disciples 'forsook him and fled'. Only women watched Jesus' crucifixion, looking on 'from afar' (Mark 15.40). Would the Romans have permitted Mary to come near enough to hear Jesus' words? Does John envisage two, three or four women present? (Probably four.) Why do John and Mark have only one name in common (Mary Magdalene)? These questions are helpfully discussed by Raymond Brown in his massive book *The Death of the Messiah* (New York: Doubleday, 1994). For the evangelists, the women who follow Jesus to the cross, and are first at his tomb on Easter morning, seem to be models of loyalty and faithfulness (though the silence of the women in Mark 16.8 remains a mystery).

Mary is not mentioned by name; Jesus simply addresses her as 'woman' (cf. John 2.4). Nor is 'the disciple whom Jesus loved' named; it is only church tradition which identifies this figure with the apostle John. This curious 'anonymity', combined with the Fourth Gospel's love of deeper meanings, has led scholars to suggest allegorical or symbolic interpretations. One suggestion is that in these verses the dying Jesus is creating a new family – a new community. The 'woman' Mary has been interpreted as the Church, the 'mother' of believers. The beloved disciple is often seen as representing the ideal follower(s) of Jesus. Some see the scene as representing Jesus' natural family, hitherto unbelievers (cf. John 7.5), becoming part of his spiritual family. Others see Mary as representing Israel, or rather part of Israel, coming to faith in Christ.

This is a difficult text on which to preach for Mothering Sunday, when our thoughts are turned to families, and gratitude to our parents (especially mothers). If we stress Jesus' love for his mother, we rely on our pious sense of what must have been the case. If we interpret this text symbolically of Israel and the Church it may seem irrelevant to the occasion, and even anti-Jewish. Although Jesus in the Gospels enjoins respect and care for parents (Mark 7.10), he does little to support traditional 'family values' (see John 2.4; Mark 3.31–35; Luke 2.49; 11.27f.); rather he stresses the priority of discipleship over family ties (e.g. Matt. 10.37; Mark 10.29; Luke 14.26). Maybe we could focus imaginatively on Mary and what it must have been like for her to be the mother of Jesus. RE

The Fifth Sunday of Lent

Jeremiah 31.31–34; Hebrews 5.5–10; John 12.20–33

Jeremiah 31.31–34

Whether or not these words derive from Jeremiah (scholarly opinion inclines to the view that they are not his work) they wrestle with a profound problem: how can God relate to us in such a way that he does not compel us to serve him on the one hand, but prevents us from spurning him on the other hand? The answer is that such an arrangement is virtually impossible. The problem with the covenant with the Israelites was that the latter were human beings, and it belongs to human nature to wish to be self-sufficient of any outside power, for all that humans constantly create outside powers in their own image. In the ancient world these were stars and planets, and magical forces. The modern world continues with astrology, to which it adds extra-terrestrial aliens and concepts such as Gaia.

It would be easy to suppose that the new covenant has been fulfilled in the New Testament and the Church, but this would be premature. Can the Church be said to have been more faithful to God in its history than the people of Israel? In what sense is God's law written on the hearts of Christians? And if everybody knew God, from the least to the greatest, would there be any need for missions?

From a Christian perspective it can be said that Jesus fulfils the new covenant in his own person and his obedience to God. His followers, alas, fall far short of this.

The Jeremiah passage must therefore be seen as a precious hope for a future kind of existence in which all mankind will love what God commands and desire what he promises. One of the forces most likely to bring about such a state of affairs is the self-giving love exhibited in the passion of Jesus. JR

Hebrews 5.5–10

See Proper 24, pp. 244–245.

John 12.20–33

'The hour has come for the Son of Man to be glorified.' References to the 'hour' of Jesus in the first 11 chapters of John point forward. 'My hour has not yet come,' Jesus announces to his mother in 2.4. When Jesus' teaching astonishes Jerusalem, the leaders attempt to arrest him, but fail 'because his hour had not yet come' (7.30). Again in 8.20 the narrator explains that Jesus could not be arrested because his hour 'had not yet come'. Abruptly, in 12.23, the situation changes, and Jesus announces that the 'hour' has now come.

What prompts Jesus to make this pronouncement about his crucifixion? Two sets of clues appear in the story just preceding this lesson, clues that seem to stand in some tension with each other. The raising of Lazarus elicits belief from many (11.45), and that very belief in turn brings about the opposition of the Pharisees and leaders of the Jewish community. 'From that day on', the narrator says, 'they planned to put him to death' (v. 53). Indeed, the reaction to the miracle of Lazarus is so great that the authorities plot Lazarus' death as well as that of Jesus (12.10–11). One conclusion drawn from the context would be that the 'hour' comes because of opposition to Jesus.

A second set of clues centres not on opposition to Jesus but on adulation of him. Several times the narrator comments that large numbers of people believed in Jesus because of the raising of Lazarus. That motif culminates in the comment of the Pharisees in 12.19: 'You see, you can do nothing. Look, the world has gone after him!' Surely there is a note of irony in this statement, since John elsewhere views the 'world' as hostile to Jesus (see the comments on John 3.14–21, Fourth Sunday of Lent).

An illustration of the fact that 'the world' has gone after Jesus is enacted in the awkward scene, 12.20–22. First the narrator introduces the presence of certain Greeks, who are presumably proselytes in view of their having come to Jerusalem for Passover. The Greeks present themselves to the Galilean Philip with the declaration, 'Sir, we wish to see Jesus.' Philip presents their request to Andrew, and the two of them in turn present the request to Jesus. Strikingly absent from this elaborate scene-setting is any clear indication that the Greeks in question actually do see Jesus or that they come to faith. Nevertheless, the elaborate stage-setting highlights their quest. In other words, what makes them important emerges in Jesus' comment in v. 23 that the 'hour' has come; that is, the arrival of 'the world' in the persons of these Greeks indicates that Jesus' death is imminent.

The 'hour' arrives because opposition to Jesus reaches its inevitable outcome: the officials will seek his death. But the 'hour' also arrives because of Jesus' very 'success' with the world. Here the world seeks after Jesus, but the world is fickle, seeking tomorrow after another who might do more astonishing signs or offer more soothing advice. The world is finally not able to believe that Jesus is from God and to follow after him. The popularity of Jesus in this passage quickly fades and turns into the hostility that confronts Pilate and demands Jesus' crucifixion (18.28—19.16). The world is a thoroughly unreliable place; neither its hostility nor its adoration can be trusted.

Perhaps because the world's favour is such a fickle commodity, the Johannine Jesus understands the 'hour' itself as a time of confrontation with the world: 'Now is the judgement of this world; now the ruler of this world will be driven out' (12.31). And that triumph over the 'ruler of this world' is coupled with the claim that, in Jesus' 'hour', he lifts all persons to himself. If we find a hint of universalism in this promise, we surely read into the text concerns distant from it, especially since this passage must be read alongside the highly dualistic language of ch. 17. Nevertheless, by drawing 'all people' to himself, Jesus anticipates the eventual overcoming of the world's opposition and opens the door for hope that 'all people' will indeed be drawn to him.

Jesus' 'hour' does not belong to him alone, nor is its significance captured by the salvific implications of drawing 'all people' to himself. Instead, the attitude of Jesus toward his impending death becomes a model for all believers, as is evident in 12.25–26. Because v. 25 and its Synoptic counterparts are often heard as life-denying assertions, it is important to see them in their context. Jesus does not propound some gnostic-like absolute denial of the goodness of physical life, but he does connect his own death with a certain understanding that life cannot be hoarded away; only those prepared to give up everything can receive the gift of 'eternal life', both now and hereafter.

John's Gospel insists that the death of Jesus is simultaneously his exaltation; a parallel 'exaltation' belongs to believers as God honours those who serve Jesus (v. 26). Both forms of honour and glory exist because, and only because, God bestows them. Believers are honoured by God for their service; Jesus is exalted, but it is God's name that is glorified (v. 28). Nowhere in this schema does John make a place for believers to bring honour on themselves, but only for them to acknowledge the God who exalts Jesus, even in his death.

Palm Sunday

(Liturgy of the Passion)

Isaiah 50.4–9a; Philippians 2.5–11; Mark 14.1—15.47 or Mark 15.1–39 (40–47)

Isaiah 50.4–9a

Although the word 'servant' does not appear in this passage, its close similarity to 49.1–6 has led most to see it as the third of the so-called 'servant songs'. It is the most intensely personal and individual of them all. While in the others the servant could well depict 'Israel' in one way or another, as well, perhaps, as an individual or group who see themselves as embodying the calling of 'servant Israel', this seems like the outpouring of someone who sees himself in the prophetic tradition of such figures as Jeremiah, called, through many setbacks and much persecution, to summon 'servant Israel' to fulfil their true destiny. One commentator entitled this passage 'the Gethsemane of the Servant'.

Among the strongly individualistic features are the repeated mention of parts of the body – tongue, ears, back, cheeks, beard and face – a forceful reminder that God uses real human beings for his purposes. His word always has to become 'flesh'.

Before he can teach others the servant has himself to be 'taught', a word which appears twice in v. 4. It can come to mean 'those who have been instructed' and who are therefore 'skilled' or 'learned' (see, in various ways, NRSV, NEB, REB, NIV). Yet the verse speaks of daily listening to God and receiving his word, so that the second use of it is indubitably passive. Anyone who speaks for God and who hopes to teach others must be lifelong and perpetual learners themselves. Only then are they able to perform God's purposes in human lives, such as sustaining those who are 'weary', God's own mission (cf. Isa. 40.30–31).

The sense of failure expressed in 49.4 is now reinforced by open and physical opposition (vv. 5–6), whether from fellow-Israelites because of his conviction that God has purposes for foreigners (for an opposed point of view see 45.9–13), or from Babylonian officials for his conviction that their power would wane (e.g. 43.14).

Yet, just as faithfulness through failure was a necessary prerequisite for the discharge of his mission (49.5–6), so persecution is an inescapable part of the 'learning' process for God's servant. Through such experiences his own faith is renewed as, in a courtroom metaphor, he becomes convinced that God will not desert him. He will be given the strength necessary for his task, his 'face set like flint' (v. 7, cf. Ezek. 3.8–9). Taught by God through his constantly renewed communion with him and by experience of his strength through persecution and rejection, he sees his mission in its true perspective. It is God's purpose that, ultimately, shall prevail (vv. 8–9). It is a lesson that was also learned by Paul through similar persecution (Rom. 8.31). RM

Philippians 2.5–11

It is usually held that though Paul's purpose in the wider passage is to urge the virtue of humility, these verses represent a separable unit, theological in character. Over the past 80 years in particular, it has become common to see them as an early Christian hymn, probably antedating Paul's use of it here in what may be his last extant letter. It may be seen to fall most naturally into three strophes (concerning Christ's pre-existent status, his self-abasement to earthly life and to death, and his subsequent exaltation to universal lordship). Thus, the passage may be taken as perhaps the oldest summary statement of Christian faith available to us, certainly in anything like poetic or imaginative form. If that is right, then its 'advanced character', in the common assessment of doctrinal terms, is all the more striking; for it seems to state a christological doctrine that is of the same order and ambitious profundity as that of the Johannine prologue.

There is dispute over the most likely sources of parts of the doctrine here stated and almost every word has its difficulties. It may be that Jesus is seen in terms of an amalgam of not wholly consistent Jewish images, with both speculation about Adam and 'wisdom' theology (like that in the Wisdom of Solomon) being prime contributors. The overall doctrine is of both the comprehensiveness of Jesus' significance and the cosmic scope of his achievement. In that way, the words are a striking example of that early Christian manner of laying hold of every possible Jewish idea and symbol and applying them to Jesus.

The final verses are the least problematic, appearing to draw on Isa. 45.23 and Ps. 110.1, that most common of all early Christian proof-texts, backing the idea of Jesus as 'lord', yet to God's glory. The background of the first part (vv. 6–8) is less clear, but the model for Jesus may best be seen as Adam; only, unlike him, Jesus accepts willingly his allotted place in God's purpose (no grasping at or retaining of equality with God), and even accepts the degradation of the cross. The two 'moves' in Jesus' drama are expressed with great vividness, even theatricality, and there is no missing the strength of the claims being made for Christ, though it is doubtful whether the 'form' of God in v. 6 carries, in context, the idea of 'divinity'; it is probably derived from the Gen. 1 picture of man as made in the image of God. So Jesus is seen as succeeding where Adam (and all of us, his progeny) failed – a doctrine used by Paul in Rom. 5 and 1 Cor. 15. Even if the comparison is less with Adam than with 'wisdom' as developed in Jewish thought, the picture is no less striking and the teaching no less powerful in its claim: Jesus' place is, for always, by God's side, his co-regent. All the more remarkable then is his foray into the world where death awaited him; and all the stronger his claim on allegiance and worship. LH

Mark 14.1—15.47

The participants in the passion are three. First, there are those who are against Jesus, directly or by desertion. Direct opponents are the high priests, elders and scribes, the Jewish authorities of Jerusalem, centred on the temple; Pilate, who goes along with them and has the decisive say on Jesus' fate; soldiers and others who mock and beat; and the crowd who urge Pilate to act (15.13f.). The deserters are the Twelve who sleep callously in Gethsemane and then forsake and flee (14.32–50), including Judas who 'hands over' Jesus and Peter who denies him – all this despite the act of the supper binding them to Jesus' own fate through sharing his body and covenant-blood (14.22–25). They are without understanding (6.52; 8.14–17) as well as simple fidelity. All these, like so much in this story, take up and fulfil Scripture: for example, Isa. 53 (especially for Jesus' silence, see below); Ps. 22 (most explicitly in 15.34, but also 15.24 etc.); Pss. 41.9 and 43.5. So we are reading of God's purpose being fulfilled. In Mark, the disciples are not graded in obloquy, all being one in their terrible conduct (just as they also all share in the brief assurance of redemption, 14.28; 16.7). Also under this heading we should put the women who can only watch, non-committally, 'from afar' (15.40; like Peter, 14.54), just as they then made their futile and uncomprehending attempt to anoint the corpse of Jesus (see p. 115) when it had been done already (14.3ff.). All are warnings to us who read.

There are, however, characters of shining and exemplary virtue: above all, the woman who does truly anoint Jesus 'beforehand' for his burial and receives an unparalleled gift of praise (14.3–9). But also Simon of Cyrene who, unlike Simon Peter who had been taught to do it (8.34), does in fact take up the cross (15.21, the Greek is identical); and the centurion-executioner who comes to at least some kind of faith (15.39), not through anything Jesus says (the words in 15.34 scarcely have that effect), nor (in Mark, contrast Matthew) through anything Jesus actively does or any outward phenomena, but at his dying. Perhaps, like Paul, Mark sees him as finding in Jesus the one 'who loved me and gave himself for me' (Gal. 2.20). It may be right to include also the young man of 14.51f. and 16.7, though he remains enigmatic (see p. 115). All these are, despite the mysteriousness of the last (though not an angel, he is plainly on their side!), models and encouragers for us who read.

There is also Jesus. He moves through the narrative into deepening isolation, along his 'way' (1.2f.) which he 'must' (8.31) tread. Gethsemane begins to show his isolation, as he leaves the Twelve with the three and then goes forward alone (14.32–42). Then, from the arrest, he is without support and in the end knows even desertion by God. Is this then what it takes to give your life 'a ransom for many' (10.45), the means of their release? Yet Mark never explains the doctrine, but leaves us to look and look until we are ready for Galilee (16.7) – so we may be unlike the outsiders of 4.12, but receivers of the secret of the kingdom.

The isolation is matched by deepening silence (15.5) and passivity, as Jesus is simply 'handed over', as if inert ('betray' is not the true sense of *paradidonai*) – by Judas to the soldiery, by them to Pilate (15.1), and by him to the executioners (15.15) (the word comes ten times in these chapters). If all this is the way to the kingdom of God, it is wholly improbable in *almost* any terms and it makes attachment to Jesus and his cause the strangest, most heroic (and most easily mistaken) of loyalties: but also the most 'true' and indeed candid in what is called 'the real world'. Only Jesus' words to the priests and elders in 14.62 speak of triumph as anywhere in sight, but they too are assurance that this is God's road (Ps. 110.1; Dan. 7.13). LH

Maundy Thursday

Exodus 12.1–4 (5–10), 11–14; 1 Corinthians 11.23–26; John 13.1–17, 31b–35

Exodus 12.1–4 (5–10), 11–14

The account of the institution of the Passover raises at least three difficulties for modern readers. The first is why it was necessary for the blood daubed on the doorposts to be a sign to God, indicating which houses should not be afflicted by the firstborn plague. After all, elsewhere in the plagues narratives God was able to exempt the Israelites from plagues that affected the Egyptians (cf. Exod. 9.22–26), so why was it not possible for the final plague? The second difficulty is the moral one of believing in a God who apparently puts to death the innocent children of the whole people, when only its ruler is in dispute with Israel. It needs further to be noted that there is a tension in the prescriptions between daubing the blood, which is essential in the Egyptian context, and consuming the lamb, which becomes the central part of the rite after the deuteronomic reform (cf. Deut. 16.1–8).

In order to explain these difficulties various theories of the origin of the rites have been proposed, such as that the blood of a lamb was daubed on their tents by herdsmen moving from winter to spring pasturage, in order to ward off misfortune; or the death of the firstborn has been explained in terms of the custom of dedicating all firstborn male humans and animals to God (cf. Exod. 13.1). It has also been pointed out that, whatever its origins, the Passover became connected with the barley harvest, at which unleavened bread marked the transition from bread made with the old grain to that made with the new.

Little of this will be of assistance to modern congregations and preachers, and a certain amount of idealizing will be unavoidable if the passage is to be used creatively. A possible starting point is the deuteronomistic observance (Deut. 16.1–8), in which the emphasis is placed upon sharing the meal in remembrance of deliverance which has affected those in every subsequent generation. This deliverance was as much political as spiritual, in that it freed people from slavery. Such deliverance was not achieved without cost and struggle, and it is an unfortunate fact of life that the innocent, including children, are caught up in and become the victims of human strife. However, the redemption of Israel from slavery is intended to bring benefits to all the nations, including Egypt. If Israel is not a light to the nations in the manner in which it establishes and practises mercy and compassion among its citizens, the Egyptians will have paid a heavy price in vain; and the Old Testament, in its narratives of the wilderness wanderings is unsparing in its condemnation of the attitude of the very generation that was freed from slavery. The path of redemption is never easy, as the whole passage indicates. JR

1 Corinthians 11.23–26

These lines concerning the sharing of bread and wine are so familiar to most Christian ministers that the act of reading the text may seem superfluous. As the 'words of institution' they are known by heart and can be recited verbatim. And, indeed, that intimate knowledge of this passage is consistent with the way in which Paul introduces it. When he writes, 'For I received from the Lord what I also handed on to you', he uses technical language for the transmission of tradition, and the Church's intimate knowledge of this passage continues that understanding of it.

The tradition itself contains the simple and direct words that connect the ordinary sharing of bread and wine with the death of Jesus and its significance for humankind. The bread signifies the body of Jesus, broken in death. The cup signifies the blood of Jesus, poured out in death. Through that death comes a new covenant, and through participation in the meal comes the remembrance of Jesus. The word remembrance (*anamnēsis*) appears in both the statement regarding the bread and the statement regarding the wine, suggesting that the Lord's Supper is vitally connected with the Church's memory of Jesus. What the exact nature of that remembrance is becomes clearer in 1 Cor. 11.26.

With v. 26 Paul no longer cites the traditional words of Jesus, but offers his own interpretation of the Supper: 'For as often as you eat this bread and drink the cup, you proclaim the Lord's death until he comes.' Two crucial points emerge here. First, Paul asserts that the very act of the meal *is* an act of proclamation. In the celebration of the Lord's Supper itself, the Church engages in the preaching of the gospel. Protestant exegetes, uncomfortable with the omission of the verbal act of proclamation in this passage, long rejected this point by attempting to argue that Paul means that preaching *accompanies* every celebration of the Supper. If understood that way, however, the verse simply tells the Corinthians what they already know (preaching accompanies the meal) and adds nothing at all to the passage. Verse 26, in fact, culminates Paul's discussion of the meal by explaining its significance. The Lord's Supper is not just another meal, the eating of which is a matter of indifference; this celebration is itself a proclamation of the gospel of Jesus Christ.

The second point Paul makes in this verse comes in the final words, 'You proclaim the Lord's death until he comes.' The Lord's Supper is a very particular kind of proclamation – a proclamation of Jesus' death. A different kind of celebration, perhaps a celebration of Jesus' miracle of multiplying the bread and the fish, might proclaim Jesus' life and teaching. Even the Lord's Supper might be understood as a celebration of the person of Jesus as a divine messenger. Building on the words of institution with their emphasis on the coming death of Jesus, Paul forcefully articulates his view that the Lord's Supper proclaims Jesus' death. Unless the final phrase, 'until he comes', merely denotes the time at which celebration of the Lord's Supper will come to an end ('you keep proclaiming in this way until Jesus returns'), what it does is to convey the eschatological context in which the Church lives and works. The Church proclaims Jesus' *death* within the context of a confident expectation that he will come again in God's final triumph.

In this passage Paul has a very sharp point to make with Christians at Corinth, who are preoccupied with factions, with competing claims about the gospel, and with what appear to be class struggles. Paul's comments about their celebration of the Lord's Supper do not make the situation entirely clear to us, but it appears that they have followed the customs of the day, according to which the hosts of the meal served the choicer foods to their social peers and the less desirable foods to Christians of lower social or economic status. The activity of eating and drinking, and the struggle over that activity, have dominated the celebration of the meal. Paul's response to that situation is to recall forcefully the nature of the Lord's Supper. This is not another social occasion. It is *in and of itself* the proclamation of Jesus' death. Because it is a proclamation, Christians must treat it as such. Whatever conflicts there are about eating and drinking, they belong outside and apart from this occasion.

As earlier in the letter, Paul emphasizes the proclamation of Jesus' death as central to the gospel itself (see 1 Cor. 1.18–25; 2.1–2). Over against the Corinthians' apparent conviction of their own triumph over death, their own accomplishments and spiritual power, Paul asserts the weakness of Jesus, whose faithfulness to God led to his death, and Paul insists that the Church lives in the tension between that death and the ultimate triumph of the resurrection.

In the context of the Church's observance of Maundy Thursday, this passage recalls again the death of Jesus. That recollection is no mere commemoration, as occurs with the recollection of an anniversary or a birthday. The remembrance, especially in the Lord's Supper, serves to proclaim the death of Jesus Christ once again, as the Church continues to live between that death and God's final triumph. BG

John 13.1–17, 31b–35

Maundy Thursday derives its name from Latin *mandatum*, 'command', referring to the 'new commandment' given by Jesus at the Last Supper. The command to love is rooted in Old Testament teaching (cf. Deut. 6.4f.; Lev. 19.18), texts combined by Jesus in his famous 'summary' of the Law (Mark 12.29–31 par.). In the Johannine writings this teaching is given new impetus as it is grounded in Christ's own love for his disciples, and the Father's love for the Son and for all who obey his word (cf. John 13.34f.; 14.21; 15.9–13; 1 John 4.7–21). It is especially poignant that Jesus gives this command after washing the disciples' feet as an example of humility and love, and before giving up his life for others.

The footwashing is unique to John's Gospel, and there has been much speculation why it replaces Jesus' sharing of the bread and the cup in John's narrative of the Last Supper. The evangelist must have included it because it was important to him and perhaps his community. What does it mean for him?

Most obviously Jesus washes the disciples' feet as an example of humble service. In the ancient world, where people walked the fields and dusty streets in open sandals or with bare feet, footwashing was a normal preliminary before meals. Washing someone else's feet was a menial task, done by 'inferiors' for 'superiors'. It was performed for guests by slaves (usually women), by children for parents, wives for husbands, and sometimes by devoted students for their teachers. It was unheard of for a teacher to wash his pupils' feet. Yet this is what Jesus does, as an 'acted parable' or visual aid, to show those closest to him that their role must be not that of 'lords', but of servants. The teaching is exactly the same as given in Luke's narrative of the Last Supper (22.27), when Jesus rebukes his disciples for disputing over who is the greatest with the words, 'I am among you as one who serves (*ho diakonōn*)'.

Yet the footwashing in John is more than a moral example. It comes at a turning point in the Gospel, as the evangelist moves from his account of Jesus' self-revelation through 'signs' and personal encounters to his 'hour', when the time has come for him to be 'glorified' (cf. 13.1, 31f.). The verbs which John uses to describe Jesus' laying aside his garments and resuming them are the same distinctive terms as were earlier used for his laying down his life on the cross and taking it up in resurrection (10.11, 15, 17f.). The footwashing illustrates Jesus' loving 'his own' to the end and prefigures his death: cf. Mark 10.45, 'the Son of Man came not to be served but to serve, and to give his life a ransom for many'. Like Peter, we have to learn to accept Christ's 'washing' of our feet, so that we may share in his work of service and reconciliation. Do we have here a neglected sacrament? RE

Good Friday

Isaiah 52.13—53.12; Hebrews 10.16–25 or Hebrews 4.14–16; 5.7–9; John 18.1–19.42

Isaiah 52.13—53.12

This final 'servant song' is undoubtedly one of the greatest passages in the Old Testament and yet, with its densely packed thought and highly symbolic poetic language and imagery, one of the most difficult to interpret. The text presents many difficulties, perhaps evidence of the problems scribes and others have found in understanding it in the course of its transmission. Commentaries discuss these in detail. Yet the grand sweep of thought is clear, speaking in the sublimest language of the deepest mysteries of God's dealings with human beings.

It opens (52.13–15) and closes (53.11b–12) with words of God about his servant. The body of the song is spoken by an unidentified group in the first person plural commenting on the action rather like the chorus in a Greek tragedy. Like the psalms of lament and prophetic passages, especially in Jeremiah, it depicts the servant's suffering, yet contains assurance of God's triumphant vindication of him.

God's opening words about his servant (52.13–15, cf. 42.1) and closing speech (53.11b–12) confirm that his role will be to bring surprised joy to the nations. Indeed, by his 'knowledge' (which he gains from his own relationship with God, cf. 50.4) he will, like a sacrificial victim, cover their sins and bring them into a right relationship with God. Thus his ministry will be triumphantly vindicated as he believed (50.8–9).

The human speakers describe the suffering of the servant which so disfigured him (53.1–3); realize that he suffered as a sacrificial victim for their sins which they now freely confess (vv. 4–6); speak of his suffering and death (vv. 7–9), but, finally, see his vindication by God (vv. 10–11a.).

Who are these speakers? They may be the Gentile kings now telling of that which before they had never heard or known (52.13b). In that case the 'suffering servant' must be Israel, who suffered innocently at their hands. Yet, by his glorious redemption of his 'servant' Israel, God has so revealed his glory that all nations come to recognize and know him (43.8–13). Or the speakers may be fellow Israelites who, having failed in their mission to be God's witness to the nations, need someone or some group who, by their faithfulness to God and suffering for his sake, bring them back to an awareness of him. In their renewed recognition of God and relationship with him the servant's ministry is vindicated.

As poetry and profound theology the symbol of the 'suffering servant' can operate at many levels, finding, as Christians believe, its supreme embodiment in Jesus. What it does show is the extraordinary power of vicarious suffering. Just as we are born into life by the pain of our mothers, advance to understanding by the dedication of our teachers, and appreciate music, literature and art through the gifts of others, so God's love reaches us through those who are ready to pay the price of being its agents. RM

Hebrews 10.16–25

Hebrews is composed of an alternation of exegetical passages, often worked out with skill and ingenuity, followed by consequent ('therefore', v. 19) exhortation, sometimes, as here, developing the scriptural material in new, but characteristic ways. The theme of the new covenant, familiar from the words over the cup at the Last Supper, appears in the suggestive text in Jer. 31.31–34, which has been quoted in full in 8.8–12 and provides a leitmotif for chs. 8—10. There, the focus was on the word 'covenant', with its dual sense as the treaty-like bond between God and his people, and a will which only comes into force with the testator's death (see the wordplay in 9.15f. – not easy to render into English). Here, it is on the more pervasive concern of this writer: the removal of sin, once by means of endlessly repeated animal sacrifices, now by the once-for-all death of Jesus.

By the time he wrote (surely after AD 70), the offering of beasts in the Jerusalem temple had ceased – in any case, he shows no interest in the rituals in practice, only in the provisions he finds in the Pentateuch. In that sense, his method is bookish. These he exploits here – yet further: this has been his subject from ch. 8. Detail after liturgical detail has been taken up and shown to be absorbed or fulfilled in some aspect of the death of Jesus, who occupies the roles of both high priest and victim in the ritual of the Day of Atonement. It is fruitless to seek tidy logic here. The pattern works by a concentration of images, even more than Johannine in its intensity. The symbolism of the entry into the Holy of Holies, seen as the counterpart of heaven, leads to a movement straight from Jesus' death to his heavenly arrival (cf. 12.2); there is no room in this scheme for his resurrection.

Then, our share in this great result awaits us, assured by the purifying water, presumably in baptism, here seen as the counterpart of liturgical purificatory washings in the old Law. Finally, there is a practical note: Christians must meet together, at least for the sake of mutual encouragement, as the future consummation approaches. SL

Hebrews 4.14–16; 5.7–9

As at Christmas, so on Good Friday a passage from Hebrews serves to affirm the full humanity of Jesus: like us in weakness, in temptation and in despair. The reference to Jesus' 'loud crying and tears' cannot fail to recall the Gospel story of Gethsemane, especially in the Lucan version which emphasizes Jesus' mental and physical anguish. His prayer was to the God who was able to save him from death, and the author states firmly that 'he was heard' – yet he died. It was not that his prayer went unheard: prayer can be answered by 'no' as well as 'yes'; but here the author probably means us to understand that Jesus' prayer was answered with the assurance that this death was not only inevitable but necessary; an answer that Jesus accepted: 'thy will be done'. Jesus was heard because of his *eulabeia*, a word the English versions find difficult to translate in this context (e.g. 'godly fear', RSV, and 'reverent submission', NRSV). It has to do with awe in the presence of God, not naked human fear, and reflects the fact that Jesus faced his suffering in prayer. There is a similar problem with the translation of the first clause of the following verse: some translations opt for the concessive 'Although he was a Son ...' so that the process of learning obedience seems a contradiction of Jesus' real role and status but a part of his emptying himself of his divinity; but it could be read as causative: it is precisely *because* Jesus is son among many children of God (2.10–14), and fully human, that obedience through suffering is his lot. (The same ambiguity is found in the 'christological hymn' of Phil. 2.) Again: he 'learned obedience' can be understood as describing how Jesus, through the repeated experience of testing learned how to obey, or that he learned obedience in the sense of discovering the full extent of the demand, what it really means to obey. And so he was made 'perfect': a term frequent in and characteristic of Hebrews, with connotations of completeness and so effectiveness. Because both Jesus' identification with humanity and his obedience to God were complete, they effect salvation, enabling us to approach the throne of God as Jesus did, and find it the source of mercy and grace in time of need. He is the great high priest, fully identified with those whom he represents, offering the only fully effective sacrifice, the sacrifice of himself, and so opening up access to God. SL

John 18.1—19.42

The four evangelists describe the story of Jesus' passion in different ways. Each has episodes or details lacking in the others, and each his own theological slant. Whereas Mark stresses Jesus' humanity and suffering, culminating in his great cry of dereliction from the cross, 'My God, my God, why have you forsaken me?' (15.34), in Luke Jesus dies calmly, fully trusting in God: 'Father, into your hands I commend my spirit' (23.46). Matthew alone mentions the legions of angels that Jesus could have called to his aid (26.53).

John's special emphasis is on the *kingship* of Jesus, and his 'autonomy' throughout his arrest, 'trials', mocking and crucifixion. John has no account of the 'agony in the garden', nor of Judas' kiss of betrayal. Jesus identifies himself to those who had come to arrest him with the words, '*Egō eimi*' ('I am [he]'), and his opponents all fall to the ground in awe. Jesus himself tells them to let his followers go free. He carries his own cross.

In the dialogue with Pilate Jesus' true kingship is a recurrent theme: Jesus makes it clear that he was born to be king, but that his kingship is not 'of this world'. Both Pilate (18.39; cf. 19.14) and the crowd (19.3) refer to him as 'King of the Jews', and Jesus dies with these words affixed to the cross – words which Pilate refuses to change, in spite of protests. Throughout all this runs the irony that what Jesus is called in mockery he is in reality, 'the King of Israel' (cf. 1.49) – and much more!

Most remarkable of all is perhaps Jesus' final 'word' from the cross, 'It is accomplished' (19.30): he has completed the work that God gave him to do.

Behind all four passion narratives lies the theme of fulfilment of Scripture, sometimes explicit (e.g. Mark 14.27; John 19.24, 37), sometimes implicit. In 19.28 Jesus' words 'I thirst' may allude to Ps. 22.15; cf. Ps. 69.21. Many commentators note the irony that the source of 'living water' (4.14; 7.37) now needs to be given a drink. But Jesus' 'thirst' in John is probably more than physical (this is not to minimize his agony). Jesus' 'food' was to do the will of him who sent him (4.34); now he has to drink the 'cup' the Father has given him (18.11).

After his death, blood and water flow from Jesus' side (in John alone). Some interpret this as showing that Jesus truly had died (perhaps from a rupture of the heart, which can produce such apparent effects); more probably the blood and water symbolize the spiritual cleansing and new life effected for believers through Jesus' death. The unbroken bones, the hyssop (19.29), and the flow of blood all point to a sacrificial understanding of Jesus' death (cf. 1.29, 36). Only John describes the role of Nicodemus in anointing Jesus' body. The huge quantities of myrrh and aloes (19.39) perhaps hint at a *royal* burial. RE

Easter Day

Acts 10.34–43 or Isa. 25.6–9; 1 Corinthians 15.1–11; John 20.1–18 or Mark 16.1–8

Acts 10.34–43

Peter's speech to the gathering at the house of Cornelius has roughly the same contents as the other major speeches by Peter in the early chapters of Acts, and indeed that by Paul in Acts 13 (though its reference to Jesus going about 'doing good', v. 38, is unique). This similarity of pattern has led to at least two not wholly consistent conclusions: that the speeches represent a standard pattern of Christian missionary preaching in the early decades, a pattern which may even be seen as one of the ancestors of the later baptismal creeds (a connection with the rite is discernible in some of the Acts episodes, including this one, v. 47f.); and that they are so similar (and the likelihood of shorthand records so remote) that, probably like all the Acts speeches, they are Lucan compositions, whatever they may or may not owe to memory and tradition – so following the practice of writers of the day. This second idea can be strengthened: the speeches are imbued with peculiarly Lucan themes and patterns, the present example being no exception. Note the universal scope of the message (v. 34), though its roots are in Israel (v. 36); the perception of Jesus as a doer of good, a fine description of especially Luke's characterization of Jesus; the post-resurrection meals with the chosen witnesses (v. 41, cf. Luke 24.35); the command to preach (v. 42, cf. Luke 24.48; Acts 1.8); Jesus as future judge (v. 42; Luke 21.36). The speeches contain what Luke saw as the core of the faith.

Cornelius is important as representing a real step forward in the mission. As promised in Acts 1.8, the preaching began in Judea, then moved to Samaria. But Cornelius is a Gentile, though one who is 'devout' and fears God (v. 2). He is one of a number of such people in Acts – a group for whose existence in at least some of the cities of the empire there is now other evidence and who may seem to be natural subjects for successful Christian evangelism: Gentiles who frequented the synagogue and valued its religious and moral teaching, but for whom conversion to Judaism seemed a step too far. Such people were perhaps social misfits of one kind or another (recent immigrants, upwardly mobile freedmen, independent-minded women, cf. Lydia in 16.14), and to whom the blessings of the Christian message may well have been both intelligible (for its roots in Judaism and in Scripture) and peculiarly attractive. It offered a spiritual home. With Cornelius the centurion (he invites comparison, like other Acts characters, with one in Luke's Gospel, the centurion in 7.1–10), the mission is on the verge of the wider move to the (fully) Gentile world. That will occupy Paul and others from chs. 13—20, and indeed implicitly to the end of the book, where Paul carries on the work even from his place of rather loose custody in Rome, 'openly and unhindered'. LH

Isaiah 25.6–9

See All Saints' Sunday, p. 261.

1 Corinthians 15.1–11

Paul reminds his hearers of the gospel that he proclaimed and they received. The introductory 'who', the balanced clauses, and some language untypical of Paul himself lead many to assume he is quoting in vv. 3–5 a very early credal confession of faith, which must go back close to the events themselves. He makes no mention of the empty tomb, or the women who discovered it, and understands his own vision of the risen Christ as comparable to those of the other male witnesses. His main concerns are to assert the reality of Christ's resurrection (which was presumably beyond dispute among believers) in order to provide a basis for insisting on belief in the future resurrection of believers, which some believers in Corinth were denying (v. 12). Unlike St Luke and the creeds that separate them, Paul saw Christ's resurrection and ours as part of the same divine mystery in which we are already caught up. He also insists on the unity of faith shared by all the witnesses, perhaps in opposition to factions in Corinth appealing to different leaders (ch. 1).

Paul also refers to the early appearance to Peter ('Simon' at Luke 24.34) and the later Gospels support an appearance to 'the Twelve' (presumably 11). An appearance to James the brother of the Lord is credible because it would help explain his subsequent leadership of the Jerusalem church. It is puzzling that Paul's strongest supporting argument, an appearance to over 500 'brethren' some of whom can still be interrogated now, some 25 years later, is otherwise unknown. This (and the differences from and between the Gospels) underlines the fragmentary character of the Easter traditions without weakening their certainty about the event itself. It should be emphasized that, like the incarnation and all divine events, the 'resurrection' is a mystery. It is expressed in the metaphorical language of being raised or got up, and elsewhere of exaltation, ascension or enthronement. Paul does not envisage a literal resuscitation – flesh and blood cannot inherit the kingdom of God (v. 54) – and as a divine event without analogy the resurrection of Jesus cannot be evaluated by historical methods. But it left traces that can be assessed by historians, notably the faith of the early Church and also the Gospel records of an empty tomb. It remains foundational for Christian faith – not as an isolated event, but as communicating and revealing God's vindication of Jesus who is the one and only foundation of faith (1 Cor. 3.11).

Which Scriptures this early creed has in mind in vv. 3 and 4 (e.g. Isa. 53 – cf. Rom. 4.25) is less important than the general conviction that the event of Christ fulfils Scripture as a whole. That Paul is content to repeat the early Jewish-Christian tradition interpreting Jesus' death as an atoning sacrifice should perhaps warn his successors against discarding older theological ideas, even if they like Paul himself place the emphasis elsewhere in communicating the gospel. We may also note that as speaking of the resurrection is speaking of God it is typically fused with speaking autobiographically (v. 9) – which to a believer means speaking of grace (v. 10), yet without false modesty. RM

John 20.1–18

Today's Gospel tells one of the best-loved resurrection stories. It is carefully constructed, beginning with Mary Magdalene's arrival at the tomb (vv. 1f.). Next, two male disciples discover the empty grave-clothes: one 'sees and believes' (vv. 3–10). They both go home. Then we return to Mary at the tomb (vv. 11–18).

John's account shares many elements with the other Gospels. In all, the first people to visit the grave are women (though their number and names vary). They find the stone rolled back, and see an angel/angels (or a man/men in white). There are, however, differences. In Mark, the women run off and tell nobody (16.8; the following verses are an addition). In Matthew, but not Luke, Jesus appears to the women and they cling to his feet (28.9). Some texts of Luke 24.12 have Peter go to the tomb, but only John has Peter and the 'beloved disciple' run there together. The 'beloved disciple' appears to be a model of faith (but why does he just return home with Peter?).

In 20.1, 11–18, John focuses on just one woman at the tomb. Mary comes while it is still dark. It has been suggested that the darkness may symbolize the disciples' desolation. In the course of our narrative she moves from bewilderment to faith. At first she stands outside the tomb, weeping. Even after the angels have spoken to her, she still assumes the body has been removed. She takes Jesus for the gardener, surmising that he was responsible for its removal (what an irony!). But when he addresses her by name (cf. 10.3, 14), she recognizes him as her 'Teacher'. After he tells her of his ascent to the Father, she acknowledges him as 'Lord'. Entrusted with his message for his 'brothers' (the disciples), she truly becomes the *apostola apostolorum*.

John's account is so personal and moving that it is tempting simply to let it warm our hearts. Yet thinking people are bound to ask 'What really happened?' The resurrection is not the sort of event that can be verified from historical evidence, and the Gospel-writers themselves seem to understand it differently. Luke, with his descriptions of Jesus eating with the disciples (24.30, 41–44), stresses its seeming physicality. Matthew, with his great earthquake and opening of the tombs (27.52–54; 28.2) heightens the miraculous. John's attitude is more ambiguous. Is his careful description of the grave-clothes and napkin (v. 7) designed merely to show that the body had not been stolen (robbers would not have left them folded)? Or does John want us to understand that the risen Jesus passed *through* them (cf. his passing through closed doors in 20.19)?

We are not likely ever (in this world) to discover exactly what took place. The main point is that the first Christians firmly believed that something stupendous happened. God vindicated Jesus. Witnesses saw him alive (cf. 1 Cor. 15.5–8). The disciples were transformed and the Church was born. Can we share in their gladness and trust, and let the risen Christ transform our lives? RE

Mark 16.1–8

No passage in the Gospel of Mark demands firmer control of its readers; here once more we must tell ourselves that the other Gospels have not yet been written (and it is even as if Paul had not given his account of appearances by the risen Jesus in 1 Cor. 15.5–8; Mark's asceticism of faith is extreme). There is no evidence to tell us that Mark ever wrote, or meant to write, anything beyond 16.8. Here, modern study has come more and more to a consensus. No lost pages, no sudden arrest.

But no wonder that, from Matthew and Luke onwards, his ending has been found unsatisfactory; so that within a century or so at least two 'better', more adequate endings had been added (see older versions of the Bible, and coyer ways of putting those endings in more recent ones). (It is true that the grammar of his last sentence, 'for they were afraid', fails him in any test of Greek; but his was not the Greek of Athens or Alexandria, and his linguistic ability, like that of many modern speakers of English in many places, did not quite match his intelligence and his literary and theological profundity.)

Here, the message of encounter with Jesus appears, but all is in prospect: there will be a meeting in Galilee and they will 'see' him. But where and what is 'Galilee'? Is it code for the place of Jesus' bringing near of the kingdom (wherever, in the atlas, that may be)? So is it then any meeting-place of Jesus' followers, then or later – at any time?

The messenger himself, a 'young man', is unexplained and enigmatic (no wonder Mark's successors give him the helpful authority of an angel – Matthew – or two – Luke and John). And is he related to the equally mysterious young man of 14.51f.? His garment there is now the word for Jesus' shroud (15.46). Is there some message, surely clear to Mark's readers but opaque to us, about the Christian neophyte as somehow sharing in Jesus' death and resurrection (Rom. 6.3–11 and the metaphor in Gal. 3.27)?

And are the women themselves to be admired or regretted? Certainly their reaction is no good at all – 'they said nothing to anyone' – and leaves us to puzzle how the message got out. Does Mark mean us not to pursue this story too keenly, for the resurrection could so easily divert us from Jesus' death, which he saw as the key to his meaning and his mission? Perhaps these women followers are as blundering as their male counterparts had been? After all, Mark had gone to lengths to have Jesus anointed 'beforehand' for his burial (14.11); so what need now? And, literarily at any rate, the women should have known there was no job for them to do: 'as he said to you' (v. 7, cf. 14.28). Nowhere does Mark face us more sharply with the question of what we can bear to mean by faith. 'Victory' seems too glib a word to describe Mark's Easter; though Galilee is of course for them as for the rest. LH

The Second Sunday of Easter

Exodus 14.10–31; 15.20–21 or Acts 4.32–35; 1 John 1.1—2.2; John 20.19–31

Exodus 14.10–31; 15.20–21

Where the sea was that the Israelites crossed and what exactly happened are questions that cannot be answered. This has not deterred commentators from attempting answers, however, even though the outcomes have often been less than satisfactory. Take, for example, the suggestion that the wind that held back the sea and dried the seabed was an actual wind that the Israelites were able to take advantage of. Even if we have never personally experienced hurricanes, we shall have seen sufficient evidence on television of their effect to know that a wind strong enough to part the sea would have been devastating for any humans and animals anywhere near it. Another, more plausible, suggestion is that the Israelites took advantage of tidal conditions to cross a strip of land at Lake Sirbonis not unlike the causeways at Lindisfarne or Mont St Michel, and that the incoming tide then swept away the pursuing Egyptians.

Most attempts to find a natural explanation for the Red Sea crossing only make it abundantly clear that the narrative as we have it goes out of its way to emphasize the supernatural. Further, similarities between Exod. 14 and 'holy war' narratives in books such as Joshua and Judges have been pointed out. Typical features of such narratives are the command not to be afraid (v. 13, cf. Josh. 10.25), the promise that God will accomplish the victory, and the fact that Israel's contribution to the outcome is little or nothing. Also, it is God who throws the enemy into panic (v. 24, cf. Josh. 10.10; Judg. 4.15).

What this means is that Exod. 14 is similar to narratives in Joshua and Judges and elsewhere, that present God as a God of war fighting on behalf of his people, and giving them victories that involve the deaths of their enemies. That this is a problem for modern readers goes without saying; but several points need to be made. First, narratives of this kind belong to rhetoric rather than reality and have parallels with other literature in the ancient Near East. Second, such narratives belong to later rather than earlier strata of the Old Testament. They are not evidence for primitive or barbaric practices in an early state of Israelite development, but functioned story-wise in the way that the violence contained in modern literature, film and television function in modern society. Third, a human race that has perpetrated the horrors of the wars of the twentieth century cannot afford to be morally superior. The purpose of Exod. 14 is to say, however problematically, that Israel owes its existence and freedom entirely to God. That it also includes a strong statement of the people's unwillingness to believe that this is possible, that slavery is preferable to freedom, should also not be overlooked. JR

Acts 4.32–35

Together with Acts 2.42–47, this passage gives a sublime picture of the idealistic, almost paradisal lifestyle of the earliest Christian community in Jerusalem in the period immediately following the resurrection and ascension of Christ. By ch. 4, the leaders have already had to answer to the temple authorities for their preaching of Jesus and for an act of healing. Nothing daunted, the life of the Church goes on under the inspiration of the Spirit.

Three comments spring to mind. First, Luke appears to have seen the circumstances described here as belonging especially to the first months: later references to the Church in Jerusalem make no reference to life as lived at this high level of mutual generosity and zeal. Second, it may be that Luke sees the early community as simply living out, on a communal scale, the commands of Jesus to his early followers, that they should abandon their goods (5.11, 28; 18.28–30) and aid the poor (19.1–10). The account in Acts thus represents the working out of a process, amounting to a whole new way of life, very different from that of the cities which Luke knew. Acts, then, picks up where the Gospel leaves off, in this as in other respects. If this is a correct reading of Luke's mind, then we note that generosity is exercised within the community and does not go beyond its bounds. But then, Luke's circumstances hardly made Christian Aid a likely prospect. It is not as if he had turned down such extramural generosity (as has been almost suggested in some quarters; charity should begin and end at home); he had never considered it. Third, this primitive 'communism' is no airy ideal, nor is everything quite as lovely as it seems. The following episode of Ananias and Sapphira (5.1–11) is the most blood-curdling passage that Luke wrote. For him, deceiving God and one's fellow-Christians, and failure to share all, especially when linked to meanness over money, is for Luke the most heinous of sins (cf. e.g. Luke 16.19–31).

Whether or not Luke's idealism or a desire to edify and stimulate his less committed contemporaries towards the end of the first century outran his historical accuracy, this is a side of Christian behaviour that has never caught on except in heroic spurts. Other New Testament evidence of church life does not show quite such standards in operation. But if you pitch it high, you may get some reward. And there are always those who, with single minds, see where true blessing lies. LH

1 John 1.1—2.2

Whether we see the Johannine Epistles as belonging to an earlier or later stage in the life of the Johannine group of Christian congregations than the Gospel of John is perhaps not of first importance. It is, however, sensible to decide whether they come from the same author or not. And the differences of perspective are such that it is most likely that the Epistles are the work of a different hand (albeit of the same 'school') from the Gospel. In brief, our present writer is not quite so audacious theologically as the evangelist.

The differences are apparent from the opening four verses of 1 John, which make a kind of prologue. They are reminiscent of John 1.1–18, yet different in sense and in originality. First, instead of daring identification of God's pre-existent Word with Christ in John 1.1–3, 14, here 'word' seems to have the more common sense of the true teaching, given by God and made available through and in Jesus. True, it might carry the stronger sense, but if so, it is undeniably muffled, as if there is hesitation to go so far.

Then, the word 'beginning' seems to have lost the abyss-like profundity and absoluteness of John 1.1 and now refers, more probably, to the start of the Christian experience and the Christian movement, made available through Jesus. It may be that in this way the Epistle shows a more pragmatic, less theoretical or mystical mind than the Gospel – and it has often been taken to point to a later date for the Epistles, after the Gospel; as if a Christian community is more likely to be moved, by the weight of life's 'realities', down from the heights of a pure sense of the divine reality, than in the reverse direction. There is a similar flattening in the use of 'joy' in v. 4; cf. John 15.11 and 16.24. There, the reference is to the fruit of sharing in the 'life' that the Son came to bring; here, it concerns the writer's simple hope that his words will be heeded.

There may be a further symptom of the same less profound, more 'common-sense' outlook in v. 5: 'God is light.' In the Gospel, Christ as 'the light' represents God, plenarily; he *is* God to us (1.4f.; 8.12; 9.5). Here, Christ is, it seems, more visible spokesman than absolute representative. The doctrine is less far-reaching, and so perhaps less adequate or innovative as a piece of *Christian* theology. Indeed, v. 6 puts to us the solidarity of Christ with us rather than with God. In his plain theocentricity (as in v. 5 notably), the writer is, despite much of his vocabulary, closer in doctrinal assumptions to other New Testament writers than the writer of the Fourth Gospel.

Finally, the writer takes up the idiom of Jewish sacrificial thinking, with the slaughter of animals as the standard means of the removal of sin. This, he says, is the real difference that Jesus has made. The Gospel had something of this – though there the image related to the sins 'of the world' (1.29), rather than 'our sins', which seem to be this writer's leading (though not exclusive) concern (1.7–9; 2.2). The eye now is more on the needs of the Christian community where sin persists (though 3.9 puts a bolder and so, it seems, inconsistent doctrine – or is it aspirational in intent?). A modern audience needs to face its light-years distance from this ancient-world sense of animal-killing as the best means of ensuring the restoration of relations between God (indeed the gods) and ourselves. That Jesus fulfilled this role and had this effect says more about Jesus than about the mechanism which that culture saw as producing the palpable and welcome effect. The experience precedes the imagery used to illuminate it. LH

John 20.19–31

The resurrection appearances in the Gospels serve two main functions: first, they witness to the fact that Jesus is alive; and second, they enable the risen Christ to instruct and commission the disciples. Today's Gospel describes two separate appearances of Jesus, followed by a brief conclusion to the Gospel (ch. 21 is believed by most scholars to be an appendix).

In vv. 19–23 Jesus appears to the assembled disciples in a house on Easter Day itself. Functionally, this corresponds to the appearance described in Luke 24.36–49. Jesus greets the disciples, identifies himself to them, and equips them for mission. There are striking links with John's supper discourses. There, Jesus promised to 'come' to the disciples (14.18), which is what he now does (20.19). He said he was giving his 'peace' to them (14.27); he does so now (20.19f.). In his 'high-priestly' prayer he spoke (proleptically) of his sending them out (17.18), he does so now authoritatively (20.21).

Of particular interest is his 'breathing' on them in fulfilment of his promise to send them the Holy Spirit or paraclete (20.22). The 'insufflation' (as it is often called) is a creative and effective act of symbolism, reminiscent of Gen. 2.7 where the Lord creates humankind and breathes into Adam the breath of life (cf. Ezek. 37.9; in the Greek text the same verb, *emphysaō*, is used in all three passages). While some have seen this as only a foretaste of what is to happen at Pentecost, this can hardly be anything other than the Johannine *equivalent of* Pentecost. There is absolutely no need to read John with Lucan spectacles and to presuppose that this dramatic gift of the Spirit is merely a preliminary to an event fifty days later.

The commission which accompanies the insufflation parallels the 'great commission' in Matt. 28.18–20, and that narrated indirectly in Luke 24.47. What is surprising is the strong focus on the forgiveness and retention of sins, without any mention of preaching or baptizing. The saying recalls Matt. 16.19 and 18.18, and may ultimately derive from Isa. 22.22. While some have seen this as conveying 'power' to one group within the Church (e.g. bishops and priests) to declare sins forgiven, more probably it should be seen as addressed to the disciples as representatives of the whole ecclesial community.

Verses 24f. prepare the reader for the fact that Thomas was not present on this occasion. The appearance a week later is unique to John's Gospel. Theologically its main function is to illustrate the nature of resurrection faith. Thomas says that he will believe only when he can see and touch Jesus' wounds. Yet when Jesus invites Thomas to touch him, he acknowledges Jesus as his 'Lord and God' without this physical assurance. The blessing that follows on those who have not seen and yet have faith is for all future believers. Has Thomas outshone even the 'beloved disciple' in his faith? RE

The Third Sunday of Easter

Zephaniah 3.14–20 or Acts 3.12–19; 1 John 3.1–7; Luke 24.36–48

Zephaniah 3.14–20

The prophet Zephaniah is generally assumed to have been active in the early part of the reign of Josiah (640–609; cf. Zeph. 1.1). His prophecies in chs. 1 and 2 and beginning of ch. 3 speak of the coming day of the Lord and the judgement that will bring, not only upon Judah and Jerusalem, but also upon surrounding peoples such as those in Gaza, Ashkelon, Moab and Ammon. At 3.8 the mood changes to one of future promise; and although it is possible that Zephaniah is responsible for some of the material in 3.8–20, the concluding verses, especially from v. 16, seem to presuppose the situation of the Babylonian exile, with its language about dealing with Jerusalem's oppressors, gathering its people and bringing them home.

Verses 14–15 have been likened to language that could have been used at a coronation. The hopes and expectations that such an occasion would arouse are related, however, not to an earthly king but to the presence of God among his people, among them not for judgement (as in the opening chapters of Zephaniah) but for salvation. The theme of God being with, or in the midst of his people is a powerful one in the Old Testament (cf. Ps. 46. 5, 7, 11). The name Emmanuel – God with us – (cf. Isa. 7.14) is an important instance.

In vv. 16–17, 'holy war' themes appear, in the command to Jerusalem not to fear (cf. the notes on the Second Sunday of Easter), and in the description of God as a warrior who gives victory. Another important theme that is present is the idea that the exile brought shame and reproach upon the people in the eyes of the other nations and, by implication, upon the God of Israel. This situation will be reversed. Israel will receive renown and praise from the other nations when God ends its captivity and restores its fortunes.

However, it would be wrong to read the passage purely in military terms. No doubt the fortunes of war, and matters such as victory and defeat, were important to the Old Testament writers; but the prophetic tradition is not interested in Israel for its own sake, but as the people that will enable the nations to desire and embrace God's rule of justice and peace. The eirenic promises of restoration imply the prior punishment, judgement and purification, so strongly stated in the preceding chapters. JR

Acts 3.12–19

In the 1930s, thanks to the work of C. H. Dodd, it became common critical orthodoxy that the great apostolic sermons in the early chapters of Acts (and indeed, less prominently, down to ch. 13) represented faithfully (though not with slavish uniformity) the pattern of the earliest Christian preaching and so, in effect, the content of faith. We were thus taken back beyond Paul to the days soon after the lifetime of Jesus himself, when the impulse given by the resurrection and the gift of the Spirit was pure and fresh.

More recently, it has become commoner to say that the sermons are more likely to tell us what Luke saw either as the gist of Christian preaching for any and every time or what he believed to have been the original message, retailed in part as a lesson for those of his own day. So, in effect, the priority of Paul among our witnesses was restored.

In ch. 3, we have the second of the sermons and in this lection just its first half, which is unkind to both Luke and C. H. Dodd. Peter and John, after the manner of Jesus, healed a lame man at the temple gate; then, a crowd having gathered, Peter speaks.

Here, and indeed in the omitted passage that follows, the appeal is to the Jewish and scriptural roots, and thus the authenticity, under God, of Jesus and all that he accomplished. As always, Luke is sensitive to the audience; compare, for example, Paul's speech in Athens (ch. 17), where the agenda is very different.

There are also Lucan emphases: the crucifying of Jesus was done in ignorance (cf. Luke 23.34; Acts 13.27) and so was, in a sense, excusable (though see Acts 28.27f.). Jesus is referred to here in some of the less common New Testament ways: 'author (of life)', v. 14, is a term found otherwise only in Hebrews (2.10; 12.2); and Acts 5.31; 'righteous one', at first sight not really a technical word at all, cf. Luke 23.50, with Wisd. 2.18, equating 'righteous one' and 'son of God'; and Acts 7.52. For the stress on the 'name', cf. p. 125. The fact that these ways of designating Jesus did not survive in wide Christian use has been seen as a sign of their authenticity here; but Luke favoured them, as we see, and it is possible to understand that they would not lend themselves easily to later developments of thought.

The appeal to Scripture, as well as being exemplified from Luke's infancy narrative onwards, was emphasized by Jesus himself in the crucial post-resurrection chapter of the Gospel (24.27, 47). And the vindication of Jesus by God after his death is the crown of all (v. 13), with repentance as the ensuing call. LH

1 John 3.1–7

The modern audience may find this passage strong meat, especially v. 6, with its unhesitating statement of the sinlessness of the true believers; and if the reading had continued to v. 9, the reaction would be stronger still. Moreover, the plain reader's impulse to say 'Steady on' turns to puzzlement when contradictory passages come to mind: in 1.8, the claim to sinlessness is self-deception (see p. 117f.); and in 5.16–17 we find pastoral provision for dealing with Christians who sin, dividing them into the serious and the not-so-serious, though v. 18 then proceeds to re-state the doctrine of 3.9.

So what are we to make of this coexistence in the writer's mind of common-sense realism and soaring spiritual ebullience? (It is worth saying that there is no evidence of an original text later corrected.) Both aspects have had their legacy: the former in the regular provision for confession of sin in private and public liturgies (with 1.8f. enduring as the common introduction to Morning and Evening Prayer in the old Anglican books), and in the developed distinction between mortal sin and venial ('... not unto death', v. 18); the latter in the logical but euphoric conviction of sectarian groups from time to time in Christian history, liable sometimes to defy the observation of outsiders.

Context is always a good key to try. The writer has the strongest possible sense of the 'set-apartness' of his people. They are Christian believers separated from the world; even more, they are the Christians who hold the faith correctly, whereas others do not – the latter being 'anti-Christs' (2.18f.), a new word coined to describe them. To be a true believer gives both present status of the highest grade ('children of God', cf. John 1.12) and (with a perspective much less strong in the Johannine mind than the sense of present gift) a future that defies description (v. 2), but is a seed of later doctrines of the believer's 'deification': 'We will be like him, for we will see him as he is.' The one seen transforms the one beholding into his own image, an idea with roots in reflection on creation (Gen. 1.26).

But this doctrine about status does not stand apart from morals. That which is one with God must share his sheer purity; and Christ has removed our sins (cf. John 1.29), so that the believer then enters Christ's sinlessness. It is a kind of logic, based on his deepest Christian convictions, that drives the writer to his surprising statement: 'No one who abides in him sins' (vv. 6, 9). In a sense, of course, it is aspirational rather than descriptive of Johannine church life (as the contrary passages show). All the same, it has a kind of theological argument to back it, though the writer has not achieved a theory that will actually accommodate both sides of his coin. A Johannine Christian must sometimes have wondered which side would have to give. And those (if any?) worried, as we might be, by the schism in the group, as itself an evil, might have wondered whether there was some self-deception. It is not without parallel. LH

Luke 24.36–48

First, as in the ethos, language-style and character-painting of the infancy narratives at the start of his book, so here at the end (v. 46; cf. v. 27), Luke is keen to root Jesus and his story in the story of old Israel. He does it chiefly by way of the old Scriptures. Jesus was no fluke, but the climax of God's whole purpose (though quite where in the Scriptures the *Messiah* is said to suffer and to rise on the third day is another matter).

Second and similarly, the risen Jesus was not mere 'spiritual' manifestation (v. 37) but as physical as could be (v. 42). (Luke is not worried by pedants' questions about the fate of the fish when Jesus had subsequently vanished.) Why does this physicality matter? Again, it roots Jesus in Jewish traditions about resurrection, e.g. Ezek. 37, the story of the dry bones. Luke and John (much more than Mark and even Matthew) mind about this. God's restored creation, like the original creation, is physical and material. God makes (and restores) real people. Luke is not interested in sophistications like Paul's idea about 'spiritual bodies' (i.e. consisting of spirit rather than flesh) in 1 Cor. 15.42ff. For Luke, it is more important to grasp the permanent value, in God's scheme of things, of our whole created selves; and Jesus paves the way. Perhaps Luke knew of Christians who were inclined to underplay such wholesome realism. For us, no doubt, the question has a different shape altogether, and we may wonder whether the way the tradition had developed in Luke's hands was wholly satisfactory, even in terms of his own day. Did he silence all questioners?

Third, this episode occurs in Jerusalem, not in Mark and Matthew's Galilee. Luke's book ends where it began, and where Acts will start. Jerusalem is the holy city, now, as it were, taken over by its true lord and by the truth of God that he speaks and represents.

Finally, the assembled proto-church, apostolic in composition and role, consists of 'witnesses' (v. 49). Their task of preaching can be well seen as testifying to what has been seen and heard. It is not therefore a creative or speculative task: let theologians and preachers beware. Perhaps Luke already knew the dangers.

Not all these points are easy now. Times have changed, and in some ways Luke seems to skate over difficulties and to be rather simplistic. But he grasps the virtues of realism and down-to-earthness, and the way God is concerned with what is real: with what is rather than with what might just possibly be. LH

The Fourth Sunday of Easter

Genesis 7 or Acts 4.5–12; I John 3.16–24; John 10.11–18

Genesis 7

Within the narrative structure of Gen. 1—11 the story of the flood is important because it is the dividing line between the original creation of Gen. 1 and the creation of our experience, in Gen. 9. The former creation is a vegetarian creation, as indicated by Gen. 1.30, that is to say, it is a world without 'nature red in tooth and claw', apart from one destructive element: the human race.

The flood as described in Gen. 7 is an undoing of creation. Creation in the Old Testament is a matter of order, of the restraining and ordering of forces which, when unleashed, can overwhelm and destroy the world. Thus the references to the fountains of the deep bursting forth and the windows of heaven being opened (v. 11) indicate that God has relaxed the forces that restrain the destructive power of nature (cf. Job 38.8, 10–11 'who shut in the sea with doors . . . and prescribed bounds for it . . . and said "Thus far shall you come" ').

Part of the order of creation is also the moral order, and the Old Testament is clear that the disruption of the moral order can affect the natural order; which is why God brings the flood upon the earth; to destroy the destructive creature, humanity, whose evil undermines the created order.

Noah and his family and the animals that enter the ark are the nucleus of a new world in the post-flood era. We are not told in what respect Noah is righteous; but the fact that he is, and that God can use this righteousness to preserve the human race that otherwise deserves extinction, is an important theme in the passage.

The story of the flood is one that provokes many reactions, from those who contend that Leonard Woolley found evidence of a flood at Ur (he did not; what he found had been caused by wind!) to those who are ever looking for, and claiming to have found, the ark.

Since 1872 it has been known that the biblical story of the flood is only one of numerous such stories from the ancient Near East, whose heroes are known variously as Ziasudra, Atra-hasis and Ut-napishtim. Flooding in the Tigris-Euphrates region of ancient Mesopotamia could have devastating results; whether there was a universal flood is less likely. Who would survive to tell us about it? Comparison with the other ancient flood stories shows how much more profound the one contained in the Old Testament is, as part of the larger narrative of Gen. 1—11, which boldly asserts both that God is the creator of the world, and that the world he originally made, the vegetarian world, is not the world of our experience. JR

Acts 4.5–12

Luke is right (v. 5) in seeing the high-priestly group as a sort of caste or royal family (though Caiaphas was *the* High Priest by this time). They were the aristocracy of Jerusalem, administering (and profiting from) the temple with its dependent activities and in a number of ways running the country on behalf of the Roman authority. As they had previously arraigned Jesus, so these people now have his senior followers before them – on the lesser charge (why a charge at all, except that they had acted in Jesus' 'name'?) of healing a sick man. Luke constantly (and edifyingly) shows us in Acts how Jesus' leading followers and missionaries act as he acted and suffer as he suffered.

As customarily, the apostles appeal to Scripture (Ps. 118.22; a familiar proof-text, cf. Mark 12.10; Luke 20.17; 1 Pet. 2.7), a powerful argument, if they can make it carry weight. In due course, and grudgingly, the apostles are released; and the mission goes on.

It is the 'name' of Jesus, not the apostles' independent power, which has had the healing effect (v. 7) and which must have the more extensive (but related in that thought-world) effect of saving us. *Sōzō* means both 'heal' and 'save' – and gets translated appropriately, in our terms, but also confusingly: see Luke 7.50 and 18.42, identical in Greek. But what is this about a 'name', or, to be specific, Jesus' 'name'? Names in the ancient world carry meaning and may carry power. Deuteronomy famously saw the sanctuary as the place where Yahweh made his 'name' dwell, e.g. Deut. 12.5, 21. In Acts especially, 'Jesus' (= Joshua = Yahweh saves) carries power in itself – for preaching (Acts 4.17), healing, baptizing (2.38; 19.5), praising God (19.17). Salvation is what Jesus signifies and what he effects. There are of course comparable modern expressions using 'name', but their sense is weaker, and any power involved is located elsewhere.

Verse 12, with its candid exclusivity, divides Christians (whether they find force in this theory of names or not). For some, it shines out in Scripture to 'prove' the uniqueness of Christ in the saving purpose of God ('no other name') – Christianity cannot somehow merge with other faiths or share with them its role as God's salvific instrument; it truly is unique. And it matters not that this first-century writer had never considered the relevant issues in their modern form. For others, this verse has no particular privilege and must be read in the light of Luke as a whole, and indeed within its historical context. Like the Nunc Dimittis (Luke 2.29–32), it tells us of Luke's confident way of seeing matters in the early days of the faith, when there was a clear-cut, uncomplicated thrust to the Christian mission and many later questions had not arisen. Luke's doctrine does not, however, overrule the effective universality of God's creative love in what we now know as a bewilderingly pluriform human world. LH

1 John 3.16–24

Two large moral questions may come to mind as one considers this passage. First, is there a hierarchy among precepts, some virtues being more urgent than others in their claims upon us; or, if God is the prescriber, do all alike carry total force? To judge from the New Testament, early Christians, and surely Jesus before them, were agreed on the priority of love, seen as God's great command. There could be disagreement on whether it eclipsed or included other well-recognized commands or duties (compare Mark 12.32–34 with Matthew's 'on these two commands hangs the whole law and prophets', 22.40); and the problem reverberates still.

But there is a second question: whom are we to love? It was Luke's Jesus who was brought to rule on the question, Who then is my neighbour? – giving the Good Samaritan as its wide and deep answer: love must be as large as need (10.25–37).

The Johannine Christians thought about these matters in their own way. In answer to the first question, they were uniquely single-eyed: love is the only moral quality that is attended to at all. And we simply cannot tell how, in practice, they tackled the moral issues that surely arose among them. It is as if they lived in the light of intuitive grace – and perhaps they did. In answer to the second question, they may disappoint many modern readers (not to mention Luke the evangelist!). We Christians are to love 'one another' (John 13.34): love is intramural. In 1 John, written in the shadow of a schism between two Johannine groups, sundered by christology, it seems that the duty of love is narrowed down further, to the true believers, those sharing one's own doctrine. (One cannot help wondering whether a few more rules might have helped to keep them in one piece.) Everything in this writing points to this being the intention of v. 17. Throughout this writing, the situation is one of stark alternatives – no longer between Christians and the rest (as in the Gospel) but between 'true' and 'counterfeit' Christians. No ecumenism here!

So the dualism of 1 John extends from faith to ecclesiology and morals. Many modern Christians would of course find little difficulty here (differing, however, on the location of 'truth'), but those looking for a more liberal faith may care to examine their hearts as to the actual extent of their love – whether in terms of practical generosity (v. 17) or readiness to give life after the model of Christ (v. 16), the former being a workaday sacrament of the latter. LH

John 10.11–18

In the other Gospels one of the most characteristic features of Jesus' style of teaching is his use of parables. In John's Gospel the word 'parable' is not used, but there is the same fondness for illustrating his teaching by comparisons with scenes from daily life in the country. So here: to illustrate Jesus' relationship with his followers we have, not just a description of Jesus as a shepherd, which would be quite conventional – great generals and political leaders were known as 'shepherds of their people'; we have a comparison with different kinds of shepherding to suggest the unique kind of 'shepherd' that Jesus would prove to be.

The contrast is with the 'hired hand', who would have little incentive to take risks when on duty. No one could blame him for not tackling a wolf single-handed for the sake of someone else's sheep, and in any case (he would doubtless argue) it would be relatively few sheep in a flock that the wolf would be likely to kill. Jesus, on the other hand, treats the sheep as 'his own'. In an earlier passage (v. 3) the 'good shepherd' has been described as one whom the sheep recognize because he knows each one of them. But he then goes on to say something totally unexpected: he 'lays down his life for the sheep'. Then, as now, such heroic conduct was hardly to be expected. At the end of the day we all believe that human life is of more value than that of an animal, and we would not particularly admire a shepherd who got himself killed by taking excessive risks when fending off danger. It is at this point that we realize that this is no longer a straight comparison with farming practice: the shepherd *is* Jesus, whose shepherding involves radical self-sacrifice, not only (as the shepherd and flock imagery would normally imply) for the sake of those already identified as his sheep but also for others who 'do not belong' – a clear reference to that breaking down of social, religious and ethnic barriers which was to be a consequence of the spread of the gospel.

In John's Gospel it sometimes seems as if Jesus moves with such confidence and serenity that he is hardly human. He knows what is in people, he knows what will happen, he is aware of the consequences for his followers and for the world. Was he, therefore, a kind of surface visitation of the divine, floating over the human realities of moral choice and agonizing decision? Any such interpretation is dispelled by the words about laying down his life; he lays it down 'of his own accord'. Far from being simply an instrument in his Father's hand, performing his divine role in sublime obedience, he is a man facing profound moral choices and resolving them out of his own free will. He fulfilled his Father's command by freely choosing to lay down his life – a new paradigm for 'the good shepherd'. AEH

The Fifth Sunday of Easter

Baruch 3.9–15, 32–36; 4.1–4 or Genesis 22.1–18 or Acts 8.26–40; 1 John 4.7–21; John 15.1–8

Baruch 3.9–15, 32–36; 4.1–4

Baruch is a pseudepigraphic work; that is, one ascribed fictitiously to an ancient author, in this particular case, Jeremiah's secretary Baruch (cf. Jer. 32.12). There were good reasons for the author to conceal his identity, because he probably wrote in Hebrew in the period 164–62 BC, during the struggle of the Jews with the Seleucids, the Greek rulers of Syria. The Hebrew has not survived; the translation is based on a Greek text. Adopting the identity of Baruch, he was able to use the time and conditions of the Babylonian exile to describe his own times and, here, to exhort his readers to greater obedience to God.

The opening words are reminiscent of the *Shema*ʻ, the prayer that begins 'Hear, O Israel', at Deut. 6.4, and that became a test of Jewish loyalty. The phrases 'land of your enemies' and 'foreign country' in v. 10 are a poignant description of the Jews' own land under foreign rule. Their present plight is attributed to their having forsaken God, and they are encouraged to seek wisdom. Wisdom is the subject of the pronoun 'her' in v. 15, and in the continuation of the entreaty for the search for wisdom in vv. 32–6 there are strong overtones of Job 28 and 38. The verb translated as 'found' in v. 32 has the sense of 'probe' or 'examine', and indicates divine approval following examination. The next verses describe the incomparability of God. The implication is that one (wisdom) approved by such an incomparable God must be eminently worthy of special attention, especially as access to her has been singularly granted to Israel (v. 36). The concluding verses explicitly link wisdom with the Torah; that is, the Law, commandments and promises of God (cf. Ps. 119). It is Israel's great privilege to enjoy a special relationship with the incomparable creator of the universe. This should give courage and hope under the suffering being endured at the hands of an alien people. JR

Genesis 22.1–18

This is the story of the *aqedah*, the 'binding' of Isaac, and at several levels it is one of the most powerful passages within the whole Bible. In one sense it is, or should be, a cause of profound difficulty. What would the present-day media make of a story of a father who set out to kill his son on the grounds that he had been commanded by God to do so? Religious believers in both the Jewish and the Christian tradition seem sometimes not to realize how utterly offensive this story would be in 'real-life' terms. It is a story told to illustrate a particular set of beliefs, and must be treated as such.

Let us first consider the character of the story. Perhaps the first thing to strike us is the extraordinary economy with which it is told. No mention is made of Sarah, Isaac's mother; no picture is given of any agonizing self-doubt on the part of Abraham. He hears a call which he takes to be from God, and without a word and without delay ('early in the morning') he obeys. He realizes that the 'young men' must suspect nothing of what is to take place, and so he deliberately misleads them ('we will come back to you'), as of course he also misleads his son ('God will provide the lamb'). Isaac is old enough and strong enough to carry the wood of the burnt offering to a place 'far away', yet he does nothing to resist his father's murderous intentions.

In these ways the story retains its intensely dramatic qualities. But it is clearly not handed down simply as a story; it has a message to convey, of an immensely difficult kind. It is a demand that God's perceived requirements must be given an absolute priority over and above the normal demands of other human beings, even of one's own family. There is a sense, of course, in which the Christian story of the death of Jesus as being part of God's plan offers a parallel, but the tension is there eased because there were human agents who crucified Jesus. Here the potential killer is the young man's own father, who has been told that the victim is to be the one through whom his own line is to continue. (We recall that Abraham has sent away his other son, Ishmael, in the previous chapter, and we have no suspicion yet that Abraham is to have several more children [Gen. 25.1–2].) Here is a word picture that envisages that God's demands take such precedence that it would be wrong to 'withhold your son, your only son' if that was the sacrifice demanded.

Later tradition has made much of this story. Apart from the Christian parallel already noted, the link between the otherwise unknown 'land of Moriah' and the site of the Jerusalem temple is hinted at later in the Old Testament (2 Chron. 3.1), and has played an important part in the traditions of both Judaism and Islam. The present-day visitor to Jerusalem is still likely to be assured that the 'rock' that gives its name to the Dome of the Rock is the place where Abraham all but sacrificed his son: Muslims believe that the son was probably Ishmael. RC

Acts 8.26–40

In the sense that it has had an enduring fascination and evocative power, the Ethiopian eunuch is one of Luke's most powerful stories; but it has still more strings to its bow.

In the first place, we note its place in Luke's ever-widening narrative of the Christian mission. In 1.8, Luke gave his programme. The gospel would move from Judea to Samaria and 'to the ends of the earth'. In this chapter we make rapid progress: with Philip's conversions and exorcisms in Samaria, ratified by Peter and John from Jerusalem, binding the new into the old (vv. 1–23), together with the skirmish with Simon (the would-be simoniac) who provides the inevitable element of grit. Now, in what follows, we appear to have moved quickly to the gospel's final phase, for surely the Ethiopian represents admirably the 'ends of the earth', not in his temporary location, but in his person. It may be so. He is certainly exotic; no place was more so to Luke's readers than the mysterious African interior. But the conversion of the centurion Cornelius in Acts 10 is made more of as a decisive move forward; though, as a 'God-fearer' (10.1–2), he was already on the fringes of Judaism, so that he was in a sort of halfway house; and Luke uses his conversion partly to validate the Church's policy, of great importance symbolically and practically, on the non-applicability of the Jewish food-laws to Gentile converts to Christ. (Mark 7.19 says Jesus already made this move, for all, and Paul had good reasons for the change, worked out, profoundly, in Galatians and Romans.) So the eunuch may indeed be the first Gentile convert, pure and simple; though he too is on the edges of Judaism, going on pilgrimage to Jerusalem and reading Isaiah. But it may be (did Luke just omit to say?) that he is an emigré Jew, powerful in the service of the Candace (a title of office, not a name, as Luke may think); so representing another category of Jewish convert (though his like abound at Pentecost). Let us say that he is probably included as a representative of those Gentiles, foretold in passages like Isa. 55.4–5 and Zech. 14.16, who will, in the day of fulfilment, worship the God of Israel, now revealed truly in and by Jesus. His eunuch status, which would disqualify him for Jewish acceptance, is made nothing of.

But beyond all these uncertain matters, the passage is notable for giving the first evidence of the formal exposition of Isa. 53 (here, vv. 7–8) as referring to Jesus, and thus giving a way of understanding his suffering and death as in God's saving purpose.

In Acts alone, Philip steps forward from the Twelve (cf. 1.13) as a character in his own right (see also 21.8–9). Luke must have had access to traditions about him, uniquely apart from Peter and John. That is, unless, as is more commonly thought, this is the Philip recruited alongside Stephen and others in 6.5–6, precisely, it seems, not to engage in the ministry of the word; in which case, both fail signally to stick to their brief (note the vigour of v. 40).

The eunuch is baptized and receives the Spirit, as occurs at all Luke's main staging-posts (in varying orders of their combination), cf. e.g. 8.14–16. But as with the Pentecost crowds, there is no sign of 'continuing church life' as being part of the process; a puzzle to later readers. What did Luke think ought to happen next?

It is suggested that the words 'what hinders me' in v. 36 had some quasi-liturgical place in Luke's experience; cf. 10.47.

The edifying drama of it is the story's great virtue, both then and (with the hesitations given by new times) now: a heartfelt and unhesitating conversion, with a reassuring theological base in the old Scriptures, then a Philip as catalyst. Fervour and sound thinking, if you can get them, make a healthy mixture. Not out of place in Eastertide, or any time. LH

1 John 4.7–21

This passage and 1 Cor. 13 are the classic reflections on love, which almost all the New Testament writers, in various ways and with varieties of emphasis, proclaim as the quintessence of virtue. We are so used to this that we forget that it might have been otherwise; various pagan and Jewish groups in the period saw asceticism, both sexual and over property, as the basis of the good life.

Whereas Paul's 'hymn to love' sets out the moral make-up of love, our writer presents the relevant theological structure that supports love's primacy. The simple basis is found in v. 8 (and repeated in v. 16): 'God is love.' This may give the impression that what is in mind is predominantly mystical – and the passage, together with the Song of Solomon, taken allegorically, can be seen as the basis of a whole powerful tradition in Christian spirituality. Yet, if we take 1 John as a whole, it is plain that a Jewish-style ethical emphasis is fundamental: see 3.17–18 (pp. 125–126) and, here, v. 20. There is also a christological route by which the divine love is mediated, exhibited and defined: v. 10, cf. 3.16. And there is the sobering realization that, for all his sublimity, our writer is not generous in his sense of the scope of God's love or the Christian's love. It is clear from the work as a whole that those who are truly born of God and know God (v. 9), and whom we count as 'brothers' (no 'sister', alas, in the text, though it is likely that the masculine is not intended to be exclusive), are those whose faith is orthodox, and do not include those Johannine 'Christians' who have 'gone out' (2.19). So the modern hearer or reader, moved to peacefully expansive emotions by the passage, may need to note the unpleasant grit in the situation; and parallels may not be absent even from the heart most confident of its generosity.

None of this does more than humanize the sublime character and concentration of the argument. The terms of the doctrine are all what we expect in Johannine writings, most of them shared with the Gospel. For example, the reference to 'the Son' as the 'atoning sacrifice' in v. 10 (cf. 2.2) perhaps invokes the common Jewish and early Christian symbol of the near-sacrifice of Isaac (Gen. 22, cf. John 3.16). And v. 12 repeats John 1.18, as v. 14 parallels John 4.42; and the mutual abiding in v. 16 is found in John 15, though some of the statements are, not untypically, rather more theocentric than christocentric compared to the Gospel parallels. But the priority and purity of love, right through to the end, is the overriding sense (v. 17f.). It is a liberating doctrine. LH

John 15.1–8

It was characteristic of Jesus to illustrate his teaching by comparison with familiar objects and occupations of the countryside. The other Gospels preserve two parables about vineyards (Mark 12.1–9; Matt. 20.1–16), but both of these focus on the labourers who worked in them. Here the comparison is with the vines themselves. Vines grow slowly – it would normally be three years before any fruit could be gathered from them; but in the meantime they would require careful tending; and this tending was a natural image for the care with which God tends his people – it is found more than once in the prophets (Jer. 2.21; Isa. 5).

But in this case the comparison involves Jesus as well. Jesus is the stem of the vine, we are the shoots; and the image is a strong one for the solidarity of Jesus with his followers and their utter dependence on him – without him they can do nothing, but if they retain their union with him whole new possibilities open up. Their prayers have a new power, and their activities bring credit, not to themselves, but to their heavenly Father, who is 'glorified' by what they do.

But this is not just a parable of comfort and assurance. There is a sterner side to it. Cultivating vines involves pruning; by no means all the shoots should be allowed to grow. If we are shoots of the vine we are necessarily under judgement. If we do not bear fruit we can expect to be pruned away and receive the ultimate penalty, which is conventionally described as being 'thrown into the fire'. But this is not just a re-statement of the traditional belief that we shall be judged on our good and bad deeds and receive our reward accordingly. The word for 'pruning' in Greek has a double meaning; it also means 'cleansing'. The kind of 'pruning' that is done to Jesus' followers is not necessarily an immediate lopping off and throwing into the bonfire. In Christian terms, 'cleansing' means, first, baptism (the means by which one becomes a shoot of the vine in the first place), and then repentance and forgiveness – which enable us, despite our failures, to be renewed and 'bear fruit'. It is only those who deliberately separate themselves from the parent stem and reject all the possibilities offered by 'abiding' in Jesus who condemn themselves to 'withering' and final rejection. AEH

The Sixth Sunday of Easter

Isaiah 55.1–11 or Acts 10.44–48; 1 John 5.1–6; John 15.9–17

Isaiah 55.1–11

It may be obvious to modern Western readers that public resources of water should be freely available to all thirsty people. This is not obvious in the Middle East where water is scarce, and where traditional sources of water may be jealously guarded and defended. The invitation to everyone who is thirsty to come to the water must therefore be seen in this light. The thirsty are also likely to be the hungry, and they, people without money, are invited to buy and eat. The invitation then spirals higher to embrace wine and milk, which are not priced.

The sequel, in which people are chided for spending money on what is not bread, makes it clear that water, food, wine and milk are not to be taken literally in this passage, although this point should not be developed in the direction of supposing that only 'spiritual' and not practical things are being spoken of. There probably is a contrast between at least two types of religion implied in these words. There is religion that involves payment and gives little in return (which was probably how the prophet thought of idolatry) and religion that depends upon the gracious and free gift of the God of Israel. Yet, as the paradox of buying food when one has no money implies, the gifts of God are not free, the cost being borne by him.

The second part of the passage moves to practicalities, and at the same time brings more surprises. God promises to make an everlasting covenant with his people, based upon his love for David. Yet its scope is not restricted to Israel. David was not a leader of the people (singular) but a leader of peoples. There are echoes here of royal ideology found, in certain psalms such as Ps. 2.8 'ask of me, and I will make the nations your heritage'; but whereas this royal ideology may have the sense of Israelite rule and thus domination over other nations, the emphasis in the present passage is different. The nations will gladly accept any invitation to be included in the covenant; indeed Israel may be knocked over in the rush to join (cf. v. 5)! This will be because of the graciousness of God made apparent in what he does for Israel, but his purpose will be to show that that graciousness is intended for everyone.

These verses bring to a conclusion that part of Isaiah that began with ch. 40, and the idea of the active word of God forms a narrative arch between 40.8 and 55.11. Whether the Israelites knew that rain and snow return to the atmosphere in the form of vapour is unlikely. The Old Testament view of these things is that God has storehouses of snow and hail (cf. Job 38.22) and that water is kept in the heavens in waterskins (Job 38.37). Presumably these were not thought of as unlimited supplies; rather, such things as rain and snow were divine messengers that were sent to do specific tasks before returning to report to God. God's word is then to be seen in these terms.

What is God's word and how does it return to him? The prophets employed a mode of speaking that has been called the 'messenger formula', which was used when kings sent messages to each other. The king would speak his message in the presence of an ambassador, and the latter would then travel to the court of the king for whom the message was intended, and repeat the message verbatim. When prophets used the formula 'thus says the Lord' they were implying that they were uttering a message that they had heard God speak. This may help us to make sense of the mechanics of vv. 10–11. Their main point is that all the words that have been spoken in chs. 40—55 will be fulfilled as surely as rain and snow help plants to grow. JR

Acts 10.44–48

These verses form the climax of the important episode concerning the Gentile centurion, Cornelius, stationed at Caesarea, headquarters of Pilate the governor. He is a God-fearer, v. 2, 22, 35; that is, he had become attracted to Judaism and affiliated to a synagogue. It is a category now evidenced from inscriptions in Asia Minor, and a number of such people appear in Acts, easily missed by the casual reader (though it has to be said that the degree of formality involved is uncertain, either in history or in Luke's usage). They are Gentiles who 'fear' or 'worship God': 13.16, 43, 50; 16.14; 18.7. It is likely that people in this position found the Christian message and movement particularly attractive; it was related to the Judaism they valued but gave them unstinted acceptance, and it is not improbable that this had been Luke's own route into Christianity. Perhaps this story is really, in Luke's eyes, less about the conversion of a Gentile pure and simple, than God's plain acceptance of God-fearers in particular. Paul's full-blown Gentile mission, after all, still lay ahead; though undoubtedly this episode (cf. ch. 11) went a good way to giving it a fair wind; and the process was completed in ch. 15. Then the stage dominated by Peter gives way to that dominated by Paul.

Here, Peter's vision leads him, by the Jewish route of table-fellowship, to be open to the full acceptance of Gentiles into the Christian community, and this new step, helping to initiate (but see above and p. 130) the final stage of the mission as laid out in 1.8, is confirmed by the Spirit, in an experience reminiscent of Pentecost (2.1–21; cf. 19.7).

We note that it is incorrect to see Luke as warranting the later sacramental pattern of initiation, which has often tended to link the gift of the Spirit particularly to confirmation subsequent to baptism. That is the order in Acts 8.14–16, a passage relied upon in episcopal churches; but cases vary and Luke is not thinking along such lines, being more interested in marking the great stages in the mission.

Peter's actual reluctance to receive Gentiles on Paul's open terms, as depicted in Gal. 2.11f., casts doubt on the historicity of this story; and it is suggested that one of its aims was to smooth away the serious difference, as a matter of historical fact, between Paul and Peter on this very issue of true Gentile equality of status in the Church. Luke is throughout concerned to present a confident narrative of the harmonious onward march of the Christian mission, ch.15 being the glorious climax (and the little problem in 15.36–41 being no more than a minor tiff by comparison with the defection of Barnabas in Gal. 2.13). In the end, Luke's version won the day, with Peter and Paul as the joint foundation-martyrs of the Roman Church and sharing a feast day for ever. Does good, edifying memory matter more than facing the facts? LH

I John 5.1–6

Theologically, the First Letter of John operates, insistently and repetitively, on a narrow front, and these verses, especially vv. 1–2, seem to be a final succinct attempt to state the message – yet again. Verse 1 gives the doctrinal core, v. 2 the immediate moral implication. Belief and love are bound together in an inseparable logic.

For all its repetitiveness in central message, this writing expresses it, in successive passages, by focusing on a particular word, usually one of the key terms of the Johannine vocabulary, already familiar from the Gospel. In these verses, it is the turn of 'world', *kosmos* (vv. 4–5); and the core of it is a statement reminiscent of that on the lips of Jesus in John 16.33: 'I have overcome the world.' Here, however, it is not Christ who does the conquering but the believer and the believer's faith. That variation makes no inconsistency in the Johannine scheme of things, for Christ and believer live in a state of mutual indwelling, and the latter, existing wholly by the gift of the former, is himself the plenary agent of God. It is a doctrine akin to that of Paul (e.g. Rom. 8.14–17; 1 Cor. 12.12f.), but developed and intensified. But in this writing there is the special factor, which we miss until we realize the writing's particular, narrowing context: these great high claims apply only to the believer who shares the writer's perception of 'true' belief. Of course we get no full or objective account of the 'false' ideas of the other party, only that they relate to the 'fleshliness' of Jesus as Messiah and Son of God (4.2), and are therefore a variant on a pervasive ground of division in second-century Christianity. This is the hidden (to the casual reader) factor in vv. 1 and 5. It seems to be about the issue: how human really was Jesus and in what manner?

It is probable that this factor, the physicality of Jesus, is the connection between v. 4 and v. 5; otherwise, the latter seems an abrupt new thought. It invokes two more potent Johannine symbols, water and blood. They were united, as here, at the crucifixion, in John 19.34f., and the former is pervasive in the Gospel (in chs. 2, 3, 4; and in 7.37f.), the latter appearing in 6.51–58. Various suggestions have been made down the centuries as to their import in the Johannine thought-world, but the most likely reference is to the two sacramental rites of baptism and Eucharist, their Spirit-filled physicality replicating the physicality of Jesus, the Word made flesh (John 1.14). As for 'not with water only', did these schismatics deny the reality of Jesus' death? It was in serious contention at the time.

Finally, what can be meant by the conquest of 'the world', surely an inflated claim, made in the exuberance of new faith? To us, it reads like an absurd piece of imperialist theological bombast coming from this minuscule group of people – who cannot even stay at one. Few at this period had much genuine and informed sense of 'the world' in the modern sense. Among the New Testament writers, only Luke and Paul show any width of knowledge of places and persons, and then only of the Eastern Mediterranean. But people compensated by an ample sense of the 'world' of the heavens, with their spiritual powers, good and bad, their layered structure, and the planets, powerful in human affairs. It is no doubt victory over those fateful powers that the Johannine Christian felt was bestowed as a result of Christ. It was a vital part of their valued liberation from all that had threatened their lives and held them in thrall. A conviction of freedom takes one a very long way. LH

John 15.9–17

The solidarity between Jesus and his followers was described in last Sunday's reading by the poetic image of the vine and its branches. This is now made more concrete: the relationship is described in terms of human experience.

Historians often ask the questions: Can we place Jesus among the customs and institutions of his time? Was he like a rabbi, attracting students to learn from him? Was his movement political, gathering recruits as he moved around? Was he like a philosopher, addressing anyone he could get to listen and hoping that some would become disciples? Was he a man with a mission, needing helpers to spread his message? All these models have been tried; none seems to fit perfectly, and here Jesus offers another one: the disciples were simply his 'friends'.

The ancient world reflected a great deal about friendship. People saw it as essentially a mutual or reciprocal relationship. To be friends, two persons need to be in a relationship of equality – a master cannot be a 'friend' with a slave – and to be able to give and receive advantages from each other. Jesus' definition seems to go along with this, in so far as he recognizes that those whom he calls his friends cannot also be his 'servants' (the Greek may mean 'slaves'). And he includes another factor in friendship. Friends should not have secrets from one another; Jesus shares with his friends everything he knows, even his privileged knowledge of God.

But this friendship is also something different. At first sight it may look daunting. 'You are my friends if you do what I command you.' We can imagine a bully saying this at school: Do what I tell you and you can be in my gang. Does our 'friendship' with Jesus depend on slavish obedience to whatever he says? But this is to take it out of the context in which Jesus is speaking. The 'commands' of Jesus are simply those that express his love for his friends and enable them to have the love for one another that he has for them – love that may even reach the point of laying down one's life for another.

This means that even friendship (as we usually understand it) is an inadequate description of this new relationship. Here there is no mutual advantage; there is nothing that Jesus can gain from his 'friends'. He 'chose' them, not because of the use they could be to him, but out of sheer love, a love that went so far as to make him lay down his life for them. In so doing, he established a principle for Christian living. This was the kind of friendship – total self-giving in love, no expectation of advantage, readiness even to lay down one's life – that was at the heart of his 'commandments' and that defines the character of that union with him and with one another, which was poetically imaged as that of the vine with its branches. AEH

Ascension Day

Daniel 7.9–14 or Acts 1.1–11; Ephesians 1.15–23; Luke 24.44–53

Daniel 7.9–14

The prescribed passage is the climax of the vision, written in Aramaic, in which the seer sees four beasts emerging from the sea (a symbol of chaos). Each beast, representing an empire, is more terrible than the one that precedes it, and on the head of the fourth beast there appears a little horn that displaces three horns, and which has eyes and a mouth.

With the beginning of the set passage, the scene switches from the source of the chaos and the destruction wrought by the beasts that emerge from it to a judgement scene on earth. The plural 'thrones' implies that there will be a panel of judges; but the dominating feature is the Ancient One (Aramaic, 'One ancient of days' i.e. years). The figure of white clothing and pure wool hair is meant to denote eternity and wisdom, and certainly not senility. The wheels of the throne are reminiscent of those of Ezek. 1, and the fire symbolizes purity and holiness. The fact that the beasts are only partially destroyed, even if their dominion is taken away, is an attempt to account for the persistence of evil in the world even after the judgement.

The climax is reached in v. 13 with the coming on the clouds of heaven of the 'one like a human being' (Aramaic, 'like a son of a human'). That this figure is in some sense 'heavenly' is indicated by his coming on the clouds of heaven, and by the qualifier 'like'. He is thus best thought of as an angelic figure. However, in the explanation of the vision in vv. 19–27, the dominion is given to 'the people of the holy ones of the Most High' (v. 27) in language almost identical with that of v. 14. These 'holy ones' are evidently those Israelites who have been persecuted and martyred by the little horn, usually taken to be Antiochus IV (175–164 BC) who banned Judaism from 168/7 to 164.

How can the persecuted ones be the same as the 'one like a human being'? This is the language of vision and symbols in which precision may not always be possible. The angelic figure may be a personification or may be a kind of heavenly guardian of the persecuted ones.

The fundamental message of the vision, however, is that the evil personified by the beasts, and embodied partly in the actions of desperate rulers, is ultimately subject to divine judgement. It is overcome not by greater, similar force, but by faithfulness to goodness and truth, which may lead to persecution and death. The dominion that is therefore given to the 'one like a human being' or the holy ones, is not based upon human ideas of power, but the experience of those who have drunk deeply from the well of suffering. JR

Acts 1.1–11

In the Lucan narrative of God's saving activity in Jesus Christ (the Gospel) and in the Holy Spirit (Acts), the story of Jesus' ascension marks the end of Jesus' post-resurrection appearances to his disciples and the prelude to the sending of the Spirit, thereby marking a transition point from Easter to Pentecost. In the liturgical tradition of the Church, Ascension is all of that and more, for it also has become a festival of the exaltation of the risen Christ.

The Acts lection for this day consists of two main components. The first (Acts 1.1–5) serves not only as an introduction to the entire book of Acts and thus to the work of the Holy Spirit in the life of the young Church, but also – in a more immediate sense – as an introduction to the Ascension miracle. The second part (vv. 6–11) is the account of the miracle itself. In both these sections, however, the primary emphasis is on the coming of the Holy Spirit.

Verses 1–5, after a brief statement of purpose (vv. 1–2) which parallels Luke 1.1–4, set forth a terse summary of the events of the 40 days following Easter, a time when Jesus 'presented himself alive to [the disciples] by many convincing proofs' (v. 3). It is perhaps assumed by Luke that 'Theophilus' has heard of these appearances of the risen Christ, since no effort is expended to provide the details of these encounters, other than what is offered in Luke 24. Following Jesus' order to the band of his faithful followers to remain in Jerusalem (Acts 1.4), he delivers the promise of God, namely, that God's Spirit is soon to be made evident in fresh ways. This coming of the Spirit is explained in baptismal terms: whereas water was the baptismal medium of old, 'you will be baptized with the Holy Spirit not many days from now' (v. 5).

The second part of our text (vv. 6–11) repeats this emphasis on the coming of the Spirit, but in a different context. Here this gracious and decisive gift of God's Spirit is compared to the political hopes the disciples had vested in the Messiah. Their question about the restoration of the kingdom to Israel (v. 6) betrays that not even the events of Easter and the succeeding 40 days had disabused them of a comfortable stereotype, that is, that God's Messiah would reinstitute the political fortunes of the old Davidic monarchy. Jesus deflects their question (v. 7) and refocuses their attention on the marvellous display of God's power and love that they are soon to see. It is not the restoration of the kingdom of Israel that will energize you, Jesus says in effect. Rather, 'You will receive power when the Holy Spirit has come upon you' (v. 8a). Thus vv. 5 and 8 lift before the reader an announcement from God that is not to be overlooked: the age of the Spirit is about to dawn.

Then Jesus is elevated beyond the limits of their physical senses, and 'two men in white robes' (compare Luke 24.4) gently chide the disciples for vacant gazing, even as they promise Jesus' second coming (Acts 1.9–11).

While the liturgical tradition of the Church has tended to make the ascension of Jesus into a festival to his glory and power, the emphasis in the biblical tradition is elsewhere. Not only is the ascension rarely mentioned in the New Testament (compare Luke 24.51 and Mark 16.19), but the interest in Acts 1 appears to be less in what is happening to Jesus than in what is about to happen in the lives of the earliest Christians. Twice in this brief passage the declaration is made that the Holy Spirit is about to infuse the life of the Church in new ways. Not that the Spirit was unknown before this. The 'Spirit of God' was the phrase that from very early times had been applied to special expressions of God's guiding and redemptive presence in human life (note, for example, 1 Sam. 11.6, and compare it to 1 Sam. 16.14). But the import of Acts 1.5 and 8 is that a new dimension to the Spirit's work is about to become evident. It is as different from what has gone before as the Spirit is different from the ordinary water of baptism. It is as different from what has gone before as the transcendent kingdom of God (v. 3) is different from the political kingdom of David and his descendants.

Just how the Spirit finds expression the disciples are not told. That is a matter of suspense, which will not be resolved until Pentecost (Acts 2). In the interim, they (and the disciples in every age) are to 'be my witness in Jerusalem, in all Judea and Samaria, and to the ends of the earth' (1.8). It will become clear only later that in this very activity of witnessing they will provide the channels for the Spirit's power and grace.

So in the New Testament perspective, Ascension is an interim time, a period – not unlike Advent – between promise and fulfilment. The disciples of Christ are called to live faithful and obedient lives and to remember that the wonder of God's love and presence revealed so radically in the cross and the open tomb still has in store fresh surprises of joy. The disciples of Christ are called to witness, little realizing how the Spirit lurks to transform all that they do into magnificent occasions for the outpouring of God's love. In this manner Ascension points to Pentecost and to all the marvellous ways of the Holy Spirit of God. BG

Ephesians 1.15–23

Like the earlier part of this opening chapter of Ephesians (1.3–14), in the original these verses are, grammatically, a single sentence. Both are statements of high rhetorical complexity and, to the modern ear, liable to be moving or even mesmerizing (rather than soberly illuminating) in their effect. The passage is such a baffling combination of Pauline phraseology and loftier-than-Pauline style that the suggestion is made that, in whole or at least in part, Ephesians is made up of liturgical forms – the prayers or hymns of Pauline Christians. The Jewish 'blessing' form of vv. 3–14 fits such a theory particularly well (though it is also found at the start of letters, even semi-artificial, literary ones).

Related to this is the still unsettled question of authorship. It can be maintained that the differences from Paul's genuine letters (long sentences, same words in different senses) are explicable on grounds of difference of purpose: this is less Paul the ethical pastor and teacher than Paul the preacher and worshipper; but the fact that Ephesians is little short of a catena of phrases from the genuine letters makes many see it as the work of a Pauline inheritor (like the Pastoral Epistles).

For our purposes the question is important chiefly as the ideas come up for consideration. Perhaps most interesting is the teaching in vv. 22–23, where Christ, very plainly in heaven (v. 20), is head of the Church, seen as his body, and now no longer in its various local manifestations but as universal in the fullest and most lofty sense. That is, there is both linkage and differentiation between Ephesians and undoubted Paul. In the more intense 'body of Christ' teaching of 1 Cor. 12, the Church and Christ are more thoroughly identified and fused: he and his people are a single entity, they in him. For all the high-flown language, the distinction here drawn makes the language of Ephesians look like a second-generation development, whereby the Church, of course dependent on Christ, nevertheless can be distinguished in its own right as a phenomenon in this world, while Christ reigns from above. It is close to the doctrine of Luke in Acts (for all its extravagance of expression), where the Church proceeds under the awesomely heavenly (and so now in effect distant?) Jesus.

Again like Luke, the writer distinguishes between the resurrection and ascension of Christ – helping, unwittingly, to warrant the Christian calendar of later years. Earlier, you could not sensibly make a distinction.

Nevertheless, Christians must themselves pray for heavenly insight: 'wisdom' and 'revelation' and 'enlightened' (vv. 17f.) are vibrant words in the piety of the time. And the cosmic perspective, as elsewhere, leans heavily on common early Christian proof-texts, Pss. 110.1 and 8.4, already part of Paul's stock-in-trade. Finally, 'fullness', part of an obscure final phrase, is again less innocent than it may seem: it was the sort of word probably to make the susceptible spine tingle, pointing the hearer to what we would see as proto-Gnostic connections, and lifting hearts to heaven. LH

Luke 24.44–53

The final verses of the Gospel of Luke are characteristic of the evangelist's picture of things and especially of his beliefs about the person and role of Jesus. On the one hand, he works with a division of history into the time of Israel, known in the Scriptures, the time of Jesus, and then the time of the Spirit-powered mission of the Church; but on the other hand, he is careful to show how the three phases interact, with the second and third 'emerging' from what preceded. So, though the Jerusalem temple had gone by the time of writing and though Jesus had foreseen its end, there is no gloating over this in Luke. Rather, he looks back to it almost fondly as the focal point of events surrounding Jesus' birth and upbringing and has shown Jesus grieving at the prospect of its fall; and here, at the end, it remains the holy place to which the disciples return to praise God at the close of resurrection day (and the motif will continue in Acts). Thus Jesus is in continuity with God's whole providential work and is, of course, its fore-ordained climax. Notice that to the formal 'law and prophets', Luke adds 'and the psalms' as giving the divine testimony to Jesus: it is a good addition for, in Luke as elsewhere, very many of the scriptural allusions and quotations come from the Psalter: it was a prime source of christological reflection and vehicle of communal self-understanding. This may be, in part at least, because scrolls of the psalms were more readily available than copies of some other parts of the old Scriptures; but many passages offered themselves, as it were on a plate, for Christian interpretation. The reference here to fulfilment is the second in the chapter: see also v. 27, in the Emmaus story. For Luke, the risen Jesus is at pains to root his work in sacred prophecy.

The passage also looks forward to the Church's mission, in effect to Luke's second volume, the book of Acts, where the horizon is no less than 'all nations', as indeed it has been since the beginning of the Gospel: see, for example, Simeon's words in 2.32 and the extension (by comparison with Mark) of the quotation from Isa. 40 in 3.4–6 to include the words, 'and all flesh shall see the salvation of God'.

Is Jesus' withdrawal in v. 51 a first shot at an account of the ascension, later rewritten and reframed, when Luke turned to write Acts? Or had he already planned his second volume, and is the idea here that Jesus withdrew at the end of this day, then manifested himself for the sacred period of 40 days (compare the temptation in ch. 4 and Israel's wilderness period) before his final bodily departure? It depends whether you think Luke had his whole narrative in view from the start – and there are many indications that he had. As generally in Luke, the ending is thoroughly up-beat and full of confidence in the Jesus-given future. LH

The Seventh Sunday of Easter

(Sunday after Ascension Day)

Ezekiel 36.24–28 or Acts 1.15–17, 21–26; 1 John 5.9–13; John 17.6–19

Ezekiel 36.24–28

This promise of the restoration of the people after the Babylonian exile tackles a fascinating problem in a way that raises further questions. Given that, from the moment of their deliverance from slavery in Egypt, the Israelites showed themselves to be selfish and distrustful of God's actions on their behalf (see especially the reading for the Third Sunday of Lent), the crucial question becomes 'How can the people of God live truly according to this calling?'

God's promise is that he will cleanse his people, replace the heart of stone with one of flesh, and put a new spirit within them. Whether the translation 'make you follow my statutes' is right, is a question that must be addressed. As it stands, it suggests a degree of compulsion that will rob the people of freedom and, in any case, make the statutes and ordinances of God redundant. This is a reason for taking the Hebrew, which is literally 'I will do (or make) that you walk in my statutes' to mean that God will create the ideal conditions for his people to follow his statutes, not that he will turn them into compliant robots.

The theme of creating the right conditions to make possible the service of God is important, because in restored Israel after the exile, as in today's world, the right conditions never existed. This is also true for any Christian interpretation of the passage which sees it as a prophecy of the giving of the Holy Spirit after the resurrection. It cannot be said of the churches that they are any nearer to exhibiting the ideal nature of the people of God than was the case with ancient Israel, in spite of the churches' claim to have the Holy Spirit. The question 'How can the people of God live truly according to his calling?' remains unresolved within the constraints of the world as we know it. JR

Acts 1.15–17, 21–26

With a note of delicacy, the reading omits the nasty accident that befell Judas (vv. 18–20) and so created a vacancy in the apostolic college. (It was particularly odd to omit the Scripture, Ps. 69.26, referring to in v. 16 and quoted in v. 20.) Despite v. 25, Luke himself was more delicate than Matthew (27.3–9), who saw the death as both self-inflicted and Judas' just deserts; and yet he was more explicitly severe than Mark, who says nothing to exclude Judas from the restoration implied in 16.7, for all had sinned and Christ had died to bring back his own.

The vacancy is filled by putting forward two names and then choosing by lot (in some respects more reminiscent of modern ecclesiastical than commercial methods). The precedents were in the Old Testament Scriptures (e.g. Lev. 16.8f.) and the aim was to give a deciding voice to God in selecting those who would lead his work. (In the eighteenth century, a pious benefactress of the Queen's College at Oxford used the same means to decide on the beneficiaries of her scholarships.)

Luke's story is, however, not without its surprises. We should hardly have supposed that Jerusalem's Christian community at this point was 120 strong, including so many of Jesus' family (though Mary may be meant, but obliquely, in Luke 24.10). And both Joseph Barsabbas and Matthias come as bolts from the blue. Odder still, Matthias never appears again (and indeed 'the Twelve' only down to the watershed of ch. 15). His role is formal in the extreme. But Luke makes rather more of 'the twelve apostles' (Luke 6.13) as an entity than other writers, as this passage demonstrates; presumably wanting to show that the Church inherits the mantle of Israel, here, now, in Jerusalem itself. He sets great store by the order and continuity of God's relationship with his people in the achieving of his purpose. Luke has nothing at all of the Marcionite about him. LH

1 John 5.9–13

There is little that is either new or distinctive in these verses and they are, in effect, yet another summation, less succinct than in 5.1–2, of the writer's beliefs – and of his position in the controversy that has, largely, moved him to write. It is hard for us to be assessors, both because it is unclear precisely what is at issue and because we cannot hear those on the other side. Our readers will do well to reread what has been said in the entries for the preceding five Sundays and reflect on this passage in the light of them.

It is hard to avoid being struck by contrasting reactions. On the one hand, by the beauty and simplicity of the writer's religious perceptions; his singleness of eye as he looks towards God who has revealed himself and acted for us in the person of Jesus; and then his sense of the overriding demand of love as the beginning and end of Christian morality. Quite how he would have unpacked its implications and its detailed requirements we cannot know, beyond that of provision for the needy brother. It is, however, significant that he scarcely envisages difficulty, it seems, though he does distinguish between greater and lesser sins (5.16f.), probably seeing as chief among the former the sin of not agreeing with his theology! The distinction is well-known in the Torah and in the Judaism of the period, including Qumran, often put as that between inadvertent and deliberate sin.

We are then faced with the other dominant impression left by this writing: that it arises from a major tragedy in early Christianity – the first known schism in the Christian community. It was of course the first of many and the modern reader is bound to reflect on what grounds can justify such a break. And it is ironic that moves for repairing schism now are so often backed on the basis of the prayer that 'they all may be one' in John 17 – though whether the Gospel had any such use in mind is surely doubtful. It was a prayer for the union of Christians in Christ and in the Father, as a matter of divine gift; and its ecclesial implications were simply taken for granted. LH

John 17.6–19

'They are in the world . . . they do not belong to the world.' Jesus' final prayer for his disciples dwells on the essential ambiguity of Christian existence – in this world, yet not of it.

John's Gospel began with an account of those who perceived Jesus' true nature and *witnessed* to him. The disciples are now to prolong that witness down the course of history. Their testimony has the authenticity that comes from the strength of their belief in Jesus' divine mission. While Jesus was with them, he carried the brunt of the disbelief and hatred that accompanied his mission. Now they have to carry this witness forward without his protection. But they will have the protection of the 'name' of God. This 'name' was an expression used in the Scriptures to convey the belief that God was present in a particular place: he had made his 'name' to dwell in the temple in Jerusalem, which became a symbol of his power to protect his people. Jesus' continuing solidarity with his disciples was equivalent to this power of the 'name', this focused presence of God on earth; and Jesus' prayer is for the disciples to be assured of this constant protective power.

What was at stake was the continuance of Jesus' work and mission after his departure. As in any religious or political movement, the unity of his followers would be essential, and there is nothing surprising in Jesus praying for it – any leader might have done the same. But in this case the unity he prays for has a deeper dimension. Jesus' own experience had been of a quite exceptional unity and closeness with his heavenly Father; the same unity and closeness is now promised to his followers. Through Jesus they can draw near to God in a new intimacy and a new sense of union. This will bind them to one another, just as it binds each of them into closeness with Jesus and his Father.

In addition to all this, they are to be 'sanctified'. The expression belongs to priests and sanctuaries. Priests 'sanctify' or 'consecrate' themselves for drawing near to God in ritual and service by separating themselves from the ordinary concerns and squalid preoccupations of the world. As a metaphor, this 'sanctifying' may simply mean no more than making certain sacrifices in order to commit oneself wholeheartedly to a particular task or form of service; yet there remains a hint of separation: 'sanctification' implies freeing oneself from certain things in order to be fully available for something else. In this sense it was and is an appropriate word for all disciples who, for the sake of Christ, enter into that ambiguous form of existence which inevitably goes with the practice of the Christian faith – 'in the world, but not of it'. AEH

Day of Pentecost

Acts 2.1–21 or Ezekiel 37.1–14; Romans 8.22–27; John 15.26–27; 16.4b–15

Acts 2.1–21

New life – sudden, unmerited, irresistible new life! That is the reality the Pentecost narrative in Acts 2 broadcasts, and the text transmits the story in the most expansive way imaginable. All the stops on this great literary organ are employed: a heavenly sound like a rushing wind, descending fire, patterns of transformed speech, and the like. It is as if not even the most lavish use of human language is capable of capturing the experiences of the day, and that is undoubtedly one of the emotions the text wishes to convey.

It is not accidental, of course, that the birth of the Church, this great 'harvest' of souls, should occur on this important festival. The Feast of Pentecost, or Weeks, as it is known in the Old Testament, marked the end of the celebration of the spring harvest, a liturgical cycle that began at Passover and during which devout Israelite families praised God for God's grace and bounty. It also was the beginning of a period, lasting until the autumnal Festival of Booths (or Tabernacles), in which the first fruits of the field were sacrificed to Yahweh. And among at least some Jews the Feast of Weeks was a time of covenant renewal, as the following text from the Book of Jubilees (*c.* 150 BC) makes clear:

> Therefore, it is ordained and written in the heavenly tablets that they should observe the feast of Shebuot (Weeks) in this month, once per year, in order to renew the covenant in all (respects), year by year. (*Jub.* 1.17; trans. O. S. Wintermute in James H. Charlesworth, ed., *The Old Testament Pseudepigrapha*; Garden City, NY: Doubleday & Co., 1985, vol. 2, p. 67.)

Pentecost/Weeks is thus a pregnant moment in the life of the people of God and in the relationship between that people and God. Or to put the matter more graphically, but also more accurately, Pentecost is the moment when gestation ceases and birthing occurs. Thus, it is both an end and a beginning, the leaving behind of that which is past, the launching forth into that which is only now beginning to be. Pentecost therefore is not a time of completion. It is moving forward into new dimensions of being, whose basic forms are clear, but whose fulfilment has yet to be realized.

Those who follow the cycle of lectionary texts (or, for that matter, those who simply read the book of Acts) have been prepared for this moment. Twice, in connection with Jesus' ascension, the coming of the Spirit has been promised: 'You will receive power when the Holy Spirit has come upon you' (Acts 1.8; compare 1.5). That promise is now realized in a manner far surpassing the expectations of even the most faithful disciples. New life for the Church! New life for individuals within the church! New life through the Spirit of God! That is the meaning of Pentecost.

No one present is excluded from this display of God's grace. Unlike other important moments in the history of God's mighty acts of salvation – the transfiguration (Mark 9.2–13), for example, where only the inner few are witnesses to the work of God's Spirit – everyone is included at Pentecost. The tongues of fire rest upon 'each' (Acts 2.3) of the disciples, and a moment later the crowd comes surging forward because 'each one' (v. 6) has heard the disciples speaking in his or her native tongue. In order that not even the least astute reader may miss the inclusiveness of the moment, the list of place names that begins in v. 9 traces a wide sweep through the world of the Greco-Roman Diaspora. That which happens at Pentecost is thus no inner mystical experience, but an outpouring of God's energy that touches every life present.

Yet not everyone responded to the winds and fires of new life, at least not in positive ways. Some mocked (v. 13) and, in their unwillingness to believe the freshness of God's initiatives, reacted with stale words (compare 1 Sam. 1.14) as they confused Spirit-induced joy with alcohol-induced inebriation. Perhaps it was the very extravagant expression of the Spirit's presence that drove them to conclude: 'This cannot be what it seems to be!' Yet what it seemed to be is precisely what it was. God's Spirit unleashed! New life – sudden, unmerited, irresistible new life! We may hope that those who mocked were among those who, on hearing Peter's sermon, were 'cut to the heart' (v. 37).

Peter's sermon begins – and this day's lection ends – with a quotation (vv. 17–21) from the prophet Joel (Joel 2.28–32a), and nothing could be more symptomatic of the nature of Pentecost than the transmutation of this text. That which in the prophet's discourse appears prominently as a forecast of destruction and death has become on Peter's tongue a declaration of new life. For Joel the signs of the outpouring of the Spirit are a prelude to disaster (see especially Joel 2.32b, c) but for Peter these wonders have been fulfilled in Jesus Christ, himself the greatest of God's wonders (Acts 2.22), and their purpose, *Christ's* purpose, is nothing less than the redemption of humankind. Again the Spirit has invaded human life in ways that shatter old expectations. It is not death that is the aim of the Spirit's visitation, but new life – sudden, unmerited, irresistible new life! 'Everyone who calls on the name of the Lord shall be saved' (v. 21). BG

Ezekiel 37.1–14

Although notions of life after death were rudimentary in sixth-century Israel, for a person not to be properly buried at death was considered to be a calamity. An individual's shallow grave was thought to be connected with Sheol, or the grave to which all the dead went, where they then existed in a shadowy, even lifeless way. People denied even this decency were more unfortunate; in a sense their lives had not been allowed to be completed.

These shared notions are the necessary background to Ezekiel's vision of the valley of dry bones. What he sees is evidently the aftermath of a battle, whose slain have been left unburied. Their flesh has been picked off by animals or carrion birds, leaving only the bones, which have become quite dry in the heat of the sun. A more hopeless scene could not be depicted, which is why the prophet gives the only possible human answer to the question 'Can these bones live?' which is, in effect, only you, God, know the answer to this question. The rest of the vision needs little elucidation, as the bones are reconnected, covered with skin and finally reanimated. The scattered, dried-up bones become a company of living individuals.

The passage is an excellent illustration of the different senses of the Hebrew word *ruach*, which is translated here as breath (v. 6), wind(s) (v. 9) and spirit (v. 14). Although in Gen. 2.7 a different Hebrew word (*neshamah*) is used for the breath that God breathes into Adam, Ezek. 37 well illustrates the Old Testament view that the difference between a living person and a dead one is that the former breathes (i.e. has *ruach*, breath) and that this phenomenon is to be related to the power of the wind, which humans cannot control, but which can have such obvious effects in the physical world. From this it is a short step to the idea of the Spirit of God as empowering individuals to do brave or noble deeds, or activities such as justice, music or artistic creation.

It has been plausibly questioned whether the application of the vision to exiled Israel (vv. 11–14) is a later expansion of the vision. The idea of bringing people from their graves does not exactly correspond with bringing to life unburied and scattered bones; and bringing people back to their land (v. 12) is no part of the vision. Whatever the original meaning of the vision, it was certainly appropriate for the restoration of Israel from exile; but that was within the world of human history. The original vision may have an eschatological dimension, that is, it may look forward to a new creation of humanity, one wrought by God after human action has produced the misery and hopelessness of a valley of dry bones. JR

Romans 8.22–27

Romans 8 contains Paul's most eloquent account of Christian existence as life in the Spirit and is therefore chosen (fragmentarily) for Pentecost and Trinity Sunday this year. Both festivals speak to us of God and therefore about ourselves. Pentecost celebrates God in action in the world, specifically God's pouring God's love into our hearts (Rom. 5.5) and eliciting our response. Paul does not separate his theological thinking from his experience of the Spirit, and both this week and next week the short extracts can encourage us to reflect on our experience as a first step towards clarifying the doctrines. It is best to read the whole chapter aloud – and then to hear Rom. 5.1–11 as its curtain-raiser before reading it again. Romans 8, like genuine poetry, communicates before it is understood.

The passage set cuts into the paragraph (which begins at v. 18) on Christians' experiences of suffering and their hope of final liberation (vv. 21, 23). Its ideas and emotions stem from Paul's Jewish eschatology, not from a dogmatics textbook, and they are activated by his experience. The anticipated new age has dawned in the death and resurrection of Jesus. It is not yet visibly present, but believers have already received the gift of God's Spirit, which Paul can also call the Spirit of Christ (v. 9), scarcely distinguishing it from the risen Lord himself, active as life-giving Spirit (cf. 1 Cor. 15.45). God as Spirit empowers all Christian ministries (1 Cor. 12) and all Christian prayer (vv. 15f. in next week's reading and here in v. 27). The Spirit will give believers life at the general resurrection (v. 11), transforming their physical bodies into spiritual 'bodies'. Between these twin poles of Christ's resurrection and the future consummation, Christians live an ambiguous existence, belonging to the new age but not yet fully free of the old (see next week), or from the sufferings and pain that accompany the birth of the new. Salvation still lies in the future. But it is possessed now in hope, and that makes patient endurance possible (v. 25, cf. 5.4). Believers have broken with the old and been transferred into the new age empowered by the Spirit. They are now children of God, adopted into a new relationship with God. This finds expression in intimate prayer to the Father and it is their experience that God is active in their prayer.

The obscurity of the passage is increased by isolating it from its context of hope for the future through believers' faith relationship with Christ in their present sufferings. The Spirit gives confident hope of future glory, and even the created order is caught up in the excitement of this anticipation. This passage is unique in Paul by virtue of its cosmic perspective. It can provide a springboard for theological reflection on the environment, and God's Spirit in the world. The relationship of that to Christian experience is a fitting topic for Pentecost. RM

John 15.26–27; 16.4b–15

It was a well-remembered promise of Jesus that his followers, when they found themselves on trial for their faith, would be prompted by the Holy Spirit with the right words for their defence. But it is only in John's Gospel that this Spirit is called 'the Advocate'. The Greek word, literally rendered *paraclete*, is a technical term for one who might appear in court for the assistance of the accused. This person was not quite an 'advocate' in the modern sense of the word; he was not necessarily a trained lawyer and his role was not to present legal arguments or formulate a defence. His effectiveness depended on the respect in which he was generally held, and his function was to persuade the judge that the accused was an honourable and deserving person whose word could be trusted and who was therefore not to be suspected of an offence.

The idea that we might have such a *paraclete* or advocate on the day of judgement was well known in Jesus' time; it was not uncommon to suggest that such things as one's good deeds or the merits of the patriarchs would perform this function. But in John, language and concepts that were normally used in respect of life after death take on new meaning when they are applied to life in the present. And this opens up new possibilities in the use of the metaphor. The advocate's role did not come to an end when he had pleaded the cause of the accused before the judge; he might then have to go back to his friend, explain to him the verdict of the court and help him to accept it. He was, in fact, a kind of go-between, representing the accused to the judge and the judge to the accused. In this sense the Advocate was also (as most older English translations render the word) the 'Comforter'.

This extension of the metaphor helps us to see how the Spirit, after Jesus' departure, would 'guide' his disciples 'into all truth'. But there is more. Once the accused is acquitted, the question arises (or at least might do so according to Jewish procedure) whether the accusers were blameless in bringing the accusation. At this point the Advocate has a further role, that of proving that the accusers were at fault in not believing the testimony that had been given, in misinterpreting the meaning of Jesus' death and in continuing to believe that the 'ruler of this world' (the devil) was justified in his attacks. All of this would take place after Jesus' departure, and would more than compensate for his absence. There was – and is – no reason for 'sorrow'. The presence of the Spirit, defending us when challenged, guiding us when perplexed and revealing more and more of the truth of God, not only makes up for Jesus' physical absence but enables others to see him as he really is – to see his 'glory'. AEH

Trinity Sunday

Isaiah 6.1–8; Romans 8.12–17; John 3.1–17

Isaiah 6.1–8

Any inner or visionary experience usually comes to people only via the symbols and thought-forms of their world. If what they tell others about their experience is to make any sense, the account of what has happened to them must also draw upon available and shared symbols. This means that descriptions of what is ultimately indescribable are inevitably located in a particular place and expressed in particular language. In the case of the present passage, the prophet's experience is described in terms of the Jerusalem temple and royal symbolism of his times. He hears the divine beings praising God in his own language, Hebrew. That descriptions of encounters with the divine can transcend the particular symbolism and language in which they are expressed is indicated by the fact that the hymn of the seraphim has become a central part of Christian liturgy (it also features in Jewish liturgy) and is repeated daily in many languages. It must not be supposed, however, that such language can be taken literally, as though the heavenly hosts actually use Hebrew to praise God; or that God is actually attended by fiery creatures with six wings. All such language merely points to realities far beyond human understanding.

These opening observations are meant as a warning against too literal an understanding of the passage. We are not told that the prophet was in the temple; indeed he could not have been in the most holy part of it. And if the hem of God's robe filled the temple and the seraphim were above him, then the temple was merely a part of a much larger canvas of his vision. Only if we accept this are we in a position to consider some of the details of the temple and royal symbolism.

The opening words may be less concerned to date the vision to the death of King Uzziah (Azariah) in *c.* 734 BC, than to contrast the dead earthly king with the enthroned and eternal heavenly king. The world 'holy' repeated by the seraphim denotes a quality of being that somehow lays bare all human self-sufficiency and self-deceit. The traditional Hebrew vowelling of v. 3c yields the sense 'the fullness of the whole earth is his glory', which some modern commentators prefer. But God's 'glory' is his ineffable presence, especially in Ezekiel, which is why the usual rendering is that the earth is full of God's glory. This is not panentheism, but the claim that God ultimately rules the whole world. The prophet's response 'I am lost' can also be translated 'I am speechless'. Both possibilities have something to be said for them. The former expresses the prophet's feeling of complete worthlessness consequent upon his vision of God's majesty; the second indicates that one who is about to be given a prophetic task has nothing to say. However, part of the revelation of God's otherness is his gracious act of removing Isaiah's sense of unworthiness. The prophet overhears discussion in the divine court. Not for the last time in human experience, his confrontation with the living God leads to his willingness to respond immediately and unconditionally to his service. JR

Romans 8.12–17

Trinity Sunday speaks of God by speaking of what it means to be a believer. That requires reference to the revelation of God in Christ and the believer's integral relationship with him and in him, but also to God as Spirit, the metaphor of wind expressing the unseen power of God at work in the human spirit, guiding the moral life and evoking passionate prayer. Later theological reflection on God as Trinity led the fourth-century Church to define doctrinally this mystery of the divine life and the relationships into which believers are drawn and caught up. Paul's sober comments are plainly rooted in experience but they rise into the rhetoric that has helped shape subsequent Christian experience. This is the raw material of a doctrine that is vacuous without that experience of life in Christ, the Lord who is Spirit (cf. vv. 9–11; 2 Cor. 3.17).

Romans 8, on being a Christian (that is, life in Christ, or in the Spirit) can be pondered in the different sections of the chapter, and this week the lectionary takes us back a section from last week. As usual Paul unfolds his thinking by way of contrasts, here between 'flesh' and Spirit; that is, dislocated human existence and the divine power that has invaded and is transforming it. His vocabulary is apt to mislead because he uses common words in an almost technical way. 'Flesh' is not the sensuous part of human nature, and has little to do with sex in Paul's usage. It refers to the human realm, created by God but overcome by hostile forces, which obstruct the development of authentic human lives. It is finite, physical and weak, but the tragedy of its weakness is that it has fallen under the control of powers opposed to God. Its natural decay therefore carries more sinister overtones. Death is an enemy with a sting (1 Cor. 15.54–56) until the victory of Christ's resurrection breaks its power and allows the Christian to speak with St Francis of 'thou most kind and gentle death'.

This chapter celebrates God's action in Christ to redeem the desperate situation and create truly human lives lived in the perfect freedom of service and dependence on God. God's initiative (v. 3) evokes human response. Those who have been transferred into the new age by baptism (6.3) have received the Spirit, but they continue to live in this dislocated world and need to be reminded to live by the norms of God's new age, not by the old self-centredness and self-indulgence, labelled by Paul 'flesh'; that is, human existence under the power of 'sin' leading to 'death'.

The motivation to live the new life comes from the knowledge of who and what and where we are, and where we are going as people 'in Christ Jesus' (v. 1), liberated by 'the law of the Spirit of life in Christ Jesus' (v. 2). We are placed in a new relationship to God – that of sons and daughters – through our faith-based, baptism-placed, Spirit-graced relationship with Christ Jesus our Lord, the Son of God. The Spirit is God's power experienced as guiding the moral life and assuring believers of that relationship with God. It (or s/he) finds voice in the prayer of believers who know they are children of God, and therefore heirs. The filial metaphor describes a present relationship, but it also implies a legal status and so speaks too of future benefits. The son and heir's knowledge of the heavenly Father, mediated by the Spirit and based on the faith-relationship with Christ (cf. Gal. 2.20) gives certainty about God's fatherly character and promise of a beautiful future. This carries believers through the sufferings of the present time (v. 18), which they shall pass through in his company. RM

John 3.1–17

In John's Gospel there is consistent opposition between Jesus and 'the world', usually represented by 'the Jews'. But the line cannot always be drawn so neatly. Here, one of those who might have been expected to belong to the opposition comes to Jesus secretly to declare his interest. But, despite his learning, his understanding of what Jesus is about is extremely limited. Indeed his main function in the episode is to provide a cue for a discourse of Jesus by asking an 'idiot question' (a typical device in this Gospel): 'How can anyone be born after having grown old?' Jesus' reply, that the kind of rebirth he is talking about is 'of water and Spirit', would have sounded enigmatic to Nicodemus; but Christian readers might have thought they knew at once what it meant: water and Spirit are the elements of Christian baptism, and this seems a clear instruction for the Church – no one can enter the kingdom of heaven without it. Jesus was laying down a principle for all Christian communities to follow: no salvation without baptism!

But it is another characteristic trait of John's Gospel to lead us up the path and then suddenly turn and show us we are on the wrong track. Here this is done by a parable. There is only one explicit parable in this Gospel (10.1–6); but there is a number of illustrations which, like the parables in the Synoptics, invite us to do some thinking for ourselves. This is one of them: 'The wind' (which also means 'the Spirit') 'blows where it chooses.' If you think the activity of the Spirit can be tied down by a rule about compulsory baptism, just think how impossible it is to chart or control the wind!

But what is the nature of this 'rebirth'? There is a subtle ambiguity in the Greek of Jesus' saying that can hardly be reproduced in English. One meaning is, 'without being born *anew*' – and this is the cue for Nicodemus' 'idiot question'. But Jesus goes on to develop another meaning, 'without being born *from above*'. And he does this by enlarging on the role of the Son of man. In the other Gospels (so far as we are able to interpret this mysterious title) Jesus speaks of himself as Son of man mainly to draw attention to the necessity of his suffering and death in this world, to be followed by his vindication and glorification hereafter. But in John's Gospel something of this heavenly destiny is brought into the present. Jesus, even on earth, is one who has a foot in both worlds, both in heaven and in earth, and therefore can give to the believer a taste and a vision of that other dimension of being which is 'eternal life'. The Israelites in the desert had been saved from a plague of snakes by looking at a brazen serpent held in front of them by Moses (Num. 21.8–9). Jesus, by being 'lifted up' (on the cross, and then in his heavenly glory) was to offer a similarly saving vision of heavenly realities to all who gazed at him expectantly enough to be brought to faith. AEH

Corpus Christi/Thanksgiving for Holy Communion

Genesis 14.18–20; 1 Corinthians 11.23–26; John 6.51–58

Genesis 14.18–20

See Third Sunday of Epiphany, pp. 45–46.

1 Corinthians 11.23–26

See Maundy Thursday, pp. 105–106.

John 6.51–58

'Unless you eat the flesh of the Son of man' – it is striking that these extraordinary words did not arouse a general reaction of shock and disbelief, but caused (according to John) a dispute among Jesus' opponents themselves. There was a sense in which people seem to have sensed that a new reality was on offer and they must ponder it before rejecting it.

But John's readers, like every Christian reader subsequently, were bound to set these words in the context of their experience of Christian worship and the sacrament of the Lord's Supper. Not that the text quotes the words of an actual church service – this would have been a banal way of alluding to it. Rather, John seems to be deliberately setting Jesus' words in a kind of counterpoint against what his readers are likely to have expected. They were familiar with the bread of the Eucharist being Jesus' *body*; but here it is called his 'flesh'. This makes the sheer carnality of the expression perhaps even more of a shock to Jesus' hearers, and enhances the drama of the scene; but we can hardly doubt that it was also intended to have a more profound meaning.

This is not the first time 'flesh' has been mentioned. The climax of the Prologue is the statement that 'the Word became flesh' – so flesh is the physical reality of Jesus the man; and 'eating his flesh' is communion with his humanity, an affirmation that the Word did indeed become 'flesh'. Yet this has to be held in tension with another implication of 'flesh', signalled later in this chapter by the warning that 'it is the spirit that gives life; the flesh is useless'. This is a contrast familiar from other New Testament writings (such as, 'the spirit is willing but the flesh is weak'). The challenge facing the Jews at the time was to recognize that the Word could become 'flesh' in a man, Jesus. But believers have to go further than that. They have to see that, to receive eternal life through the true bread that is Jesus' flesh, they have to understand that the bearer of that 'flesh' is the Son of man whose true home is 'above', the realm of the Spirit.

If ever there was a warning against taking the words of this Gospel too literally it is in the last sentence of this reading: 'the one who eats this bread will live for ever'. 'Living for ever' is a way of speaking of 'eternal life', and everyone knew what that was: it was the blessed existence promised to the righteous after death. The startling originality of Jesus' language was that this was brought forward into the present: eternal life can begin *now*. AEH

Proper 3

(Sunday between 22 and 28 May inclusive, if after Trinity Sunday)

Hosea 2.14–20; 2 Corinthians 3.1b–6; Mark 2.13–22

Hosea 2.14–20

Verses 14–15 (Hebrew 2.16–17) are the conclusion of a long accusation by God against Israel, which has probably been cast in the form of an accusation in a court of law by a husband against an unfaithful wife. The woman, as befits the legal language, is not addressed directly, but spoken of in the third person. The conclusion, however, after many forms of punishment have been mentioned, is that God will seek to renew the relationship with Israel that existed in the beginning, when God brought the people out of Egypt (v. 15d). This view of the wilderness relationship, one which sees it in terms of courtship and young love, stands in sharp contrast to the picture presented in Exodus or Numbers. There, the people are constantly complaining about the hardships of the wilderness! The precise location of the Valley of Achor (v. 15b) is disputed, but there is general agreement that it was a route from the Jordan Valley to the promised land, and that 'Achor' means 'disturbance' or 'trouble'. It will be made a door of hope by the establishment of conditions in which the relationship between God and Israel will lead to perfect harmony. Those conditions are described in vv. 16–20 (Hebrew 18–22). Abundant fertility will do away with the need for the fertility god Baal (the Hebrew word also means 'lord' and 'husband'). Wild animals will be no threat to the people, neither will the land be disturbed by war.

The view that Israel can be pictured as a faithless wife and that God can be seen as a faithful husband has angered some feminists; and one does not have to be a feminist to agree that the symbolism is unfortunate if it gives rise to the idea that wives are always faithless and husbands are always paragons of virtue. It is also indisputable that the passage reflects a society in which men have much formal power over women. On the other hand, the text is a product of its time and place, and within those limitations it tries to present a picture of God that rises above the limitations of a human husband. A crucial, and unanswered, question is that of the conditions that are needed to enable humans to respond adequately to God. By picturing a situation from which all external danger has been removed, the passage at least recognizes that there are hindrances to the response of humans to God that are often beyond their control. Salvation is not, then, just a spiritual matter. It has material and political dimensions. JR

2 Corinthians 3.1b–6

Paul here defends his own apostolic mission and ministry in Corinth against new Jewish Christian missionaries who apparently bring testimonials, perhaps even from the Jerusalem church. He suggests that the validity of his gospel is evident from its results (a dangerous argument) – the proof of the Spirit and power (cf. 1 Cor. 2.4). The conflict between these written testimonials and the activity of the Spirit among the Corinthians, with themselves (metaphorically) Paul's letter of recommendation, leads into a far-reaching contrast between the old Mosaic covenant (Exod. 24) and the new covenant (cf. 1 Cor. 11.25) in Christ, a contrast developed by means of a midrash on Exod. 34. This contrast between the letter and the Spirit, found also at Rom. 7.6, does not correspond to that current in English (and Greek) between the letter and the spirit of a law (cf. Rom. 2.29), or between the literal and the figurative, but refers to the character of the old, with its written code, and the new where the Spirit is now poured on the community of the new age. What that meant for some of the Corinthian believers can be inferred from Paul's earlier epistle. Now he draws conclusions from it about the nature of his own ministry. God in Christ is at work in him through the Spirit, and this brings life (authenticity, wholeness of life, or salvation) to them. Paul no doubt has in mind the promise of Jer. 31.31–34, when he speaks of the 'new covenant', and probably Ezek. 11.19; 36.26, with its new spirit and heart of flesh. The old covenant resulted in death because it was broken (cf. Gal. 3.12). The new, written in the heart by God, will mean that they 'know the Lord' (Jer. 34.34), which Paul refers to the Lord Jesus (v. 16), the source and focus of his confidence in the ministry with which God has entrusted him.

Paul's polemical antithesis between the old and the new does not lead him to deny the divine origin and intention of the Mosaic covenant, or to doubt that its 'commandments' (with love their criterion and scope) remain binding (1 Cor. 7.19). Circumcision is irrelevant but Paul's account of the Spirit giving life has a strong moral component. Like Jesus he can quote Lev. 19.18 (Gal. 5.14; Rom. 13.9) as a summary of God's will stated in the law of Moses, and probably sees this love of neighbour as 'the law of Christ' (Gal. 6.2). This right and proper requirement of the law is fulfilled by those who live in and walk according to the Spirit (cf. Rom. 8.4). RM

Mark 2.13–22

It is important to read today's Gospel in one of the more recent translations (e.g. REB or NRSV) and not in the Authorized Version. The reason for this is that there is a variant reading in the Greek manuscripts in v. 17; some have: 'I did not come to call the righteous, but sinners'; while a very few others add the words: 'to repentance'. The latter is the version in Luke 5.32, where Luke seems to have added these words to the shorter version as he found it in Mark; but scribes who were copying Mark (and Matthew) added them, from Luke, and in this way they became part of the Greek manuscripts used for the translation for the AV in 1611. It is thanks to the work of textual critics that the majority of translators of the Gospels now omit 'to repentance'.

The shorter text, omitting these words, makes far better sense. No one would have objected to Jesus if he had called sinners to repent; that was what everybody wanted sinners to do. His offence was that he did not; he invited toll-collectors to meals and ate with them. (The word translated here as 'call' can also be used of invitations to a meal, as it is, for example, in the parable of the wedding in Matt. 22.1–14.) This may mean that when Mark says that Jesus was having a meal 'in his house' (v. 15), he is referring to Jesus' house, not Levi's (as the editors of NRSV thought). Jesus is the host, and the guests are his choice, and they are the people who are outsiders of Israel, who habitually break the Law of Moses, such as Levi the toll-collector, to whom Jesus has said, 'Follow me'. His mission is to them, and the way in which he fulfils it is by associating with them; eating with them in his house.

This paragraph in Mark (2.13–22), and indeed the larger unit to which it belongs (2.1—3.6), have one theme running through them: the time of the Law of Moses is over; now is the season of new wine, and it requires new wineskins. The Law is the old wineskins, and the new wine is the good news of the kingdom of God.

Among Christians of the first century there was a variety of answers to the question, Is the Law of Moses still obligatory for the followers of Jesus? Paul believed it was no longer in force, certainly for Christians who had not been Jews before they were baptized. Mark seems to have shared Paul's radical attitude. His view is that God's grace comes first, 'preventing' us in all our doings; there is no minimum standard of entry into the company of Jesus, only the invitation issued by the host.

Jesus' exercise of this invitation was one of the most offensive things about him, and it remains so, still. JF

Proper 4

(Sunday between 29 May and 4 June inclusive, if after Trinity Sunday)

1 Samuel 3.1–10 (11–20) or Deuteronomy 5.12–15; 2 Corinthians 4.5–12; Mark 2.23—3.6

1 Samuel 3.1–10 (11–20)

See Second Sunday of Epiphany, p. 42.

Deuteronomy 5.12–15

The sabbath command in its form in Deuteronomy (for a slightly different version see Exod. 20.8–11) ends with an imperative of redemption; that is, a command based upon God's redemptive work in delivering his people from slavery (v. 15). The implication is that the purpose of God's redemptive act was to create a society in which there would be no exploitation, and which would in its practical arrangements express and achieve graciousness.

From a modern standpoint, the conditions described in v. 14 leave something to be desired. They presuppose the existence of male and female slaves, for all that Old Testament laws restricted the length of time of slavery to six years (see Exod. 21.1–6; Deut. 15.12–18). It has also been pointed out that a man's wife is not mentioned among those who are to rest on the sabbath! At the same time the command is not without graciousness. The male and female slaves are explicitly mentioned as deserving rest as well as the male addressees of the command; and the domesticated animals and the livestock are included. (See Exod. 23.12 for a version of the sabbath command that puts the ox and ass at the head of the beneficiaries!) Nor should the resident alien be overlooked among those mentioned. These were most likely Israelites who, for some reason, were banished or absent from their own nearer kinsfolk, and who took refuge with families with which they had no connection.

All attempts to discover from whom the Israelites borrowed the idea of a rest every seven days have so far failed. It remains a uniquely Israelite gift to the world. It is also to be noted that the sabbath is not here a day of religious observance, but one of abstinence from work, although there is a hint of the sabbath as a religious festival at 2 Kings 4.23. The main purpose of the command is both humanitarian (i.e. to prevent exploitation) and to affirm that part of what it means to be human is to acknowledge God's lordship over time, by regular rest and recreation. Although there have often been absurd types of sabbatarian observance in Christianity, the movement towards a seven-day, 24-hour society in Britain raises the question whether things have gone too far in the opposite direction. JR

2 Corinthians 4.5–12

Paul has spoken at length about his apostolic ministry since 2.14 and the theme will dominate the rest of this letter, or edited collection of letters. He claims that his own activity and suffering are both sign and vehicle of his message, and he has already had to fend off the misunderstanding that he is commending himself (3.1). His point is to communicate the crucified Lord in whom believers see the glory of the revelation of God. The light, which God made shine in creation (Gen. 1.3) and which Isa. 9.2 heralded, has shone in their hearts giving the knowledge of God that the prophets foretold. This knowledge is found in the face of Jesus Christ (v. 6), in his dying and his resurrection. Paul's topic here is the communication of this counter-intuitional message of the cross, which 1 Cor. 1.18 has described as offensive and foolish, and gaining converts who (v. 26) were mostly of low social status and lacking power. Here it is the apostle himself whose very weakness makes plain that the power of his message is not his own but comes from God. His apostolic existence reflects the dialectic of the crucified and risen Lord. The pain of it is borne by the apostle himself but the benefits accrue to those who accept his message: life, wholeness, salvation, are already a present reality.

Like the Gospels, which call some to renunciation of possessions and family life (e.g. Mark 10.21–30; Luke 14.25–33) without perhaps making this the norm, Paul's contrasting his own apostolic existence with the Christian life of the congregation in Corinth seems to imply two quite different callings, or ways of being a Christian, without claiming that one is intrinsically superior to, or more 'perfect' (despite Matt. 19.21) than the other. The apostle Paul, and some disciples in every age, bear witness to the self-emptying of God in Christ by their whole lifestyle. Like the speaker in Isa. 53, the rest can recognize the finger of God in the affliction of the dedicated one; supremely in the figure of Christ but also in those who bear his marks. The rest who see this and believe are beneficiaries of God's gift of life, like the Corinthian congregation. The life, death and resurrection of Jesus, his teachings, his healings, and his example, are intended by God to benefit everyone and are actually good news for all who respond. All believers are called and empowered. They have their tasks and responsibilities commensurate with their gifts, but not all are apostles. Not all exhibit in their bodies the marks of crucifixion. Yet all can exhibit something of the risen life of Christ, the fruit of the Spirit which is love, joy, peace, etc. (Gal. 5.22f.).

The contrast that Paul draws between his own religious vocation (as distinctive as Samuel's call in today's Old Testament lesson) and the rest of God's people led by the apostle and prophet suggests, in a society where the boundaries between church members and wider population are less clear, a further distinction in the light of Jesus' own ministry. His teaching was addressed to the crowds and still is intended for all. Christians today can therefore rejoice in the existence of a broad 'fringe' of those who hear and are influenced by Jesus even if not (yet) full members of the Church, sharing in the risen life of Christ through word and sacrament. Paul's churches were open to interested enquirers (1 Cor. 14.23), even though his letters are addressed to converts, and he was clear that the visible life of a congregation should lead others to acknowledge Jesus as Lord. He does not measure anyone's commitment, but he challenges those who hear and read his letters to test themselves – and be transformed. RM

Mark 2.23—3.6

The two stories in this passage have commonly been seen as the concluding instalments in a long Marcan section, running probably from 1.21, that is made up of sample episodes from the ministry of Jesus, mostly healings and not more than one of a kind. Helpfully (on this not watertight view), and as a rough sort of designation, it has been described as 'a day in the life of Jesus'.

Whether or not that view gets anywhere near what Mark had in mind, the two final stories are both on the same theme: how to look at (and carry out) the observance of the sabbath. There are at least two quite different ways of looking at the passage. The first is historical. Supposing the episodes to have a good basis in Jesus' life and teaching, how radical do they really show him to be? Or, to put it another way, if Jesus took the lines here depicted, would he have provoked the startling reaction given in 3.6 – a plot to do away with him? Or is that a piece of Marcan hindsight, based on a misjudgement of what the episode can have meant at the time? There has been a tendency recently for critics skilled in the Judaism of the period to say that the statements by Jesus, though radical and challenging, are not outside the limits of current Jewish opinion. For instance, danger to life and health was seen by many, with varying degrees of readiness, as justifying the mitigation of strict sabbath observance. We are, after all, in a period when Judaism was diverse and far from the kind of codification that ensued after AD 70 when rabbinic authority became more prominent. Mark has read back from the passion, here foreshadowed, and from the state of Jewish-Christian disputings in his own day.

But perhaps we do better to try to enter into Mark's intention from the start. There are strong signs that this writer, working about AD 70, had been formed by some of the leading perspectives of Paul – including the rendering obsolete of food rules (7.19) and the keeping of sabbath (cf. Gal. 4.10; Col. 2.16). These were no longer relevant for the followers of Jesus. The basis of their relationship with God lay in the new covenant established by Jesus' death. Hence the fiercely uncompromising tone of Jesus' statements in these two stories. Neither Matthew nor Luke (each from his own angle) could tolerate Mark 2.27 and omitted it. And Matthew (12.1–14) particularly transformed the discussion in the two stories into a seminar on scriptural passages or legal principles, issuing in perfectly reasonable answers that make the concluding judgement on Jesus perverse as well as cruel. Opposition to Jesus is shown as wicked from the start.

For Mark this issue transcends the matter of sabbath-keeping. He takes the discussion to a quite different plane: What kind of a God do we have dealings with and what is the character of the life he wills for us? Is it a matter of this rule and that, to be interpreted thus and so? Or is it a matter of a whole new world in which we are to live with God in freedom, truly a question of life or death (3.4)? LH

Proper 5

(Sunday between 5 and 11 June inclusive, if after Trinity Sunday)

1 Samuel 8.4–11 (12–15), 16–20; (11.14–15) or Genesis 3.8–15; 2 Corinthians 4.13—5.1; Mark 3.20–35

1 Samuel 8.4–11 (12–15), 16–20; (11.14–15)

We noticed when looking at 1 Samuel 3 that it seems as if we are intended to see the whole collection from Joshua to 2 Kings as one continuous work, and that impression of unity is strengthened by the presence of several sermon-like passages, spelling out the implications of the action being described. 1 Samuel 8 is one of these sermon-like passages. (It seems as if ch. 11.14–15 are added as an optional extra to the reading, to spell out what happened as a result of the exchanges described in ch. 8.)

This chapter is important for us because it illustrates very vividly a tension which runs through much of the Old Testament. On the one hand Israel is pictured as a people like all the other surrounding peoples of the time, subject to the usual vicissitudes of national life. In the ancient Near Eastern world the only conceivable form of government for such a people was monarchy, and the elders (v. 4) and the people as a whole (v. 19) express their desire for a king 'to be like other nations'. Such a wish is not regarded wholly negatively; it is based on a legitimate dissatisfaction with the sons of Samuel (v. 5). But the story as a whole also illustrates another strand within the Old Testament, one which is very concerned to show that Israel was *not* like other nations, and that its success or failure was dependent upon its loyalty to God, who had been their ruler 'from the day I brought them up out of Egypt to this day' (v. 8).

Whether this sermon was based on events in Samuel's lifetime seems doubtful; it is much more likely that one of the causes underlying it was the compiler's knowledge of the eventual defeat and overthrow of the two kingdoms of Israel and Judah, by the Assyrians and the Babylonians. In the final editor's mind this could only have been due to disloyalty to God, and here the view is being put forward that loyalty to an earthly king was likely in practice to mean disloyalty toward God. Of course there are other views of kingship to be found in the Old Testament; most notably perhaps in the Psalms, such as Ps. 72. (You might find it interesting to look at that Psalm and compare the picture of royalty found there with that set out in the present passage.) Some parts of the story of David also take a more positive view of kingship, and we shall see when we reach 2 Samuel 7 that our compiler found no difficulty in offering a much more favourable presentation of monarchy. The picture in vv. 12–15, of the demands which a king would make on his subjects, is presented here in very negative terms, but it probably gives a good idea of the sort of requirements that were laid down; there was no such thing as 'constitutional monarchy' in the modern sense in the ancient Near East. RC

Genesis 3.8–15

The denouement of the story of the disobedience of the first man and woman is told with great narrative artistry. Commentators have long since pointed out the oddity of God apparently not knowing the whereabouts of the hiding couple, as well as his apparent ignorance of their having eaten fruit from the forbidden tree. One ancient Jewish solution has pointed to what is undoubtedly a narrative device, in which God asks questions to which he perfectly well knows the answers, in order to initiate conversation. A good example is God's question to Cain, 'Where is your brother Abel?' (Gen. 4.9). In the present narrative the divine questions provoke human responses that are aimed to avoid the truth and responsibility. Thus the man's answer to the question 'Where are you?' gives his nakedness as his reason for hiding, whereas the real reason is his disobedience. Again, the answer to the question 'Have you eaten . . . ?' is not a direct yes. It puts the blame upon the woman. The woman, similarly, puts the blame upon the serpent. Whether consciously or not, these narrative devices portray a fundamental human weakness, which can be observed from childhood onwards: a tendency to avoid responsibility and to put the blame on others.

The curse upon the serpent, which follows in vv. 14–15, has been called the proto-evangelium, because it was taken by Christian interpreters to foretell the vanquishing of Satan (the serpent) by one of the woman's descendants, Christ (see Luke 3.23–38 where the genealogy of Jesus is traced back to Adam). This interpretation was assisted in the Latin version of the passage by the presence of the feminine pronoun ('she will bruise'), which was taken to be a reference to Mary, the mother of Jesus. The NRSV 'he will strike' makes it unclear as to who 'he' is. The NEB and REB use the plural: 'they will strike . . .' in order to indicate what is probably the original intention of the text, that humans and snakes will always experience mutual hostility. By choosing this passage in connection with Mark 3.20–35, the lectionary obviously has something like the proto-evangelium in mind. It is arguable, however, that the human attempts to avoid moral responsibility, presented so artistically in the narrative, deserve the main focus of attention. JR

2 Corinthians 4.13—5.1

Some readers may find themselves rushing past the beginning of this lection to make their way to the more familiar and, indeed, more beautiful section that begins in 2 Cor. 4.16. The opening lines of this passage are profoundly important, however, for they assume a radical continuity between the faith of Israel's past and the faith of the Church's present. At the same time that these lines reflect that continuity, they also demonstrate the profound discontinuity introduced by the gospel of Jesus Christ.

Paul's assertion that 'we have the same spirit of faith that is in accordance with scripture' quietly forges a connection between past and present that the Christian Church has often neglected, to its detriment. Admittedly, the exact nuance of the phrase the NRSV translates 'the same spirit of faith' is debatable, but the identification between past and present is not. The gift of faith that inspired the psalmist now enables the Christian preacher.

The quotation in v. 13 ('I believed, and so I spoke') comes directly from the Septuagint of Ps. 115.1 (the equivalent of Ps. 116.10), although the Greek here departs significantly from the Hebrew, so that this wording will not be found in English translations. In this particular instance, the continuity Paul finds concerns the movement from faith to speech, the way in which faith necessitates proclamation. As Paul indicates elsewhere, he does not view his preaching of the gospel as an optional activity, but as necessity (e.g. 1 Cor. 9.16).

Despite this strong continuity between the psalmist and Paul (and his co-workers), 2 Cor. 4.14 recalls the radically new element that has entered the picture: 'the one who raised the Lord Jesus will raise us also.' The 'same spirit of faith' now manifests itself in the new conviction *both* that God raised Jesus from the dead *and* that God will also raise those who belong to Jesus.

Here Paul expresses resurrection faith in a slightly different way than elsewhere. While he elsewhere expresses the conviction that the resurrection of humankind follows from that of Christ (as in Rom. 6 and 1 Cor. 15), here he distinguishes between the resurrection of the apostles and that of Corinthian believers ('will bring us with you into his presence'). The future of the apostle and that of the Church are intertwined so that extricating either party from the relationship is impossible. Even in the final triumph of God, apostle and congregation belong together (see 2 Cor. 1.13–14).

Verse 15 removes any impression that the final goal of Christian proclamation or of the resurrection itself is anthropological. Even if Paul grandly insists that 'everything is for your sake', he takes a further step that qualifies that generalization. 'Everything' exists so that grace as it extends 'to more and more people, may increase thanksgiving, to the glory of God'. Some interpreters of Paul have argued that he indeed understands the glory of God as something that can be enhanced objectively by human thanksgiving; human gratitude actually increases the glory of God. Whether or not that interpretation captures Paul's thought, it does draw attention to the *telos* of the gospel, which is the glorification of God.

Verse 16 employs a phrase from 4.1 to resume the topic of apostolic boldness. 'We do not lose heart' refers not to the fear of death (or the absence thereof) but to the courage to proclaim even in the most adverse circumstances (4.1–12). Even as the psalmist proclaimed ('I believed, and so I spoke'), Paul will continue to speak, because of his conviction about the power of God (4.13–15).

The remainder of the passage amplifies the motivation that lies behind Paul's courage to preach. Here he speaks once again by means of contrasting that which appears to be significant now with that which will be significant always. The 'momentary affliction' is visible, it is real, but it lasts only a brief while. Chapter 5.1

brings this line of reasoning to a head: 'If the earthly tent we live in is destroyed, we have a building from God, a house not made with hands, eternal in the heavens.' Debate flourishes as to the origin and meaning of the imagery employed in this verse, and the commentaries will provide the options. One important suggestion is that Paul draws on Jewish apocalyptic thought which anticipates a new eschatological temple in the newly restored Jerusalem (see e.g. 2 Esd. 10.40–57; *2 Bar.* 4.3). A 'building from God, a house not made with hands', then, would graphically depict the eschatological home of God's people. This interpretation does not rule out the implications of such a new home for individuals, but it does mean that Paul does not refer here to the resurrected body of individuals so much as to the new creation in which believers will find a home. It is because of the certainty of this new home that Christian preachers can speak and act boldly.

Because the section of 2 Corinthians pertains so directly to the nature of Christian preaching, some Christians may conclude that it has little to say to them (except as the recipients of preaching). Of course, that near-sighted reading of the text neglects the continuity between the task of the apostle and that of every believer. If the apostle (or the contemporary preacher) proclaims the gospel in one way, all believers become proclaimers by their lives as well as their words. The need for courage ('we do not lose heart') does not pertain to the preacher alone. BG

Mark 3.20–35

As so often in Mark, the passage is an *inclusio*, with the beginning and end sections (vv. 20–21, 31–35) engaging with the middle by way of support or dialogue. It is true that this analysis depends on translating the description of those who appear in v. 21 as 'his family'. The Greek means 'his own', and versions have often shied away from the obvious sense in favour of 'his friends' or some such expression. Indeed, if it were not for their appearance in vv. 31–35 and for Mark's habit of *inclusio* one would indeed think the reference was to the disciples. But to balk at 'his family' would be to read Mark in the light of Matthew and Luke who take a more positive, even devout, view of Jesus' family (and indeed of the disciples); both of them omit this troublesome verse! Mark takes no such view (see p. 185): the family are at best indifferent, here hostile or uncomprehending, as their peremptory summons in v. 31 confirms. Like those to whom 'everything comes in riddles' (4.11), they stand 'outside' where the person and message of Jesus are concerned.

The passage tells how family and scribes encountering Jesus fail utterly to comprehend, let alone accept him and his pure preaching of the kingdom. The reactions of the two groups are in tandem: he is mad and he is the devil's instrument. The latter calumny is defined as sinning against God's Holy Spirit (vv. 29–39); that is, it is to judge good as evil, the best as the worst. Failure can go no deeper. It is as stark a confrontation as any Mark has given us so far, though the plotting of Jesus' death in 3.6 approaches it; and the dispute with the scribes takes up the paradigmatic struggle with Satan in 1.12f.

The episode with Jesus' family is of course not simply part of a literary-theological polemic against Jesus' family as a real human group. Its sense is illuminated in this Gospel by the instruction to quit one's family if one will be a follower of Jesus (10.28–30) and the prophecy of family division on the issue of Jesus in 13.12. Jesus is no friend of 'family values' as a top priority; the times and the cause are too urgent. The kingdom has drawn near (1.15) and normal arrangements are turned upside down (though it appears that the paradisal character of true marriage makes it exempt, 10.2–12). Of course one can say that this is preacher's hyperbole,with drastic 'either-ors' like those of the Old Testament prophets. Matthew and Luke both thought it worth modifying this passage, but chiefly because of their different view of the role of Jesus' family; so that Luke even makes Jesus' words wholly ambiguous: 'My mother and brothers are those who hear the word of God and do it' (Luke 8.21). (Try reading it aloud!) They are quite as drastic about family renunciation (Luke including even the wife, 18.29). In context, and putting the matter rather formally, the subject is church life, even ecclesiology: for all of them, the Christian community should (had to, in many cases) take over the role of one's family. Moreover, the 'Jesus-movement' itself was surely in its first years a young people's affair. Only later are Christian families fully in view.

One must then think out exactly how to read these drastic statements in the Gospels. Are they the rash views of idealistic youth; or are they preserved and/or included as paradigmatic for the severity of Christian commitment or the true understanding of the overriding claims of the Christian community? In any case, what then of Christians in post-Christian society? Would 'imitation' quite meet the case? LH

Proper 6

(Sunday between 12 and 18 June inclusive, if after Trinity Sunday)

1 Samuel 15.34—16.13 or Ezekiel 17.22–24; 2 Corinthians 5.6–10 (11–13), 14–17; Mark 4.26–34

1 Samuel 15.34—16.13

Modern readers of the Bible may well find themselves more in sympathy with Saul than was the editor of 1 Samuel. Whether the unfavourable portrait is due to Saul's apparent failure as a leader, or is a deliberate literary contrast with his successor David, is difficult to tell. Sometimes Saul's changes of mood have been explained in terms of various modern psychological theories, but this is unlikely to contribute to our understanding; we cannot know enough of the details of his life and character for this to be realistic.

The beginning of our reading makes clear that Saul's failure is now virtually certain. Samuel had been the agent of Saul's call to kingship; now we are told that the two men never met again, though this sits awkwardly with 19.18–24. Still more drastic is the fact that the editor asserts that God himself regretted having allowed Saul to become king. Such a presentation is scarcely compatible with the views of God's unchanging nature and foreknowledge expressed in traditional Christian doctrine, but passages like this can act as a valuable reminder of a different perception of the divine character and plan.

But if Saul is rejected, what is to be done? At the beginning of ch. 16, by contrast with the presentation of Samuel elsewhere, he is pictured as rather feeble and indecisive, and anxious about Saul's reaction. God provides clear instructions, even telling Samuel what to do to allay Saul's suspicions. No longer are there any doubts about kingship as an institution. A new ruler must be found!

Samuel's arrival at Bethlehem causes initial anxiety whether so distinguished a visitor might be an ill omen. That problem resolved, familiar folk-tale motifs follow – seven sons, rejection of the handsome oldest one, choice of the youngest. And of course it is not just a random statement that the youngest is 'keeping the sheep', for that is a regular way of describing both divine and human kingship, as fulfilling the role of a shepherd. Ps. 23 provides an obvious example. RC

Ezekiel 17.22–24

These verses are the sequel to an elaborate allegory, which is concerned with the fate of the Judean kings Jehoiachin (597–*c.* 560) and Zedekiah (597–587). In the allegory, a mighty eagle breaks off the top of a cedar of Lebanon and takes it to a land of merchants, where he plants it. This refers to the taking of Jehoiachin into exile to

Babylon by Nebuchadnezzar in 597 BC. The eagle provides a replacement for the removed part of the cedar from the 'seed of the land', which becomes a low, spreading vine. This refers to the appointment of Jehoiachin's uncle, Mattaniah, as king, whose name Nebuchadnezzar changed to Zedekiah (2 Kings 24.17). The vine, however (i.e. Zedekiah) inclines its shoots towards another eagle (i.e. Egypt). This leads to rhetorical questions about the fate of the vine. Surely it will be pulled up and wither away, a reference to the punishment visited by Babylon upon Zedekiah when he rebelled against his overlord.

Verses 22–24 are a deliberate reworking of the allegory of the eagles and the plantings. It is God who takes the sprig from the top of a cedar and who plants it not in a land of merchants but upon the mountain height of Israel. Given that in the allegory the cedar top represents the house of David and its transplantation the exile of the king, in the present verses the allegory envisages the divine restoration of the house of David. However, this restoration will have universal implications. The nation ruled by a king of the Davidic line will enjoy universal rule. He will provide safety and shelter for people far and wide (the birds sheltering in the tree); all trees (i.e. kings and rulers) will recognize God's rule. What is high will be brought low; what is low will be exalted. What flourishes will wither; what is dry will enjoy fertility. God's rule reverses human estimates of rank, success and failure.

It is generally agreed that vv. 22–24 represent a post-exilic reworking of an allegory that goes back to the warnings uttered by Ezekiel against Judah during his ministry. They are a noble expression of a hope for a new world, to be inaugurated by God following the judgement that he brings upon his people at and during the exile. JR

2 Corinthians 5.6–10 (11–13), 14–17

For all the beauty and power of Paul's language in 2 Corinthians, the letter makes turns and twists that are often difficult to follow. Just as the reader glimpses what 'tablets of stone' might be, Paul shifts to language about the veiling of Moses or about houses not made with hands. The Corinthians are Paul's letter of recommendation, but he needs no letter of recommendation. The apostles are at home in the body, but they would prefer to be at home with the Lord.

Whatever the problems in understanding these individual passages, it is clear that many of them reflect a struggle to articulate differences between the way things appear (in the world, to those who are not Christians) and the way they really are (to those who are Christians). Nothing is the way it seems to be – real letters are written where they cannot be read in the usual way, the gospel is hidden but transparent, the apostles seem to be close to death but they bear life within them.

The assigned lection begins with still more such contrasts and paradoxes. Christians seem to be at home in their bodies, in the physical world, but their real home is with the Lord, and to be in that home is their preference (vv. 6–10). Unlike others, Christians must make judgements based on what is inside persons, not on 'outward appearance' (vv. 11–12). The apostles themselves appear to be crazy ('beside ourselves'), but they are the most sane of all (v. 13).

Finally, beginning in v. 14, Paul gets to the heart of the matter, identifying why it is that this conflict exists between what the world sees and what Christians know to be real. First, he explains the grasp of the gospel by reference to a bit of Christian tradition. With the words 'one has died for all' Paul cites a creed he uses elsewhere in a somewhat different form (see e.g. 1 Cor. 15.3; Gal. 2.20, 1 Thess. 5.10). These words are too compact to associate them with any particular theory of the atonement. Whatever it means to say that Christ's death is 'for all', that death also involves the death of all (v. 14) and, more important, that death claims the lives of all.

That Christ's death was 'for all' means somehow that believers are bound up in that death. For Paul, Christians do not watch the cross as if it were a scene 'out there' or 'back there' somewhere, displayed for them now so that they can understand the historical ramifications of this event. Nor is the cross connected with believers only by virtue of some influence it has with God, so that the cross persuades God to forgive human sin. The death of Christ on the cross involves believers directly, in that they die in it and now have lives that are not their own but belong to Christ.

With vv. 16–17 Paul undertakes to state the implications of the cross for the present course of human lives: 'We regard no one from a human point of view.' Now all the language about conflicting perceptions comes back into view. Because of the cross, Christians see things differently. They simply do not think, perceive, assess, judge in the way they did before. The crucial case for this change of perception comes in v. 16b: even if they once viewed Christ 'from a human point of view' (as a common criminal, or perhaps a fool), they no longer see him in that way. Here it becomes clear why Christians look to the heart rather than the face, and even why they see the cross itself differently (see 1 Cor. 1.18, 24).

Particularly given the stress on the individual in Western Christianity, the question might arise whether Paul here refers to some private experience that the individual savours. Is this, to put it crudely, an early Christian form of New Age thought, in which what is valued is the individual's personal growth and enriching experience? The final verse in the lection should silence any such responses.To say that there is a 'new creation', that 'everything old has passed away', that 'everything has become new' is to locate the individual's experience in a context as large as the cosmos itself.

The verses that follow further locate this experience of changed perceptions, even new creation, in the action of God: 'All this is from God, who reconciled us to himself through Christ.' God's action of sending Christ, thereby reconciling human beings to himself, is the objective act that results in a change in human perception.

Christians experience a radical change in their way of thinking, a change tantamount to a 'new creation'. When Paul makes this observation, he certainly acknowledges a personal, subjective experience. That comment about experience, however, stands between two unequivocal statements about the origin of this new experience. If Christians have new eyes, it is because and only because of the death of Christ on the cross, a death that includes them and simultaneously grants them new life (5.14–15). If Christians have new eyes, it is because God has reached out to them, initiating reconciliation, sending Christ as the agent of that reconciliation, and establishing ambassadors of that reconciliation. The new vision comes because the eyes are a gift. BG

Mark 4.26–34

It is likely that Mark would like us to read this passage only in the light of the long allegory about the sower and the seed in 4.1–20, and especially vv. 10–12. Those verses tell us what Mark means by parables and make clear the great importance he gives to them. 'To those outside, everything comes in *parables*' (v. 11). *Parabolē*, literally 'comparison', seems to carry a range of senses similar to the Hebrew *mashal*: pithy saying (so vv. 21–25); allegorical story (so vv. 1–20, complete with explanation; the only example of such a story in Mark apart from 12.1–12); and riddle.

It is this last sense that seems to dominate (though 12.1, 12?) Mark's use of the word, even when apparently combined with other literary forms, like the allegory here. It is almost certainly this meaning in v. 11 – and it carries over into the picture-stories in vv. 26–33. Also, it makes sense of v. 34; though what follows in the rest of the Gospel shows that the disciples absorbed little of Jesus' explanations, cf. e.g. 6.52; 8.14–17, 27–33. (Matthew and Luke took a more obviously useful view of what parables are for, and tended to adjust Mark accordingly; they are for enlightening people, as common sense indicates, plain tales designed to hit you between the eyes.) For Mark, people's rejection of the 'secret of the kingdom of God' (v. 11) raises a profound difficulty. Why should they do it? It must surely be because, for his own inscrutable reasons, God means it so; and Isa. 6.9–10 told it to us.

So what we call the 'Parable of the Sower' seems to be a crucial passage in Mark, helping us to fathom the whole mystery of Jesus' success and failure – as they are before the world and for God. It is a passage whose ramifications can be traced throughout the book; and, as one study puts it, the good news itself is, for Mark, a riddle or mystery (a *parabolē*) whose depths we must plumb – if it is 'given' to us to do so. Even more clearly, a grasp of vv. 1–20 is necessary for seeing the bearing of our present passage.

The good news is the kingdom of God (cf. 1.14–15) and the two stories in vv. 26–33 emphasize its twin qualities of mysterious hiddenness and assured future. We cannot tell how (and in Mark we never really shall), but the harvest will assuredly come, the vast growth will take place. It prepares us for the assurance of the Galilee 'seeing' that so cryptically lightens even the passion (14.28; 16.7). Hiddenness is not the last word and openness will surely follow (vv. 21–23). So Mark plumbs the 'mystery' of faith, which some receive and others do not – on which we are now inclined to consult the sociologist. Mark is less inclined to be content with what people say; see 8.27–33; 14.29–31. LH

Proper 7

(Sunday between 19 and 25 June inclusive, if after Trinity Sunday)

1 Samuel 17.(1a, 4–11, 19–23), 32–49 or 1 Samuel 17.57—18.5, 10–16 or Job 38.1–11; 2 Corinthians 6.1–13; Mark 4.35–41

1 Samuel 17.(1a, 4–11, 19–23), 32–49

An earlier, less hurried generation was able to savour the build-up of stories at length. In effect all 58 verses of 1 Samuel 17 are one story, telling of Philistine domination of Israel, and the mockery of Saul and the Israelites by their giant champion. We all know his name, Goliath, though in most of the story he is actually anonymous, simply called 'the Philistine'. Perhaps this anonymity is due to the name being given only at a late stage in the tradition, and the name Goliath may have been 'borrowed' from a different episode found in 2 Sam. 21.19. It is also possible that the namelessness is intended to belittle anyone who challenged the Lord's army; such a one is not even worthy to be given a name.

The greater part of the chapter is devoted to the build-up of dramatic tension: the inability of Saul and the Israelites to find anyone who could resist the Philistine giant; the apparently chance arrival of David on the scene, with some cheeses for his brothers (v. 18, not included in our selection of verses); the irritation of David's oldest brother at the lad's presumption. The account of the confrontation is also superbly told; no doubt it was customary for fighting men to taunt one another, and point out their opponent's inadequacies (politicians and sportsmen continue that tradition), but at last all the preliminaries are over, and in one dramatic verse the deed is done; David's slingstone brings the Philistine crashing to the ground.

By all means feel free to read a variety of moral lessons into this story, of the overcoming of powerful evil and the like. Do not overlook, however, the sheer skill of the story-teller. Not much biblical material still resonates in the contemporary world, but the image of David and Goliath certainly does. Treasure the story for its own sake. RC

1 Samuel 17.57—18.5, 10–16

David has killed the Philistine giant; now he is introduced to Saul and his court. The literal-minded will find a problem here, for according to a different tradition David was already well known to Saul, and had become his armour-bearer, and Saul 'loved him greatly' (16.21). The biblical editors were quite content to set down side by side two apparently irreconcilable accounts of the rise of David to a position in the royal service.

The picture of David's introduction to the court has both positive and negative elements. On the positive side we are alerted to David's alliance with the king's son Jonathan, a linkage that will be important in the stories that follow. But David's skill and success bring out negative reactions also; in the verses omitted from our reading (18.6–9) we hear how David was more highly esteemed in popular opinion than Saul. So Saul becomes jealous of David, and is pictured as trying to kill him. Much of the remainder of 1 Samuel is devoted to this story of rivalry. Saul both admires David and sees in him a threat to his own position. It is striking that this development in Saul's character is here (v. 10) specifically attributed to 'an evil spirit from God'. In the writer's eyes, human weakness and divine judgement are inextricably bound together.

It is important to remember, both in our present reading and in the fascinating story that develops in subsequent chapters, that the story is told from David's point of view. It would have been perfectly possible to tell the story in terms of a vassal rebelling against his legitimate master, but that aspect is never brought out. From the point of view of the story-teller Saul's reign ended in ignominious failure, whereas David succeeded and became the chosen vessel of God. RC

Job 38.1–11

The climax of the book of Job is the reply of the Lord (YHWH – the first time the name has been used in Job since ch. 2), who speaks from the whirlwind. It deserves close reading. In the first place it is in no sense an answer to the questions that Job has posed during his defence. Second, although God says that he will question and Job will answer, it is clear from the outset that Job will be quite unable to deal with the questions. He was clearly not in existence when God laid the foundation of the earth, and can therefore know nothing of what went into this process. Whether because he is unable to answer, or because he is given no opportunity to answer, Job remains silent until 42.2, where he confesses his complete submission to God's power and knowledge. It is also to be noted that the highest example of human speculative probing into the meaning and injustices of life in Job are described as darkening counsel by words without knowledge.

There are many charming touches in this passage and elsewhere in Job 38—41 regarding the origin and organization of the created order. In vv. 8–10 the sea is described as bursting from the womb, and clouds and darkness are its clothes at birth. Yet the dangerous potential of water is recognized, as the sea is shut behind doors, and limits to its encroachments are prescribed. Another charming picture is that of heavenly rejoicing when the cornerstone of the structure that would support earth was laid (v. 7).

Is there no point in the human quest for knowledge? Must we ultimately passively submit to the divine will? This is not the message of Job. God judges that Job has spoken what is right (42.7) in his railings and fulminations about God's apparent unfair and even malicious treatment of him. The point of chs. 38—41 is to say that humans are not able to see things from God's standpoint. They would not be able to make any sense of reality even if they could. This means that while the human quest for knowledge and for answers to the most perplexing questions of human existence must never be discouraged, humans must never forget that they represent a tiny speck in an immeasurable universe; and that God deals compassionately with humans in spite of their inhumanity to each other. JR

2 Corinthians 6.1–13

Throughout 2 Corinthians the apostle is having to defend his ministry. This passage follows a powerful reference to his ministry of reconciliation rooted in the reconciliation of the world that God was achieving in Christ. To call himself and them co-workers with God (cf. 1 Cor. 3.9) seems bold, but it is all God's gift or 'grace' and Paul's comment on his quotation from Isa. 49.8 shows how he sees them all caught up in God's work of salvation. One might compare this with what Jesus says at Matt. 13.16f. par. Luke 10.23f. or at Luke 4.21 – and contrast it with the perspective of Luke for whom the presence of Jesus in his ministry 'today' has become yesterday. For Paul the presence of Jesus is as real in his own time as in Jesus' ministry, and his own apostolic work is part and parcel of God's saving revelation in Christ. There is no question of God's gracious initiative being downplayed or anyone earning their salvation, least of all the former persecutor himself

However, the significance of the Christian ministry is also given due weight, and obstacles to its functioning properly are to be removed. The validity of Paul's ministry, as an apostle of the crucified Lord, may be seen in the hardship he endures and by the Christian character that shines through it all. In a highly rhetorical passage he describes its ups and downs, the truth of it in God's eyes and the false slanders that come its way, the dialectic of dying and living that reflects the cross and resurrection of Jesus. In Paul's mighty crescendo one may sense the power of God breaking through the weakness and humiliations of the apostolic ministry, summed up in the paradox of 'having nothing and yet possessing everything'. Paul has opened his heart to the Corinthians and implores them to do the same. His concern that the ministry be not blamed (v. 3) provides a useful rule for clergy in a media-hungry generation (cf. Matt. 18.6f.), and is applicable to the nonsense perpetrated by the institution no less than to the occasional idiocies of its office-bearers. His account of the marks of an apostle (the plural of v. 4 includes others than himself) should humble them – and elate. Twenty-eight words or phrases describe his ministry in vv. 4–10, moving into a crescendo of paradoxes and a glorious climax best translated by Alan Dale in *New World*. One senses the tide of feeling rising. It is how Paul says it as much as what he says that makes an impact, but the rhetoric would be worthless without the apostolic life that stands behind it. The power of the gospel is from God, but its credibility owes much to its ministers. The apostle's expression of love for his congregation and his final plea for understanding and generosity have been echoed through centuries of Christian ministry. RM

Mark 4.35–41

The early part of Mark's Gospel relates in dramatic ways the in-breaking of God's reign in the life and actions of Jesus. The statement in Mark 1.14–15 of Jesus' preaching in Galilee ('The time is fulfilled, and the kingdom of God has come near') sets the agenda for the rehearsal of the incidents of his ministry that follow in the narrative. The section that begins at 4.35 and continues through 6.6 contains four extraordinary deeds (the calming of the storm, the healings of the Gerasene demoniac and the woman with a flow of blood, and the raising of Jairus' daughter), followed by a response to these deeds by the citizens in Jesus' home town. In the unfolding of the story, the reader begins to get a sense of what it means that 'the kingdom of God has come near'.

The Gospel lection for this Sunday confronts us with the astounding event of the stilling of the winds and sea (4.35–41). The event is so remarkable that it is easy to get caught up in the interesting but not very fruitful question of whether, and how, Jesus did it. Historical probes are not totally unimportant, but going behind the text to question or verify the happening tends to divert the reader from the text itself and what it says. What has the preacher really accomplished if they convince a congregation that the stilling really happened, or that there is a rational explanation for the phenomenon, or that the story is a pious fraud? Better to concentrate on the meaning of the story in its context.

The incident takes on added meaning in the recognition that the sea symbolizes throughout the Old Testament the abode of chaos. Repeatedly in the psalms God is praised as the One who 'divided the sea by your might' and 'broke the heads of the dragons in the waters' (Ps. 74.13; see Job 38.8–11). God's power at the time of the exodus from Egypt is described as a rebuke of the sea and a control of the waters (Pss. 106.9; 114). Thus, when Jesus calms the storm it is not merely a brute demonstration of power over nature, but a redemptive act in which the chaotic forces of the sea, like the demons, are 'rebuked' (Mark 4.39). The miracle has a purpose in the rescue of disciples from fear and disorder.

With this recognition, a number of details of the narrative, including Jesus' dialogue with the disciples, make good sense. First, the trip at night across the sea was Jesus' plan (v. 35). This was not a diversion hatched up by the disciples to have a leisurely time with their leader away from the pressures of the crowd. Jesus took the initiative, and the disciples went along at his direction. They had every reason to blame him when the weather changed. After all, the journey was his idea.

Second, the narrator wants us to know that the squall was frightful. Verse 37 provides a picture of a boat in great distress, 'already being swamped'. The anguish of the disciples, then, was not ill-founded. They were not overreacting when they awakened Jesus with the frantic cry, 'Do you not care that we are perishing?' Their situation was desperate, and they turned to the one who brought them on this trip in the first place.

Third, Jesus' sleep is revealing. His own trust in God brings remarkable peace, even in the face of the storm, and contrasts dramatically with the panic of the disciples at the chaos of the sea. His sleeping while the disciples fret is reminiscent of the scene, later, in Gethsemane when the situation is reversed – Jesus frets and the disciples sleep (14.32–41). There is a time for fretting and a time for sleep.

Fourth, it is difficult to type the disciples in light of their words and actions. Jesus' only words to them carry a gentle criticism (4.40). Their panic shows that they have not yet reached a point of profound trust. Though they have received special instructions from Jesus himself (v. 34), they are still asking, 'Who is this?' At the same time, they are awe-struck by what Jesus has done. They tremble with the fear appropriate to those who have been in the presence of God's Son, and at least pose the critical question.

Investigating the details of the narrative leads one to the conclusion that the story recognizes those times in the life of the Church when it is threatened by the forces of chaos and confusion, forces that turn out to be no match for the reign of God present in the person of Jesus. Certainly the account of the incident found in Matthew's narrative (Matt. 8.23–27) has moved clearly in such a direction – a story of fearful disciples ('you of little faith') and the calming and reassuring Jesus. But the stories present us not merely with the presence of Jesus, who shares our predicament amid the storms of life, but with the power of Jesus,who can do something about the storms. The text confronts us not so much with a strategy for coping, as with a promise of salvation. CC

Proper 8

(Sunday between 26 June and 2 July inclusive)

2 Samuel 1.1, 17–27 or Wisdom of Solomon 1.13–15; 2.23–24; 2 Corinthians 8.7–15; Mark 5.21–43

2 Samuel 1.1, 17–27

The previous reading in this sequence showed David just entering Saul's service. Now Saul is dead, killed in the battle against the Philistines on Mount Gilboa. David, through actions which some (though not the biblical writer) might consider treacherous, had not been involved in that battle. Indeed he had been acting as a vassal to the Philistines, but they feared that he might not be loyal in a close fight, and so had not used him and his followers in the battle. Some will see in this the literary skill of the compiler, maintaining the tension to the end of the story of Saul; others will see a closer reflection of the political intrigues of a divided country. Historically, Israel and the Philistines may not have been two such implacably opposed forces as the biblical story implies. Probably they were two groups with much in common, struggling for control of the land. David will not have been the only one who supported both sides at different times.

However that may be, news is brought to David of the death of Saul and of his son (and David's companion) Jonathan. David's first act had been to have the messenger killed, but in our passage the mood quickly changes, and we have this wonderful lament, one of the most moving poems in the whole Bible. In its immediate context it enables the narrator to end the story of Saul in a positive way. His weaknesses have been described; here his achievements are pictured in a way that also presents David, once his vassal and for a long time his rival, in very generous terms.

Though specifically applied to Saul and Jonathan, its language of mourning can be applied much more widely. (I personally have a vivid memory that when I heard, one Sunday morning a few years ago, of the death of Diana, Princess of Wales, it seemed natural to read this passage instead of the appointed lesson at the service I was to take that day; and the congregation appreciated it greatly.) Traditional biblical phraseology is less familiar than once it was, but many phrases from this poem are still occasionally found in wider usage. ('How are the mighty fallen'; 'Tell it not in Gath' and so on.) If you are looking for biblical material by which to express grief for a death, various psalms are appropriate for close friends; but for a more public figure the pathos here is incomparable. RC

Wisdom of Solomon 1.13–15; 2.23–24

Verses 13–15 are part of a poem that begins in v. 12 with a warning against people bringing about their own death by the errors of their ways. This introductory verse is necessary, for without it the statement that God did not make death (v. 13) becomes problematic. Death as the natural end to biological life is an inescapable part of human existence, and as such is part of the created order. What God did not make, and what he does not desire, is death in the sense of life lived in opposition to or ignorance of, life-giving wisdom. The terms 'life' and 'death' in this passage, therefore, mean more than bare physical existence. Similarly, the word 'exist' in 14b has more to do with the quality than the mere fact of existence. The positive side of God's creative acts (which is probably how the NRSV 'generative forces' is to be understood) is emphasized. The whole purpose of bringing things into being was so that they should be positive and enjoyable. Hades, a shadowy and miserable realm, has, or should have, no place in earth. In v. 15 there is a distinctly Jewish slant on belief in immortality. Humans are not immortal simply by being human. It is righteousness that is immortal, and human immortality cannot be conceived or expected apart from participation in righteousness.

Verses 23–24 of ch. 2 are again a fragment plucked from a larger context. This begins with a condemnation of the wicked who persecuted the righteous (2.12–20), because their understanding of the nature of God and reality was at fault (2.21–22). They were challenged by goodness, which called into question their pessimistic and cynical view of the world. The truth is that in spite of the existence of physical death, God's purpose in creation was to endow humankind with a mode of being that, in fellowship with God, would endure beyond physical death. This possibility, granted to mere humans, aroused the envy of the devil, through whom death in the sense of belonging to the realm of evil, entered the world.

The text takes it for granted that readers will be familiar with the existence of the devil and of how death entered the world. We have here, in fact, an interpretation of Gen. 3 in which, under the influence of the dualism that became increasingly a feature of later Judaism, the serpent is identified with the devil. In Gen. 3 the serpent is condemned to go on its belly as one of God's creatures. In later interpretation it has become the ruler of a realm opposed to God. This development is designed to make sense of an ambiguous world in which evil is all too apparent and powerful. The Wisdom of Solomon insists, however, that what is seen is not the clue to what is real. It unequivocally affirms the goodness of God, and of the will of the creator to enjoy fellowship with humankind, such that evil and death ultimately lose their power to spoil and harm. JR

2 Corinthians 8.7–15

2 Cor. 8 and 9 may originally have been separate notes. Both chapters advance Paul's project, already discussed in 1 Cor. 16.1–4, of raising money for the Jerusalem church. Here he describes this 'collection' (1 Cor. 16.1) in spiritual terms that

express the givers' dispositions, rather than talking cash. It might have been part of the agreement at the Jerusalem meeting (Gal. 2.10) and we hear more about it at Rom. 15.25–28 on the eve of its delivery. Its importance to Paul as a sign of the acceptance by Jerusalem of his Gentile mission and the Gentiles' membership in God's now expanded people is plain, but the silence of Acts 21 (despite a mention at Acts 24.17) is ominous.

Paul's difficulties in eliciting funds from his congregation have a certain resonance and add interest to his rhetorical strategies. He tries to motivate the Corinthians by referring to the generosity of poorer churches in Macedonia, presumably Philippi and Thessalonica, and to their relationship with Titus (vv. 1–6). Here he appeals to their own spiritual self-consciousness (v. 7), well documented in 1 Corinthians, and later (9.4) he will hint at the shame they would suffer if they did not match the Macedonians' generosity. Giving is voluntary, but Paul makes it plain that the authenticity of their Christianity is at stake in this sign of love, increasing the moral pressure by referring to the incarnation itself (v. 9). His appeal to the self-impoverishment of Jesus Christ in the self-abnegation of his incarnation is reminiscent of the Christ-hymn in Phil. 2.6–11 which like this passage probably speaks of the incarnation of a heavenly being, but 2 Cor. 8.9 speaks also of the saving benefits of the incarnation in terms that echo what Paul said a little earlier (6.10) about the benefits (to them) of his own ministry.

The motif of Christ becoming what we are in order to make us what he is (2 Cor. 5.21 as well as here) would soon be taken up in a different form by Irenaeus and the Greek Fathers to speak of salvation through human nature being divinized. Here there is no question of 'natures', only a rhetorical and mythological flourish which motivates the appeal for generosity. Paul's embarrassment about asking for money, even where it is not for himself, is appropriate in an age when begging was (as it still is) the hallmark of religious charlatans. But the gospel implies giving, and that regardless of any financial incompetence which may (or may not) explain the mother church's needs. Despite the christological motif he does not ask for a sacrificial giving that would impoverish them (such as Jesus demanded of some) but the rational, Hellenistic principle of equalization or fairness involving redistribution. His text from Exodus (16.18) confirms that this will have reasonable results, and even in his next chapter – where scriptural allusions become more frequent, and the prayers of those the Corinthians help are a further argument – Paul remains reasonable and persuasive. All the terms in which Paul speaks of financial matters invite his readers to think of their giving not as a tax, nor as buying God's favour, but as a sign of their love and so of the authenticity of the Christian fellowship of churches. RM

Mark 5.21–43

This passage is an example of what commentators sometimes refer to as a 'Marcan sandwich': two stories have been brought together so that one is placed in between the two parts of the other. Mark seems to have done this half a dozen times in his book. An obvious example is the cursing of the fig tree and the cleansing of the temple in ch. 11. The two parts are always related to one another in such a way that one story throws light on the meaning of the other.

In the case of Jairus' daughter and the woman with the haemorrhages, both are female and in both stories the figure 12 plays some part. Also, both are excluded from society, the woman according to the Law (Lev. 15.19–30), the girl by the fact of death; in both parts there are references to fear and to faith. There is also an element of contrast: the woman herself seeks her cure, whereas the girl's father seeks it for his daughter.

It would almost certainly be a mistake to think that Mark believed that the girl was not literally dead but only asleep, and thus that no miracle was involved. Had that been Mark's view, he would not have told the story. He tells it in order to bring those who are hearing his Gospel, that is being read to them, into a specific relationship with Jesus; that is, he is the one who saves them from all kinds of evil, everything that separates people from one another, including the last enemy, death. The good news that Mark wants his congregation to hear is to do with someone who can be known by his deeds even more than by his words. (Matthew and Luke took the other view and devoted more space in their books to the teaching of Jesus, of which Mark records much less.)

Jesus is shown as the healer who has more power than doctors (and makes no charge for his treatment) and frees us from mortality. The presence of such a person could well provoke fear and amazement, which have no positive value. Mark's purpose is to promote faith in Jesus and nothing else. This may be the reason for the final remark: the strict instructions not to let anyone know about the raising of the girl; miracles outside the context of the gospel and of faith in the good news have no effect except to frighten and to fascinate. JF

Proper 9

(Sunday between 3 and 9 July inclusive)

2 Samuel 5.1–5, 9–10 or Ezekiel 2.1–5; 2 Corinthians 12.2–10; Mark 6.1–13

2 Samuel 5.1–5, 9–10

In tradition David and his successors are strongly associated with Jerusalem, and here we have the story of how he came to be established as king there. He is pictured as having ruled Judah at Hebron for seven years. Hebron is in the far south of the land, well away from the main centre of Israel, which was much further north, and in this story we are told that it was the people of Israel themselves ('all the tribes of Israel') who came to David with the request that he become their ruler.

It is not known why Jerusalem should have been singled out as the appropriate capital. In the Hebrew Bible its previous inhabitants are called 'Jebusites', but we have no definite knowledge of them from any other source. Jerusalem was certainly a more convenient spot from which to rule over both north and south, and it is possible that having been a Jebusite stronghold made it in a sense independent of both north and south and thus acceptable to both. We may call it David's 'capital', and the last verse of our passage may speak of David becoming 'greater and greater', but this should not mislead us into supposing that it was a 'city' in any modern sense of the term. Its inhabitants will have been numbered in hundreds, and it was in reality little more than an easily defensible fortress. The reference to 'the Millo' in v. 9 is not very clear, but the word might mean 'filling', and could refer to the steep slopes, which formed a kind of defensive barricade.

Whatever the details of its original capture, the symbolic importance of Jerusalem for something like 3,000 years has been enormous. Whether one turns to a Christian hymnbook, or to the TV news, it is likely that there will soon be a reference to Jerusalem. We may be thankful that, since the time of the Crusades, Christians have been content to 'spiritualize' Jerusalem, for they are among the least attractive episodes in Christian history. Now 'Jerusalem the golden' and other such expressions from Christian hymns do not refer to any earthly city. But the importance of the earthly city for both Muslims and Jews means that tensions in that part of the Middle East are likely to be with us for a long time to come. RC

Ezekiel 2.1–5

The selected passage actually begins with a phrase taken from 1.1, 'The heavens were opened and I saw visions of God', which is then combined with the concluding words of 1.28 with the NRSV 'it' altered to 'this' in the lectionary version. The passage thus implies the chariot vision of God so vividly described in ch. 1, which leads to the prophet falling prostrate (1.28). It is significant of the way in which the mystery of divine communication is presented in the passage that the prophet hears someone unspecified speaking (the Hebrew simply has 'I heard a voice speaking'). The address to him, 'mortal' (NRSV margin gives the literal Hebrew 'son of man') emphasizes that the prophet is a mere human, as opposed to the transcendent beings he has witnessed in his vision of the chariot and its four living creatures. Yet this mere human is to carry out the commission of the living God whose glory Ezekiel has glimpsed. The spirit that comes into him is probably best understood as that enabling power granted to God's special servants (cf. Judg. 11.29).

The declaration that God is sending Ezekiel to the people of Israel gives him the status of ambassador, and recalls the messenger formula. This was the procedure whereby a king spoke a message for another king in the presence of a messenger, who then journeyed to the other king and repeated the message to him verbatim, beginning 'thus says the king of . . .' In the case of God, the message begins 'thus says the Lord GOD' (v. 4).

Ezekiel's task may seem hopeless from the outset. The people throughout their history have rebelled against God and been impudent and stubborn (vv. 3–4). Why is God sending yet another prophet? It may be in order to underline the people's continuing guilt. It may be to give them no excuse for their guilt, for they will not be able to deny that there has been a prophet among them (v. 5). Most likely, however, Ezekiel's commission derives from the fact that however wayward Israel has been, God will not give up on them. Ezekiel's first task, until he heard the news of Jerusalem's destruction (Ezek. 33.21), was to announce impending judgement. Thereafter he was able to deliver a message of hope and restoration. JR

2 Corinthians 12.2–10

Exegetical imaginations occasionally run out of control with this passage. Attempts to coordinate Paul's comments about the 'third heaven' with biographical details gleaned from elsewhere in his letters produce accounts that are interesting if not convincing. Speculation about Paul's 'thorn in the flesh' ranges wildly from physical to psychological causes and even to marital distress. Along the way, unfortunately, the trees of such fanciful reconstructions obscure the forests of the letter's larger context.

Attention to context here is essential, or the passage will remain a collection of enigmas. In 2 Cor. 10—13, Paul constructs a sharp defence of his ministry by waging an equally sharp attack on some other Christian preachers who have made their way to Corinth. Portions of 1 Corinthians and preceding sections of 2 Corinthians already demonstrate that Paul's authority at Corinth is an unstable commodity, but here the situation is desperate. The so-called 'super-apostles' (11.5) have attacked Paul on the ground that he does not sufficiently exhibit the powers appropriate to an apostle. He does not accomplish great deeds, he has not been the recipient of marvellous spiritual experiences, and he accomplishes no miracles. If he had such achievements, he would surely boast of them.

In response to these charges, Paul begins in 11.16 what is customarily referred to as his 'fool's speech', a section of the letter in which he parodies his opponents. While he refuses to play their game of boasting about his real accomplishments, he does humour the Corinthians' need for apostolic boasting by boasting of things that are the mirror image of their expectations. Instead of boasting of things that show his strength and power, he boasts of those that demonstrate his weakness and vulnerability.

When Paul speaks of 'a person in Christ', he almost certainly refers to himself (12.2). The remainder of the discussion of this vision makes little sense if Paul is not the recipient of it. Throughout this tiny narrative, Paul both tells of the vision and simultaneously distances himself from it, and referring to himself in the third person may serve to reinforce the attitude toward visions that he wishes to inculcate. Similarly, when Paul twice comments 'whether in the body or out of the body I do not know; God knows', he attributes both the cause of this experience and its proper understanding to God alone.

Verses 5–7a reinforce Paul's reluctance about boasting. Although he could boast about himself, he insists that he will not do so (again with tongue in cheek). He will speak only of others or only of his weaknesses.

Verses 7b–9a move from 'boasting' about visions to 'boasting' about great deeds. Lest Paul become too elated with his own achievements, God gave him 'a thorn', 'a messenger of Satan'. Whatever particular malady or difficulty this 'thorn' might be is utterly insignificant, because the question is whether Paul can prevail over it or persuade God to do so on his behalf. Rather than boasting of his powerful ability to work wonders, Paul recalls three occasions on which he prayed for relief and three occasions on which his request was denied. If the scene depicted in vv. 1–4 is an inverted vision, this is an inverted miracle.

What response did the Corinthians make to Paul's dramatic, even outrageous, comments? Virtually no evidence exists that permits a historical answer to that question. As much as it is attractive to imagine that they saw the error of their judgement and adopted Paul's view of things, the arguments of Paul's detractors were strong ones. The arguments continue to be strong, even if not necessarily couched in terms of healings and visions. How are congregations and ministers assessed if not in terms of their powers, powers to attract quantities of people and quantities of money? That ongoing phenomenon may suggest that the question with which Paul and the Corinthians are struggling in this section of 2 Corinthians is not a question for only one moment in Christian history, but for every moment.

The closing lines of this passage sound themes that are familiar from 2 Cor. 1—9. Paul does not need a miraculous resolution of his difficulty, whatever its nature, because the Lord said, 'My grace is sufficient for you, for power is made perfect in weakness' (12.9). This is not a glorification of weakness as such or for its own sake, but because in weakness 'the power of Christ' dwells in Paul. Paul's very weakness is transformed into strength (v. 10).

An earlier lection from 2 Corinthians drew attention to the integral relationship Paul sees between the apostle and the congregation (see Proper 7 on 2 Cor. 6.1–13).

Here the theological undergirding of that relationship becomes clear. Paul, like the Corinthians and all believers, experiences the life of Christ in his own person. The 'body of Christ' imagery of 1 Cor. 12.12–31 draws on this same understanding. Because of the deep and abiding connection between the apostle and Christ, Paul is able to see his own weaknesses as instances in which the strength of the gospel can be manifested. BG

Mark 6.1–13

The choice of the parameters of the Gospel lesson for this Sunday seems unusual. The passage is composed of two fairly discrete sections. In most structural outlines Mark 6.1–6a serves as the conclusion to a section that has highlighted not only Jesus' mighty works but also the responses to him by particular individuals and groups. Mark 6.6b–13, in relating the call and sending out of the disciples, introduces a new section in which the ministry of Jesus moves out beyond Galilee and includes Gentiles as well as Jews. The preacher may want to select one or the other of the two sections as the text for the sermon.

The sceptical rejection of Jesus by the people of his home town (vv. 1–6a) provides a fitting ending to the earlier section of the Gospel. On the one hand, the Pharisees, offended by Jesus' activities on the sabbath, 'conspired with the Herodians against him, how to destroy him' (3.6). Jesus' family, troubled by his behaviour, 'went out to restrain him' (3.21). The scribes from Jerusalem accused him of operating as an agent of Beelzebul (3.22). On the other hand, the woman with a 12-year haemorrhage (5.34) and Jairus, the leader of the synagogue, demonstrate remarkable faith in Jesus, even in the face of detractors. Some seed fell along the path or on rocky ground or among the thorns, but some fell on good soil and bore fruit.

Two questions arise with this text. First, why do Jesus' fellow townspeople reject him? They are initially astonished at his teaching in the synagogue, but then begin to wonder how all this could come from the mouth of Mary's boy, the one with whom they had grown up. Then they reject him. The Greek verb translated 'took offence' (6.3) is used elsewhere in Mark to depict those who begin but then fall away (4.17), those who start walking but then stumble (9.42–48), those who become deserters (14.27–29).

The defection of the Nazareth citizens is obviously linked to Jesus' roots. Their expectations preclude the possibility that he could be anything more than a home-town lad who is putting on airs. Their preconceived notions prevent their entertaining the thought that Jesus could be the embodiment of God's promised rule. And so another group who could, like Jesus' family, be called insiders turn out to be outsiders.

It is the same old story at the heart of many rejections of Jesus. When measured by the criteria set by the world as to what a religious leader worth his salt ought to be, he simply does not stand up well. He is not successful enough or influential enough or prestigious enough to merit a wholehearted commitment. His invasive presence is forestalled by the carefully constructed preconceptions that enable people to dismiss him.

The second question that arises is: Does the story provide a clear statement about the necessity of faith as a precondition to Jesus' doing mighty works? Can God act only when we pray for it and expect it to happen? That appears to be the point of 6.5–6 and could be supported by the many miracle stories in which the faith of the recipient is mentioned *prior to* Jesus' action; for example, the leper (1.40–41), the paralytic (2.5), the woman with haemorrhaging (5.28, 34), and Jairus (5.22–23). The prominent exceptions however, such as the exorcisms, prevent an unambiguous answer to the question, and perhaps suggest that the rejection at Nazareth is not primarily intended to provide a solution to the relation of faith and miracle. It seems more to serve as a dramatic contrast to the stories of other characters in need who simply trust Jesus' power and receive his help.

The second section of the lection (6.6b–13) describes the third call of the disciples (1.16–20; 3.13–19) and their mission in the surrounding villages. They are empowered and instructed by Jesus and apparently carry on a successful campaign, consisting of preaching, healing and exorcism.

Three features of the commissioning are particularly instructive. First, the disciples are authorized by Jesus (6.7). At the very heart of their mission lies a call of Jesus to be engaged in just this venture. This means that not only do they derive their direction from him, but also he gives them power to do the same mighty works that he has done. By his decision and not theirs, they become the extension of his ministry.

The point is worth repeating regularly in most congregations. Before the Church is a voluntary organization it is a community constituted by the call and commission of Christ. Only then is it able to fulfil its mandate to preach and heal in the name of Jesus.

Second, Jesus' instructions call for lean, unencumbered disciples. The order to dispense with extra food and clothes and money is to be construed as a demand not for asceticism, but for simplicity. Travelling light has its dividends. The traveller is free from bearing unnecessary burdens and is not tempted to turn the journey into a venture for profit. Again, the point is worth reflection in these days when the Church faces its own loss of status and power and struggles to know how to position itself for the future.

Third, the reality of rejection must be taken seriously. The shaking off the dust from the sandals may be a visible 'testimony' to just how significant such a rejection is, done in the hope that a change of mind may yet taken place. In any event, the disciples do not go with the promise that every listener of their sermons will repent. They should be neither surprised nor discouraged when doors are slammed in their faces. After all, Jesus has received just such a response from religious officials, from the citizens of his home town, and even from his family. CC

Proper 10

(Sunday between 10 and 16 July inclusive)

2 Samuel 6.1–5, 12b–19 or Amos 7.7–15; Ephesians 1.3–14; Mark 6.14–29

2 Samuel 6.1–5, 12b–19

Ancient Israel seems to have known two contexts for the worship of its God. One was a fixed building, the temple. The other was a movable shrine usually described as 'the ark'. (It may be helpful to remember that in Hebrew this is quite a different word from the one used to describe Noah's vessel in the flood.) The exact nature of the movable shrine is not entirely clear, but it was regarded as important in many different biblical traditions. In the Books of Samuel it has not been mentioned since 1 Sam. 7.2, but now it is clearly important for the author of the story of David that he should be associated with the ark. In particular the story of the ark being brought to 'the city of David' (i.e. Jerusalem) provides a further opportunity to stress that David and his line are acceptable to God, whereas the former king, Saul, and his family are rejected. Michal, the daughter of Saul, was one of David's wives, but she takes a negative view of his 'leaping and dancing', and is in turn rejected by David. It might be that she represents a stricter, more 'puritan' approach to worship; more likely this is simply a literary device to emphasize David's acceptability over against the rejection of the house of Saul. It will be for individual readers to decide to what extent they can simply accept the unexamined masculine assumptions of this and many other parts of the biblical narrative; we are told that Michal 'despised David' but never told why. Characteristically no explanation of her reaction is offered; equally characteristically many modern male commentators have blamed Michal for her attitude.

There is another negative aspect to this story, which is hidden by the omission of vv. 6–11. from the prescribed reading. In that section the procession was marred by the death of Uzzah, who is pictured as being struck down and killed because of God's anger. One can understand why this section was omitted, but it is nevertheless important for our full understanding of the biblical picture that God is sometimes presented as dangerous and unpredictable. One of the most difficult problems for religious believers in many traditions is how to maintain a proper balance between picturing a God in dangerous, threatening terms, including an expectation that his followers will also engage in violent behaviour on his behalf; and a God who is so anaemic that it scarcely seems worthwhile to take him seriously. RC

Amos 7.7–15

Verses 7–9 are the third of three visions, each of which indicates imminent and devastating judgement upon the northern kingdom, Israel. In the case of the first two visions, Amos intercedes for the people. 'How can Jacob stand? He is so small!' (7.2, 5). God relents and promises that the indicated judgement will not take place. Whether or not the vision of the plumb line indicates a judgement smaller in scope than those of the first two visions is hard to say. At any rate, it is not followed by an intercession from the prophet. The vision means that God is to establish a standard, a means of measuring behaviour. He will no longer be indifferent to how his people lives.

Verse 9, which restricts the coming judgement to the cultic centres and which makes explicit reference to Jeroboam II (782–747 BC) is an editorial transition to the prose account of the attempt to ban Amos from preaching in the northern kingdom. Whether or not Amos publicly predicted Jeroboam's violent death is uncertain. If he did, the prophecy was unfulfilled because, according to 2 Kings 14.29, Jeroboam died a peaceful death after a reign of 41 years, which saw him restore much of Israel's material greatness. The prophecy of Israel going into exile agrees with Amos 3.11–12 and 4.2–3, and would be sufficient to arouse hostility. It was also fulfilled in the events of 734–721, when the northern kingdom was reduced to nothing by the Assyrian Tiglath-Pileser III.

The attempt of Amaziah to silence Amos leads to a well-known, and much disputed, statement about Amos's relationship to prophets and prophecy. The NRSV margin offers the simple solution, that Amos says in effect, 'I was not a prophet nor a prophet's son; I was a herdsman, and the LORD took me from the flock and said, Go, prophesy.' Although this is attractive, and possibly correct, there is no 'was' in the original Hebrew, and the NRSV text is more faithful to the original. Another solution has presumed that by the word 'prophet' (Hebrew *navi'*), Amos understood someone belonging to a professional guild, and that he wished to dissociate himself from this idea. At the greatest extreme is the suggestion that 'I am no prophet' is a forceful way of saying 'I *am* a prophet'! The view that Amos is dissociating himself from 'professional' prophets can at least be justified by the fact that Amaziah twice used the verb for 'to prophesy' that is directly connected with the word for 'prophet'. Amos is saying, in effect, that he is not doing what Amaziah accused him of, that is, carrying out the normal activity of an institutional prophet. It is as one called unexpectedly by God out of the tasks of daily living that Amos delivers his message of judgement. JR

Ephesians 1.3–14

See Second Sunday of Christmas, pp. 32–34.

Mark 6.14–29

The story of the beheading of John the Baptist is hardly a text one would spontaneously choose for a sermon. Despite the fact that it is an intriguing tale that has been retold through the centuries in various media, its details of violence are too graphic, and its tragic ending leaves little room for good news. Furthermore, it is the only passage of this length in any of the Gospels not immediately focused on Jesus. Yet Matthew (14.1–12) and Mark (6.14–29) both include a detailed account of the incident, and Luke (9.9) at least alludes to it.

What function does the story, with its gory details, have in the broader narrative of Mark's Gospel? The most obvious thing concerns the parallelism between John and Jesus and between Herod and Pilate. John is initially introduced in Mark as the forerunner of Jesus, the messenger who prepares the way of the Lord and baptizes the beloved Son (1.2–11). The narrator dates the beginning of Jesus' public ministry from the arrest of John (1.14). While Luke establishes the connection between John and Jesus through parallel accounts of their conception, birth, naming and childhood development (Luke 1—2), Mark ties the two together through their deaths.

Each innocently suffers at the hands of a vacillating political figure. Herod and Pilate both see good in the accused men brought before them, and left to themselves both would choose freedom over capital punishment. Yet, because of their own weaknesses, both let themselves be trapped by external circumstances and permit a violent death. In both stories disciples come, take the body, and place it in a tomb.

Readers of Mark's narrative already know that a conspiracy to destroy Jesus is under way (3.6). The brutal slaying of John alerts them to the fact that such things happen to righteous people and they have every reason to expect that it will happen to Jesus. Perhaps there is even a hint of Jesus' resurrection in the rumour voiced by Herod himself and spread among the people that Jesus was John-risen-from-the-dead.

The story serves yet another function. It is interjected between the sending out of the disciples on the journey through the surrounding villages (6.6b–13) and their report to Jesus of the successful mission (6.30), another example of Mark's 'sandwiching' technique. In the midst of a positive account of the disciples' exorcisms, healings and preaching comes this jolting description of the slaying of 'a righteous and holy man' (6.20), who had provoked the political authorities by speaking the truth. Not only is the parallel drawn between John and Jesus; it is also drawn between John and the disciples. Just as the account prepares readers for Jesus' coming trials, it also prepares readers for the coming trials of disciples.

Mark's Gospel, much like the letters of Paul, is amazingly realistic about the fortunes of disciples. Even when there is reason for optimism, when exorcisms, healings and effective preaching are taking place, the threat of political and even religious opposition is not far away. Believers should not be too surprised when the declaration of God's judgement and mercy is met with hostility.

In a striking detail in the story, we are told that Herod has a fearful fascination with

John. Though challenged by him for this marriage to his sister-in-law, Herod shields John from his wife's rage. Is he scared of John, or perhaps attracted to his fiery preaching? Who knows? But as is often the case in political contexts, personal respect is easily abandoned when circumstances ('regard for his oaths and for the guests', 6.26) warrant it. Although grieved, Herod orders John's death.

John's tragic end in a sense anticipates Jesus' words spoken to the disciples later at the temple, when they are warned about being dragged before governors and kings and beaten in synagogues for the sake of the gospel (13.9–11). Truth-telling becomes a perilous venture in a world of Herods and Pilates. Even when one has friends in high places, there is little security. CC

Proper 11

(Sunday between 17 and 23 July inclusive)

2 Samuel 7.1–14a or Jeremiah 23.1–6; Ephesians 2.11–22; Mark 6.30–34, 53–56

2 Samuel 7.1–14a

This reading lacks the exciting narrative power of some of the other readings from Samuel, but theologically it is of major importance if we wish to understand the viewpoint of the final editor. In particular it brings out two basic themes.

First, there is the question of where God is to be perceived as dwelling. The usual picture, in the religious traditions of the ancient Near East, was of gods dwelling in particular 'houses' or temples, and in due course that became the norm in Israel also. When we reach the last reading in the present section we shall find a description of the dedication of Solomon's temple (1 Kings 8). But in today's passage, after his initial enthusiasm, which is presumably that of the loyal servant eager to please his master, Nathan warns David not to go ahead with his temple-building plan. The word of God coming to someone at night is a frequent theme of our readings, as we saw with Samuel in 1 Sam. 3 and shall discover again in the reading about Solomon, from 1 Kings 3. This may be a deliberate device linking the chief characters in the story. For the moment, however, we know, and the final editor of the book knew, that Solomon's temple was going to be destroyed, and an important part of his message was that the God whom Israel worshipped was not dependent on the provision of a special building. Here is a question that continues to exercise religious believers today (or should do so): To what extent is God's presence to be linked with particular buildings?

The latter part of our reading introduces another major theme. The Hebrew word *bayith*, like its English translation 'house', can mean either a building or a family, and vv. 11–14a play on this double meaning. God promises a 'house' for David. The last phrase of our reading, 'I will be a father to him and he shall be a son to me' is an expression frequently found in the Old Testament, usually in the context of establishing a covenant between God and the chosen representative. Often the covenant is pictured as being with the whole community, but here and in some psalms the king is the chosen partner (e.g. Ps. 89.3–4). The importance of this covenant with David explains the care shown in the New Testament to emphasize the tradition that Jesus of Nazareth was a descendant of David. RC

Jeremiah 23.1–6

The use of the figure of the shepherd to indicate a king is well-established in the ancient Near East. Some Egyptian pharaohs included the shepherd's crook among the symbols that denoted their royal status. Jeremiah has already criticized shepherds; that is, rulers, in poetic oracles at 10.21 and 22.22, and the present passage in prose may be a reworking of these ideas. At any rate, only vv. 1–2 of ch. 23 probably derive from Jeremiah, with vv. 3–4 and 5–6 constituting two enlargements from later times. There are two ways of understanding vv. 1–2, depending on whether the translation 'concerning' is retained, or whether 'to' is preferred. In the second case there is a direct address to the condemned rulers. Another matter of translation that affects the interpretation is whether to follow the NRSV in v. 1 or to prefer the REB 'who let the sheep of my flock scatter and be lost'. The REB implies negligence, whereas the NRSV conveys the sense of deliberate oppression on the part of the rulers. Again the NRSV 'driven them away' suggests a different image from the REB's 'dispersed'. The NRSV also raises more acutely than REB whether the verbs used are to be confined to the shepherd imagery or whether they have wider reference. Are vv. 1–2 saying that the (or an) exile has already occurred? If they are, then the whole passage will be post-exilic.

Verses 3–4 certainly envisage the exilic or post-exilic situation, with their promise to gather the remnant of the flock 'out of all the lands' where they have been driven. It is noteworthy that this disaster is attributed to the rulers of Judah and Israel, and not to foreign powers.

The opening words of v. 5 'the days are coming' look to the longer-term future. The tree imagery (cf. Isa. 11.1) suggests that the defunct Davidic line will sprout once again. The king provided by God will do all that the condemned shepherds failed to do, and his name will sum up the longed-for situation. The word 'righteousness', which probably looks back to the phrase 'righteous branch', has the active sense of vindication in Hebrew. God's righteousness is what he does to vindicate and uphold what is right. The GNB's 'the LORD is our salvation' gets the flavour of this. JR

Ephesians 2.11–22

The doxological motif in Ephesians makes a sharp turn in this familiar and important passage. Earlier portions of the letter offer praise to God for God's blessings to humankind; there the emphasis falls on God's actions in Jesus Christ and their consequences for the relationship between God and humankind. Believers receive 'every spiritual blessing' (1.3) and the 'riches of his grace' (1.7). In 2.11–22, by contrast, God is praised less for what is conventionally called the 'vertical' result of God's action than for the 'horizontal' result, its consequences for human beings. Three times in this passage the author employs the emphatic pronoun *hymeis* ('you Gentiles' in v. 11; 'you' in v. 13, 'you' in v. 22), which draws attention to the anthropological implications of the doxological motif.

The passage begins with a series of astonishing contrasts between the past of believers and their present. Those 'Gentiles by birth' were formerly uncircumcised, 'without Christ', 'aliens from the commonwealth of Israel', 'strangers to the covenants of promise', 'having no hope', and 'without God in the world'. Each of these characterizations powerfully depicts a situation of alienation and estrangement. In the world of the first century, dominated as it was by the Roman state, being an outsider meant being rootless and isolated. The two references to 'aliens' and 'strangers' play on that need for belonging. Whether or not these Gentile Christians would have agreed with the description of themselves as 'having no hope', the author's depiction of them summons up despair. That despair is only increased by the claim that they were 'without God in the world', a claim that is at the same time objectively impossible (no human being can be without God) and yet subjectively true.

By contrast, 'now in Christ' these believers have come near. No longer outsiders, they are part of one new group. They belong to 'one new humanity', 'citizens with the saints and also members of the household of God'. This description reverses the earlier situation almost element for element. Believers no longer exist in alienation from God's people, but have been brought near. They no longer experience the powerlessness and alienation of strangers, but have become full citizens. Moreover, they are part of a household. Like all households, this one confers on its members a certain status; because the household is God's, the status here is unimaginably high.

This dramatic reversal came about because of God's action in Jesus Christ. Ephesians 2.13–14 identifies that action specifically with Christ's death ('by the blood of Christ', 'in his flesh'), complementing the author's earlier reference to the salvific character of Christ's resurrection (1.20). It is Jesus' death that brings down the 'dividing wall, that is, the hostility between [Jew and Gentile]' and that enables the creation of 'one new humanity'.

One question in the ongoing debate regarding Pauline authorship of Ephesians concerns the likelihood of Paul's having thought of Jews and Gentiles becoming a single new humanity (by contrast with the language of grafting Gentiles on to the tree of Israel in Rom. 11.7–24). As important as that question is, it ought not to eclipse the fundamental point; namely, that the dramatic reversal of the Gentiles' situation comes about because, and solely because, of the death of Christ. They did not 'earn' the disappearance of the 'dividing wall', any more than Jews voluntarily opened the 'commonwealth of Israel' to Gentiles. Both events occur as a result of God's initiative.

The final section of this passage abounds with imagery depicting the communal nature of this new humanity. Believers are members of God's household (v. 19), part of 'a holy temple in the Lord' (v. 21), 'a dwelling place for God' (v. 22). All of these images connect believers firmly both with one another as part of the 'one new humanity' and with God. Christ, the 'cornerstone' of this new edifice, provides the crucial link between believers and God.

Much in this passage dramatically insists on the ways in which the new life of believers differs from their old life. Their identity has radically changed. Their alignments and loyalties are new. The destruction of the dividing wall has created a new era. The death of Christ has brought about a new situation for humankind. Nevertheless, at least one element in this passage points toward the continuity of this new situation with what has gone before, and that is the reference in v. 20 to the 'apostles and prophets' as the foundation of God's household. Even the new humanity, in which the categories of Jew and Gentile no longer exist, builds nevertheless on the earlier teaching of the 'apostles and prophets'. The edifice of faith is not simply a new spiritual life, lacking any contact with the past. Those who have gone before form the very foundation of the household.

In the face of a contrast such as the author of Ephesians here depicts, many contemporary Christians would advise that the past be forgotten. 'Put it behind you', 'let it go' would come the admonitions. Here, however, the admonition is one to remembrance. The passage itself begins with a call to remember the life of the past and its alienation (v. 11). This remembrance serves not simply as a kind of intellectual reminder of the past but as a means to thanksgiving, praise and service. After all, those who are now part of God's household must inevitably reflect that status in their actions. CC

Mark 6.30–34, 53–56

The writers of commentaries on the Synoptic Gospels often compare them to jewels in settings: the units of narrative and discourse are the jewels, and the linking passages are the settings. The idea is that the evangelists composed the settings, having received the stories and sayings by means of tradition. It may also be possible to show that later evangelists (Matthew and Luke) made the same distinction and paid closer attention to Mark's traditional material, resetting it in their own ways.

The two paragraphs for this Sunday are both sections of Marcan editorial writing, and the traditional material that he was presenting here has been omitted (i.e. vv. 35–52, the feeding of the 5,000 and the walking on the lake). The lectionary is about to leave Mark, and to use John 6 for the next five Sundays, where there will be the Johannine accounts of the feeding and the crossing of the lake; after which it will return to Mark 7 for Proper 17. It is a surprising procedure, to insert a chapter of one Gospel into the more-or-less continuous reading of another; but, in defence, it must be said that what has been done leaves us with a point to consider that might otherwise have gone unnoticed.

The disciples have returned from their mission and told Jesus what they have done, and he takes them away in order that they may rest. But this becomes impossible. There will be 5,000 to feed, a storm to endure and crowds to be healed. The crowd is not a menace to Jesus; he has compassion on them, because they are like Israel in the past: sheep without a shepherd (Num. 27.17; 1 Kings 22.17; Ezek. 34.5). The situation shows him what his mission is. He feeds them. The reaction of the disciples is the opposite to that of Jesus: 'Send the people off to the farms and villages round about, to buy themselves something to eat' (v. 36).

Mark draws a sharp contrast between Jesus and his chosen followers: patience runs out for them, but not with him. The sick are brought to him from the whole district, and all who touched him were healed. In Mark's Gospel, it is Jesus who is destroyed by his mission; he brings life through dying. And it is the disciples who save their own lives, but do not hear the message about the resurrection (16.7f.). This is the central Marcan paradox: 'Whoever wants to save his life will lose it, but whoever loses his life for my sake and the gospel's will save it' (8.35). JF

Proper 12

(Sunday between 24 and 30 July inclusive)

2 Samuel 11.1–15 or 2 Kings 4.42–44; Ephesians 3.14–21; John 6.1–21

2 Samuel 11.1–15

We saw in our reading last week, from 2 Sam. 7, that God had promised a son to David who would succeed him on the throne. But who was that son to be, for David had several children by different wives? (Polygamy among the rich and powerful is taken for granted and not condemned in the Old Testament.) One of the most gripping stories in the whole Bible can be found as this question of the succession to David is spelt out. The Sunday readings only offer extracts, but try to make time to read 2 Sam. 9—20; once you have started you will find yourself gripped by it, for in sheer drama it far surpasses any TV soap opera.

By the time that our extract begins the scene has been set. The army is away, waging war in Trans-Jordan, against the Ammonites. The army, and thus most of the young men, are out of Jerusalem. But David has not gone with his troops; he has time on his hands. The story of his liaison with Bathsheba follows. Little is said about Bathsheba, save for the reference to her physical beauty. We do not know whether she was caught by surprise, or had deliberately calculated that to bathe where she did was likely to attract the king's attention. As always the story is told from a male viewpoint, and it is made very clear that to David at least the news of her pregnancy was unwelcome.

Bathsheba was a married woman, and so David's first ploy is to have her husband, Uriah, a prominent member of the army (one of the chosen 'Thirty' leaders according to 2 Sam. 23.23–24, 39), come back to Jerusalem. Perhaps if he slept with Bathsheba the child could be passed off as his. But Uriah either suspects something is afoot or is too naive for his own good. And so David compounds his sexual folly by arranging for Uriah to be killed in the fighting.

Next week we shall see some more theological reflections on this story. But the story itself is told in a remarkably neutral way. The actions of the various characters are described without evaluation or criticism. Those who hear or read this story have to make their own decision about the morality of what is described. Some will surely find this to be a great relief; so much religious talk is enclosed in moralizing. The other point that we must notice about this story, and indeed the whole of 2 Sam. 9—20, is the willingness of the story-teller to tell the story without feeling it necessary to put a gloss on David's actions. He may be God's chosen ruler, but in this account of his life he is as liable as any of his subjects to engage in actions that infringe any moral law. RC

2 Kings 4.42–44

To both Elijah (cf. 1 Kings 17.14–16) and Elisha (the present passage) are attributed miracles of multiplication of food. The lectionary has omitted the words 'from Baal-shalishah' before 'bringing' in v. 42, and while the place name will mean nothing to modern worshippers (its actual location is disputed, although many commentators locate it around 12 miles north of Lydda) it is unfortunate that the lectionary has removed the passage from its context.

If it is legitimate to read vv. 42–44 in the context of vv. 38–41, we learn that the prophetic groups over which Elisha presided were being affected by a famine in the land. Although the location of Gilgal (v. 38) is also disputed, the whole passage taken together (i.e. vv. 38–44) can be presumed to indicate that the man from Baal-shalishah had come from an area not affected by famine in order to relieve the prophets. The barley harvest, the earliest of the harvests in ancient Palestine, occurred in late March/early April. The willingness of the man from Baal-shalishah to help is contrasted with the scepticism of Elisha's servant that the help will be of any value (v. 43). Although no miracle is explicitly described in v. 44 it is certainly implied. The miraculous multiplication of food will not be an easy idea for modern readers. What the passage has in common with John 6.9 (the feeding of the 5,000) is that the miracle could not happen without the willingness of someone to go to the trouble of gathering food, and of taking it to where it was needed. That is not such a difficult idea for modern readers. JR

Ephesians 3.14–21

The prayer that stands at the heart of this lection constitutes a significant challenge for the preacher. While the language of the prayer is powerful and moving, it begins with a depiction of God that many contemporary Christians will find problematic or even offensive, and it elsewhere employs language that is abstract and difficult to untangle. It may be important to acknowledge at the outset that this prayer, like much in human thought about God, seeks for far more than can be articulated in common speech.

The opening reference of Eph. 3.14–15 to 'the Father, from whom every family in heaven and on earth takes its name' will provoke complaints that the Bible promotes a masculine God. That question is far too complex to be addressed here, apart from recalling that the Bible also employs maternal imagery with respect to God and everywhere insists that God is not merely a larger-than-life human being, either male or female. Here God the Father is connected with the naming of 'every family'. The note in the NRSV is slightly misleading, in that the word there translated 'family' does not mean 'fatherhood'. The Greek word *patria* refers concretely to family, extended family, larger units of people who are somehow connected to one another, not to the abstract notion of 'fatherhood'. Because *patria* is a cognate of *patēr*, the word for father, however, and English does not allow an adequate way to demonstrate that connection, the editors offer 'fatherhood' as a substitute.

This tricky problem of moving from Greek to English is important here, since what the writer asserts is the connection between *patēr* and *patria*. That is, God who is called Father is the one through whom every family is named. The point is less concerned with 'Father' than with the intimate and profound connection between God and the human family. Indeed, here 'family' itself is no longer simply 'human' family, as the writer invokes families both 'in heaven' and 'on earth'. Whatever connectedness exists among human beings either here or elsewhere exists by virtue of their first and primary connection with God. To that connection the writer does obeisance, and dares to articulate a prayer on behalf of his correspondents.

In Greek, the prayer itself contains three main petitions of decreasing length, each of which is introduced in the same way (by a *hina*, or purpose, clause). The first petition consists of vv. 16–17, which primarily seek spiritual strength and growth for the author's addressees. Earlier parts of this letter celebrate the dramatic change God has brought about in the lives of these Gentile converts (e.g. 2.1–3, 11–22), but the prayer recognizes that such change is never final or complete. Strength comes as God's gift through the Spirit, as God's gift through the indwelling of Christ, as God's gift through love. Attempts at describing each of these gifts analytically or parsing out various forms of growth will be futile, as the prayer piles up images of the growth invoked for believers. What is crucial, however, is to understand that the growth anticipated poems about and because of God's ongoing and even intimate relationship with believers.

The second petition consists of v. 18 and the first half of v. 19 (including the words 'that surpasses knowledge'). Here the prayer for growth takes on specificity in the request for understanding and for love. To comprehend 'what is the breadth and length and height and depth' is surely to understand all that – and more than – human beings can indeed comprehend. Even beyond that knowledge, however, lies the love of Christ, beyond the very frontier of the human capacity for knowledge.

Because of its brevity, the final petition ('so that you may be filled with all the fullness of God') may appear to be an afterthought. On the contrary, the prayer for the 'fullness of God' is the culmination of all prayer, in that it seeks the realization in fact of the connection posited in the introduction to the prayer, the connection between God and the human family. The final lines of the passage adequately summarize this petition and the prayer itself as 'far more than all we can ask or imagine'.

The petitions of this prayer necessarily involve gifts to individual believers. There are, nevertheless, indications that these gifts are not private but have a deeply corporate significance. To begin with, the 'you' in the passage is a plural 'you', suggesting that all the addressees are connected here. More important, the phrase 'with all the saints' (v. 18) places the addressees in the context of believers both local and distant. These gifts pertain to the whole people of God, not to a special few who are somehow spiritually talented. In addition, the phrase 'glory in the church' (which sounds an odd tone to Protestant ears, but would be welcome in Orthodox Christian circles) identifies the addressees with the assembly of those who together bow before God. The gifts are individual in that they must be granted to and appropriated by individual Christians in their daily, individual and sometimes achingly private lives. At the same time, however, the gifts are corporate in that those individual Christians do not exist apart from the larger community of faith. CC

John 6.1–21

A version of this miraculous provision of food occurs in the four Gospels no fewer than six times; it was clearly remembered vividly. But it is only John's Gospel that draws detailed lessons from it. These will be the subject of subsequent readings; but even at the start there is a hint that there is more to it than just a demonstration of Jesus' power. In the other Gospels the hour is late, the place deserted, the people hungry and liable to faint on the way; the feeding is an act of humanitarian relief. John says nothing of this – and indeed it is not particularly plausible. Galilee was densely populated in Jesus' time, and it was difficult to get far away from towns and villages. The traditional site of this miracle is within sight of the ruins of Capernaum, and even if this one is not authentic it would be hard to find another that was really remote and that was not high up in the mountains. Instead, John drops an early hint of the occasion's significance. 'The Passover was near'; that is, an annual festival when a meal had profound religious significance. What was to be the significance of this one?

It is characteristic of this Gospel to pass off what we would regard as the most remarkable moment in the story in a throwaway line: 'When they were satisfied'. Five thousand people had been fed from five loaves and two fish. It is important to visualize the quantities. The loaves were the small flat ones still used among Semitic peoples: not fewer than three was the usual meal for a man. But the scale of the miracle is conveyed in a detail that all the Gospel accounts emphasize – the amount left over. A sceptic might have said that the people were not hungry at all, or that they had brought their own picnics – but no one could possibly explain *12 baskets* full of scraps afterwards.

At any rate, what had been done was enough to convince people that Jesus was no ordinary person. Indeed they called him 'the prophet'. Moses had foretold that God would 'raise up for them a prophet like himself' (Deut. 18.15), and had not Moses provided a miraculous supply of manna? Jesus was showing signs of being the one whom Scripture pointed to right from the beginning.

Before any teaching is given, there is another episode to record. The threat of making Jesus 'king' is something that occurs in the other Gospels in the form of a temptation of the devil; this is the only place where we are told it was an actual event. To avoid it, Jesus withdrew; and the story of his apparently walking on the water is again one that is shared with the other Gospels. Again, the sceptic can come up with an explanation: the fact that the boat reached the land 'immediately' suggests they were already in shallow water and Jesus was just wading. But this is certainly not how the writer saw it. The disciples were 'terrified'; and Jesus' words, reported here exactly as in the other Gospels, have in this one a particularly solemn sound. 'It is I' is literally '*I am*', the formula Jesus uses for some of his most significant statements about himself. It was the one who could say '*I am*' with this powerful resonance of authority who was bidding them not to be afraid. AEH

Proper 13

(Sunday between 31 July and 6 August inclusive)

2 Samuel 11.26—12.13a or Exodus 16.2–4, 9–15; Ephesians 4.1–16; John 6.24–35

2 Samuel 11.26—12.13a

We saw last week that the story of the succession to David for the most part avoids passing judgement on the actions of the characters involved, but here we have a rare exception. We are told that 'the thing that David had done displeased the LORD'. Perhaps the final editor wanted to make certain that readers and hearers got the message right.

However that may be, there follows a parable. Christian readers may associate parables particularly with the teaching of Jesus, but they are found in a variety of religious traditions. Like some of the more extended parables of Jesus this story engages in deliberate exaggeration in order to make the point more vividly. Nathan's story is told in such a way that in effect it demands an immediate response. The king asserts that justice must be done in such a case. Nathan's response is brilliant: 'You are the man!' David is condemned out of his own mouth.

We know little in detail about the status of figures like Nathan who came to be regarded as prophets, but certainly in this story his authority seems to be unquestioned. He is able to spell out all that God had done for David (vv. 7–9), again with a measure of exaggeration (Saul's wives?). This enables him to warn David of the disasters that now lie ahead (vv. 10–12). There is no suggestion that Nathan is under threat when he makes these devastating announcements. Perhaps the intention is to set out with approval the ability of David to recognize when he had done wrong. This provides a contrast with the attempts of later kings such as Ahab who tried to silence the prophet Elijah and others who spoke against them. Certainly our reading ends in the most edifying way, with David acknowledging that he has done wrong. He is assured of God's forgiveness without any requirement that he should offer any form of sacrifice. RC

Exodus 16.2–15

This passage is one of several in Exodus and Numbers that deal with the complaints of the Israelites in the wilderness and divine intervention to satisfy their needs. They have their origin in natural phenomena that occurred in the wilderness. Quails (*coturnix coturnix*) arrived in northern Sinai in August-September in great numbers from the Sudan and Ethiopia and, exhausted from their journey, could be easily hunted and gathered. Manna is a secretion from a flowering tree such as the tamarisk bush, assisted by the sting and secretion of a tree louse.

This 'natural food', well known to anyone used to living in the wilderness, has become the basis of accounts of miraculous feeding of the Israelites; but it should be noted that the narratives have also become object-lessons that must have figured in religious instruction.

This is most obvious in vv. 4–8. The sabbath has not yet been instituted (cf. Exod. 20.8), but the Israelites are instructed to gather twice as much on the sixth day as they normally gather, the implication being that they will then not need to gather any manna on the seventh (sabbath) day. Later in the chapter, there is an explicit command to the people not to gather any manna on the seventh (sabbath) day (v. 23) and the Israelites discover that if they keep manna overnight on days one to five it will go bad, but that if they gather twice as much on the sixth day to be used on the seventh, it will keep. Israelites who ignored the instruction about gathering twice as much on the sixth day and who went looking for manna on the seventh day are disappointed (vv. 27–30).

Another charming feature of the story (not included in today's reading) in vv. 17–18 is that however much people gathered it amounted to the same: those who gathered much had nothing over, and those who gathered little had no shortage (v. 18). This is not a charter for laziness, but a way of saying that God met each person's needs completely, and independently of the human competitiveness that would undoubtedly result in some getting more, at the expense of those who gathered less.

This passage, then, shows God graciously responding to the people's complaints. Later episodes show how the people redeemed from slavery began to try God's patience. JR

Ephesians 4.1–16

The reader who is schooled to any degree in the traditional beliefs and formulas of the Church may arrive at this passage of Ephesians with something of the relief of a sailor reaching landfall after drifting in impressive but baffling waters. The first three chapters, rich and sonorous, are not always easy to grasp in detail, though modern translations sometimes seek to simplify, while disguising, the complex grammatical structure of many of the ultra-long sentences in which they are composed. But here is relative simplicity, and one looks ahead in time to the often bare expressions of creeds and liturgies.

If we suppose that Ephesians is likely to come, in part or whole, from the hand of a follower of Paul rather than Paul himself, then this passage may be seen as supporting such a case, for it is in effect a digest or confection of Pauline phrases and ideas, especially in vv. 4–6, on the theme of oneness. Almost every term is paralleled, somewhere and somehow, in Paul's undoubted letters; for example, 'one body and one Spirit' in 1 Cor. 12.13; 'one Lord' and 'one God' in 1 Cor. 8.6; 12.3, 6. Here, they are concentrated in sentences that are a foundation for the writer's beliefs about the Church, its structure of Christ-given ministry, its centredness on Christ, and its proof against subversive forces within and without. As suggested above, it is a kind of charter of confident catholic stability and ever-onward progress (vv. 7–16).

The ordered institutional concern, based firmly on central doctrine abut God, is probably itself evidence of a second-generation date for this writing – and its familiar congeniality (to us still) is perhaps a sign that, in certain basic sociological ways, 'second-generation' features and factors persist, whatever the often huge shifts of context in which the Church exists. Times and places may change, but we still hear much of this passage with a kind of ease of recognition and edification.

Yet it is likely that by the time of Ephesians there was beginning to be unease precisely about the cohesion of Christ's people (v. 14; cf. Acts 20.29f.). The latter part of the passage certainly sets out to build up a sense of the Church's unifying structure of ministers (v. 11), which Christ himself had provided. This is probably seen as a gift at Pentecost (with which Ps. 68, quoted in v. 9, was associated); that is, the 'descent' and the giving follow the ascension (rather than the reference being to either the incarnation or a descent to the sphere of the dead after the crucifixion). It is, then, a picture similar to that of Acts 1—2. We note that in v. 8 the original ('received gifts from men') is altered – to accord with what God's providence had actually done. Jewish exegetes did the same, making it refer to the gift of the Law.

But there is still a destiny in view (vv. 13–16) – the fulfilment of the close corporeity of the Christian people, with Christ as their sole and essential unifying principle. Here, different from 1 Cor. 12.21, but as in Eph. 1.22, Christ as head is distinct from, while still being one with, his own; it is his authority that needs now to be explicit. Yet there is a moral dimension too, for the whole is filled with the spirit of love (vv. 15, 16). So doctrine, ecclesiastical arrangements and ethics work together, and Christ fills all, now and in the future that is assured. LH

John 6.24–35

Somewhat mystified by Jesus' apparent disappearance from the site of the miraculous feeding, the crowd followed him as soon as they could to the other side of the lake. Whatever their motives may have been – the hope of more such miraculous provision, a chance to see another sensational 'sign', or just sheer curiosity – Jesus sees the need to lead them towards a deeper understanding.

He begins at a level they do not find difficult. The contrast between 'food that perishes' and 'food that endures' sounded like conventional religious teaching – short-term materialism over against lasting spiritual benefits. And if they were familiar with the Son of man of Daniel 7, they would have known that he might well be instrumental in securing long-term rewards for the faithful. So they responded by asking what kind of conduct would assure them of these rewards. The same question is asked of Jesus in the Synoptic Gospels, and the answer is to 'follow' Jesus. Here (in typical Johannine fashion) it is to 'believe in' him.

But how were they to know that they *should* believe in him? They needed some 'sign' that would decisively identify Jesus as the person he claimed to be. Moses, after all, had secured many days' provision of manna in the wilderness. Could Jesus claim similar credentials, such that a sentence from Scripture would fit him as well as it fitted Moses, 'He gave them bread from heaven to eat'?

Oddly enough, this sentence does not exactly occur in the Old Testament, though it was close to a more or less standard formula for summarizing the manna episode (Neh. 9.15; Ps. 78.24). But it becomes, in effect, the text of Jesus' sermon and is treated as preachers have always tended to do, a word or two at a time. First, Jesus comments on 'He'. *He* does not mean Moses. It was God who provided the manna; and possibly there is some resonance here with the Lord's Prayer (not given in John's Gospel), where the Father is prayed to 'give us this day our daily (or perhaps it meant "our special") bread'. Second, Jesus interprets the word 'bread'. The manna may have been supernatural, but it was merely to satisfy physical hunger. The *bread* of the scriptural text meant more than this, just as what Jesus had just provided was more than an emergency supply of bread. But the crowd still does not get the point. They ask to be given this bread 'always', just as the woman at the well had asked Jesus to give her a supply of water that would prevent her having to come for it each time herself (John 4.15).

Instead Jesus offers true bread, indeed he is himself (as he will go on to show) 'the bread of life'. And this is for any- and everyone who will genuinely ask for it – the invitation deliberately evokes the figure of Wisdom crying out, 'Come, eat of my bread and drink of the wine I have mixed' (Prov. 9.5). AEH

Proper 14

(Sunday between 7 and 13 August inclusive)

2 Samuel 18.5–9, 15, 31–33 or 1 King's 19.4–8; Ephesians 4.25—5.2; John 6.35, 41–51

2 Samuel 18.5–9, 15, 31–33

David's family troubles have continued. Between last week's episode and today's reading comes some of the most vivid narrative in the whole Bible. Part of the problem was the rivalry between the children of different royal wives. One of David's sons, Amnon, had raped his half-sister Tamar. Tamar's brother Absalom had had Amnon killed when he was drunk, and then had taken flight. Eventually he returned, but the tension between David and Absalom continued until it led to open war. At first it had seemed as if Absalom's rebellion might succeed, but he dithered at a crucial time and David's superior organization led to Absalom's death and the rout of his followers.

The verses chosen for today's reading show David torn between love of his son Absalom and the need to put down the rebellion. His command that his army should 'deal gently' with Absalom may strike us as somewhat unrealistic, but it heightens the dramatic tension. In the flight after the battle Absalom is trapped in the scrubland ('forest' may give a slightly misleading impression). David's senior general, Joab, is shrewd enough to realize that he would be unwise to be held personally responsible for Absalom's death, and so in vv. 10–14 he arranges how it can best be brought about. In any case the macho young men around him have no scruples and Absalom is killed.

Today's part of the larger story focuses on the news being brought to David. Joab had foreseen David's reaction and had tried to ensure that the news would be brought, not by Ahimaaz, a member of the royal entourage, but by a foreign servant, 'the Cushite'. The plan had nearly misfired when the eager Ahimaaz took a short cut and got to David first, but it was only when the 'official' messenger arrived that news of Absalom's death was formally conveyed to David. Our reading ends with David's grief over the death of his rebellious son outweighing any pleasure and relief that his kingdom was still intact – a reaction for which he was to be taken to task by Joab in the verses following our reading.

There is no neat-and-tidy, right-v-wrong approach to this story. Family solidarity and public good cannot be put on the scales and measured against one another. It is important, too, to remember that the verses in the public reading are no more than an extract; try to find time to read the whole story in which they are set. At one time this story, of the succession to David, was accepted as largely reliable history; scholars nowadays are much more sceptical about that, but the power of the story, with its unveiling of and reflection on the tensions of public and family life, remains. RC

1 Kings 19.4–8

Elijah had just won a great victory on Mount Carmel (1 Kings 18.20–40). He had demonstrated that the God of Israel was more powerful than Baal, and had had the prophets of Baal killed. It is therefore surprising that Queen Jezebel's threat against him, sworn by gods whom Elijah had proved to be powerless, should cause the prophet to flee headlong. Elijah's journey into the wilderness had Beer-sheba as its point of departure (v. 3). He finds refuge under a broom tree, which is probably the white broom, a common shrub in the desert regions of Arabia, which has very long roots that can reach down to sources of water in even the driest conditions. The irony of Elijah's situation is pointed up by the fact that the God in whose name he won the contest, but whose power he now no longer seems to trust, is able to provide him miraculously with water and a cake baked on hot stones. He is eventually persuaded to give up his view that life is hopeless (v. 4b) and to proceed to Mount Horeb (i.e. Sinai), where his commission as a prophet will be renewed.

Whether or not we take this story to be historically true, it is a powerful narrative that skilfully charts some of the contradictions of being human, as well as being a servant of God. A great triumph can be a hard cross to bear, especially if everything is then expected to turn out as the successful person desires. A slight disappointment can bring the whole house of triumph crashing down like a pack of cards, and lead to judgements that are totally unrealistic in their negativity. Self-pity takes over, and the person tries, unsuccessfully deep down, to enjoy, and to justify, being a failure. Fortunately, God does not allow the situation to persist. Through some messenger or by some other way, reality gradually returns, life continues and God's work is done. It is when Elijah looks away from himself (v. 6) to what God has provided that his journey back from self-pity begins. JR

Ephesians 4.25—5.2

Sometimes ethical teaching is free-standing, in the sense that its content is uttered for its own sake and in its own right; more commonly, outside the traditional educational setting, it tends to respond to need. People are behaving in such-and-such a way, it is wrong, and they ought to desist, for the following reasons.

Here, the doctrine laid down earlier in this chapter, about the oneness of God and of the believers' life 'in Christ', united in the one Church, is the ground of the subsequent teaching on matters of behaviour. Its content is in itself not remarkable or unusual, though (on the principle stated above) it may indicate that relations in the Christian community, as known to this author, were not free of malicious and unkind behaviour. There can scarcely have been a time or place where these admonitions were not in season. Ephesians is at least an antidote to golden-age illusions! At the same time (as in Paul's letters), there are some signs of stereotyped rather than strictly relevant teaching, especially perhaps the injunction not to steal (v. 28), familiar from the Decalogue.

What is remarkable is that, at every turn, commonplace moral instructions are backed by doctrinal convictions; more than that, they spring straight out of those convictions (no problem here about 'is' not leading to 'ought'). You must forgive because you are forgiven by Christ; it is of course the doctrine familiar from the Lord's Prayer in Matthew and Luke (and already in Mark 11.25). As ever in Ephesians, most of what we have in this passage has parallels, chiefly in Paul's undoubted letters. There are images that belong to those times rather than to ours. 'Members (= limbs) one of another' (v. 25) is in Romans 12.5 and is based on a familiar political metaphor of the period, especially for the relations of citizens to each other. The idea of being 'sealed' (v. 19; cf. 1.13) may relate to the branding of slaves – baptism asserts both God's claim and his dependability – or, more specifically, be reminiscent of Ezek. 9.4f., where God's own are marked for recognition by him on the last day (cf. Rev. 7.4f.; 9.4). The Church is the secure community of God's own. Finally, Christ is a sacrificial offering to God (5.2). In the first-century world, both Jewish and pagan, it is as commonplace a metaphor drawn from life as one could imagine, its allusions visible every day in the cities where by far most Christians lived. LH

John 6.35, 41–51

The word 'complain' translates a word that properly means a kind of disgruntled murmuring; and it is indeed because they had heard something which they found somehow shocking, rather than something they wanted to 'complain' about, that the word is used of the Pharisees. Part of their objection was the very ordinariness and familiarity of Jesus' background. They knew his family, and found his relatively humble and unacademic upbringing incompatible with the extraordinary claims he was making. Jesus recognized their difficulty, and accepted the consequence that it would only be some who were able to believe in him.

And how would they do so if their teachers did not give them a lead? *Teaching* in Jesus' culture, as in most cultures, was a matter of handing on tradition. One would say, 'I was taught by so-and-so', and this would give weight and credibility to what one had learned. But none of the accredited teachers was prepared to acknowledge Jesus and pass on students to him. So how was anyone to come to believe in him? Jesus' answer was radical: he was appealing over the heads of the entire body of past and present teachers. It was God himself who would 'draw' people, it was God who would 'teach' them – for which (like any good teacher himself) he could quote a text, 'They shall all be taught by God' (cf. Isa. 54.13).

'Whoever believes has eternal life.' That would not have sounded too difficult. Eternal life was the lot of the righteous after death, and 'believing' was an understandable way of describing the qualification for it. But on Jesus' lips the phrase has a different meaning. The 'bread' that Jesus gives (unlike the manna, which just provided physical sustenance) is such that 'one may eat of it and not die', one will 'live for ever'. 'Eternal life' is being given a new meaning; the new life which comes from believing in Jesus and eating the bread is as different from the old as life is from death. The old life is 'death'; the new life is what people used to think only began (for the righteous) after death. In Jesus' language, it begins *now*.

The bread was Jesus' *flesh*. However familiar, this phrase can still startle us. To its first hearers it would certainly have caused a frisson, and the consequences are felt right through this chapter of the Gospel. But John's readers were accustomed to 'the Lord's Supper'; they were already used to calling bread and wine the body and blood of Christ. In the other Gospels, the little that is said to explain this startling language is concentrated in the account of the private meal with the disciples the night before the crucifixion. Here the narrative context is different; but John has used this episode as the point at which to gather together all the teaching he could about what Christians soon came to call 'the Eucharist'. AEH

Proper 15

(Sunday between 14 and 20 August inclusive)

1 Kings 2.10–12; 3.3–14 or Proverbs 9.1–6; Ephesians 5.15–20; John 6.51–58

1 Kings 2.10–12; 3.3–14

It is understandable, but at the same time rather frustrating, that those who compile lectionaries highlight only the happy and agreeable parts of the biblical material. The beginning of this reading gives the impression that Solomon peacefully came to the throne when David his father died in a good old age. If we look at the whole story, however, we receive a very different presentation. As we have seen in the readings of the last few weeks, there was a bitter struggle within David's family as to who should succeed as king. Right to the end it seemed as if not Solomon but his half-brother Adonijah would be the successful contender. Only after intense palace intrigue was Solomon's claim recognized, and the remainder of 1 Kings 2 gives some indication of the brutal measures he took to ensure that his position was not threatened by those who had supported other contenders. You might find it an interesting topic, either for self-reflection or for discussion with your friends, whether you think the biblical readings in our liturgy should largely be confined to the obviously acceptable passages. (And don't forget that the New Testament has some pretty horrifying material too!)

The main part of today's reading is concerned with a topic that has become proverbial: the wisdom of Solomon. The Jerusalem temple had not yet been built, so he goes to Gibeon, here regarded with apparent approval as 'the principal high place' ('high places' are usually condemned) and there has a dream. Again, dreams are not always regarded favourably in the Old Testament, but this one is, and what is seen in the dream is taken as reality. Solomon already shows his wisdom by describing the dream in the way that he does. By asking for wisdom, Solomon is said to obtain all the other gifts that he had not asked for.

Wisdom has many different meanings, but in the Solomon tradition it does not seem primarily to be concerned with religious matters. Rather it denotes the ability to discern the right and effective answer to the problems that arise and to know how to put that answer into effect. (The story of the two prostitutes, which follows in 1 Kings 3, provides a good example of the application of this kind of wisdom.) It might also be expressed in pithy sayings, summing up the inner realities of a situation, and in this sense Solomon came to be regarded as the patron of proverbial wisdom, including the books of Proverbs and Ecclesiastes, which came to be attributed to him. RC

Proverbs 9.1–6

The book of Proverbs reaches the climax of its first main section (chs. 1—9) with Wisdom's invitation to the uninstructed (NRSV 'simple', v. 4) to attend her banquet. This invitation is in opposition to other invitations in chs. 1—9 by the harlot woman (7.10–23) and the foolish woman (9.13–18). These latter figures denote actual physical temptations, such as prostitution, but also point to the attractions of other forms of religion, especially ones that embrace sacred prostitution and sexual licence.

The precise nature of Wisdom's seven-pillared house is uncertain. Some experts regard it as a rather superior seven-roomed construction, much larger than the average house. There is also the view that a kind of temple is envisaged, even possibly the Jerusalem temple. This could be supported by the reference to the slaughter of Wisdom's animals. Temples were the main centres for the slaughter and sale of meat in the ancient world, although this consideration is not conclusive when it comes to identifying Wisdom's dwelling. Because she is preparing a feast and inviting guests, Wisdom employs servant-girls, whom she now sends out to invite the guests (cf. Matt. 22.3). The Hebrew of vv. 4–5 can be taken in more ways than is represented by the NRSV. It is possible that each servant-girl is given the following words of invitation to speak: 'You that are untutored, turn in here; and whoever lacks sense, to him I say, come . . .'

The sense of 'the highest places in the town' is also uncertain. It may refer to the location of Wisdom's house, or be a way of indicating that the invitation is intended to be heard by all. Another question that is disputed is whether 'bread' in v. 5 means what it says, or whether it means food in general. In v. 2 Wisdom has had animals slaughtered and, meat being an expensive commodity in the ancient world, its provision at the banquet would mark it out as being a grand occasion.

The passage, of course, is not about eating and drinking, but about acquiring the knowledge and insight that will constitute and lead to life lived in accordance with God's will. That it should be presented in terms of an invitation to a banquet, however, is meant to indicate that what is on offer is deeply satisfying to those who are prepared to follow the path of Wisdom. JR

Ephesians 5.15–20

This is not the most striking passage in the New Testament or indeed in Ephesians, and the preacher who takes it on may find it hard to rise above platitude; hard too, in most likely cases, to urge his congregation to eschew drunkenness in favour of surrender to the Spirit.

However, there may be more of value here than meets the casual eye. It is the conclusion of a long section (5.3f.) of stern moral instruction, based on a conviction of unity, in Christ. The essence is the contrast between 'light' and 'darkness', each associated with its associated deeds; in the latter case chiefly sexual ills but also covetousness and silly talk. On the positive side, life in the light is marked by 'wisdom', a long-held and much explored Jewish ideal that Paul had redefined in 1 Cor. 1—2. The context here is eschatological, so that there is urgency in adopting the true way of life. One must 'buy up (make the most of) the time'; that is, the chance now offered and available, in view of the end (v. 16). Like much in these verses, it is probably taken from Col. 4.5. The other main parallel, virtually verbatim, is in v. 19f., cf. Col. 3.16f. The question is then raised how far this writing is close to real church life as the author knows it or is instead a literary work, done from the desk. In any case we get, first- or second-hand, one of our few glimpses of the content of early Christian worship and discover what a tenaciously conservative phenomenon it has remained in aspects of its make-up. LH

John 6.51–58

See Corpus Christi, pp. 155–156.

Proper 16

(Sunday between 21 and 27 August inclusive)

1 Kings 8.(1, 6, 10–11), 22–30, 41–43 or Joshua 24.1–2a, 14–18; Ephesians 6.10–20; John 6.56–69

1 Kings 8.(1, 6, 10–11), 22–30, 41–43

1 Kings 8 is a very long chapter. The three previous chapters have described the construction of the temple in Jerusalem. Now it is completed, and our reading picks up two themes. The first, in the bracketed verses, describes the actual dedication of the temple. We noted in an earlier reading in this series (2 Sam. 7) a tension between the understanding of God as being associated with a small movable shrine, the ark, and the construction of a fixed dwelling-place. The tension is said to be removed when the ark is brought into the temple; in fact nothing more is known about the ark. The temple and its ideology now becomes dominant. That is where 'the glory of the LORD', pictured as if it were a material substance, was to be located.

The required part of today's reading, however, takes the construction of the temple for granted, and is concerned with the prayer uttered by Solomon at its dedication. Notice first that the prayer is spoken by Solomon himself, not by any minion. Kingship was itself regarded as a religious office, and the temple was a royal building; some have even called it a royal chapel. (It may be helpful to remember that its dimensions were quite modest; it would be wrong to envisage anything comparable in scale with the great cathedrals of Christendom.)

The whole of Solomon's prayer touches on many points, but in the selection made for this reading the particular emphasis is on the tension within the idea of a God who cannot be contained in heaven, even the highest heaven, and who yet has a special care for a particular people. So vv. 22–26 stress that Solomon is regarded as the heir to the promise made to David, which we looked at in 2 Sam. 7. But in vv. 27–30 there is a wider perspective. While there is a special concern for the house where God's 'name' dwells (this idea of the 'name' signifying the divine presence is found often in this chapter), God's presence is not to be confined to the temple.

This is a tension that is perhaps even more acute in the modern world, and it is good for Christians to reflect on their understanding of a God whom they regard as both special to Christianity and also as the unique ruler of the whole universe. An example of what this kind of tension may mean concludes the reading. The conviction is expressed that foreigners may wish to join with Israel in the worship of this God; their prayers too are to be welcomed and accepted. It hardly needs to be emphasized that here is another issue that is of fundamental importance for all those who adhere to the great monotheistic faiths – Judaism, Christianity, Islam – in the contemporary world. RC

Joshua 24.1–2a, 14–18

At the end of the book of Joshua, when the occupation of the land of Canaan has been successfully completed, Joshua assembles all the Israelites at the central and ancient city of Shechem (present-day Nablus) in order to renew the loyalty of the people to their God YHWH (the Lord). There is an oddity about the logic of the passage, because in vv. 16–18 the people readily agree that it was the Lord who brought them out of slavery, conducted them safely to the promised land and drove out the peoples who lived in it. If they had such a clear view of things, why was it necessary for Joshua to challenge their loyalty?

In fact, it is the way in which the verses have been selected for the purposes of the lectionary reading that has created the odd logic. In the omitted verses (2b–13), Joshua gives a brief outline of the people's history, beginning with the ancestors of Abraham, who served other gods. Particular stress is placed upon the greatness of what God had done, especially at crucial points, such as when the Israelites cried out to God because they were being pursued by Egyptian chariots and horsemen (v. 7). It is emphasized that they now occupy a land on which they have not laboured, in cities they have not built, where they enjoy the fruits of orchards and vineyards they did not plant (v. 13). Faced with such overwhelming evidence, it is little wonder that the people's response is so positive!

The passage may reflect the custom of annual or periodic gatherings of the people at which their sacred history was recalled and the people were invited to renew their pledge of loyalty (cf. Deut. 31.9–13). A modern equivalent might be the practice of renewal of baptism, marriage or ordination vows.

The passage raises the question of the nature of loyalty and commitment. If the Israelites needed such heavyweight reminding of what they owed to God, one wonders whether their day-to-day loyalty to him was very sincere. The same can be said of renewal of vows. Does it do any more than generate some immediate piety or resolution to do better, that quickly fades? On the other hand, loyalty can quickly fade if it loses touch with God's loyalty to us. This latter has the function of keeping our loyalty fresh, not as a set of facts to shame us into temporary, manufactured commitment, but as the dimension within which we live our daily lives. JR

Ephesians 6.10–20

The ghastly wars of the past century have reduced the appeal and commendability of the military metaphor for the Christian life exploited in this final main section of Ephesians. Hymns that survive from an earlier period and the greater popularity then of military-looking organizations attached to the churches testify to an ethos in which the stout-hearted spirituality here proposed seemed beyond reproach.

But the Christians of the first century lived in an era largely of peace for the citizens of the Roman Empire and were not engaged in the agony of present or imminent bloody strife. In fact they were rather like British Christians who sang J. B. Monsell's 'Fight the good fight' and S. Baring-Gould's 'Onward, Christian soldiers' lustily in the nineteenth century. In that sense, the imagery is certainly not drawn from every-day life. It is in fact scriptural; see Isa. 40.3, 9; 52.7; 59.17; Ecclus. 46.6; and Wisd. 5.17f. Moreover (nearer to home), Paul had taken it up; Rom. 13.12; 1 Thess. 5.8; Col. 3.12, perhaps. Still, it is our writer who has drawn these aspects together and made of them a highly memorable and concentrated whole, perhaps with liturgical use in view. And of course it speaks forcefully of the seriousness of the Christian's commitment, which is, once accepted, total and inescapable, for enemies are all around.

The most notable point, however, is that the armour is that of God, handed to the believer, who is thereby endued with a strength that goes beyond the human. It is, therefore, language parallel to that of the Spirit; divine gift empowering the believers. The crisis atmosphere of the passage has suggested a baptismal association, the outward sign of commitment and of separation from the realm of the devil's operations, now and on the final day (v. 13). This would chime in with the linkage with one's fellow-Christians (v. 18); and Paul the apostle is the particular example (vv. 19–20).

Judaism had its own tradition of both literal and metaphorical warfare in God's cause. The War Rule of Qumran offers a much more intricate parallel, with the same basic awareness of the cosmic struggle between the two powers for the spiritual mastery of all things. But whereas for Qumran the battle lies ahead, for this writer it is already fully engaged and Christ has won the decisive victory. How does this way of reading the universe look now? LH

John 6.56–69

It comes as something of a surprise to read that Jesus 'was teaching in the synagogue at Capernaum'. This is the conclusion of a long discussion with a crowd that had pursued him for more teaching (and perhaps more miraculous feeding) from the far side of the Sea of Galilee. But the style of Jesus' discourse has had something of the sermon about it, and given that it appears to gather together much of his teaching about 'the bread that comes down from heaven' the synagogue was a perfectly appropriate place for the public part of his exposition.

All the Gospels contain instances of Jesus holding private conversations with his disciples to clarify points in his public teaching. On this occasion it was not merely that they were puzzled (as well they might have been). They shared the general sense of shock at Jesus' notion of 'eating his flesh' and expressed it (like 'the Jews') by a disgruntled murmuring (misleadingly translated 'complaining' in the NRSV). And no wonder. Taken literally, Jesus' words about being 'bread' to be 'eaten' could not but be disconcerting, and when it came to 'drinking his blood' the sensitiv-ities of any Jewish person would have been aroused, however figurative the language was supposed to be.

In reply to his disciples, Jesus does not soften his language; but he does give them a clue to its meaning. Jesus was not offering his flesh to be eaten as an ordinary man but as the Son of man; and this was a person who belonged to both heaven and earth. When he had been 'lifted up' on the cross to his place at the right hand of God, talk of 'eating his flesh' would have a different and more profound meaning. Jesus would then exist in a world of the Spirit, and this same Spirit would give meaning to words that at present seemed startlingly physical.

Even so, the shock was too great even for some of those who were closest to him. The theme of opposition to Jesus is common to all the Gospels, and is particularly prominent in John. Normally there is a clear distinction between his followers on the one hand and his adversaries on the other (with the crowds vacillating between). But here the division runs through the group of disciples themselves, leaving only the Twelve as the remnant who remained faithful. (The text goes on to say that even this group had its waverer who eventually betrayed him.) As in the other Gospels, Peter was their spokesman and was able to make a decisive confession of faith: Jesus was 'the Holy One of God' – the title that in Mark (1.24) is given to Jesus by a demon; and demons, being supernatural beings, knew who Jesus really was. AEH

Proper 17

(Sunday between 28 August and 3 September inclusive)

Song of Solomon 2.8–13 or Deuteronomy 4.1–2, 6–9; James 1.17–27; Mark 7.1–8, 14–15, 21–23

Song of Solomon 2.8–13

The Song of Songs (to give it its Hebrew name) is a series of independent poems with some overlap and some recurring themes. How the poems are to be related to each other, however, is not always clear. In the present poem the words 'wall', 'windows' and 'lattice' (v. 9) are important. If the poem is read independently, there is no suggestion that the woman cannot go out and meet her lover. If, on the other hand, notice is taken of the restrictions to which the woman is subject elsewhere in the collection (cf. 8.1–4) the poem takes on a different meaning; and this line will be followed in the present explanation.

Granted that the woman is not necessarily free to join her lover, the poem expresses human frustration. On the one hand is the world of nature, which is all innocence, beauty, expectation and invitation (vv. 11–13). Anyone who has experienced the ending of the winter rains and cold in Palestine in late March and early April (although it can vary!) will know what a beautiful aspect the land presents. It is a time for adventure and for throwing off restraints; and this aspect, which the world of nature presents, is matched by feelings within the man and woman in the poem. Some commentators have seen in the figure of the beloved leaping upon the mountains an image deriving from the storm god, which is here pressed into secular use. In other words, there are two separate images in vv. 8–9. In v. 8 the image is that of an almost superhuman figure; in v. 9 the image switches to that of the expectant gazelle or the young stag eager to respond to the sexual urges within him.

Over against the spontaneous world of nature stands the conventional world of human culture, with its restrictions, particularly on what women may be allowed to do. Some of the restrictions are no doubt necessary, to defend not only females but vulnerable males from an unrestrained law of the jungle. Yet these restrictions also express power relationships, often to the advantage of men.

The poem can be read, then, as an expression of the ambiguity of being human. As part of nature, humans experience the rhythms of nature, respond to its moods, and are moved by its sublimity. But human society, in the way that it is organized, often requires and demands a renunciation of deep human feelings. In this sense, the poem is eschatological; that is, it evokes desires and longing beyond what human ingenuity can provide. It yearns for a different, a better, world. JR

Deuteronomy 4.1–2, 6–9

The words 'So now, Israel . . .' (the introductory words 'Moses spoke to the people' do not actually occur, and have been invented by the lectionary compilers) mark the beginning of a new section in which Moses switches from rehearsing the story of Israel's journey from Mount Horeb (Sinai) to the plains of Moab, to addressing the Israelites gathered before him. The aim of the passage is to provide two reasons why Moses' hearers, and all subsequent generations of Israelites, should obey the commandments delivered by God to Moses. First, these commandment are not simply just and good because God has commanded them; they are self-evidently good and just (v. 8) and will be recognized as such even by people who do not acknowledge the God of Israel.

Second, because other nations will be able to perceive the excellence of the laws given by God, they will recognize the eminent wisdom and greatness of Israel in obeying these laws wholeheartedly. In the wider context of the passage these arguments are backed up with rather more carrot and stick! There are warnings about what will happen if the people do not obey (vv. 25–28) while the authority of Moses the lawgiver, and thus of the laws themselves, is bolstered by a reminder of the awesome conditions of blazing mountains and dark clouds under which the laws were conveyed.

The arguments contained in the selection of verses for the lesson, however, have much to be said for them, without the need of carrot and stick. From the Church's point of view, it ought be to be possible to present what faith is about in such a way that even non-believers see that there is something of excellence and worthy of consideration at stake. In which case, they may not only respect the Church for adhering to faith; they may be drawn to it themselves. JR

James 1.17–27

Typical of the letter of James, this lection presents several challenges to the preacher. Its primary interest lies less in articulating the theological implications of the gospel (in fact, Jesus is scarcely mentioned) than in clarifying what it means for Christians to live with the gospel. For that clarification, the writer draws on a number of traditional sources for ethical guidance and covers a disparate array of topics. The result resembles Jewish wisdom literature more than it does many other early Christian writings.

This particular lection touches on a bewildering variety of themes familiar from other literature. That Christians have received a new birth is familiar from John 3.1–10 and from 1 Pet. 1.3; 2.2. The language of firstfruits is used by Paul in reference to Jesus' resurrection (1 Cor. 15.20). Similar advice about listening quickly and speaking only slowly appears in Ecclus. 5.11 (see Eccles. 5.2), and warnings about anger appear in Eccles. 7.9 and Prov. 15.1. The imperative of caring for orphans and widows both anticipates the lengthy discussion later in James and recalls prophetic imperatives regarding justice.

The verses that begin the passage (vv. 17–18) actually conclude the preceding discussion about temptation. By contrast with the notion that temptation comes from God (v. 13), the writer insists that good gifts (and not evil temptations) come from God. By contrast with the birth of sin and death described in 1.15, v. 18 describes the birth given to believers; they come into being 'by the word of truth' in order to be 'first fruits of his creatures'. God's plan is for goodness and for life, not for evil or for death. As the note in the NRSV suggests, the saying at the end of v. 17 ('there is no variation or shadow due to change') is somewhat unclear in the Greek manuscripts. What does seem clear, however, is the author's conviction that God may be relied on to continue to act in favour of God's creation.

With v. 19, the topic changes from God's actions to those expected of human beings. Despite the traditional, even folksy, character of the opening of this section, the movement within it is difficult. It begins with a statement about the importance of listening (by contrast with speaking or growing angry), suggesting that hearing is in itself an important act. However, v. 22 introduces the contrast between hearing and doing, in which hearing is subordinated to doing. Verse 26 returns to the dangers of speech, but only in order to move to the prophetic imperative of caring for those in need.

Any generalization about the twists and turns in this passage takes the risk of oversimplifying it, but it may nevertheless be helpful to see the author as struggling (here and throughout the letter) with the integrity of the Christian life. What gives Christian life some wholeness? What identifies the Christian life? How can belief and action be held together in a unity – or can they possibly be separated?

In vv. 19–27, that desire to articulate the integrity of the Christian life addresses two distinct issues: the character of speech and the character of action. The dangers of inappropriate speech reappear in the well-known discussion in 3.1–12 (see proper 19). In this initial discussion, speech seems to be a metonym for human thought. The author moves quickly from the admonition to be 'slow to speak' to warnings about anger and wickedness (v. 21). More revealing still is v. 26, which equates the unbridled tongue with the heart that deceives itself. Writing centuries before the development of depth psychology, the author of James understands that even what purports to be casual speech reveals thoughts and feelings deep within the human heart.

Verse 22 moves from the integrity of thought and speech to the integrity of hearing and doing. The most characteristic theme of the letter, the demand to be 'doers of the word', appears here for the first time and in its most theoretical form. Those who hear the gospel but do not act on it 'are like those who look at themselves in a mirror' and 'immediately forget what they were like'. Given the prevalence of mirrors in contemporary Western society and the preoccupation with taking advantage of them, this analogy may seem inadequate. In common with other ancient writers, however, biblical writers refer to the ephemeral or insufficient nature of the mirror (e.g. 1 Cor. 13.12). What is seen in a mirror must be viewed again and again, because the impression is gone as soon as one looks away. By contrast, the 'perfect law, the law of liberty', enables people to live with what they see and to live out what they believe. The imperative of caring for orphans and widows (v. 27) provides a concrete example of this call to integrate hearing and doing.

The brief note at the end of v. 25 warrants close attention. Those who both hear and act on the gospel 'will be blessed in their doing'. In the never-ending quest to be sure that faith is 'worth something' like any other commodity or acquisition, Christians often resort to calculating (privately if not publicly) the rewards they may receive because of their belief or because of their action. The writer of James does indeed identify a reward for those who act on the gospel, but the reward – the blessing – comes in the action itself. SL

Mark 7.1–8, 14–15, 21–23

Almost as far back as we can go, the evidence points to divisions among the followers of Jesus. Paul, for example, refers to groups sharply divided from each other, and he says that it must be so; even if it is only to show which members have the maturity to deal with such difficulties (1 Cor. 11.18f.; cf. also Rom. 14.1—15.13). The argument in Mark 7 about what is clean and what is unclean illustrates first-century disagreements (among Christians, and indeed sometimes in Judaism) on this very live issue; Mark, Matthew and Luke each deals with the situation in his own way.

In Mark, the earliest of the three as it is now thought, Jesus is said to have declared all foods clean (7.19, part of the chapter that is omitted from the lectionary); in Matthew, on the other hand, where those words are not included, this freedom is limited to not washing before meals (15.20); and in Luke the whole passage is omitted from the Gospel, and the subject is dealt with in Acts (10.1—11.18). This and other passages in these three Gospels and Acts suggest that Mark comes from the Pauline wing of the Church, Matthew from the Jewish Christians who continued to keep the Mosaic Law; and that Luke was a writer who was trying to unite them. He does this by ascribing the freedom from the Law to the guidance of the Church by the Holy Spirit, rather than by including it as part of the teaching of Jesus.

Mark's explanation is that Jesus distinguished between the commands of God and human traditions; in this case, the Pharisees are accused of using such traditions (which they raised to a high status) to avoid keeping the commands of God. Washing before meals was part of the oral law, whereas honouring parents was part of the Decalogue, and one should not find spurious ways of evading it. (It would be surprising if in fact Pharisees did not agree.)

The disagreements between members of the churches (as we can see them in Rom. 14 and 15), with some claiming the authority of Paul and others the authority of the more traditional James, must have been deep and bitter. Paul's solution (motivated by the needs of his Gentile missions) is acceptance of one another, not an attempt to prove some right and others wrong.

Anything to do with food and purity could raise irrational and insoluble problems. The really extraordinary thing is that some Jews (such as Paul himself)

were able to overcome lifelong taboos and believe that Jesus had given them this freedom. Mark shows that he believed this too, and he makes it clear in this Sunday's Gospel. JF

Proper 18

(Sunday between 4 and 10 September inclusive)

Proverbs 22.1–2, 8–9, 22–23 or Isaiah 35.4–7a; James 2.1–10 (11–13), 14–17; Mark 7.24–37

Proverbs 22.1–2, 8–9, 22–23

This selection of verses crosses what scholars take to be divisions within Proverbs, because similarities have been perceived between 22.17—24.22 and the Egyptian *Wisdom of Amenemope* (written towards the end of the second millennium BC). Thus 22.17—24.22 is usually treated as a separate section. A case in point is v. 22, which can be compared with the following words from Amenemope:

> Guard thyself against robbing the oppressed
> And against overbearing the disabled
> (J. B. Pritchard, *Ancient Near Eastern Texts*, p. 422).

Whether or not that part of Proverbs is dependent on the Egyptian text and, if so, what this implies for the date of the material, are disputed questions. But they are a reminder that Proverbs contains material in common with other collections of proverbial teaching from the ancient Near East.

Verses 1 and 2 raise interesting questions and can be interpreted in ways that make them contradictory. Verse 1 can be taken to mean that wealth and riches are not approved by God, while 'the rich man in his castle, the poor man at his gate' possible implication of v. 2 suggests that God makes people rich (and poor)! On the other hand, and perhaps preferably, the verses can be interpreted in the reverse order. That rich and poor both have God as their maker indicates no advantages for the rich when it comes to the things of God. Verse 1 is then not condemning wealth, but saying that there is something better. A 'good name' and 'favour' can be understood in secular terms; that is, they are about having a good reputation in the eyes of other people; in context they can also have a religious dimension.

Verses 8–9 are different from each other. The first of these verses describes the consequence of bad action in a moral universe (although the Old Testament is well aware that life is not, unfortunately, so predictable!). The second verse is located within the world of human consequences. It is not easy to bring out the force of the words translated as 'generous'. Literally 'good of eye', they describe a disposition to be creatively good by seeing and seeking out need, and responding to it. Such people may be blessed by God, but their virtue and generous character are also a blessing to them.

With vv. 22–23 the passage moves to yet another position. Rewards and punishments are no longer confined to the impersonal operation of a moral universe or of virtue being its own reward. The active concern of God for the poor could not be more clearly stated. He is both their defending counsel and the one who carries out judgement on their behalf. JR

Isaiah 35.4–7a

This magnificently poetic picture of the future salvation of God's people follows the account of the judgement of Edom in ch. 34, in which Edom is seen as a type of the enemies of God. Evil must be overcome before salvation can be experienced. The chapter contains many of the themes and much of the language and imagery of chs. 40—55, not surprisingly considering that they are separated only by the historical interlude of chs. 36—39. Second Isaiah's picture of salvation as deliverance from exile in Babylon has here been broadened to promise salvation from all conditions of human suffering and all 'Babylonish captivities of the people of God', of which the miraculous deliverance through the wilderness from bondage in Egypt was prototype and promise, supplying much of the imagery here.

The yawning desert separating all dispersed Jews from their land of promise will be miraculously made as fruitful as Lebanon with its forests and Sharon with its rich pasturage (cf. Ps. 104.16). Indeed the natural world will reflect the very character and nature of God as he bestows 'glory' and 'majesty' on it, the qualities he himself possesses and which he will reveal to his people (v. 2). The vision which Isaiah had in the temple will be fulfilled as 'the whole earth becomes full of his glory' (6.1–3).

It is such a vision and such a hope that form the basis for the encouragement given by the prophet to all who are in present despair. If it is true that people perish without a (prophetic) vision (Prov. 29.18) it is essential that God's messengers make God and his certain action the centre of their message (v. 4).

The result is that the mission of the Servant (Isa. 42.7; cf. 61.1–3) will find fulfilment as those who have been blind to the signs of God's presence, deaf to all encouragement to hope, and crippled from taking any constructive action will find the release of the newly saved (vv. 5–6). Their journey from despair to deliverance will be possible since the aridity of the desert will be transformed, as once the wilderness of Sinai provided manna and water, and the wild beasts who made it dangerous to travel will no longer terrify them (v. 7). The way across the desert promised by Second Isaiah (40.3–4) will be open to God's people, 'holy' since it leads to the temple in Zion and thus to worship of, and fellowship with, God (v. 8).

They will be the 'redeemed' of the Lord, those for whom God has acted as nearest kinsman in their need (Lev. 25.25–28) and whom he has 'ransomed' from the powers of evil on whom he has shown his vengeance (v. 4, cf. 34.8).

Matthew 11.5 and Luke 7.22 show how naturally the early Christian Church found a promise here, which was more fully to be realized in Jesus Christ. RM

James 2.1–10 (11–13)

This passage illustrates two of the leading themes of the Epistle of James: the importance of integrity and consistency; and the special place of the poor in God's care. The scene is set in a meeting, presumably for prayer. The word used for the meeting, or meeting-place, is *sunagōgē*, so the scene may reflect the early days of the Church, when Christians still belonged to the Jewish community, or ordered their meetings after its pattern; and their meetings are, like those of the Jewish synagogue, open to visitors. Christians seem, however, already to have come under suspicion and attack for their distinctive faith; the name called over them is presumably the name of Jesus into which they were baptized. It is not surprising that a vulnerable community might welcome the arrival of an influential visitor who might be a potential protector or benefactor; but such a welcome offends against the imperative to treat all alike, and also against God's especial choice of the poor. Is there an inconsistency here – does God show the partiality that in human beings is condemned as sin? James's answer is that God offers his gifts generously to all (1.5); it is the actions of the rich that lay up for them a different treasure (5.1–6).

In a New Testament document notorious for its lack of Christian theology, this passage contains an explicit reference to Jesus, giving him the title 'Lord' that is elsewhere particularly an expression of faith in his resurrection (Rom. 10.9). It also describes him in terms of 'glory': perhaps drawing on the Jewish idea of the sign of the presence of God (Exod. 16.10, 2 Chron. 7.1–3). No two Christian documents could be less alike than James and the Fourth Gospel, but this author may share something of the belief that in Jesus 'we beheld his glory' (John 1.14). There may also be deliberate, though unacknowledged, allusions to the teaching of Jesus. The affirmation of God's choice of the poor to be rich in faith and to inherit the kingdom recalls Jesus' beatitude on the poor, not exactly in the Matthean or Lucan forms (Matt. 5.3, Luke 6.20), but perhaps reflecting a still live oral tradition. The appeal to the 'royal law', again, may indicate that Lev. 19.18 has an especial primacy because Jesus singled it out (Mark 12.28–31). (James's argument in vv. 11–13 about commitment to keep the whole law has been taken to show that he belongs to a fully observant Jewish Christian community, but it is spelled out in terms of core commandments of the Decalogue rather than 'every jot and tittle'.)

The passage gives a picture of a particular style of Christianity, which could belong to early days, but may have continued for some time – and may have analogies in modern (especially perhaps English) practice: with emphasis on an ethos grounded in the teaching of Jesus, but without the need for a developed or dogmatic Christology. It affirms, however, an uncompromising 'bias to the poor' that echoes both the prophetic tradition of Israel and the challenging actions and words of Jesus and that requires the community to look beyond itself to the contemporary world with its exploitation and inequality. SL

Mark 7.24–37

The contrast between the children and the dogs refers to the distinction between Jews and Gentiles, and what is surprising about this is that Mark reports it as part of the speech of Jesus. It was an insult to Gentiles to call them dogs, and we would not have expected Mark to attribute it to the Lord. Attempts have been made to explain this away: Jesus was testing the woman's faith; the word for dogs is a diminutive, and means little dogs, and it expresses affection. In this strange book, nothing should be explained away, but its oddness should be accepted. Mark believed that Jesus was a first-century Jew, and that he deliberately confined his activities almost entirely to Jews; the time for the Gentile world would come later (13.10). This passage comes within a limited excursion by Jesus into Gentile territory adjoining Galilee; so it is perhaps meant as a hint of greater things to come. The Syrophoenician woman is one of three women in Mark's book who are all examples of faith; the other two are the poor widow (12.41–44) and the woman who anointed Jesus (14.3–9).

Jesus is presented to us as one who puts people and their needs before fixed ideas. He defends the disciples for plucking ears of corn on the sabbath, and he heals a man's withered arm also on the sabbath (2.23—3.6). Mark is content to allow his readers to think that a sharp-witted woman changed his mind about the Gentiles and their 'hunger'.

'Had an impediment in his speech' (v. 32) is the translation of a single word in Greek (*mogilalos*), and it is a rare word, of which there are few examples in contemporary Greek writers. One such instance is the Greek translation of Isaiah: 'Then the eyes of the blind will be opened, and the ears of the deaf will hear. Then the lame will leap like a hart, and the tongue of the *stammerer* will be clear' (Isa. 35.5–6). Matthew picked up the allusion to Isaiah and rewrote the paragraph, bringing in the dumb, the crippled, the lame and the blind (15.29–31), replacing Mark's specific story of the man with a more general summary of Jesus' healings.

Mark can be seen as making two points: Jesus goes beyond what might have been expected by those who studied the Scriptures with their promise of fulfilment for Israel; but he also takes up what prophets had said and done. In particular, he imitates both Elijah and Elisha in their good deeds for Gentiles living just beyond the boundaries of Israel (see 1 Kings 17—21 and 2 Kings 1—9). In the transfiguration in ch. 9, Jesus would shortly be seen to transcend Elijah. God's fulfilments exceed the hopes and deeds of the prophets. JF

Proper 19

(Sunday between 11 and 17 September inclusive)

Proverbs 1.20–33 or Isaiah 50.4–9a; James 3.1–12; Mark 8.27–38

Proverbs 1.20–33

Ancient cities, especially in Palestine, were usually built upon mounds that did not provide a great deal of open public space. Such spaces as there were, such as the entrance to the city gate (v. 21), were therefore much in demand, and the ideal place for wisdom teachers and prophets to proclaim their message. Wisdom, personified as a woman (the Hebrew *chokmot* is actually feminine plural, but to be taken as a singular), thus takes her stand. It was presumably not normal for there to be women preachers; but we are concerned here with a literary device.

It is often supposed that Proverbs implies a view of the universe as embodying an abstract moral principle according to which wickedness is always punished and virtue is always rewarded. Sentiments to this effect can certainly be found (cf. Prov. 22.8) and such a view seems to inform Job's so-called comforters. Wisdom's words here show that things are more complicated. If there were a clearly perceived correlation between goodness and prosperity, and wrongdoing and disaster, presumably even human beings would realize where their best interest lay. But Wisdom charges her hearers with having refused her advances, of having ignored her counsel (vv. 24–25). This was no doubt because, from her standpoint, they were simple, scoffers and fools (v. 22). Yet they were no doubt also calculating people who could see no advantage in goodness.

Wisdom seems certain that calamity will indeed strike them (v. 26), in which case they will get no sympathy or help from her. Those, on the other hand, who acknowledge her 'will live at ease, without dread or disaster' (v. 33). If these sentiments have any meaning for today, it can only be in an eschatological sense; that is, within a dimension in which God's love and mercy will have undone the effects of human wickedness. Without this dimension, Wisdom's teaching runs the very real danger of turning good news into a threat, and of making enlightened or even selfish self-interest the main reason for loyalty to God. A difference between what Wisdom says here and the prophets say elsewhere is that God does not give up on his people when calamity strikes; and this involvement leads ultimately to a cross. JR

Isaiah 50.4–9a

See Palm Sunday, p. 101.

James 3.1–12

James draws on a whole range of imagery to illustrate his theme of the dangers of speech, showing that he belongs to a world where cultures meet and mingle at the popular level. There are proverbial similes of horse and ship that could function in any society; a reference to *Gehenna*, the place of destruction in Jewish eschatology; even an apparent allusion to Hellenistic philosophy in the 'the wheel of nature', a phrase suggesting derivation from the Pythagorean idea of the transmigration of souls. He has two main targets. First, the destructive power of words. His warning here sounds clearly in a modern world of mass communication where propaganda, spin and incitement to hatred or violence are all too familiar. 'It's good to talk' is a well-known advertising slogan, but the harm done by words, whether used carelessly or deliberately, is just as well known. Second, and here developing a broader theme that runs through the epistle, he attacks inconsistency in speech. James is very concerned with personal integrity; whether in wholehearted prayer (1.5–8), in equal treatment of individuals (2.1–4) or in consistency of belief and action (2.14–16). Here he attacks the use of words both to bless and to curse. It is not just that these are diametrically opposed forms of speech, but that their use reveals a deeper-seated division. For blessings and curses to come from the same mouth, the same person, shows that that person's own character is confused and distorted. It also shows a failure to recognize the true nature of the object of destructive speech: another human being made in the image of God (there is, of course, a clear allusion to the creation narrative of Gen. 1.26). Respect and honour for God should be worked out in a similar respect and honour for one's fellows: his creatures and his children.

Before launching into the more colourful part of this passage, James had issued a simple and pragmatic warning to teachers, among whom he seems to count himself. Paul also refers to teachers as having a recognized role in the Christian community, distinct from prophets (1 Cor. 12.28). They may have been responsible for expounding the Scriptures in a Christian meeting, like the rabbi in a Jewish synagogue. The teacher would be regarded with respect, which might make the role seem desirable; but it carries responsibility. A teacher has power to influence what is learnt, and how it is learnt, and to form attitudes that may be taken out into the wider world and influence relationships there for good or ill. The most important lesson to teach and to learn is that of personal integrity and of equal treatment of others in the sight of, and as in the image of, God. SL

Mark 8.27–38

To read Mark aright, it is always necessary, where there are parallels, to divest oneself of what Matthew and Luke made of him. (They had not yet written and Mark did not know what they would write!) In many ways, they understood him, disagreed with him, and sanitized (even fumigated) his message.

Nowhere is it more helpful to think thus than in the so-called Confession of Peter.

So great is the weight of preaching that says 'Can *you* be like Peter?', and so immense the fame of the encomium (Matt. 16.17–19) on Peter, the rock on which the Church is built (whether taken papally or not), that it requires attention strictly to Mark to see that he probably meant something quite different.

The question is: Is Peter admirable or flawed? Is he here the one who 'followed' without a thought in 1.16–20 (see p. 271) or the one who sees without perceiving at the transfiguration (9.2–5; cf. 8.14–17) and forsakes then denies Jesus in the passion?

Out in Gentile territory (the big wide world of the kingdom's future mission), Jesus is 'in the way' (cf. 1.2–3). Peter acknowledges Jesus as Messiah. Hitherto, the term has not been applied to him, though 'Son of God', probably meant as synonymous, has come to Jesus' ear alone (in Mark) at the baptism (1.11) and from demons, having knowledge of the invisible world and its secrets (3.11). Of course we readers know that Jesus is both from the moment we take up or first hear the book (1.1). At his trial, Jesus will – at last – accept that he is Messiah (14.62), for the passion is the heart of his Messiahship. But has Peter got it right?

Jesus says that Peter's affirmation must not get out. But is that because early Christians knew it had not been generally known and needed to explain why (so no original tradition here), or because Peter's claim is, in the flow of Mark's narrative, so inadequate as to be erroneous? The rebuke Peter administers to Jesus when he hears what 'Jesus as Messiah' entails brings Peter's failure of understanding into the open (v. 32). Worse is to come. This is no simple little mistake, but satanic: Peter is on the other side, like the scribes of 3.22–30. (Matthew made the rebuke by Peter into a courteous demurral, and Luke dropped the identifying of Peter as Satan. Mark's literary-theological depiction of Peter is too much for his successors who know the heroic role of the great apostles, see p. 146f.)

The true and necessary doctrine about Jesus and how to follow him comes in vv. 34–38. It is the essence of tough Marcan realism, brooking no softening for now. Yet the ultimate hope is wholly sure (v. 38); and 9.1 may suggest that, for those who do indeed 'see', the passion will bring the start of fulfilment. LH

Proper 20

(Sunday between 18 and 24 September inclusive)

Proverbs 31.10–31 or Wisdom of Solomon 1.16—2.1, 12–22 or Jeremiah 11.18–20; James 3.13—4.3, 7–8a; Mark 9.30–37

Proverbs 31.10–31

This passage has annoyed some feminists and some liberation theologians. It is easy to understand why. While, from the point of the Hebrew, it is a skilfully constructed poem of 22 verses in which each verse begins with a successive letter of the Hebrew alphabet, its gender and class assumptions are disturbing even for those who may not be feminists or liberationists.

In the first place, it is not only written from a male point of view; it offers a stereotype of what a 'capable wife' should be like. Even worse, it suggests in v. 10 that such women are rare commodities! Another unfortunate impression created by the poem is that while the 'capable wife' not only runs the household but the whole estate (v. 16) her husband seems to live a life of comparable idleness (v. 23). From the class point of view, she is clearly not poor; and the fact that her husband is an elder of the land, that she has servants (v. 15) and owns, or at least manages, property certainly marks her out as highly privileged. At the same time, it is possible to admire her competence and shrewdness, as well as her sheer hard work. Here is certainly a very 'strong' woman within the context of the male-dominated upper class of later Jewish society; and it would be churlish to overlook her kindness to the poor and needy (v. 20). The poem also ends with a warning comment about charm and beauty (v. 30) while the final verse could be directed against male exclusivity and superiority. Her achievements should be publicly recognized. Some, however, may feel that this only compounds the problem for modern readers, by widely advertising a stereotype of the 'capable wife' that has little resonance with the demands upon women today, and their legitimate aspirations.

Like all writings, this text is a product of its times and conditions. If it has a latent meaning beyond what its author intended, it will be by way of challenging modern readers to consider their own attitudes to gender and class, and whether these are informed by the spirit of Christ. JR

Wisdom of Solomon 1.16—2.1, 12–22

Anyone considering basing a sermon on this powerful reading would be well advised to read the whole passage, including 2.2–11. Rightly or wrongly, it has been described as a Jewish expression of the principle of *carpe diem* (enjoy the day), not, of course, that the principle is commended here. It is to be noted that the ungodly are not merely people who have intellectual hang-ups about God. They certainly have intellectual hang-ups, but they translate these not only into a nihilistic philosophy of life, but into active persecution of those who seek to be loyal to God (2.12–20). The section 2.1–5 sets out their philosophy and the grounds for it. The language is reminiscent of some of the observations in Ecclesiastes (cf. 2.23; 12.7); but unlike that book, the philosophy here leads away from God to a covenant with death (i.e. 1.16; death is not mentioned in the Greek, but commentators take 'him' to refer to death). Their point is that since no one returns from death, since we were put on earth without our knowledge or agreement and since after death we will be forgotten, life might as well be lived as though the only reality is enjoying the present to the full. What this entails is spelled out in 2.6–11, and it is a pity that v. 11 does not appear in the reading: 'But let might be our law of right, for what is weak proves itself to be useless.' This principle certainly guided some fascist regimes of the twentieth century.

But the ungodly are not content to get on with their own pleasures. The existence of goodness and of the godly is a profound challenge to all that they stand for. They cannot let it go unnoticed, and are moved to carry out the persecution of God's servants. Hopefully, it is not true, but only their perception, that the godly consider them to be base and unclean.

In considering the implications of the passage, it has to be stressed that the ungodly do not draw the only conclusion from their perception of the world and human existence. It is possible to agree with the apparent purposelessness of human life and yet still to believe that goodness and kindness are worth pursuing. The sentiments of 2.11 are, thank God, not the only possibility. But the passage does throw up the challenge of the problem of good; the problem of why it is that people continue to believe in God and goodness in the setting of an ambiguous world and active persecution. The passage speaks of the 'prize for blameless souls' (2.22), but the godly do not live as they do solely to gain a prize at the end. Their lives, and what they stand for, are evidence that an ambiguous world need not be understood in an entirely negative and pessimistic way. The problem of good is far more difficult to handle than the problem of evil. JR

Jeremiah 11.18–20

Verses 11–19 are in prose in the Hebrew, with v. 20 being a fragment in poetry. Because 'their evil deeds' (v. 18) has no antecedent in either the Hebrew or the selected portion for the reading (!) (i.e. to whom does 'their' refer?) many commentators have assumed that 12.6 ('for even your kinsfolk and your own family . . .') originally followed 11.18, in which case the 'their' would refer to members of Jeremiah's own family. Whether or not this is right, Jeremiah is clearly grateful to God for having revealed to him that his life was in danger because of his activity as a prophet. In his innocence he was as defenceless as a gentle lamb. REB 'pet lamb' brings out even more strongly the vulnerability of an animal that had come to trust the very people who were now plotting against it. This could strengthen the view that the threat came from within Jeremiah's own family. The reported speech of the adversaries ('Let us destroy . . .') contains one difficult point of interpretation. NRSV 'its fruit' renders the Hebrew 'in (or "with") its bread', and the REB, for example, has followed many interpreters in reading the Hebrew consonants to produce the English 'Let us destroy the tree while the sap is in it'. The language of the adversaries is very strong. Not only do they want to end Jeremiah's prophetic work; they want to obliterate all memory of it as well as of him. Jeremiah's violent poetic outburst (v. 20) may disturb some readers for its lack of charity, but the prophet was only human and the conflict was a matter of life and death.

The passage has been chosen because the Gospel records a prediction of Jesus' betrayal and death. Taken together, the passages are a reminder that servants of God are called to work in a world that does not wish to know or hear God's truth. Under both the old and new covenants this may lead to persecution and death and, in both cases, the figure of the pet lamb may appropriately indicate the vulnerability of the servant of God. Why does God not protect and publicly vindicate those he calls to his service? In fact, he does, but in unexpected ways. Jeremiah may not have lived to see his vindication, but the fact that we are reading his words today indicates that his adversaries did not, after all, efface all trace of him! JR

James 3.13—4.3, 7–8a

James returns to a subject he has discussed before: the question of unanswered prayer. In 1.6–7 the reason lay in the subject: someone who prays without conviction or wholeheartedness must not expect an answer. Here the reason lies in the object of prayer: God will not give what is asked for selfish ends. In 1.5 a proper object of prayer is wisdom: that gift God will always give. Now wisdom is defined. It is the necessary underpinning for the good life, giving a character that is totally free from the destructive and divisive aggression that almost amounts to murder (James's use of hyperbole is similar to Jesus' in Matt. 6.21–22). Most importantly for James, wisdom will also create a character of complete integrity in dealing with others (compare his example of failure in that regard in 2.1–9; Proper 18). This characterization of wisdom as the key to action recalls passages in the 'wisdom literature' of Israel that also deal with the way to live the good life (e.g. Prov. 1.2–7), and James may be seen as inheriting and carrying on the wisdom tradition.

His list of the characteristics of wisdom – pure, peaceable, merciful – also recalls Jesus' beatitudes (Matt. 5.7–9), for Jesus too, in his teaching and especially in his use of parables, may be seen as a 'sage': a teacher in the wisdom tradition. There is a major difference, however. The wisdom tradition of Israel, and indeed of other parts of the ancient Near East, for it is a very international tradition, is very much concerned with maintaining the status quo, and with guidelines for the individual to live in harmony with a stable and well-ordered society – Jesus was concerned with turning the values of contemporary society upside-down in the light of the kingdom of God. James may, like a teacher in the ancient tradition, urge his readers to ask God for wisdom, and to let it be manifested in their lives, but it is clear elsewhere in the epistle that in his bias to the poor and the powerless he is following the wisdom of Jesus. The contrast between the wisdom of God 'from above' that underpins the work of peacemaking and a 'devilish' wisdom that leads to dispute and conflict is echoed in the concluding exhortation to submit to God but to resist the devil. This sequence is found also in 1 Pet. 5.6–9, and it may be that a common pattern of early Christian ethical teaching underlies them both; another indication that despite the Epistle of James's few overt references to Jesus, its author is firmly among his followers. SL

Mark 9.30–37

There are three predictions of the passion and resurrection in Mark; they punctuate the journey from Caesarea Philippi to Jerusalem (8.27—11.1) and provide an interpretation of it: to follow Christ is to share his humiliation and his glory (cf. 8.34—9.1).

This, the second of these predictions (see also 8.31 and 10.33–34) is the briefest of the three, mentioning only the essential points: Jesus will be handed over into the power of human beings, will be killed by them, and will rise after three days. Mark explains that Jesus did not want anyone else apart from the disciples to know, so emphasizing the importance of his teaching; it is central to Mark's understanding of the gospel.

What is also much emphasized by Mark is the failure of the disciples to understand what Jesus is saying to them. After each prediction Mark gives an example of their incomprehension: that of Peter in 8.32–33; that of James and John in 10.35f.; and here their argument as to which of them was the greatest – totally inappropriate, since what matters is the opposite of greatness, namely being last and being a servant.

The child is the symbol of what is required of the followers of Jesus. We must be careful here, because our ideas about children may be different from those of people who lived in the ancient world – and in fact earlier than the nineteenth century, when a new and romantic idea of childhood entered Western thought. In general, the ancients thought of childhood as a time to be passed through as quickly as possible, a necessary evil. The child stood for what one should *not* be: uninformed, immature, having no status in society, incapable of owning property, quarrelsome, ignorant. 'Do not be children in your thinking' (1 Cor. 14.20). 'We are no longer children' (Eph. 4.14). 'When I grew up, I finished with childish things' (1 Cor. 13.11).

The choice of a child as the role model for disciples is therefore surprising. We do not find it in the letter-writers of the New Testament, but only in the Synoptic Gospels. It stands for absence of status, lack of respect, being a non-person, one who has been rejected by society – all the things that were true of someone who had been crucified. JF

Proper 21

(Sunday between 25 September and 1 October inclusive)

Esther 7.1–6, 9–10, 9.20–22 or Numbers 11.4–6, 10–16, 24–29; James 5.13–20; Mark 9.38–50

Esther 7.1–6, 9–10; 9.20–22

This reading presumes a knowledge of the whole story of Esther, otherwise congregations will not be able to identify Haman and Mordecai, nor will they know the risky circumstances and purpose of Esther's audience with her royal husband. Again, the point of the concluding verses (9.20–22) will be lost on anyone unfamiliar with the Jewish festival of Purim, and the use of these verses as the basis for its observance (whatever its origin) in Judaism. Unfortunately, this extract is the only occasion in the entire Revised Common Lectionary (i.e. covering all three services on Sundays) where the book of Esther appears. If it is decided to use this as an opportunity to make congregations familiar with the whole story, it is worth considering using the Greek version of Esther, which is Scripture for the Catholic and Orthodox churches, and available in NRSV, REB and NJB. Greek Esther contains a beautiful prayer uttered by Esther prior to her dangerous approach to Ahasuerus: 'O my Lord, you only are our king; help me, who am alone and have no helper but you, for my danger is in my hand' (Greek Esther 14.3–4). Theologically, the book of Esther can be taken to describe the fragile existence of the people of God in a world hostile to God, even if modern readers may find the wholesale slaughter of the enemies of the Jews less than edifying. JR

Numbers 11.24–30

Numbers 11 is an odd narrative, in that the problem that stands at its heart is not the problem that endowment with the Spirit of God remedies. The story begins with a complaint of the people in the wilderness about their food. Manna is evidently too boring a diet, and the people remember with nostalgia the culinary delights of their time of slavery in Egypt. The irony of slaves enjoying a rich diet should not be overlooked. At the end of the chapter the craving for meat is satisfied by the provision of quails (birds whose Latin name is *coturnix coturnix*) and by divine punishment of the ungrateful former slaves. The material that intervenes hardly fits this scenario.

Moses complains to God that he cannot bear alone the burden of leading the people, a complaint similar to the story in Exod. 18 of Moses being persuaded to appoint other judges to help him deal with the people. God promises in Num. 11.16–17 that he will ease Moses' burden by putting some of Moses' spirit upon elders who can then help. What this has to do with the miraculous feeding of the complaining people by sending quails into their camp is hard to see.

The passage set as the reading deals with the carrying out of the promises to give some of Moses' spirit to elders, in this case 70. The proof that the transfer has been carried out is that those affected 'prophesy'. This is to be understood along the lines of 1 Sam. 10.9–13, a frenzy of ecstatic utterance and behaviour that was not necessarily edifying in itself, but which identified people as belonging to a particular group or sect. Nowhere in the narrative is it indicated that those endowed with the spirit subsequently assisted Moses either to judge or to feed the people.

The heart of the story is the endowment of Eldad and Medad, two otherwise unknown Israelites, with the spirit. It is tempting to see, but impossible to identify, the struggle of groups for legitimacy behind the story. Eldad and Medad then symbolize 'outsiders' who, contrary to what 'official channels' expected or encouraged, were clearly designated as ones approved by God. Moses' support for them and his sublime prayer 'would that all the Lord's people were prophets' need to be read, in the first instance, in the context of prophesying as frenzied, ecstatic activity. The groups that displayed these external symptoms were, in the stories of Samuel and Kings, groups fanatically loyal to the God of Israel, and prepared to take drastic action in support of their faith. In the context of Numbers, Moses' wish is for a people wholly committed to God, although the story clearly looks different, if read through Christian eyes. JR

James 5.13–20

Two themes have run through the Epistle of James: the dangers of divisiveness, both internal and personal and in relationships, and the dangers of speech, which express these divisions. Now, in conclusion, he paints a picture of an integrated and supportive Christian community in which speech is properly used: in prayer, praise, confession and conversion. The use of song in the early Church is also encouraged by Paul (Eph. 5.19). It may include the psalms, new Christian hymns, such as are often identified in Phil. 2.5–11 and Col. 1.15–20; maybe also the canticles of Luke 1—2 and the outbursts of praise that punctuate the vision of the Apocalypse of John. Singing in tongues (as in 1 Cor.14.15) may also be included, though James does not seem here to be familiar with charismatic gifts.

The ministry of healing, taken for granted as a regular and familiar part of the life of the Church, is not conducted by those regarded as having a special spiritual gift, but by the elders of the Church by virtue of their office. (If James represents a very early stage in Christian history, as is often thought, structures of leadership have already emerged, perhaps taken over from those of the synagogue.) Olive oil was widely used in the Mediterranean world in the treatment of the sick (as by the good Samaritan in Luke 10.34) but the elders' anointing is clearly a ritual act, conducted as it is 'in the name of the Lord', Jesus, whose healings would be the model and authority for their own. Clearly, this prayer and anointing is carried out in the expectation of recovery: James's picture does not provide a model for the anointing of the dying. He shares, as indeed Jesus does (Mark 2.5), the assumption that sickness may be connected with sin, and the 'healing' may be both physical and spiritual.

It is surprising that, in a passage explicitly related to Christian practice and to the example and authority of Jesus, James should return to the Old Testament (1 Kings 17.1; 18.42–45) for an illustration of effective prayer. The gospel tradition might have supplied him with the example of Jesus as a man of prayer. Elijah, however, is part of the tradition inherited from Judaism, and finds a special place in Christian imagination when his role is seen to be fulfilled by John the Baptist (Matt. 11.12–13). The final exhortation is, again, typical of James: prayer must be carried into action. As prayer for the poor must be carried through into supplying their needs (2.4–17), so mutual prayer and confession, important as this is, is not enough; there must be an active effort to convert and reclaim the wanderer. This is not a one-way activity, with all the merit on one side and all the benefit on the other. There is an ambiguity in the last clause, which could be read as equivalent to the preceding one; but the verse is best understood as relating to both parties. Both need and experience forgiveness: the converter may help to 'save a soul from death', but he will also 'cover a multitude of sins' of his own. SL

Mark 9.38–50

Mark does not use the word 'church' in his Gospel, but there can be little doubt that he belonged to one (perhaps one that looked to Paul for its origins or at any rate for its way of seeing its faith). Little doubt either that he wrote his book in order that it might be read out to a congregation. We know from the work of Justin Martyr in the mid-second century that this is what happened and, in a mostly illiterate society, reading aloud was certainly normal. The problems that face any community, religious or secular, seem to be on his mind as he gathers together here various sayings of Jesus that will help to bring peace to those who are at variance with one another.

The community of Jesus is not to overvalue itself; they are not to think of themselves as having exclusive rights over the use of his name. They are to be 'open', in the sense that the presumption will be that people are in favour of them rather than against, unless it is clearly seen that this is not so. (Mark's congregation seems to feel itself much less threatened than Matthew's church; he omits this paragraph in Mark, and changes the saying of Jesus to its opposite, 'He that is not with me is against me' (12.30), perhaps deliberately 'hiding' it in a new context.

Those who act out of kindness to the believer will be rewarded by God at the judgement. The opposite of kindness is offence – leading people into sin; God will punish those who do so. And there is another direction from which offences can come: from inside the human heart. 'All these evil things come from within' (Mark 7.21–23). What might lead to our downfall is to be excised ruthlessly, because it is obviously better to lead a restricted life here and now and enter eternal life in the kingdom of God than a 'full' life now with no future at all.

This brings Mark to a saying that sums up much of the teaching in his book:

'Everyone will be salted with fire.' It is a revised, Christian version of a rule in Leviticus: 'With all your offerings you shall offer salt' (Lev. 2.13). (Some copyists of Mark have even inserted this into his text.) Just as salt made the sacrifices of the old covenant acceptable to God, so what makes the believers' sacrifice of themselves (what Paul calls 'your bodies', Rom. 12.1) acceptable is their surrender of themselves to fire, that is destruction. Losing your life is the only way to save it (Mark 8.35). Such self-sacrifice is to mark their communal life. It is also the only way that leads to peace in a community: 'In humility count others better than yourself. Let each of you look not only to his own interests, but also to the interests of others' (Phil. 2.3–4).

Mark's picture of the followers of Jesus is of people who welcome those who are not members of the community and who are aware of their own weaknesses (recall his depiction of the Twelve!) and sensitive to the needs of others. JF

Proper 22

(Sunday between 2 and 8 October inclusive)

Job 1.1; 2.1–10 or Genesis 2.18–24; Hebrews 1.1–4; 2.5–12; Mark 10.2–16

Job 1.1; 2.1–10

For the next four weeks, Track 1 has extracts from the prose and poetic parts of the book of Job. While it has often been pointed out that there are noticeable differences between chs. 1—2 (in prose) and 3—37 (in poetry; the divine name YHWH, the Lord, is used in the former but not the latter; there is no allusion in the latter to the origins of Job's misfortunes) the book in its final form is intended to be read as a whole. In this case, the reader has privileged information about Job's sufferings, information not available to Job, his wife or his 'comforters'. In this regard it is most unfortunate that the lectionary chooses 2.1–10 rather than 1.6–12 from the prose introduction, because this deprives congregations of the reason for God allowing the Satan to afflict Job. The Satan's argument is that Job's piety brings him good returns in terms of God's blessing, and that Job's attitude will change radically if Job suddenly suffers misfortune (1.9–11). God, who knows Job's reasons for his loyalty better than the Satan, is certain that the Satan will be proved wrong, but gives the Satan permission to afflict Job. The lectionary portion assumes all this, and restricts the argument of the Satan to the view that Job will renounce this piety if his own person is afflicted (2.4–5).

It is unfortunate that the NRSV renders the Hebrew 'the Satan' as Satan (but see the NRSV footnote of '*the Accuser*'), because congregations will readily associate this figure with Satan in the developed demonology of later Judaism and of Christianity. In Job, the Satan clearly has an adversarial role (cf. REB 'the Adversary, Satan' at 1.6) but he is still clearly one of the heavenly beings (2.1), and God's questions to him do not indicate divine ignorance of his activities but are a narrative device to initiate a conversation.

Within the terms of the prose prologue, the narrative raises the problem of good. If there were an obvious connection between loyalty to God and material blessing (as in some versions of the 'prosperity gospel'), religion would be a worthwhile investment; and it has to be admitted that most believers are not wholly altruistic in the exercise of their faith. The bottom line is that many people persist in their faith and their belief in goodness when there is much in the world and their personal lives to count against such commitments. Their persistence may puzzle those for whom the Satan speaks. Only God, and the faithful, know the real reasons. JR

Genesis 2.18–24

This passage has been chosen because its concluding verse (2.24) is quoted in the Gospel for the day. What preceded 2.24 has featured in feminist discussions, because it presupposes the anterior existence of the male, with the female being made from part of the male. This presumption is strengthened by the interpretation of the passage in 1 Tim. 2.13, where the creation of Adam before Eve is used as the basis for the view of female subordination to the male. Some feminists have also been angered by the description of the woman as the 'helper' of the man (v. 18).

In the view of the present commentary there is no point in trying to make the text say what it does not say, for example, by arguing that the man is actually an androgynous creature that does not become male until the female is created. As has long been recognized, Gen. 2 contains a number of origin stories, which were part of popular folk wisdom. The whole story of the making of the woman turns on a Hebrew pun, the fact that the Hebrew for woman, *'ishshah*, can be understood as the word for man, *'ish* with a directional suffix, hence the explanation 'out of man' (v. 23). If a folk etymology has become a theological justification for the subordination of women, this is an unwarranted use of the passage.

The interesting thing about v. 24 is that some nineteenth-century interpreters saw it as a survival of an ancient custom of matrilocal marriage; that is, marriage in which a man moved to live with his wife's family. This is not implied by the text, which is simply saying that marriage entails a shift of loyalty and affection, from parents to spouse. The attempt to use the verse as a biblical justification for monogamous heterosexual marriage as the only form ordained by God is as misguided as using the preceding verses to justify male superiority. Whatever may have been the interpretation put on the passage in New Testament times, it must not be forgotten that Old Testament society was polygamous. Many characters – for example, Jacob, Elkanah (the father of Samuel) and David – have more than one wife without being censured, and Old Testament law made specific inheritance provision for the elder son in a family where there was more than one wife (Deut. 21.15–17). JR

Hebrews 1.1–4; 2.5–12

These two non-consecutive passages of Hebrews are presumably juxtaposed to bring out on the one hand the heavenly grandeur and on the other the redemptive humanness of Christ. The intervening passage is mostly devoted to dense and subtle exegesis of scriptural texts designed to prove Jesus' superiority to the angels; when read on Christmas Day as set in the Book of Common Prayer it did not always fall on wholly comprehending ears.

The first four verses, having asserted the claim to root the Christian case in prophecy, place Jesus as the very highest level in the heavenly hierarchy and see him as God's climactic spokesman. They go alongside the opening of John's Gospel and passages in Paul (e.g. 1 Cor. 1.24; 8.6; Phil. 2.6–11) that see him as pre-existent and the agent of creation. The word rendered 'reflection' (perhaps better the more active 'radiance' or 'effulgence') is used in Philo and in Wisd. 7.26 of the 'Wisdom' of God, the personified agent of his creative activity (cf. Prov. 8). The language here reflects the early Christian conviction that Jesus the Son of God is the wholly comprehensive agent of God's saving purpose for the world, in every dimension and at every level.

The writer turns easily to what we see as quite other strands in the Jewish Scriptures, here first Ps. 110.1, that most widely used of all early proof-texts (v. 3b). The 'name' in v. 4 has all the resonance that filled the idea in scriptural tradition – the name being 'Son', cf. 1.5, where he applies to the moment of Christ's return to heaven the text, Ps. 2.7, attached in the first three Gospels to his baptism and the transfiguration.

In 2.6–8, the author engages in yet another of those learned exercises in exegesis that dominate his work, this time working in Ps. 8.4–6 (cf. also 1 Cor. 15.27). He exploits the fact that the Septuagint text, seen as just as inspired as the Hebrew, has a useful ambiguity. In v. 7, the Hebrew sees man as a 'a little lower than the angels', that is, in the hierarchy of creation. For our writer's purpose, however, it is a godsend that the Greek can bear the temporal sense: he (man or son of man, v. 6) became '*for a little while* lower than the angels' en route to his triumph. Taken thus, Ps. 8 describes exactly Christ's saving act.

Yet this human phase is no charade, no painless visitation by royalty, but is as wholly genuine as it is vital. Our author is fully convinced of Jesus' self-identification with the human lot – suffering and death included. It is indeed essential to his mediatorial role (vv. 10–12). LH

Mark 10.2–16

By the time Mark included it in his Gospel, Paul had already said that Jesus deplored divorce (1 Cor. 7.10); though Paul gave no context to Jesus' teaching on the subject, and he proceeded to qualify it in cases, new since Jesus spoke, where a Christian is married to an unbeliever (7.12–16) – though by no means does he encourage separation even in such cases.

Mark gives the teaching a context, and offers no mitigation. It is the classic text for those who take an absolute 'no divorce' view. But the least we can do is to try to grasp Mark's intent. He presents Jesus' teaching in the setting of the Jewish debate on the subject. There is this view and that view; what then does Jesus say? Some Jewish teachers of the day were permissive, as the Law itself was taken to be; others were more restrictive. None that we know of were rigorous. How could one be, in the light of the Law (Deut. 24.1–4)?

Jesus proceeds to undercut this way of reading the Torah in favour of its deeper message. (It was a strategy also used by Paul when he appealed to Gen. 15.6 to relativize the subsequent law of circumcision, Rom. 4.) So God's provision for Adam and Eve in Eden has priority, if we would grasp God's purpose for human life. Later rules were a concession to our weakness – or, candidly, hardness of heart (v. 5), a kind of faithless obtuseness such as the disciples displayed in 6.52.

The life of the kingdom, which Jesus both announces and inaugurates among us, has then the character of a renewal of Paradise – Eden remade. This graphic vision is akin to Paul's doctrine of Christ as second Adam (Rom. 5.12f.; 1 Cor. 15.22) and life in Christ as new creation (2 Cor. 5.17; Gal. 6.15). It is taken up again in, for example, Rev. 21—22; the end will be as the beginning, though *now* city, *then* garden. It is a sense of the gospel that has sublime beauty. More than any other image perhaps, it astonishes us who have grown used to Christianity being 'there', and gives us a fresh sense of its force.

It remains to consider the status of the teaching. Mostly, it has been taken as law. Yet Mark is oddly free of such provision – and Christians have been in no rush to take the subsequent passages, on the great evil in wealth, in any such way. So did he really mean, here virtually uniquely, to turn canonist? Matthew took him so, and found Mark's 'rule' needed mitigation: 19.9; 5.31f. But then, Matthew provided means of enforcement: 18.15–17. Mark has no such interest. His picture of marriage is of life as it is to be in God's kingdom, when all shall be renewed and perfected – and it can begin in the here and now. Jesus had given a preview of it in his victory over Satan's testing, 1.13 (see p. 271). Where Jesus is, there is Eden. LH

Proper 23

(Sunday between 9 and 15 October inclusive)

Job 23.1–9, 16–17 or Amos 5.6–7, 10–15; Hebrews 4.12–16; Mark 10.17–31

Job 23.1–9, 16–17

The opening words of the reading are not what the Bible actually has (the text reads 'Then Job answered'), and the need of the Lectionary to add 'his companions' indicates that congregations are expected to know what the poetic part of the book is about; that is, a series of speeches in which Job's companions try to convince him of their point of view (that he must have sinned grievously to have deserved punishment on such a large scale) and Job rebuts their arguments.

In the preceding chapter Eliphaz has accused Job of being like the ungodly, who oppress the poor and weak and argue that God is either indifferent to such action or powerless to prevent it. Job is urged to repent and to pray to God for forgiveness, and his life will once again enjoy blessing. In reply, Job does not bother to answer the slanders of Eliphaz. His problem is more pressing; namely, that he cannot find God. He is convinced that God would give him a fair hearing if only he could present his case to God; the problem is that wherever he looks, God is not to be found.

What does it mean to 'find' God? How do people know that their prayers have been heard and that their arguments have proved to be convincing? These are very difficult questions to answer, and Job's realistic refusals to persuade himself that God has heard him are in striking contrast to the glib certainties of his companions, not to mention the glib certainties of some present-day believers who appear to have God well under control. The book of Job makes it clear that God makes himself known in his own ways and in his own times. Job has to endure much abuse from his companions and much agonized questioning of God's ways until there is a divine response from the whirlwind (cf. 38.1) that totally ignores all the arguments that the human disputants have so painstakingly rehearsed.

For modern readers, the following points may be made: that human experience of God's absence or elusiveness is nonetheless an experience of God, if there is a determination to be satisfied with nothing less than God himself. God enables seekers to trust in his justice and mercy. These ensure that God will be found, in that way and time that serve the seeker best, from God's perspective. JR

Amos 5.6–7, 10–15

These words, which derive substantially from the prophet Amos who was active before the fall of the northern kingdom, Israel, in 722/1 BC, raise a fundamental theological question about the nature of divine judgement. Clearly, the behaviour of the ruling élite in Israel was unacceptable by humanitarian, let alone divine, standards. The chief evil was the corruption of justice. The gate of the city (v. 10) was one of the few public spaces in an Israelite city, and it was where justice was administered (cf. Ruth 4.1–2). As if it was not bad enough for those who sought to uphold justice to be hated, active measures were taken to subvert justice by the offering of bribes (v. 12). The outcome is summed up in v. 7. Justice is turned to wormwood (white wormwood, a dwarf shrub frequently coupled in the Bible with poison hemlock, and thus considered poisonous), and righteousness is pushed to the ground.

What is to be done in such circumstances? The threat that God will break out against the house of Joseph like a devouring fire (v. 6) is probably an editorial interpretation of vv. 4–5 (which have to do with cultic rather than strictly ethical matters), which predicts judgement for the sanctuary at Bethel. However, this only points up the problem. If God destroys his people, who or what will take their place? Will they be any better than those destroyed? If the people reform, will this be only because they have been frightened by the prospect of judgement? Does Goes want loyalty to him to be based upon a threat?

It is impossible to answer these questions, for all that it is necessary to pose them. The passage hovers between threat and promise. The call to 'seek good and not evil, that you may live' (v. 14) is not a call to superficial repentance in order to avoid punishment, but a call to a radical change of life, which will lead to a new quality of existence based upon love of what is good. It will lead to a proper understanding of what it means to say that God is with us (v. 14). But is a group of people so deeply mired in evil capable of such repentance or even of wanting it? The last two lines (v. 15b–c), which also hover between threat and promise, leave the question unanswered. JR

Hebrews 4.12–16

The strength of the imagery in the opening lines of this passage will initially attract readers, but many will find the implications of that imagery uncomfortable and unwelcome. Contemporary reflections on God as redeemer, as liberator, even as friend, leave little room for thinking of God or God's word as a 'two-edged sword'. Judgement language is out of fashion.

This particular depiction of 'the word of God' is more than simply judgement language, however. It appears in the text as a response to Christian understanding of the gospel and the role Scripture plays in that gospel. The preceding passage (Heb. 4.1–11) reflects on Ps. 95 and the notion of entering into God's 'rest'. The author sees in that concept a challenge to God's people to continue to be faithful; hence, the psalm *becomes* an instance of the discerning, judging, probing word of God. Verses 12–13, then, come as an afterthought, expressing warning but also thanksgiving and praise.

The personification of the word of God in this passage led some commentators in the early Church to assume that the *logos* here refers to Christ. Although that identification is familiar from the Prologue to John's Gospel, the context suggests that the word of God is understood as an aspect of God, as God's power of critical discernment, God's capacity for judgement. In addition, the personification of God's word in Scripture (see e.g. Ps. 147.15, where the word 'runs', and Wisd. 18.14–16, where the word 'leaps' and touches heaven) and in other early Jewish writers suggests that here also the word refers to God rather than to Jesus.

Consistent with this personification of God's word is the vitality attributed to it. The word is 'living and active'; it is 'piercing until it divides'. The first of these descriptions of the word's vitality refers to the way in which God's speech continues to play a role in the present life of the believing community. God spoke through the psalm discussed in Heb. 4.1–11, but God also continues to speak through that same psalm. This speech of God, past and present, plays an important role throughout Hebrews, beginning in 1.1–4.

The word of God also 'pierces', with its characteristic discernment and judgement. Associations between judgement or the spirit and the sword are familiar from other New Testament writings (Eph. 6.17; Rev. 1.16; 2.12; 19.15). In this passage the imagery appears to fall apart when the word is said to divide 'soul from spirit' and 'joints from marrow'. Since the places at which soul and spirit or joints and marrow are joined are non-existent, such surgery is beyond the human imagination. That is just the point, of course: God's word accomplishes feats of discernment of which the human mind cannot even conceive.

This vivid portrait of the word of God and the inevitability of judgement concludes with the reminder that all are vulnerable to God 'to whom we must render an account'. That last word, 'account', translates the Greek *logos*, as does 'word' earlier in the passage. To the divine 'word', then, a human 'word' must be given in answer.

With v. 14, the writer takes up a different topic, that of the priesthood of Jesus, and vv. 14–16 have little literary or theological connection with vv. 12–13. (For more detailed comments on 4.14–16, see the discussion under Good Friday.) For readers who find the notion of God's discernment terrifying, however, as most surely do, the promise of the great high priest and his sacrifice comes as a word of comfort. God's judgement never stands without God's mercy. BG

Mark 10.17–31

When this writer heard an actor recite the Gospel of Mark by heart at the Mermaid Theatre in London, only one episode produced a palpable sense of discomfort in the largely middle-class audience: it was not the passion or the injunction to take up the cross or to 'follow' that embarrassed us, but the idea that wealth and the kingdom of God do not mix. After all, we had been trying to mix them for years.

At one level, this is as radical a piece of social teaching as any Jesus gives in Mark, rivalled only by that on the upside-downing of power in 10.35–45. But Mark's eye may have been not so much on macro-political or social policies as on the radical character of life in the kingdom in general: it follows the teaching on divorce, with its paradoxical ideal (or rather norm) for human relations, at least between men and women, making Adams and Eves of us all and giving us back our paradisal freedom (see p. 239).

Not that this is a teaching meant simply to shock rather than to evoke obedience. We know that as soon as urban Christian congregations came into being, questions of class relations, between haves and have-nots, began to arise: see 1 Cor. 11.17–end for the church in Corinth in the 50s; and the Letter of James is obsessed with the subject, disliking the rich but at the same time assuming that the church consists of the middling sort, the poor being noticeable when they venture in. Indeed, it was not long before a congregation's dependence on at least a decent number of richer members (initially for houses big enough to meet in and charitable giving to the destitute) started to be a virtual necessity of church life – as it has remained ever since, in ever more complex ways. In practice, such teaching of Jesus, here and elsewhere, has been both an incentive and a reproach. Paul, with his urban churches, does not mention it.

But that social reality of early church life may skew the theological force of this teaching. It is, as has been suggested, about the singleness of mind and loyalty that the kingdom requires – a call to a kind of asceticism, which, in Jesus' day, both Cynic philosophers and, in more communal mode, the members of the Qumran community would have understood. Mark, however, in this spirit quickly moves on beyond the matter of possessions to that of family, also dispensable, and then to that of reward (and high idealists got embarrassed). One must relinquish – but one will receive; a new – and secure – community to replace that given up ('with persecutions' says Mark's 'cross' theological realism, v. 30). So it becomes teaching on the Church as a theologically live entity, here and now – where the kingdom can be found. Is this where, for Mark, we are, in a way, to 'see Jesus come in power' (9.1) and find our Galilee (16.7)? It is interesting that Matthew, by contrast, placed the reward wholly in the future (19.28–29) and had the leaders chiefly in view. For him, here, eschatology replaces Mark's ecclesiology.

This is of course the most disquieting and least faced of all Jesus' teaching, other aspects of biblical ethics being found less threatening to so many decent Christian selves.

But perhaps the most astonishing feature of this passage comes in the opening exchange with the virtuous man who cannot part with his ample property. In Mark, it is a rule that the 'bit-part' characters, appearing once, are examples to us of devotion and salvation – with the apparent exception of this figure. Yet he, uniquely, is, for all his failure at the vital fence, loved by Jesus – nowhere else is it said (v. 21). Is it the case then that devotion so great (v. 22) rather than full success assures the divine love? Or does the man's refusal (v. 22) endanger the loving (v. 21), or at least leave it hanging in the air, unmet? LH

Proper 24

(Sunday between 16 and 22 October inclusive)

Job 38.1–7 (34–41) or Isaiah 53.4–12; Hebrew 5.1–10; Mark 10.35–45

Job 38.1–7 (34–41)

See Proper 7, pp. 174–175.

Isaiah 53.4–12

See Good Friday, pp. 108–109.

Hebrews 5.1–10

The author of Hebrews has introduced his distinctive description of Christ as the 'great high priest' in 4.14, and now proceeds to explain why it is appropriate. Here he selects three points that are characteristic of any high priest: he must be chosen and appointed; he must be human, able both to empathize with human weakness and to represent human beings before God (Hebrews nowhere suggests that a priest represents God to humanity); and his key function is to offer sacrifice. The model is taken from the scriptural tradition of the priesthood of Aaron, from which the priesthood of the Jerusalem temple from the exile to its final destruction derived its origin, rather than from any experience of that later priesthood in practice. In the Pentateuch, Aaron is not 'called' directly in the dramatic way that Moses is in Exod. 3; rather Moses is instructed to single out his brother and his brother's sons, to equip them and to consecrate them by ablution, anointing and the sprinkling of the blood of animal sacrifice (Lev. 28–29; and Num. 8–9, where Aaron's priesthood is inaugurated by his first acts of sacrifice to atone for his and for the people's sins). Immediately there are points of difference as well as similarity. It will be crucial for the author later that Christ is the high priest who does not need to offer for his own sins (thus 7.27 and 9.25–26); and he will also explain why Christ's high priesthood is distinctively 'after the order of Melchizedek', fulfilling Ps. 110.1–4 and Gen. 14, rather than simply after the model of Aaron. (Thus 7.1–19: Melchizedek's priesthood is seen to be 'better', since he blesses Abraham, ancestor of Levi and so of the levitical priesthood; and because Genesis gives him no genealogy, he must be a 'once-for-all' priest, neither following a predecessor nor followed by a successor.) Here the author emphasizes that Christ's high priesthood derives from the direct call of God. He finds the expression of this in the conjunction of the two messianic psalms, Pss. 2 and 110, which he has already quoted in 1.5, 13 in a catena of quotations with which his readers were clearly expected to be familiar (see Christmas Day, p. 26).

Although differences between the priesthood of Christ and the general model are thus signalled, one basic similarity is firmly emphasized. Christ the high priest is fully identified with those whom he represents: fully human in his weakness and suffering, to which he responded with prayer. The picture unmistakably recalls the gospel story of Gethsemane, especially in its Lucan version (Luke 22.41–44). In his anguish, the author says, he 'was heard' – yet he died. He was heard for his *eulabeia*, which some versions translate as 'godly fear' or 'reverent submission'; it is not raw human fear of pain and death, but fear as awe in the presence of God, and reflects the tradition of Jesus' acceptance that 'not my will but thine be done' (Luke 22.42). He accepted his suffering 'although he was a Son'. Most translations thus render the clause as concessive: the suffering seeming to stand in tension with the exalted state of sonship declared in ch. 1; but it could be precisely *because* he was a son among many brethren (2.10–14) that obedience through suffering was proper for him. (The same ambiguity is found in the 'christological hymn' of Phil. 2.) Through his suffering his humanity was made 'perfect': a term frequent in Hebrews, with connotations of completeness and so effectiveness. Because he is the high priest chosen and appointed by God, who is also fully identified with those he represents, Jesus can perform the one sacrifice that can finally achieve their salvation. SL

Mark 10.35–45

Matthew altered the beginning of this passage, so that it is the mother of James and John who asks for top places for them rather than the brothers themselves. Thereby he transforms a piece of blundering, barefaced ambition into a touching example of maternal pride. Why has Mark no compunction in writing as he does? Perhaps there was a tradition that he was not prepared to shrug off, for all its shame. What is undeniable is that this story is at one with Mark's dominant portrait of the disciples of Jesus. True, they were called and they 'followed', unhesitatingly – including the sons of Zebedee (1.16–20, see pp. 270–271). True, they were given the secret of the kingdom of God (4.11). But for the rest, they blur the vision, fail to rise to the kingdom's call, and will ultimately fall into the darkness of betrayal and flight.

And en route we have this instance of crude failure to grasp the nature of Jesus' role and their place within it. Jesus gives two answers to their specific request, then explains the positive nature of his mission.

The first of the two answers is reminiscent of that to Peter in a not dissimilar episode in 8.27–38 (cf. pp. 226–227). Using the two scriptural images of being put into water and being given a cup to drink (cf. 1.9–11; 14.23–25), Jesus points to suffering as his destiny – and theirs too if they are truly of his company. The second answer is that the bestowal of honours is in the apparently inscrutable purpose of (we suppose) God; Jesus has no role in such matters. He is God's willing agent, not his arbiter in any eschatological honours system.

This brushing aside of quasi-political ambitions leads to the positive doctrine that underpins it (vv. 44–45). The kingdom of God is wholly countercultural, the very reverse of all power-seeking and authority-exerting. The basis of this vision of the structures of the new life and the new society is in Jesus' own character and destiny: to 'serve' and to 'give his life as a ransom for many' – that is, probably, the means of ransom and redemption for any who can or will receive it. (The image is likely to be from the manumission of slaves.) And the passion is imminent.

Whether and how a Church could possibly maintain such a vision or at any rate such a way of life, without precedence, honours and the exercise of power, for century after century, is another matter. But at least Mark's Gospel (and Matthew's too, despite the adjustment at the beginning, 20.20–28) survives to tell the tale – and we read it still. LH

Proper 25

(Sunday between 23 and 30 October inclusive)

Job 42.1–6, 10–17 or Jeremiah 31.7–9; Hebrews 7.23–28; Mark 10.46b–52

Job 42.1–6, 10–17

There has either been some disarrangement within vv. 1–6, or phrases and material from elsewhere in Job has been interpolated into vv. 3–4. The NRSV recognizes this by using different types of inverted commas, but these will hardly help those who are looking at a Bible, and certainly not members of the congregation who are simply listening to a reading. REB solves the problem by adding words such as 'you ask' and 'you said' in vv. 3–4, and this is probably the best way of making the passage intelligible, unless the NEB is followed, with its radical omission of all the offending material.

The climax of Job comes in vv. 5–6, where Job confesses that his knowledge of God has changed from second-hand report to first-hand encounter. None of his questions have been answered, and the reasons for his suffering remain unknown. But he has encountered God in some mysterious way, which has possibly included his suffering and his vain quest for answers. It has also involved his experience of the sublime, as he has been required to contemplate the awesome nature of the created world and the peculiar and irrational behaviour of some of the creatures in it. Job's despising of himself (v. 6, if this is what the Hebrew means; cf. REB 'I yield') comes not from disgust at what he had said when arguing, but from a realization of the great gulf between God's reality and his own transience. He no longer needs answers to his questions; the vision of God makes everything else irrelevant.

Verses 10–17 are part of the resumption of the prose story that began in chs. 1—2, although the prose framework would be meaningless without chs. 3—42.6. Many commentators have felt that the restoration of Job's fortunes spoils the book. It seems to confirm the arguments of Job's companions that goodness always results in blessings, a point strongly denied by Job! But vv. 7–8, not included in the reading, are important here, because they state God's view that the companions had not spoken well, whereas Job did speak as he should have done about God. The restoration of Job's prosperity means that the Satan who deprived him of it does not get the last word. Neither does the ending prove the Satan's point that Job does not fear God for nothing (1.9). Job has more than proved that his loyalty is based upon firmer foundations than enlightened self-interest. It is precisely because Job has come to a new and first-hand understanding of God that he can put the restoration of his prosperity into proper perspective. JR

Jeremiah 31.7–9

See Second Sunday of Christmas, pp. 31–32.

Hebrews 7.23–28

This lection provides a summary of the discussion of Jesus' priesthood that was introduced in Heb. 4.14 and preoccupied ch. 7. It also reintroduces the theme of Jesus' sacrifice, which will come to the fore in the section that follows. As a transitional passage, it aptly epitomizes Hebrews' treatment of Christ as the supreme and perfect high priest. Despite the importance thereby attached to the lection, by this point in Hebrews the comparison between the priesthood of Jesus and the earthly priesthood may have worn a bit thin. What began as a lively comparison and contrast between the role of the human priest and that of Jesus, by virtue of the detail given grows somewhat tedious. Surely such a lengthy discussion might have been avoided.

Readers even minimally aware of Israel's traditions will, of course, recall the importance of the sacrificial system for many forms of Judaism in this period. If it was written in the aftermath of the destruction of the temple in Jerusalem, as is often thought, Hebrews may reflect an early attempt at interpreting that event for a Jewish Christian audience; that is, because of the true sacrifice made by the priesthood of Jesus, the Jerusalem temple is no longer needed. Jesus has replaced the temple and its sacrificial system. Such an event would warrant the considerable detail lavished on it by the author of Hebrews.

Something else is at stake in this comparison between Jesus and the temple priesthood that merits the attention given it, however, and that concerns the overcoming of routine. Few contemporary readers can appreciate the extent to which the sacrificial system is associated with the routinization of religious life. The use of that word, 'routinization', is not intended to suggest in this instance that the temple becomes less important or less meaningful, but that the system must ever be given attention. New priests must be found as the old die (7.23), and sacrifices must be offered 'day after day' (v. 27), making the system part of the routine in human relationships with God. In this respect, the notion of Jesus as the perfect priest is similar to the Fourth Gospel's story of Jesus' encounter with the woman at the well. She comes routinely to draw water, and he offers her water that she will not need to draw again, shattering her routine and creating genuinely new possibilities for her life (John 4.7–30). Like the water offered the Samaritan woman, then, the priesthood of Jesus is not simply a 'new and improved priesthood', but a priesthood that brings to an end the need for human priests.

In three distinct but closely related ways this lection insists on that point. First, Jesus is superior to the 'former priests' by virtue of the fact that he 'holds his priesthood permanently' (Heb. 7.24). The way this point is made differs slightly from what might be anticipated. The passage begins with the observation that 'the former priests were many in number, because they were prevented by death from continuing in office' (v. 23), prompting the expectation that Jesus would be said to continue because he does not die or because of his resurrection. What v. 24 actually says differs just slightly from that: 'he holds his priesthood permanently, because he continues for ever'. Christ 'continues', or, a bit more literally, 'Christ remains', 'Christ abides.' The point is not merely that he lives longer than the 'former priests', even as long as for ever, but that he endures, persists, continues. The priesthood of Christ may be counted on because, like the God whose Son he is, Christ stands at the beginning and end of time (see 1.1–4).

Second, because of the fact that Christ continues for ever, he offers the supreme intercession for humankind. The text scores this point in two ways, by asserting first that Christ is able to save 'for all time' (or 'completely' – the Greek is ambiguous), and then by recalling that Christ 'always' lives to make intercession. The repetition involved in 'all time' and 'always', as in the Greek *pantelēs* and *pantote*, emphasizes the ultimacy of what is being said.

Third, Christ brings an end to human priests because, being perfect, he made the perfect sacrifice of himself. The description of Christ's perfection ('holy, blameless, undefiled, separated from sinners, and exalted above the heavens', v. 26) explains why he could become the perfect, the final sacrifice. Although Old Testament traditions serve constantly as a resource for the author of Hebrews, so do rhetoric and philosophical tradition. In this motif of perfection, the influence of Platonic thought can be detected, in which the physical world represents only shadows of the ideal world that lies beyond human grasp.

That preoccupation with the realm of the perfect, unattainable in human life, may seem remote from contemporary thought when cast in Platonic terms, but the pastoral force of the passage remains unchanged. What the notion of Jesus as the final, true, supreme high priest offers is the assurance that salvation continues as a possibility for human beings. No matter the ugliness of human life, the depravity of individual or corporate sin, the perfect sacrifice of Jesus brings forgiveness close by, an ever-present possibility. CC

Mark 10.46b–52

To the innocent modern reader, coming upon it in isolation, this economically told little story tells of Jesus' powerful aid to one disabled. But it would have had further echoes for Mark's original audience. Jesus makes the blind to see, so fulfilling Isa. 35.5 and 6.1 (in the Septuagint), cf. Luke 4.18; Matt. 15.31. It is the work of God, long purposed, a sign of the kingdom. Beyond that, there are many signs of personal Christian meaning – for those with ears to hear (or eyes to see).

Bartimaeus is a blind beggar: he is without perception and is in dire need. His condition is symbolized by his location – off the road ('by the way' – just like the futile seed in 4.4, the Greek being identical). As his story proceeds, the recent or perhaps potential convert can easily identify with him. For members of a first-century congregation, especially if (as seems to be the case in Mark) there had been exposure to the terms and images of Pauline teaching, there would be baptismal allusions, pinpointing conversion to the Christian movement. 'Get up' (v. 49) is the standard word of resurrection, and in baptism, one dies and rises with Christ (Rom. 6.3–11; Col. 3.1). Perhaps already the removal of one's old clothing and the donning of new was a baptismal custom, v. 50; cf. Gal. 3.27. The man's sole desire is to 'see again'; to 'be enlightened' will equally catch the sense, though English translation forces us to choose at which level to operate (vv. 51, 52). Similarly, 'has made you well' means equally 'has saved you' (as the phrase is usually rendered at Luke 7.50, where illness is not involved). The gift is salvation, the man's cure is his conversion, so that he becomes Jesus' follower (v. 52). He who was formerly 'by the roadside (way)' is now 'on (literally "in") the way'.

'The way' is the road that Jesus has come to the world to tread, from the start (1.2, 3); and throughout, its end is in Jerusalem at the cross. Mark placed a blind man's healing at either end of the passage in the Gospel more literally relating Jesus' journey ('way') from Galilee to Jerusalem: see 8.22–26 (cf. 8.27; 10.32); as if to say that this is the necessary journey for those who would 'see' and be saved (cf. 8.34). LH

Bible Sunday

Isaiah 55.1–11; 2 Timothy 3.14—4.5; John 5.36–47

Isaiah 55.1–11

See Sixth Sunday of Easter, pp. 133–134.

2 Timothy 3.14—4.5

Naturally enough, references to the commendations of 'Scripture' are put down for reading on this day. But it is as well to be clear what is referred to: the expression 'sacred writings' (v. 15) is a standard Hellenistic Jewish way of referring to Scripture. In context, that means the Septuagint; that is, (in Protestant Christian terms) the Old Testament (= Hebrew Bible) plus, more or less, the Apocrypha. We are still some decades away from collections of Christian writings and a sense of such collections as 'Scripture', that is, authoritative writings, to be used in liturgy and decision-making. (Nevertheless, one might say that the use of Mark as a source by Matthew and Luke, combining acceptance with additions and alterations, was not unlike the way Jewish writers had, in the past, developed existing authoritative works in the furtherance of quasi-canonical use; cf. the dependence of Ephesians on Paul's undoubted writings and our present writer's appeal to the authority and example of Paul, whose mantle he wears.) This text, if viewed in context, is then of only modified usefulness to an unsubtle modern propagandist for the authority of Scripture.

Moreover, there is irony in the fact that this writer is notable in the New Testament for his scant use of what Christians came to call the Old Testament whose merits he advocates: 2.19 stands alone in this book. In that way, his appeal to Scripture is on all fours with his campaign for true doctrine – whose content he states only in brief formulas and does little to expound. 'All scripture', v. 16, conceals a multitude of problems that are never touched here, and 'inspired by God' is in practice too general to solve them, and has often served more as a weapon than a serviceable tool.

No, our writer's overwhelming concern is for unity and for the elimination of dissent. It is evident that at this time, probably around the end of the first century (note the hint in v. 15), the Christian movement was at a dangerous stage in its development (4.3–4), looking for criteria of true faith and authorities to define and legitimate it, whether in terms of documents or dependable human leaders (cf. 1 Tim. 3). Gone is the time when a chief task was how to define oneself over against Judaism; here, the problems are internal to the Church and the old Scriptures are part of the Christian equipment. Wearing his Pauline hat, the writer, having leaders especially in view, urges sober fidelity in the task of holding the line, before the Lord returns. His is the predicament, endlessly replicated, of the person of goodness and sound sense trying to grapple with the strident and the eccentric. Or at least, we can be sure that that is how he viewed the situation – and it does beg the question. Even the neutral commentator risks showing his colours. LH

John 5.36–47

On what grounds can one believe that Jesus is the Messiah, the Son of God, the Saviour of the world?

This is the question that runs through John's Gospel; but for the most part the question is asked within a particular frame of reference. On what ground could '*the Jews*' believe Jesus to be what he claimed to be? And by 'the Jews' (since this clearly does not mean all Jews: Jesus and his disciples were as much 'Jews' as anyone else) John meant the representatives of the Jewish religion and culture. Why were they so implacably opposed? Should their opposition deter others?

When we want to prove a case, we naturally look for *evidence*. What proof can we give for the statements we make? But in the Jewish culture it was not so much a question of evidence as of *testimony*: whose word can we believe? The first chapter of John's Gospel assembled the key witnesses in Jesus' case, of whom the most important was John the Baptist. There followed a series of 'works' or 'signs', which led some people to believe that Jesus was indeed an agent of God and 'worked' with his authority, but which left others unconvinced. Now Jesus invokes a form of witness that is the very word of God himself – the Scriptures.

On the face of it, this should have settled the matter. All believed that the Scriptures were the word of God and contained the key to 'eternal life'. But no written word yields its meaning unless it is interpreted aright. The true interpretation of 'Moses' would show that Jesus was all he claimed to be – Jesus offers clues to discovering this in all the Gospels, and the early Church soon developed its own interpretation, which seemed to confirm the Messiahship of Jesus. But there were other ways of reading the sacred text, which amounted to 'not believing' its underlying message. 'The Jews' – who have in fact been followed by all those Jews who ever since have remained faithful to their own religion – could not accept this way of reading the Scriptures, and so failed to receive what Jesus (and subsequently his followers) claimed was the testimony of God himself.

There was one other way in which they might have been convinced. In public life, whom do we most easily respect and believe? Those who are widely respected and honoured by others? The point is made here by means of a play on words that can hardly be reproduced in English. The Greek word *doxa* means both 'honour' and 'glory' – the glory we ascribe to God when we worship and adore him. The choice Jesus presented to his contemporaries (and still does to us) is whether to accept the standards by which human beings 'honour' one another or whether Jesus possessed 'honour' of a different kind altogether, the 'honour' that is nothing less than the glory of God. AEH

Dedication Festival

The First Sunday in October or Last Sunday after Trinity

Genesis 28.11–18 or Revelation 21.9–14; 1 Peter 2.1–10; John 10.22–29

Genesis 28.11–18

The stories relating to Abraham are essentially separate episodes, though concerned with connected themes. The main body of material relating to Jacob in Gen. 28—35, however, is more closely integrated. Its basic concern is the relation between Jacob and those around him, especially his twin brother Esau and his uncle Laban. Jacob was pictured as the forefather of the later nation Israel, a name which he was himself to be given, and so relations between Israel and its neighbours were an important concern.

The setting of the present passage is Jacob's flight from Esau to seek hospitality (and, hopefully, a wife) from Laban's family, pictured as living at Haran in Mesopotamia. The accounts of both his outward journey (this episode) and his return (ch. 32) offer descriptions of an important encounter with the divine. Departure from and entry into the holy land represent important rites of passage.

Here, then, we have an account of a theophany, a manifestation of God to his worshipper, with a particular message. Stories of this kind are frequently used by the biblical writers to picture encounters with the divine; we may think of Moses at the burning bush (Exod. 3) and Isaiah's vision (Isa. 6), as well of course as the accounts of Jesus' transfiguration (Mark 9) and Paul's 'Damascus Road' experience (Acts 9) in the New Testament. The appropriate response is one of godly fear and awe, and both of these are found here (v. 17). A slightly unusual feature of this story is that the name of the place where it happened is provided: Bethel, which continued to be an important holy place in Israel, often as a rival to Jerusalem (1 Kings 12.29–35). Tensions between different religious claims were a feature of ancient Israel, as they continue to be in much of the modern world.

Tension is inherent, too, in the promise made in the theophany. On the one hand it can be seen as a restatement and a development of the promise made to Abraham at 12.1–3, and that brings out the universal aspect of God's commitment (vv. 14–15). On the other hand there is a strongly local basis, linked to the particular holy place. The expression 'Jacob's ladder', based on v. 12, has become traditional, but it is easier to envisage it as a stairway or ramp (cf. NRSV footnote); the holy place was similar to the famous ziggurats excavated in Mesopotamia (modern-day Iraq). RC

Revelation 21.9–14

Beyond the cycles of suffering and judgement, when the powers of evil are finally defeated, and the dead judged, John sees the new heaven and the new earth, and from that new heaven comes the new Jerusalem. This is the Church as it will be in the new age, transfigured with the glory of God himself, shining with the jewel-like radiance that belonged to the vision of God in heaven in 4.3. The imagery clearly derives from the vision of the new city that is the subject of the last chapters of Ezekiel (40—48) and expresses that prophet's hope for the future restoration of his exiled people; but it is significantly adapted. The city is the bride, the wife of the Lamb; the people of God are the people of Christ, united to 'him who loves us' (1.5). The gates of the city bear the names of the tribes of Israel, for the Church is the people called by God, but the foundations of the city bear the names of the twelve apostles, for the new people of God has its beginnings in those called by Jesus. The city stands four-square, facing all ways, and unlike the city of Ezekiel where gates may be shut to exclude the alien (44.1–2, 9), John's readers will be told that the gates of his city are always open (21.25).

How is this image of the heavenly Church of the future to be applied to an earth-bound church building of the present? The medieval builders of Gothic churches caught the vision. Churches should be full of light, for God is light, and so to enter a church was to come into his presence; they were orientated west-east, facing Jerusalem the symbol of heaven, so that the journey into a church could become a spiritual journey from the world to heaven; with their statues of saints and angels and with their shrines and relics, they brought the people of God on earth into contact with the host of heaven. Not all churches in post-Reformation England can still convey those ideas, but any church may, or should, serve as a place where Christ is seen to be present with his people in a union of love that is open and available to all. SL

I Peter 2.1–10

This passage usually appears in discussions of the priesthood of all believers, or the spiritual priesthood. Within the context of First Peter, however, as John Elliott has demonstrated, this passage serves to introduce the notion of the 'household of God', which v. 5 signals with the unusual expression 'spiritual house', or 'spiritual household' (*A Home for the Homeless*; Philadelphia: Fortress Press, 1981, 23, 75). The household code of 2.18—3.7 underscores the importance of this motif, as does the use of the 'household of God' in 4.17. Recurring language that describes believers as 'newly born' or 'reborn' and that seeks the unity of believers within the community further enhances this motif.

Chapter 2.4–5 introduces the household language, which vv. 6–10 develop through a variety of biblical quotations and editorial comments. Indeed, the profusion of biblical quotations and allusions in vv. 6–10 seems bewildering apart from the underlying theme of the unity of believers in a single household. Understanding Jesus as the living stone, believers are also to see themselves as living stones, whom God builds into a single, spiritual house (vv. 4–6). Again, like Jesus, these stones will be rejected by unbelievers, by the world at large, but will be affirmed by God (vv. 7–8). The various descriptions of vv. 9–10 serve to reinforce this notion that the community of believers is *one* community. Together it constitutes 'a chosen race, a royal priesthood, a holy nation, God's own people'. These expressions, like that of the 'household', underscore the collective nature of the community.

The imagery in this passage may seem exotic, and perhaps even exclusivistic ('a chosen race, a royal priesthood'), until the author's specific pastoral goals become clear. First, the insistence on the unity of believers in *one* body – household, race, priesthood, nation – serves to create and maintain a social identity. If recent research is correct in its understanding that the audience of this letter consists of persons who are displaced and dispossessed, not only spiritually or religiously but socially, economically and politically, then what the author does here asserts that in Christ, God creates a new place for those who have none. The language of the household erects boundaries that provide place, purpose and community for those who 'have tasted that the Lord is good' (v. 3).

Second, the passage links this particular community with Jesus Christ. Commentators have often ignored the concrete social dimensions of this passage, but correcting that misreading should not lead to the conclusion that the social dimension constitutes the whole of the passage. This 'spiritual house' is not a social club, which exists solely for the needs of its members. It is, rather, a household of which the head is God and the cornerstone Jesus Christ. As much as believers belong to one another within this household, they also belong to God. God builds the house (v. 5), God lays the cornerstone (v. 6), the house is known (and accepted or rejected) by its cornerstone (vv. 7–8). By virtue of God's own mercy and nothing else, this household has come into being (vv. 9–10).

Third, as a result of their identification with one another and as members of God's household, believers within this new household have a new standing. No longer outcasts, marginalized by their social condition, believers may be described in powerful and positive terms. Like the prototypical 'living stone', Jesus, believers are 'chosen and precious in God's sight' (v. 4). The language of v. 9 exalts the community and implies its privileges before God. Even if the household was once 'not a people' and 'had not received mercy' (v. 10), it now can rightly claim to be the people of God's own possession.

Given the historical setting in which the author of 1 Peter wrote, the language of this passage serves an important pastoral need. That need continues in every Christian generation, for the Church constantly requires the recollection that God created it to be a single household, taking its identity from Jesus Christ and set apart from the world. Given the intractable human temptation to convert a gift into a possession, however, Christians have too often read passages such as this one to mean that *their* standing before God came as a result of their own goodness and permitted them to exclude others from membership in the same household. The text grants no such licence for exclusivity or condescension. The householder, God, has sole authority over admission at the doorway. BG

John 10.22–29

Each of Jesus' visits in John's Gospel is related to a festival. Often some feature of the festival is relevant to the story; on this occasion it serves merely as a date. Dedication was a December festival, celebrating the purification and rededication of the temple by Judas Maccabaeus in 164 BC after its profanation by the pagan ruler Antiochus Epiphanes. The temple area, as rebuilt by Herod the Great, was bounded by great 'porticos' or colonnades, which provided shelter from wintry weather and served for meetings, instruction or (significantly) even a legal hearing. For the word used here – 'gathered round' – has a threatening sound: it would describe an army besieging a city or a circle of judges assembled round a defendant. And this gives us a clue to the interpretation of the dialogue that follows. The Jews' question and Jesus' answer both recall Luke's account of Jesus' formal trial before the Sanhedrin (22.67–71): the challenge to declare himself the Messiah was at the heart of Jesus' final confrontation with the authorities and Jesus' response to it, reported somewhat differently in each of the Gospels, is a key to understanding his identity.

There has been a number of alleged 'Messiahs' in Jewish history. One thing they have in common is that it is not they who make the claim: it is others who believe they recognize them and lead them to acknowledge what they are. The onus, that is to say, is not on the claimant himself but on those who are confronted by the challenge of a person who seems to raise a genuine possibility that the promised Messiah has come. So it is here; and Jesus responds by showing why the disbelief of the majority is not a reason to doubt his Messiahship. His 'works' have been done, not on his own account, but in such a way as to reveal God's purpose working through him; but to recognize this, people have to establish a close relationship with him, such as he has already illustrated by his comparison of himself with a good shepherd, his followers with personally known and cherished sheep.

On this occasion Jesus draws one more inference from the shepherd-sheep comparison: 'they will never perish'. This shepherd will not allow his sheep to be snatched away (indeed he has said he will lay down his life for them). And the reason he can say this with confidence (though here we are hampered by the obscurity of the original Greek in the last sentence of the reading) is that it is nothing less than the Father's power that guarantees their safety. AEH

All Saints' Day

(1 November)

Isaiah 56.3–8 or 2 Esdras 2.42–48; Hebrews 12.18–24; Matthew 5.1–12

Isaiah 56.3–8

The community centred upon Jerusalem that rebuilt the temple around 515 BC and restored the religious life of the people, was one split by deep divisions, if Isa. 56—66 is anything to go by. There were those who seem to have questioned whether there was any need for the temple to be rebuilt at all (Isa. 66.1–4) while others were sharply critical of some of the religious observances (Isa. 58.1–9).

The present passage, with its inexplicable omission of vv. 2–5, is evidently concerned with the problem of non-Jews belonging to the chosen people and participating fully in its temple worship. Its sentiments are only understandable if there were people in the Jerusalem community at the end of the sixth century BC who maintained that non-Jews could not belong to the Jewish community.

We can only speculate about who these non-Jews were who had joined or who wanted to 'join themselves to the Lord' (v. 6). They may have been non-Jews who had moved into Palestine during the exile, from southern Trans-Jordan, or they may have been Babylonians who had been involved in the administration of Judah during the period 597 to 548. It is less likely that they were Babylonians who deliberately journeyed back to Jerusalem because they wanted to embrace faith in the God of Israel.

On the face of it, that there were such people should have been a cause for satisfaction if not joy. After all, Isa. 45.2 contains a call to 'all the ends of the earth' to turn to God and to be saved. Foreigners, however, cause problems in all societies in all ages. If they are too successful they arouse resentment; if they perform below the average they are blamed for a society's troubles. We may also detect in the passage disputes about the layout and accessibility of the rebuilt temple. Unfortunately, we know nothing about its layout; but the temple that Herod the Great enlarged and rebuilt at the close of the first century BC certainly allowed access to certain parts only to Israelite males. The passage certainly promises to non-Jews who observe the sabbaths and hold fast to the covenant that they will be able to join fully in the worship of the temple, and that their sacrifices will be acceptable. We do not know how the dispute over non-Jews was resolved at the end of the sixth century. Sixty years later, Ezra and Nehemiah made a determined, and apparently successful, attempt to exclude the non-Jewish wives of Israelites from the community (Ezra 9.1–4; 10.1–15; Neh. 13.1–3, 23–29). The implications of the passage for today's churches with regard to their attitude to all 'outsiders', especially those of African and Asian ethnic origins, should not be difficult to discern. JR

2 Esdras 2.42–48

2 Esdras (also known as 4 Ezra) is a composite work. Chs. 3—14 were written in Hebrew or Aramaic around 100 AD as a response to the destruction of the second Jerusalem temple by the Romans 30 years earlier. The Semitic original is lost and the chapters are known only in translation, in Latin, Syriac and Ethiopic to name only three languages. The Latin version contains additional material in the form of chs. 1—2 and 15—16 which are often referred to as 5 Ezra and 6 Ezra respectively.

Chapter 2, from which today's reading is taken, is a Christian addition, probably dating from the second century AD. We therefore have the phenomenon of the Old Testament (Apocrypha) reading being later than the New Testament readings!

A comparison of the reading with parts of the book of Revelation (cf. Rev. 7.9–14) indicates that Revelation is the probable source for the material in 2 Esd. 2. However, 2 Esd. 2 is more explicitly Christian than Revelation in the sense that it features a young man of taller stature than any other, who places crowns on the heads of the martyrs (v. 45). He is later identified (v. 47) as the Son of God. In this reading the focus is arguably mostly upon the tall young man. In Rev. 7.9–14 the focus is more upon the martyrs. JR

Hebrews 12.18–24

The opening verses summarize the description of Sinai in Exod. 20, the place where God is present, but a frightening, dangerous and inaccessible presence. Even Moses, the only one who can go into the presence of God and bring back his message to the Israelites, is full of fear. This is the setting for the making of the old covenant between God and his people, and the giving of the ten commandments. By contrast the author of Hebrews invites his readers to Mount Sion, the heavenly Jerusalem. (The contrast between Sinai and Jerusalem is reminiscent of Paul's allegory in Gal. 4, though the purpose of the comparison is very different.) There is now access to God, and also to a great community with him. First are the angels, as if at a festival (the word suggests the great public celebrations of the gods in the hellenistic world). Then there is the assembly (*ekklēsia*, the word used for the Church) of the firstborn enrolled in heaven: their identity is more uncertain. Hitherto Jesus has been called 'the firstborn' (1.6), but with brothers and sisters, and in Rom. 8.28, in Col. 1.18 and Rev. 1.5 he is the 'firstborn of the dead'; it is possible that the group of firstborn here in Hebrews are the Christian dead who have already followed him to heaven. The 'spirits of the just made perfect' are easier to identify: they are the saints of the Old Testament whose faith was celebrated in ch. 11 but who would not reach the city to which they looked forward 'without us' (vv. 10, 39–40).

The image is like the great west door of a gothic cathedral, the ranks of angels, saints and prophets welcoming into heaven the Church on earth. In the midst of them is God; he is still judge, but with Jesus not Moses as the mediator between him and his people. Moses in Exod. 24 sprinkled the blood of sacrificed oxen on the altar and the people. The author of Hebrews has already alluded to this in ch. 9

in the course of his explanation of the sacrifice of Jesus on the analogy of the Day of Atonement ritual: the blood of sacrifice that Jesus presents in the true Holy of Holies that is heaven, is his own. Here in another link in a chain of allusions, the sprinkled blood of the covenant at Sinai suggests to him the shed blood of Abel (Gen. 4). That blood called on God the judge to avenge it in punishment of the brother-slayer; Jesus is the brother whose blood gives forgiveness of sins (a comparison drawn in Edward Caswall's passiontide hymn, 'Glory be to Jesus', *NEH* 83). Finally, this access to God through Jesus is not a vision of the future but an experience of the present: the author twice uses the perfect tense, we 'have come' to where we are. SL

Matthew 5.1–12

Matthew has arranged his Gospel in alternating sections of narrative and teaching. There are five sections of teaching, each ending with virtually the same formula that marks the transition from direct speech to narrative (see e.g. 7.28–29). The first of these speeches is the Sermon on the Mount (5.3—7.27), and today's Gospel is the beginning of it.

In the previous narrative (chs. 1—4), Matthew has prepared his readers for this section of his book by comparing Jesus to Moses: both were threatened by wicked kings; both escaped, one out of Egypt and the other into Egypt; Moses received, and now Jesus commends and revises, the Law of God, on a mountain.

John the Baptist and Jesus have proclaimed the coming of the time when God will rule and the need for repentance (3.2; 4.17); so the first speech addresses the question that this raises: who is it that will enter this new age?

There are eight Beatitudes, marked out by an *inclusio* – the repetition of the promise: 'The kingdom of heaven is theirs' (5.3, 10). Each beatitude consists of two parts: the statement that certain people are blessed, and the promise of their reward. After the eighth beatitude, the form of the language changes, from third person plural ('Blessed are the . . .') to the second person ('Blessed are you . . .'); these eight sayings can be read as the 'text', or as a kind of prologue, for the rest of the Sermon, which then begins at 5.11.

The order of the eight sayings is different in some of the manuscripts and ancient versions from that which is found in most printed editions of the New Testament, and it is not certain which arrangement is original; there is much to be said for following the witnesses that place v. 5 before v. 4. If this is done, then the Beatitudes form four pairs: the poor and the meek; those who mourn and those who fast; the generous and the single-minded; the peace-makers and those who are persecuted.

The seven different promises in the second halves are in effect all one promise (just as the petitions in the Lord's Prayer are in effect one and the same), because each of them refers to entry into the kingdom of heaven, the time when God will rule on the earth (see 6.10). They are not alternative options, so that one cannot choose some and reject others, for example preferring comfort and mercy to seeing God. The future passive verbs (shall be comforted, filled, receive mercy, be called God's children) are all ways of describing God's actions in the coming end-time of fulfilment; he will comfort, fill, be merciful, and he will declare who are his children.

Similarly, the eight statements in the first halves of the Beatitudes refer to everyone who is to enter the coming age: all of them are poor, meek, mourning for the way things are in the world, longing for God to rule, abandoning status and privilege, peace-makers, and (inevitably) persecuted by those who do not want God to rule. Again, these are not alternatives.

A major theme that runs through the Beatitudes and the Sermon on the Mount, and indeed this Gospel as a whole, is: many who are first will be last, and the last first (19.30; 20.16). Discipleship means the acceptance of a life that is not what the majority choose. What is required of those whom God will bless is poverty and the giving up of any compensating 'religious' rewards in the present (see. 6.1–21; 23.1–33). The character of the follower is, of course, the same as that of the one whom we follow. JF

All Saints' Sunday

Wisdom of Solomon 3.1–9 or Isaiah 25.6–9; Revelation 21.1–6a; John 11.32–44

Wisdom of Solomon 3.1–9

The opening word 'But', omitted by the Lectionary, indicates that this passage is closely linked to what precedes it. The wicked have persecuted the righteous man even to the point of torture and death, because of their conviction that God is powerless to intervene. 2.21–24 provides an interlude of reflection (cf. Proper 20, pp. 228–229) before 3.1–9 rebuts the supposition of the wicked.

The idea of people having souls is a Greek rather than a Hebrew idea (Wisdom of Solomon is a Greek text). In Hebrew thought, a person *is* a soul rather than *has* a soul; and at Wisd. 1.15 immortality is inextricably linked to righteousness (see Proper 8, p. 179). Thus although there is use of Greek terminology here, the Greek idea that the soul is necessarily immortal is not present. The righteous survive death because they are in the hand of God, and they are in the hand of God because they have cared for righteousness. It must not be supposed that this is simply a crude works and reward version of religion. That would entail a good life lived with little concern for God in the hope of life after death that also had little to do with God. What is envisaged is a life lived in fellowship with God, fellowship that death cannot break because God is more powerful than death. Although the text of 9d is uncertain, the last two lines of the verse emphasize God's close concern for those who trust him.

There are similarities between vv. 7–8 and Dan. 7.27, where kingship and dominion are given to the holy ones of the Most High, the ones who have suffered for the sake of God. Precisely what the governance of the righteous entails is not stated; but if immortality is inextricably linked to righteousness, there is more than a hint of the existence of a better world to come, the hope for which had sustained the righteous against the cynicism and hostility of the wicked. JR

Isaiah 25.6–9

Isaiah 25 is part of the so-called Isaiah apocalypse (chs. 24—27), a section that is among the latest parts of Isaiah to be written, and in which the idea of resurrection is hinted at (Isa. 26.19). The set passage falls into two parts: vv. 1–5 are in the form of a song or psalm of thanksgiving, while vv. 6–9 are a continuation of 24.23.

Dealing with the second part first, the apocalypse begins (in 24.1) with a sombre account of God's impending judgement on the earth. The link between moral order and the order of creation entails that the wickedness of earth's inhabitants is so great that all that sustains human life physically will no longer be available, with the result that civic life will completely break down. The judgement will be so complete that it will also embrace the stars of heaven, the kings of the earth and the sun and moon (24.21–23). This will be the prelude to God assuming kingship on Mount Zion.

Verses 6–9 describe the joyful outcome of this divine enthronement. In contrast to the devastation of the earth, God will invite all nations to take part in a banquet which celebrates his kingship (v. 6). The 'shroud' and the 'sheet' that he will destroy are probably those that are worn by people mourning the dead. They will become unnecessary objects because God will destroy death, that personification of the greatest power that confronts God, and which causes most perplexity to human attempts to make sense of the world. Tears will be wiped away from all faces (v. 8) and those who are invited to the celebration will hail it as the better world for which they have hoped and waited (v. 9).

Verses 1–5 interrupt the sequence of 24.23—25.6, and were probably inserted to help make the transition from the deep gloom of ch. 24 to the brilliant light of ch. 25. They are a song celebrating the demise of a city (v. 2); whether a particular one is meant or whether it is a city personifying the power of evil is not clear. The point is that the destruction of this city is an assurance to the poor and needy that God is ultimately on their side (v. 4). For the powerful and ruthless peoples of the world, the downfall of the city is a warning to them that they will not have the last word.

The verse about the sun and moon being abashed and ashamed (24.23) is possibly alluded to in Mark 13.24 prior to the coming of the Son of man on the clouds with great power and glory. The passage about the banquet on Mount Zion is reminiscent of the saying in Matt. 8.11, that many will come from east and west and eat with Abraham, Isaac and Jacob in the kingdom of heaven. The passage is thus extremely rich, not only in its own context, but with echoes into the New Testament. JR

Revelation 21.1–6a

At the end of his vision, John sees the new creation and the union of heaven and earth. All that separated God and humanity in the present age, all the rebellion and conflict that called for judgement has been overcome. There is no more sea, because the sea is a powerful symbol of the forces in the old creation unsubdued by God. In the beginning, in Gen. 1.1, the Spirit of God moved over the waters of chaos, and it was from the sea that John saw the beast emerge to launch his attack upon the saints (13.1, 7). In the Old Testament, the myth of the primordial sea (which may itself be an adaptation of earlier Near Eastern creation myths of the battle between god and monster, as in Ps. 74.13–14) may be merged with the tradition of the exodus, so that the story of deliverance becomes a story of new creation (Isa. 51.9–10). The essential characteristic of this new age is the presence of God with his people, with no distance and no barriers remaining. His 'tabernacle' will be with them, as the tent of God's glorious presence travelled with Israel during their wilderness wanderings (Exod. 40.34–38); and the new covenant between God and his people is established, in the terms foretold by Jeremiah (31.31–33).

With God's victory won, there is no room for the sorrow and pain that have haunted so much of John's vision, and in the presence of the eternal God who is Alpha and Omega there is no room for death. John's vision is like that of Paul, for whom death is the 'last enemy', to be swallowed up in victory in the great transformation of the mortal into the immortal at the last trumpet (1 Cor. 15.26, 51–55). Paul's and John's visions are both of the new age of the future, in which they both believed, but both passages are now used at funerals, expressing a hope for the individual believer at death. There is justification for this use, for John's hope for the new age is anticipated earlier in his vision. In 6.9–11 the martyrs have been seen already waiting under the altar in heaven; in 7.9–17 the great multitude of those who have come through the great ordeal already stands before the throne, and their tears are wiped away; in 14.1–4 the Lamb's army have already been redeemed from the earth to be with him always. For John, the martyrs have a special place among Christian believers and a special and immediate place in heaven; others would extend this privilege more broadly to the saints. Yet surely all the Lord's people are saints, and the presence of God among his people is already anticipated by Christ, called 'Immanuel', God with us, and the Word who dwelt (or 'tabernacled') among us revealing God's glory (Matt. 1.23, John 1.14). John has already seen him among his churches, the living one who holds the keys of death, and who is ready to come in to anyone who opens the door to him (1.17–18, 3.20). SL

John 11.32–44

'Jesus began to weep.' In its traditional translation (which is probably also more accurate) – 'Jesus wept' – this verse is both the shortest in the Bible and one of the most famous. To countless people it has conveyed the precious information that Jesus shared our humanity to the point of weeping for a friend's death. This may well be true; but is it all that we are meant to understand?

It is a characteristic ploy of this Gospel to let people draw the wrong conclusion from Jesus' words and actions in order to throw into sharper relief their true meaning. When the Jews said, 'See how he loved him!', had they judged rightly? The question is raised by two expressions that are used just before: 'greatly disturbed' and 'deeply moved'. These words may just express a natural grief; but in Greek, when used elsewhere, they have more to do with indignation and agitation than with mere sorrow. So what is the meaning of Jesus' tears? Are we to accept the conclusion drawn by 'the Jews'? Or should we ask whether those other words do not have their usual sense and show that Jesus was not so much grieving as *angry*? What moved Jesus to anger on other occasions was hypocrisy and narrow-mindedness. Here, he was surrounded by people who professed to believe in resurrection and life after death, yet who were crying their eyes out because someone had died (and there may well have been professional mourners adding to the din). Would it not have been entirely characteristic of him to shed tears of anger at their lack of faith?

That someone could bring a person back from the dead was hard to believe under any circumstances; according to the other Gospels Jesus achieved it twice, but each time very shortly after the moment of death. Folk religion could cope with this.

For three days, it was thought, the soul was still attached to the body; it was conceivable to restore it to life. But after that it was impossible; the body had begun to decompose (as we are sharply reminded here) and the life force had gone for ever. What Jesus was now about to do exceeded all possible expectations. The drama is palpable; and in the structure of the Gospel, which has worked through a number of astonishing 'signs' performed by Jesus, it is a powerful climax.

What did this 'sign' signify? That Jesus was the greatest miracle worker of all time? It was to dispel any such crude interpretation that Jesus prayed aloud. The miracle would be a demonstration, not of his own power, but of God's; he was merely God's agent, 'sent' to act on God's behalf. And his purpose was more than just to prolong a friend's life; it was to act out a parable. The quality of living offered by Jesus was such that even death could not destroy it. AEH

The Fourth Sunday Before Advent

Deuteronomy 6.1–9; Hebrews 9.11–14; Mark 12.28–34

Deuteronomy 6.1–9

A new section is introduced by the words 'Now this is the commandment . . .' ('Now' is omitted from the Lectionary version), but the emphasis moves from an address to the generation that stood at Mount Horeb (Deut. 5.4) to instruction to children and children's children. If the generations are obedient they will multiply greatly in the promised land (6.3). Verse 4 begins the opening section of the most famous prayer in Judaism, the Shema', so named because of the Hebrew imperative *shema'* meaning 'hear!'. The whole prayer consists of Deut. 6.4–8, 11.13–22 and Num. 15.37–42, and is recited twice daily by observant Jews. The translation and interpretation of the opening words are problematic, as indicated by the various alternative renderings provided as footnotes in the NRSV. The Hebrew is literally, 'YHWH our God YHWH one', with the NRSV representing YHWH as LORD. On the basis of usage elsewhere in Deuteronomy it is unlikely that 'YHWH our God' should be rendered as 'YHWH is our God', and more likely that 'is' should be added between 'YHWH' and 'one'. This yields the translation 'the LORD our God, the LORD is one'. It is then necessary to explain what is meant by 'one'. This most likely refers to YHWH's uniqueness. He alone is God and needs no other gods to assist him.

However, this unique and incomparable God is also, for Israel, *our* God, not because of what Israel deserves or merits, but because of God's graciousness (cf. 7.7). The uniqueness of God leads to a unique claim upon Israel: the Israelites must love God with heart, soul and might (6.5). 'Love' in this context includes an emotional element, as indicated in Deut. 7.7–8 where it is said that God set his heart on Israel (Hebrew *hashaq* meaning 'to love' or 'become attached to') and chose and loved them. But it also entails loving obedience to God's commandments.

The phrase 'with all your heart, and with all your soul' is a trade mark of Deuteronomy and of books influenced by it. The metaphors do not mean the same as in English. The 'heart' is the seat of the intellectual faculty of a person, while 'soul' (Hebrew *nephesh*) is the seat of emotional and spiritual faculties. *Nephesh* can also mean 'person'. Heart and soul taken together thus mean a person's total life, physical, mental and spiritual. In 6.5 'might' is added, probably referring to a person's material possessions. The injunction to recite 'these words' when a person lies down and rises up and that they should be placed on the hand, forehead and doorposts has given rise in Judaism to the recitation of the Shema' prayer evening and morning, to the wearing of phylacteries at times of prayer, and the placing of *mezuzot* on doorways. These practices continue to this day. Phylacteries contain Deut. 6.4–9, 11.13–21 and Exod. 13.1–10, 11–16, while *mezuzot* contain Deut. 6.4–9 and 11.13–21. In the original context of 6.6–8, 'these words' refers to all that is to be commanded, and the injunctions about why the words should be recited and where they should be placed is powerful rhetoric stressing the abiding importance of what is enjoined. It may also be based, however, on the fact that, in the ancient Near East, people wore amulets to give them protection, and that doorposts inscribed with sacred words have been found in Egypt. JR

Hebrews 9.11–14

Among the standard interpretative devices of the first century was the practice of arguing 'from the lesser to the greater' (*qal wahomer*). If a characteristic could be attributed to something smaller or lesser, it was assumed a fortiori that the same or even greater characteristics could be attributed to something larger or greater. The New Testament provides many examples of such reasoning. When Jesus argues that, because God 'clothes the grass of the field, which is alive today and tomorrow is thrown into the oven' (Matt. 6.30), God will also clothe human beings, he is using an argument 'from the lesser to the greater'. Another good example of such interpretative logic comes following Jesus' question, 'Is there anyone among you who, if your child asks for bread, will give a stone?' (Matt. 7.9). The conclusion is clear that, if limited human parents care for their children, 'how much more' will God, the supreme parent, care for God's children (Matt. 7.11). Paul employs the same technique when he contrasts the accomplishments of the finite trespass of Adam with Jesus Christ's gift of grace (Rom. 5.12–21).

Because these examples are familiar, it is easy to overlook the fact that this means of reasoning goes against modern notions of logic. After all, perhaps God provides clothing for plants because they are not able to fend for themselves! Recognizing the tremendous differences among human parents, can one reason the nature of God's parenting style by looking at that of human parents? Despite these problems, argument 'from the lesser to the greater' needs to be understood in order to see how these various passages 'work'.

Much of Hebrews presupposes this kind of thinking by presenting Jesus as the high priest who is even greater than human high priests and who, therefore, accomplishes far more for humankind. This lection meticulously contrasts certain features of the atonement accomplished by human priests and that accomplished by Christ. As elsewhere, however, the author employs the contrast not only to embroider around a theme but also to encourage behaviour that is appropriate to Christian faith.

The lection opens with what might appear to be an incidental reference: 'But when Christ came.' In Hebrews, however, references to the arrival of Christ often serve to recall his becoming Son or high priest. For example, 1.4 speaks of Christ as having 'become [literally, arrived] as much superior to angels . . .' and 6.20 of his 'having become [literally, arrived] a high priest for ever'. Here, an intensive form of the customary verb (*paraginomai*, rather than *ginomai*) makes the arrival even more dramatic.

The initial contrast implied in v. 11 is between the place of Christ's atonement and the place of the atonement accomplished by the customary sacrifices. He entered 'through the greater and perfect tent'. Lest the contrast with the temple be missed, Hebrews further identifies the tent as 'not made with hands' and 'not of this creation'. In other words, this place is made by God. Often interpreters allegorize this tent, seeing in it reference to the body of Christ. The context makes such conclusions unnecessary, for Christ is said to go 'through' the tent to the 'Holy Place'. The discussion in vv. 6–9 clarifies the contrast, for there the author talks about the Yom Kippur sacrifice, in which annually the high priest enters into the 'second' tent. Here Christ enters not annually into the 'second' and more sacred place, but into the most sacred place imaginable, and only once.

Verse 12 introduces the second contrast, that having to do with the means of the sacrifice. What the human priests sacrifice are 'the blood of goats and calves', but Christ sacrifices 'his own blood'. Verses 13–14 restate this part of the contrast; here it is the 'blood of goat and bulls, with the sprinkling of the ashes of a heifer'. The reference to the slaughter of the red heifer puzzles exegetes, for that ceremony is not connected with the Yom Kippur sacrifice. Possibly the association here arises because, by this time in Jewish tradition, the sacrifice of the red heifer has been associated with the high priest.

With v. 14, the 'how much more' phrase identifies the point of this long series of contrasts; if the annual sacrifice of animals in a tent erected by human hands accomplished sanctification, what sanctification will be accomplished by the sacrifice of Christ in a place erected by God? The answer comes quickly. That earlier sacrifice covered things that defiled the flesh or things that caused ritual impurity; this new sacrifice cleanses 'our conscience from dead works'. The familiarity of language about 'works' from the Pauline letters should not lead to the conclusion that these 'dead works' are works of the Mosiaic law. Elsewhere in Hebrews, the phrase 'dead works' clearly refers to immoral actions (6.1), and that is its referent here as well.

The sacrifice of Christ, then, brings about cleaning from ritual impurity and forgiveness of sins. Something even greater is at stake, however, as the last words of the passage indicate: 'to worship the living God!' This purification has a purpose beyond that of rectifying the individual's standing before God. It enables the worship of God. The verb 'worship' translates the Greek *latreuein*, which connotes both cultic and ethical service (see e.g. *latreuein* as 'serve' in Luke 1.74; Rom. 1.9; 'worship' in Acts 24.14). Purification finally results in the sort of devotion to God that is as total as the sacrifice of Christ, who gave 'his own blood'. CC

Mark 12.28–34

The scribe's question is one of a number of ensnaring puzzles placed in Jesus' path by various kinds of interlocutors. In this case, however, the question is one that was debated in scribal and rabbinic circles. May we think in terms of a hierarchy among the provisions of the God-given Torah, or are they all equally the beneficent will of

God? Some rabbinic opinion gave distinct priority to the command to love, as Jesus does in this passage.

The interesting issues that follow such a judgement are: What then of the subordinate commands? Are all still valid but to be obeyed in a manner imbued with love for God or neighbour, as appropriate? Or are some relativized, even perhaps to the point of extinction, by the priority of love? It is, after all, not hard to think of cases of possible conflict once the priority of love is admitted – unless love be always defined so as to rule out such conflicts. Rabbinic opinion tended to an inclusive view, and the Jesus of Matthew's Gospel agrees: 23.23; 22.40 in his parallel to our passage. Paul was less clear: see Rom. 13.8–10; and his refusal to enforce Torah relating to circumcision, sabbath and food laws on Gentile converts was a major move, justified in part on the positive side by the umbrella priority of love (Gal. 5.6), though other arguments, for example of an exegetical kind, were also adduced. (In due course, Christians came to distinguish, helpfully as it seemed, between the ceremonial and moral provisions of the Old Testament law, but that division was not known in the first century.)

Mark's subordinating of the sacrificial law to love, put on the lips of a scribe improbably won over to Jesus by his not out of the way reply, was a daring step – too daring or at least too ambiguous for Matthew to retain; it could easily seem like a brushing aside – as was indeed natural in a Gentile Christian congregation, especially in or after AD 70 when the regime of sacrifices was obsolete in any case.

The question of the relation of the love command to the rest of a moral system remains live, with Christians tending to divide along lines not dissimilar to those found in Mark and Matthew, for all the huge differences in religious context between then and now. Is love to be defined by the rest of the moral imperatives or are they firmly its subordinates and servants, to be ready to cede in cases of conflict? But if the latter, whence do we derive our idea of love: from mere personal preference or hunch? Or is it, for the Christian, defined by the self-giving of Jesus (cf. Gal. 2.20), in such a way that the faithful believer will acquire, from the Spirit, a kind of rudder or intuitive charism indicating what love requires (Gal. 5.22)? Is this in effect implied by Mark as the scribe makes his almost ecstatic (and surprising) response to Jesus in v. 33, so willingly endorsed in the final words of the story? In the kingdom of God, love suffices. LH

The Third Sunday Before Advent

Jonah 3.1–5, 10; Hebrews 9.24–28; Mark 1.14–20

Jonah 3.1–5, 10

This is another passage that presupposes a knowledge of the whole story of the book from which it is taken (cf. Proper 21, p. 232). The Lectionary compounds the problem by omitting the words 'a second time' after 'Jonah'. Congregations unfamiliar with the book of Jonah will thus be unaware of the high drama of the book, and of Jonah's unsuccessful attempt to escape from his commission to preach judgement to Nineveh. If opportunity arises, the whole book offers a story with many ironies, that can be easily and effectively dramatized.

Within the limitations of the verses selected, the first point to be noted is that God sends a prophet to warn a foreign city, and a city that has done no favours to Israel. In 722/1 the Assyrians brought to an end the political existence of the northern kingdom, Israel, and the book of Nahum in its present form exults over the downfall of Nineveh in 612 BC. Although prophetic books of the Old Testament often contain oracles directed against foreign nations and their cities, it is rare if not unique for a prophet to be specifically sent to a foreign nation. The fact that the book of Jonah is a novel rather than a prophetic book is irrelevant here. The idea is what counts, and it is highly unusual.

The other main point is the reaction of the people of Nineveh to Jonah's message. It is a continual complaint of books such as Jeremiah that God persistently sent prophets to warn Israel, Judah and Jerusalem, and that the rulers and people took no heed (e.g. Jer. 35.15). By contrast, the non-Israelite Ninevites repent immediately. There is irony in the fact that such a large city responds to the preaching of a prophet from a tiny nation that was no match for the might of Assyria.

The story of Jonah shows, among other things, that God is concerned for nations other than Israel and that he finds ways to cause his word to be heard in unexpected places. Further, there may be a more ready response to his word from those outside the household of faith than from those within. JR

Hebrews 9.24–28

Through chs. 7—9, the author of Hebrews has been exploring the model of priestly activity to explain his understanding of the person and work of Christ, and in particular that of the high priest on the Day of Atonement, when on that one occasion of the year he offered a sacrifice for all the people, and entered the Holy of Holies to present it before God (thus Lev. 16). Now the author summarizes his conclusions. Christ fulfils this model, by making it effective in a way never achieved before, and so making it unrepeatable. 'Once' is a favourite word in Hebrews: it means 'once for all': what has been done, is done; and never needs doing again. To repeat an action is not a sign that it works, but precisely that it has *not* worked. As the fully human yet sinless high priest, Christ was able to offer the one sacrifice that could meet the need of human sinfulness, that of himself; and having offered it in his death, he has passed into the true holy of holies, heaven itself, presenting humanity before God. A new situation has been created; a new age inaugurated. In the opening verses of the Epistle, the author contrasted the past of God's communication through the prophets with 'these last days' in which he has spoken through the Son (1.1–2); now again he sets Christ's work at 'the end of the age'.

However, the fact that Christ's work was the full, final, and effective priestly act means that it has consequences. The author shares the belief found in many parts of the New Testament that Christians stand between the completion and the consummation, in the tension of 'already' and 'not yet'. Christ will appear again, not in any sense to finish off or supplement his atoning work, for that would make him like the high priests of old, endlessly repeating the mere shadow of what they could never make real. His second coming will be 'not to deal with sin', but to answer the expectations of those who are 'eagerly waiting'. What are they waiting for? The author's analogy of human death followed by judgement is puzzling. It might suggest that Christ's two appearances are first to die and second to judge; and certainly in 10.26–31 there is a 'fearful prospect of judgement' with no second sacrifice for sin. This is, however, for those who betray Christ, not those who wait for him. The meaning of his second coming for those who wait will be explained in ch. 11, the roll-call of the heroes of faith who looked for the city of God and therefore committed themselves to being exiles and wanderers on earth because their true homeland was in heaven (11.13–16). Those whose sins Christ has borne wait for him as their saviour who will take them where he has gone before, as the 'pioneer and perfecter of faith' (12.2). In some parts of the Epistle, the author criticizes his readers for their lack of perseverance and enthusiasm as time passes (6.9–11; 10.32–36); here he underlines for them both the grounds and the goal of hope which will sustain them through whatever lies ahead. SL

Mark 1.14–20

If it is helpful to think of the first part of the Gospel of Mark as having the character of a prologue (see p. 40), made up of a series of theologically powerful cameos, each succinct and pregnant with meaning, then we have to decide where the prologue-like material ends. Publishers of Bibles may nudge us in one direction or another. Some leave a gap after v. 13, and the brief narratives of the baptism and temptation of Jesus may seem to bring this kind of material to an end. But there is a good case for including at least vv. 14–15. No one could suppose that these verses give other than an epitome of Jesus' message, the gist of what he stood for and what it signified. It is scarcely a sermon long enough to detain an audience in real-life time.

Our question is more difficult when it comes to vv. 16–20: does the 'prologue' go even as far as this? To use an anachronistic shorthand: if one sees v. 14–15 as concluding Mark's normative statement, then he is being taken as a sort-of-Protestant. Jesus' preaching is the climax, and the good news of the kingdom is the heart of the matter. But if vv. 16–20 form the end of the prologue then he is a sort-of-Catholic. The climax is the call of followers, the establishing of the Christian community around Jesus. In other words, the Church is then of the essence of the gospel. Certainly, this depiction of disciples has a purity and positivity not borne out in most of what follows in the narrative. Here we are presented with the ideal.

The temptation story (vv. 12–13) was full of symbolism and scriptural echoes. Jesus, like Israel with its 40-year time in the wilderness, is tested by the force of evil. Then in his victory, he assumes the mantle of Adam, now restored to his unfallen role, at peace with the animals and with angels serving him, not barring the gates of paradise (Gen. 3.24). The temptation here is balanced at the end by the temptation or testing (*peirasmos*) in Gethsemane, 14.32–42; just as the call of the followers, with the ideal immediacy of their response, to be ruined by their subsequent conduct, especially in the passion, is redeemed in the hope and promise of restoration in Galilee (16.7). In the end, as at the start, what can one do but 'follow' when the summons of Jesus reaches one's ears? For Mark, 'disciples' are not really 'pupils' in the school of Jesus: they are walkers in his 'way' (1.2f.) – and 'fishers' who will see that the community grows apace, just like the seed in ch. 4. They are vital to the very reality of the kingdom's coming (3.14; 6.7–13). LH

The Second Sunday Before Advent

Daniel 12.1–3; Hebrews 10.11–14 (15–18), 19–25; Mark 13.1–8

Daniel 12.1–3

The opening words of the lectionary reading are a shortened form of the beginning of Dan. 10.1, which introduces chs. 10—12. The third year of Cyrus was around 536 BC whereas Daniel was written in the second century BC even if some of its stories in chs. 1—6 are much older. The attributions of books to persons and times well before those of the actual author is a familiar device in the ancient world, and in the case of Daniel afforded protection to the author and his book in a time of persecution.

The background to the mention of Michael is the belief that nations have heavenly, supernatural counterparts who watch over their interests. Traces of this are evident in Old Testament passages such as Deut. 32.8–9 and Ps. 82, but in later Judaism there is a more developed angelology and demonology in which to express this view. The belief that supernatural beings engage in conflict is also found (cf. Dan. 10.18–21; Jude 9). The passage is meant as reassurance to Jews suffering persecution. They have a protector and they will ultimately be delivered.

Verse 2 contains the clearest reference in the Old Testament to resurrection; but it must be noted that this is not necessarily resurrection to life after death. It is probably closer to the thought of psalms such as 16.10, which speak of God rescuing his servants from the power of Sheol, the shadowy underworld. Sleeping in the dust of the earth (v. 2) has allusions to Gen. 3.19 as well as to the dead being placed in a grave that was believed to be the door to Sheol. The idea of awaking to new life is implicit at Ps. 17.15: 'As for me, I shall behold your face in righteousness: when I awake I shall be satisfied, beholding your likeness.'

What is envisaged in the first place, then, is an awakening of the dead into an earthly existence that is necessary for judgement to take place. However, the nature of this post-mortem existence hovers between this world and a world to come, as indicated by the reference to the wise shining like the stars for ever and ever.

It is probably best not to press the imagery too far in a literal direction. Although the mediation of Michael may indicate the felt remoteness of God, the purpose of the passage is to affirm that God has the final word. JR

Hebrews 10.11–14 (15–18), 19–25

The first part of this lection (Heb. 10.11–18) brings to a conclusion the discussion of Christ's priesthood. Psalm 110 again provides an important basis for the author's reflection on Christ's role (v. 12). By contrast with the priests who must stand daily to offer sacrifices for sin, Christ's singular sacrifice enables him to sit at God's right hand, his work completed for all time. The quotation from Jer. 31.33–34 once again interprets Christ's act in light of the promise of a new covenant and the forgiveness of sin.

With the second part of the lection, Hebrews employs this theological treatment of Christ's priesthood and sacrifice as the grounds for exhortation. Verses 19–21 recall the outlines of the indicative, what has been accomplished by the 'blood of Jesus'. Verses 22–25 consists of three exhortations (hortatory subjunctives), each of which is taken up and developed in the section that begins with 11.1. Taken together, vv. 19–25 are one long sentence, suggesting the close connection between the actions of Jesus and the resulting consequences of those actions for Christian behaviour.

In recalling the priesthood of Jesus, the writer appeals to the 'confidence' believers have ('since we have confidence to enter the sanctuary', v. 19). The noun 'confidence' (translating the Greek word *parrēsia*) refers to the boldness of Christians, a boldness that enables them to act in ways that will seem strange, even incomprehensible, to the outside world. In Acts, the 'boldness' of Peter and John stuns the authorities, who know that they are not educated men (4.13; cf. 4.29, 31; 28.31). Paul speaks of proclaiming the gospel with 'boldness', by contrast with the veiling of the law (2 Cor. 3.12). In this lection confidence or boldness enables Christians to 'enter the sanctuary' of God and provides them with the strength to fulfil the three admonitions of Heb. 11.22–25 (cf. 4.16).

The first admonition urges faith, 'Let us approach with a true heart in full assurance of faith' (v. 22). This can occur since 'our hearts [have been] sprinkled clean from an evil conscience and our bodies washed with pure water.' The relationship between these two conditions is worth noting. Hebrews does not explicitly identify purification as a cause of faith, but neither is purification an end in itself. The purification brought about by Christ's sacrifice is a condition to which the response should be the 'full assurance of faith'. And faith enables believers to make their 'approach'. Exactly what approach this is remains unspecified, but the context suggests that it cannot be limited to cultic experience alone. Christ's priesthood makes possible an 'approach' to God that involves all of life, inside and outside the sanctuary.

The second admonition is the shortest and reflects traditional Jewish and Christian convictions about the reliability of God's sovereign word: 'Let us hold fast to the confession of our hope without wavering, for he who has promised is faithful.' As elsewhere in the New Testament, for the author of Hebrews 'hope' is not the equivalent of merely wishing for something; rather, hope suggests confident expectation about the future. Precisely because God has already fulfilled promises (6.13–15; 8.6–7; 11.11), God may be relied on to fulfil those promises that remain. For similar reasons, the long recitation of the faithful deeds of the 'cloud of witnesses' results in the call to perseverance (12.1–2). The past serves as the basis for hopeful action in the future.

The most lengthy of the admonitions comes last (vv. 24–25). Initially, the notion of Christians 'provoking' one another to 'love and good deeds' may sound odd, as if Christians are being enjoined to manipulative behaviour. Probably what the author intends is that believers should act in ways that become enticing for others, something like Paul's (presumably exaggerated) comment that the Thessalonians became such an example that Paul had no need to preach (1 Thess. 1.7–10). The sheer insight into human behaviour here is impressive; both authors recognize the value of the living model through whom instruction comes indirectly.

The one 'good deed' singled out in this exhortation may seem painfully contemporary: 'not neglecting to meet together, as is the habit of some.' Although it is notoriously difficult to reconstruct the situation of the community addressed in Hebrews, here surely a specific problem comes into view. 'Some' are absenting themselves from the gatherings of the community for worship and instruction. The placement of this comment in a section that introduces general exhortations suggests that, for the author, the gathering of the community is a vital aspect of faithful existence and not to be taken lightly.

Finally, Christians are to encourage 'one another, and all the more as you see the Day approaching'. As often in the New Testament, exhortation and eschatology stand hand in hand. The section that follows reminds readers of the judgement that accompanies this 'Day' and warns against moral laxity. The forgiveness acquired through Christ's sacrifice does not license believers to moral indifference but, on the contrary, enables them to act with confidence. CC

Mark 13.1–8

This is the last of the Sunday gospels from Mark, and it is the setting – and the first paragraph – of the only lengthy piece of continuous teaching in this Gospel. It will help towards understanding it, if the chapter is considered as a whole, and not just the first few verses of it.

Mark is giving his hearers the final speech of Jesus, spoken in private to the first four disciples (see 1.16–20), but to be passed on to others. The conclusion of it is: What I say to you, I say to everyone: Keep awake (13.37).

The first words of Jesus in Mark had announced that the time of preparation for the new world had come; God's time of ruling both in heaven and on earth would soon be here (1.15); and Jesus demonstrated this throughout the book, by casting out demons, healing sickness, feeding the hungry and raising the dead. But now, as he has also said, he is about to die. How can the rule of God begin?

It will begin with his resurrection after three days and with his coming again with great power and glory (13.26f.). But just as his way to glory is to be through shame and humiliation, so it will be for the world also: evil will have its way and work itself out, destroying everything. It is parasitic, and can only live by consuming its host. The disciples are not to underestimate how long this will take; they are not to be misled by those who think it is the end before it really is.

The end (vv. 7, 13) is, from another point of view, the beginning. The Jesus of ch. 13 is the Jesus of chs. 1—12: the exorcist, the healer, the giver of health and sanity, the Saviour, the Lord of wind and sea, the one whom God will not leave in death. He is the one whom the disciples are praying for when they say, *Marana tha*; Come, Lord! (1 Cor. 16.22), or when they say to their Father:

> Hallow your name,
> Begin your rule,
> Make your will done.

Just as the suffering of the Lord and the suffering of his followers are the same, so also the glory of the Lord and the glory of his followers will be the same. The gathering of the chosen (13.27) is the beginning of the age of eternal life, which is that for which every creature of God waits and longs.

Mark ch. 13 was, for Mark and his contemporaries, the completion of the gospel – the good news of God (1.14), Maker and Saviour of all that is. And the rest of the book of Mark showed it being realized at grievous cost. JF

Christ the King

Daniel 7.9–10, 13–14; Revelation 1.4b–48; John 18.33b–37

Daniel 7.9–10, 13–14

See Ascension Day, p. 138.

Revelation 1.4b–8

The affirmation of Christ as 'the King' would have had tremendous resonance for John and his readers in the context of the contemporary Roman Empire. They were faced with a state that required the payment of divine honours to its ruler. Although this was mainly a matter of ritual and ceremony that expressed the loyalty of the subject, there were emperors who came to believe in their own divinity and expect it to be recognized accordingly. Some modern commentators set the Apocalypse in the reign of Nero, the first emperor to persecute Christians, but the traditional and still most popular setting is in the reign of Domitian, who required to be acclaimed as 'Our Lord and our God'. To Christians this would be a gross parody of their recognition of Jesus as, in the words of Thomas, 'My Lord and my God' (John 20.28); and in Revelation the Roman Empire appears as the Beast, the great enemy of the Church and a blasphemous parody of the Lamb (13.1–9). In opposition to its claims, in his opening address to his readers, John proclaims Christ as 'the ruler of the kings of the earth', the Davidic king-messiah of Ps. 89.27; about to be universally revealed on the clouds of heaven like Daniel's Son of man (Dan. 7.13). This kingly Christ is, however, one with the man Jesus; and therefore exercises his rule because of his death and resurrection. When the conquering Lion of the tribe of Judah is proclaimed in heaven, John will see the slaughtered Lamb (5.5–6).

The supreme power is, of course, that of God 'the Almighty', one rendering in the Greek Old Testament of the Hebrew *Yahweh Sabaoth*. The divine name revealed to Moses in Exod. 3.14 was translated into Greek as 'He who is', and John develops this into a ringing statement of God's eternity. God is past, present and future; but so also is Christ. As 'the faithful witness' who died *he was*; as 'the firstborn of the dead' and 'him who loves us', *he is*; and *he is to come*, still as the one who was 'pierced' (an allusion to Zech. 12.10). This is more than analogy. At many points the Apocalypse clearly suggests the divinity of Christ, and in its conclusion John will hear the living Jesus apply to himself the language used here of God, Alpha and Omega (22.13). In an irony of history, as the Roman Empire became Christian after the conversion of the Emperor Constantine, its distinctive symbol for Christ was the *chi-rho* monogram often combined with those Greek letters *alpha* and *omega*.

Christ's kingly power is a sharing in the power of God – and it is also experienced by his followers. Those whom he has freed from sin (a variant reads 'washed', perhaps in allusion to 7.14) become a kingdom of priests: the description of Israel as God's redeemed people in Exod. 19.6; also applied to the Church in 1 Pet. 2.5. As such they are able through Christ to offer God the honours due to him alone, and that no earthly regime can claim. SL

John 18.33b–37

That the formal charge against Jesus was that he claimed to be 'King of the Jews' is one of the best attested facts of ancient history. All four Gospels record that a notice to this effect was attached to the cross, and it is difficult to think of any reason why they should have invented it – any suggestion that Jesus was a political threat to Roman rule was exactly what they most wanted to avoid, and they would hardly have mentioned this apparently incriminating piece of evidence unless it had been actually seen by a number of people.

Yet at the same time it was obvious to every Christian that Jesus was not, in any ordinary sense, 'King of the Jews'. He had made no such claim and was plainly uninterested in any form of political power. In the other Gospels, when Jesus is asked this question by Pilate, his answer is neither yes nor no: 'You say so'. In John this is spelled out more fully. Of course Jesus is not a 'king' in the usual meaning of the word; yet there is a sense in which he has a 'kingdom', which in the Greek has the same meaning as 'reign': Jesus has an authority that comes to him, not 'from this world', but from his intimacy with his heavenly Father, such that one could say that he is 'reigning' over the world.

But in the matter of religious authority, it is never sufficient just to appeal to divine authorization, as if one had a direct line to God (as we know only too well from our experience with fundamentalist groups who try to justify their extreme views in this way). The will of God for human beings is never something that can simply be read off a sentence in Scripture or a dogma of religion. It has to be discerned in the context of our perpetual pursuit of the *truth* – truth about ourselves, about the world and about God. Even Jesus did not claim to give us this truth in its entirety; some of this truth would be made known to us by the Spirit in later times, some we would have to continue to search for ourselves. But Jesus had taken the first crucial step in *testifying* to this truth. He was a witness to be trusted above all others, testifying to the truth about God and human beings, not only by his words but by his acts and his death. For truth has a cost. If we pursue it and 'listen to his voice' we are caught up in the same destiny as his – to suffer for the truth but at the same time to know that our testimony is another vital component in the structure of his 'kingdom', which is the establishment of his reign, his authority, on earth. AEH

Harvest Festival

Joel 2.21–27; 1 Timothy 2.1–7 or 1 Timothy 6.6–10; Matthew 6.25–33

Joel 2.21–27

This passage is part of the divine response to the people's prayer and fasting (2.15–17) in the face of disaster (1.2—2.11). The exact nature of the disaster is disputed. It is possible to see it wholly in terms of a devastating plague of locusts (cf. 1.4; 2.25) or to see a series of disasters, including drought, locusts, fire and invasion by an army.

The word of hope follows to some extent the order of 1.4–20. Thus v. 21, with its promise to the soil, reflects 1.10; v. 22b with its reference to trees and vines alludes to 1.12; and the promise of food in v. 24 can be paralleled by 1.16. Whether or not the order of 2.21–27 is wholly determined by 1.4–20, it is noteworthy that the prophet addresses the soil and the domestic animals directly (vv. 21–22) before addressing the inhabitants of Jerusalem (v. 23).

An intriguing question of translation and interpretation is raised by the Hebrew of v. 23a, which mentions the instructor, or teacher in, or for, righteousness. Jewish, and some older Christian, interpreters have seen here a reference to the Messiah, and given that a 'teacher of righteousness' is known from the Dead Sea Scrolls, the question has been raised whether Joel 2.23a is the origin for this title. Because of the similarity between the Hebrew *moreh* 'teacher' and 'former rain' (i.e. rain that falls ideally in October) most modern versions render the word as 'rain' or 'autumn rain' although the NIV margin also offers 'the teacher for righteousness'.

The concluding verses must be taken either eschatologically – i.e. looking to an ideal future – or must be admitted to be unrealistic. If they imply that there will be no more famines, then they are wrong. One of the challenges of preaching at Harvest is that there is no easy correlation between thanking God for his bounty, and living in a world plagued by famines, famines caused partly by human greed and selfishness. If a passage as Joel 2.21–27 can help, it is only by way of looking beyond what humans achieve when they ignore God. JR

1 Timothy 2.1–7

It is virtually impossible to find New Testament passages that accord at all closely with the themes now customarily (and appropriately) taken up in Harvest Festival sermons. Both 'creation', as a theme in itself, and (still less) environmental responsibilities were not in the forefront of these writers' minds. And, though thanksgiving is a commonly urged disposition of the Christian heart, its subject is usually the gracious saving work of God in Christ rather than the fruits of the earth. In certain circumstances indeed, it may be helpful to explore this dichotomy between New Testament Christianity and more modern observances. It is of course not unheard of for clergy at any rate to feel that in celebrating the harvest they are making a concession – perhaps to unrealism, for they are urban (so they bring in the products of local factories); or to deep pre- or sub-Christian, quasi-pagan instincts, an older religion centred on the fertility of the natural world; and some look over their shoulder to Roman Catholic and other non-established church clergy who tend not to notice this half-secular rite where the gospel of Christ is, it may seem, easily muted.

But 1 Tim. 2.1–2 is salutary. It marks an early stage in such accommodation (if that is the right word for it). It is one of the evidences for what is often seen as the bourgeois character of the Pastoral Epistles, their tendency to sober respectability (cf. the qualities urged for Christian ministers in 1 Tim. 3), and their lack of a sense of the deeper and more dangerous aspects of Christian allegiance. At the same time, political loyalty of what we (in a very different world) are likely to see as a rather naive and uncritical kind is commanded by Paul (Rom. 13.1–7) and indeed (with whatever sense) in the tradition of Jesus' teaching (Mark 12.13–17). Here, a Pauline inheritor states the attitude more unequivocally than ever, and the general disposition is plain. Here is the charter for all civic services and prayers for royal families and rulers that have ever been – the kind of open Christian ministry often disliked by Catholic and principled Protestant alike. Yet its justification here lies in something deeper than the tendency to live at ease in one's social niche; and it goes beyond even the great and gracious good of social stability that only those who enjoy it can take easily for granted and which later Christian thinkers were to make much of. The doctrine is that God desires the salvation of all and Jesus gave himself for all. The only question then is how best to further the divine purpose in the societies of which we are part. Even Harvest Festivals may help! LH

1 Timothy 6.6–10

In this alternative passage, we move from general principles and reflections on them to sharp ethical injunctions, all of them in tune with many other passages in early Christian writings and in the teaching of Jesus.

There can be no doubt that early Christians had little room for the accumulation of wealth. It is true that there is some havering on the matter, a measure of indecision between the strictest asceticism, the renouncing of property, on the one hand and, on the other, working with the demands of practical, settled church life. Thus, while the Jesus-movement – engaged, it seems, in itinerant mission – comes across as wedded to property-less existence, in the manner of Cynic teachers of the time; though for reasons connected, perhaps with joyful lightness of being, to the dawn of God's kingdom, once settled congregations were established, by Paul and others, in urban settings, the accent moves away from the total renunciation that Jesus enjoined. There should preferably be a few Christians who were reasonably substantial householders able to host Christian meetings and act as centres for the group. It is very likely indeed that such people stepped naturally into the role of 'seniors' or 'overseers' of the churches. Thus, in Paul for example, the accent moves from renunciation to almsgiving, a very different matter.

All the same, there is, if not always a bias to the poor (as in the teaching of Jesus), at least a bias against the rich: we see it in the Revelation of John, in the Letter of James – and in our present passage. There has of course always been a good deal of hypocrisy in this area, striking many as barefaced, as for most of its history the Church has not only been, in many places, a major property-owner, but also always in need of the rich to finance its good endeavours (people with consciences that New Testament teaching could strike). But the message of our present passage has deep resonances in our own day, in many contexts and with many nuances. The theme is inseparable from life in human society and never out of season, though often highly complex in the details of the ethical policies involved. LH

Matthew 6.25–33

The appropriateness of this passage for the purpose of harvest raises questions. If the choice arose because this is about the only passage that (seemingly) veers towards the rhapsodic about nature, then it may be necessary to rescue it from such a Wordsworthian association. As also in so many of the parables, notably in Mark, rural imagery arose naturally in the Palestinian environment, as well as having numerous Old Testament precedents – in parabolic stories and in 'wisdom' teaching, for example. But if the choice arose because of the message – that we are not to be anxious about the necessities of life – then in the modern as in the ancient world, the message needs careful understanding and sensitive presentation if it is not to come over as sick indeed. We cannot read it as straightforward moral teaching of universal validity.

As usual, sensitivity to context is a key. Apart from the typically Matthean 'and his righteousness' in v. 33, the passage is widely seen as surely authentic to Jesus: partly because its emphasis is not one that is in the forefront of later church life, but more because we have here a prime symptom of the lightness of soul in the mission of Jesus when the dawning of the kingdom was seen as near. That fully explains the life-stance urged here, and is all of a piece with the exhortations to renounce wealth and family ties. God rules and we can shrug off all that binds us to the present age. Modern application is, therefore, not easy, especially when the material things of life decorate the church and occupy the attention. There may be, however, an interiorizing of what began, surely, as a practical message.

At first sight, we seem to see Jesus as the practical psychotherapist: don't be anxious because anxiety will get you nowhere (v. 27). But in fact the message is theological. It is the simple question of the direction of faith: Do you, in the heart, trust God, or do you not? The answer then forms one's inner priorities.

Stanley Spencer made a painting that has the title 'Consider the lilies of the field'. It depicts a large, ungainly and unkempt Jesus kneeling in a field of daisies. (Easter daisy may actually be the meaning of the Greek *krinon* – and are not lilies unlikely in 'the field'?) Jesus is 'considering' them, as the traditional versions say. Of course

Spencer mistook the sense: the word means 'learn from' or 'take for instance', not 'contemplate'. But the idea of interiorizing one's priorities may be the best modern reflection on words that had their exuberant heyday when the Christian movement was very young. As in life, age can debilitate. LH

Biblical Index

Made in the USA
Coppell, TX
22 October 2022

85121956R00164